Palgrave Politics of Identity and Citizenship Series

Series Editors: **Varun Uberoi**, Brunel University, UK; **Nasar Meer**, University of Strathclyde, UK; and **Tariq Modood**, University of Bristol, UK

The politics of identity and citizenship has assumed increasing importance as our polities have become significantly more culturally, ethnically and religiously diverse. Different types of scholars, including philosophers, sociologists, political scientists, and historians make contributions to this field and this series showcases a variety of innovative contributions to it. Focusing on a range of different countries, and utilizing the insights of different disciplines, the series helps to illuminate an increasingly controversial area of research, and titles in it will be of interest to a number of audiences including scholars, students, and other interested individuals.

Titles include:

Parveen Akhtar
BRITISH MUSLIM POLITICS
Examining Pakistani Biraderi Networks

Heidi Armbruster and Ulrike Hanna Meinhof (*editors*)
NEGOTIATING MULTICULTURAL EUROPE
Borders, Networks, Neighbourhoods

Peter Balint and Sophie Guérard de Latour
LIBERAL MULTICULTURALISM AND THE FAIR TERMS OF INTEGRATION

Fazila Bhimji
BRITISH ASIAN MUSLIM WOMEN, MULTIPLE SPATIALITIES AND COSMOPOLITANISM

Rosi Braidotti, Bolette Blaagaard, Tobijn de Graauw, and Eva Midden (*editors*)
TRANSFORMATIONS OF RELIGION AND THE PUBLIC SPHERE
Postsecular Publics

Bridget Byrne
MAKING CITIZENS
Public Rituals, Celebrations and Contestations of Citizenship

Jan Dobbernack
THE POLITICS OF SOCIAL COHESION IN GERMANY, FRANCE AND THE UNITED KINGDOM

Jan Dobbernack, and Tariq Modood (*editors*)
TOLERANCE, INTOLERANCE AND RESPECT
Hard to Accept?

Romain Garbaye and Pauline Schnapper (*editors*)
THE POLITICS OF ETHNIC DIVERSITY IN THE BRITISH ISLES

Nisha Kapoor, Virinder Kalra and James Rhodes (*editors*)
THE STATE OF RACE

Peter Kivisto, and Östen Wahlbeck (*editors*)
DEBATING MULTICULTURALISM IN THE NORDIC WELFARE STATES

Dina Kiwan (*editor*)
NATURALIZATION POLICIES, EDUCATION AND CITIZENSHIP
Multicultural and Multi-Nation Societies in International Perspective

Aleksandra Lewicki
SOCIAL JUSTICE THROUGH CITIZENSHIP?
The Politics of Muslim Integration in Germany and Great Britain

Aleksandra Maatsch
ETHNIC CITIZENSHIP REGIMES
Europeanization, Post-war Migration and Redressing Past Wrongs

Derek McGhee
SECURITY, CITIZENSHIP AND HUMAN RIGHTS
Shared Values in Uncertain Times

Tariq Modood and John Salt (*editors*)
GLOBAL MIGRATION, ETHNICITY AND BRITISHNESS

Nasar Meer
CITIZENSHIP, IDENTITY AND THE POLITICS OF MULTICULTURALISM
The Rise of Muslim Consciousness

Ganesh Nathan
SOCIAL FREEDOM IN A MULTICULTURAL STATE
Towards a Theory of Intercultural Justice

Therese O'Toole and Richard Gale
POLITICAL ENGAGEMENT AMONGST ETHNIC MINORITY YOUNG PEOPLE
Making a Difference

Momin Rahman
HOMOSEXUALITIES, MUSLIM CULTURES AND IDENTITIES

Michel Seymour (*editor*)
THE PLURAL STATES OF RECOGNITION

Katherine Smith
FAIRNESS, CLASS AND BELONGING IN CONTEMPORARY ENGLAND

Paul Thomas
YOUTH, MULTICULTURALISM AND COMMUNITY COHESION

Milton Vickerman
THE PROBLEM OF POST-RACIALISM

Eve Hepburn and Ricard Zapata-Barrero
THE POLITICS OF IMMIGRATION IN MULTI-LEVEL STATES
Governance and Political Parties

Palgrave Politics of Identity and Citizenship Series
Series Standing Order ISBN   978–0–230–24901–1 (Hardback)
(*outside North America only*)

You can receive future titles in this series as they are published by placing a standing order. Please contact your bookseller or, in case of difficulty, write to us at the address below with your name and address, the title of the series and the ISBN quoted above.

Customer Services Department, Macmillan Distribution Ltd, Houndmills, Basingstoke, Hampshire RG21 6XS, England

Transformations of Religion and the Public Sphere

Postsecular Publics

Edited by

Rosi Braidotti
Professor and Director of the Centre for the Humanities, Utrecht University, The Netherlands

Bolette Blaagaard
Assistant Professor, Aalborg University, Denmark

Tobijn de Graauw
Manager Academic Programme, Utrecht University, The Netherlands

and

Eva Midden
Assistant Professor, Utrecht University, The Netherlands

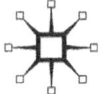

Editorial matter, selection and Introduction © Rosi Braidotti, Bolette Blaagaard, Tobijn de Graauw and Eva Midden 2014
Remaining chapters © Respective authors 2014
Softcover reprint of the hardcover 1st edition 2014 978-1-137-40113-7

All rights reserved. No reproduction, copy or transmission of this publication may be made without written permission.

No portion of this publication may be reproduced, copied or transmitted save with written permission or in accordance with the provisions of the Copyright, Designs and Patents Act 1988, or under the terms of any licence permitting limited copying issued by the Copyright Licensing Agency, Saffron House, 6–10 Kirby Street, London EC1N 8TS.

Any person who does any unauthorized act in relation to this publication may be liable to criminal prosecution and civil claims for damages.

The authors have asserted their rights to be identified as the authors of this work in accordance with the Copyright, Designs and Patents Act 1988.

First published 2014 by
PALGRAVE MACMILLAN

Palgrave Macmillan in the UK is an imprint of Macmillan Publishers Limited, registered in England, company number 785998, of Houndmills, Basingstoke, Hampshire RG21 6XS.

Palgrave Macmillan in the US is a division of St Martin's Press LLC, 175 Fifth Avenue, New York, NY 10010.

Palgrave Macmillan is the global academic imprint of the above companies and has companies and representatives throughout the world.

Palgrave® and Macmillan® are registered trademarks in the United States, the United Kingdom, Europe and other countries

ISBN 978-1-349-48632-8   ISBN 978-1-137-40114-4 (eBook)
DOI 10.1057/9781137401144

This book is printed on paper suitable for recycling and made from fully managed and sustained forest sources. Logging, pulping and manufacturing processes are expected to conform to the environmental regulations of the country of origin.

A catalogue record for this book is available from the British Library.

Library of Congress Cataloging-in-Publication Data

    Transformations of religion and the public sphere : postsecular publics / Rosi Braidotti, Professor and Director of the Centre for the Humanities, Utrecht University, The Netherlands, Bolette Blaagaard, Assistant Professor, Aalborg University, Denmark, Tobijn de Graauw, Manager Academic Programme, Utrecht University, The Netherlands, Eva Midden, Assistant Professor,Utrecht University, The Netherlands.
    pages cm.—(Palgrave politics of identity and citizenship series)
    Includes bibliographical references.

    1. Europe – Religion – 21st century. 2. Postsecularism – Europe. 3. Secularism – Europe. I. Braidotti, Rosi, joint author.
BL695.T73 2014
200.94'09051—dc23   2014023292

Contents

Notes on Contributors   vii

Introductory Notes   1
Rosi Braidotti, Bolette Blaagaard, Tobijn de Graauw, and Eva Midden

1 Is There a Crisis of 'Postsecularism' in Western Europe?   14
   Tariq Modood

2 Reawakening Enlightenment? Contesting Religion and Politics in European Public Discourse   35
   Anders Berg-Sørensen

3 (Pro)claiming Tradition: The 'Judeo-Christian' Roots of Dutch Society and the Rise of Conservative Nationalism   53
   Ernst van den Hemel

4 Re-examining an Ethics of Citizenship in Postsecular Societies   77
   Christoph Baumgartner

5 The Eradication of Transcendence   97
   William Egginton

6 The Unprecedented Return of Saint Paul in Contemporary Philosophy   115
   Gregg Lambert

7 More Proof, If Proof Were Needed: Spectacles of Secular Insistence, Multicultural Failure, and the Contemporary Laundering of Racism   132
   Alana Lentin and Gavan Titley

8 Remediating Religion as Everyday Practice: Postsecularism, Postcolonialism, and Digital Culture   152
   Koen Leurs and Sandra Ponzanesi

9 Mentality, Fundamentality, and the Colonial Secular; or How Real Is Real Estate?   175
   Pamela Klassen

10 Religious Aspirations, Public Religion, and the Secularity of
   Pluralism 195
   Patrick Eisenlohr

11 Towards a More Inclusive Feminism: Defining Feminism
   through Faith 210
   Eva Midden

12 Blasphemous Feminist Art: Incarnate Politics of Identity in
   Postsecular Perspective 228
   Anne-Marie Korte

13 Conclusion: The Residual Spirituality in Critical Theory:
   A Case for Affirmative Postsecular Politics 249
   Rosi Braidotti

Index 273

Notes on Contributors

Christoph Baumgartner is Associate Professor of Ethics in the Department of Philosophy and Religious Studies at Utrecht University in the Netherlands. Principal topics of his research and teaching are religion in the public sphere, freedom of religion and freedom of expression, citizenship, secularity and postsecularism, environmental ethics, and ethical dimensions of climate change.

Anders Berg-Sørensen is Associate Professor at the Department of Political Science, University of Copenhagen, Denmark. He holds a PhD in Political Theory. His dissertation was titled 'Paradiso-Diaspora: Reframing the Question of Religion in Politics' (2004). He has researched the democratic negotiations of religion and politics in European political thinking and public culture and is currently associated with the research project 'Religious Citizens: Religious Affect and Varieties of European Secularity' focusing on the political thinking of secularism. He is currently investigating the relationship between political ethics and real politics with a special interest in political cynicism, among other things, as part of the research project 'Compromise: Democratic Ideals and Real Politics'. He has recently published the book *Contesting Secularism: Comparative Perspectives* (2013).

Bolette Blaagaard is Assistant Professor in Communications at Aalborg University, Copenhagen. She works and has published in the intersectional field of journalism and cultural studies. She is the co-editor of *Cosmopolitanism and the New News Media* with Lilie Chouliaraki (2014), *After Cosmopolitanism* with Rosi Braidotti and Patrick Hanafin (2013), and *Deconstructing Europe: Postcolonial Perspectives* with Sandra Ponzanesi (2012).

Rosi Braidotti is Distinguished University Professor at Utrecht University and Director of the Centre for the Humanities in Utrecht. Her research and writing engages feminist philosophy and cultural studies, poststructuralism, and critical theory as well as epistemology and Deleuze studies. Recent books include *The Posthuman* (2013), *Nomadic Subjects: Embodiment and Sexual Difference in Contemporary Feminist Theory* (2011a), and *Nomadic Theory: The Portable Rosi Braidotti* (2011b). For more information, visit www.rosibraidotti.com.

viii Notes on Contributors

Tobijn de Graauw is Manager of the academic programme at the Centre for the Humanities at Utrecht University, the Netherlands. Her background is in political philosophy, and during her MA at Utrecht University she specialized in global justice and human rights. Her current projects and research interests include the postsecular, religion in the public sphere, the cultural roots of citizenship, and the environmental humanities.

Patrick Eisenlohr is Professor of Modern Indian Studies at the University of Göttingen and Professor of Anthropology at Utrecht University. He obtained a PhD from the University of Chicago in 2001 and previously held positions at Washington University in St. Louis and New York University. He is the author of *Little India: Diaspora, Time and Ethnolinguistic Belonging in Hindu Mauritius* (2006) and has conducted research on transnational Hindu and Muslim networks, language and diaspora and the field of linguistic anthropology more generally, and media technology in Mauritius and India. In his most recent research, Patrick is interested in how media practices shape situations of ethnic and religious diversity, and how they contribute to the non-deliberative and everyday dimensions of citizenship.

William Egginton is Andrew W. Mellon Professor in the Humanities and Vice Dean for Graduate Education at the Johns Hopkins University, where he teaches courses on Spanish and Latin American literature, early modern European literature and thought, literary theory, and the relation between literature and philosophy. He is the author of *How the World Became a Stage* (2003), *Perversity and Ethics* (2006), *A Wrinkle in History* (2006), *The Philosopher's Desire* (2007), *The Theater of Truth* (2010), and *In Defense of Religious Moderation* (2011). His next book, *The Man Who Invented Fiction*, is to be published in 2015.

Ernst van den Hemel is a research fellow at the Centre for the Humanities, University Utrecht. His research focuses on the postsecular, nationalism, and early-modern theology. He completed his PhD on John Calvin's Institutes at the University of Amsterdam in 2011. His publications include a monograph on Calvinism and the right to resistance (2009), and a co-edited volume on the work of Alain Badiou (2012). He is co-editor of the forthcoming edited volume *Words: Religious Language Matters* (2014).

Pamela Klassen is Professor in the Department for the Study of Religion at the University of Toronto, and directs the Religion in the Public Sphere Initiative. Her book *Spirits of Protestantism: Medicine, Healing, and*

Liberal Christianity (2011) won the 2012 American Academy of Religion Award of Excellence for Analytical-Descriptive Studies. Her other publications include *After Pluralism: Reimagining Religious Engagement* co-edited with Courtney Bender (2010) and *Blessed Events: Religion and Home Birth in America* (2001). For more information, see http://projects.chass.utoronto.ca/pklassen/.

Anne-Marie Korte is Professor of Religion, Gender and Modernity in the Faculty of Humanities at Utrecht University. She is also the Director of the Netherlands School for Advanced Studies in Theology and Religion (NOSTER). Her major research interests are classic and contemporary miracle stories and the role of gender and sexuality in contemporary accusations of blasphemy. Her latest publications include *Everyday Life and the Sacred: Re/configuring Gender Studies in Religion* co-edited with Angela Berlis and Kune Biezeveld (2014) and *Contesting Religious Identities* co-edited with Bob Becking and Lucien van Liere (2014).

Gregg Lambert is Dean's Professor of the Humanities and founding Director of the Syracuse University Humanities Center in New York. He has published extensively on contemporary issues of the humanities, critical theory, and continental philosophy, especially on the philosophies of Gilles Deleuze and Jacques Derrida.

Alana Lentin is an associate professor in Cultural and Social Analysis at the University of Western Sydney. She is the co-author of *The Crises of Multiculturalism: Racism in a Neoliberal Age* with Gavan Titley (2011), and has also edited *The Politics of Diversity in Europe* (2008). Her other books include *Racism and Anti-Racism in Europe* (2004) and *Racism: A Beginner's Guide* (2008).

Koen Leurs is a Marie Curie Postdoctoral Fellow at the London School of Economics. He is the author of *Digital Passages: How Diaspora, Gender and Youth Culture Intersect Online* (forthcoming 2015), co-editor of the anthology *Everyday Feminist Research Praxis* (2014) as well as the special issue on *Digital Crossings in Europe* published in *Crossings. Journal of Migration & Culture* (2014). His research focuses on digital networks, youth culture, multiculturalism, urbanity, migration, and gender. See www.koenleurs.net.

Eva Midden is Assistant Professor in Gender Studies at the Media and Culture Studies Department at Utrecht University (Netherlands). She wrote her PhD thesis, 'Feminism in Multicultural Societies', at the University of Central Lancashire (United Kingdom) and was recently involved in the European Research Project 'MIGNET' for which she conducted research on migration, gender, and religious practices in new media. Her general research interests include feminist theory, postcolonial theory, intersectionality, postsecularism, whiteness, and media analysis. Her latest publication is 'Feminism and Cultural and Religious Diversity in *Opzij*: An Analysis of the Dutch Feminist Magazine' in the *European Journal of Women's Studies*.

Tariq Modood is Professor of Sociology, Politics and Public Policy at the University of Bristol and is also the founding Director of the Centre for the Study of Ethnicity and Citizenship. He was awarded an MBE for services to social sciences and ethnic relations in 2001 and was elected a member of the Academy of Social Sciences in 2004. His latest books include *Multiculturalism: A Civic Idea* (2nd ed., 2013), *Still Not Easy Being British* (2010), and as co-editor *Secularism, Religion and Multicultural Citizenship* (2009; co-editor), *Global Migration, Ethnicity and Britishness* (2011), *European Multiculturalisms* (2012), *Tolerance, Intolerance and Respect* (2013), and *Religion in a Liberal State* (2013). His website is tariqmodood.com.

Sandra Ponzanesi is Head of Humanities at University College Utrecht and Associate Professor of Gender and Postcolonial Critique at the Department of Media and Culture Studies/Gender Graduate Programme, Utrecht University. She is the author of *Paradoxes of Postcolonial Culture* (2004), *The Postcolonial Cultural Industry* (2014) and co-editor of *Migrant Cartographies* (2005), *Deconstructing Europe* (2012), *Postcolonial Cinema Studies* (2012), and editor of *Gender, Globalization and Violence* (2014).

Gavan Titley is Lecturer in Media Studies at the National University of Ireland, Maynooth. He is the co-author of *The Crises of Multiculturalism: Racism in a Neoliberal Age* with Alana Lentin (2011), and they have also edited *The Politics of Diversity in Europe* (2008). Forthcoming books include the edited *National Conversations? Public Service Media and Cultural Diversity* (2014) and *Hate Speech Online: Principles and Politics, Platforms and Practices* (2014).

Introductory Notes
Rosi Braidotti, Bolette Blaagaard, Tobijn de Graauw, and Eva Midden

This collection of edited essays aims to explore the so-called 'postsecular condition' from a variety of disciplinary angles and from different but intersecting theoretical and political perspectives. Originally coined by Jürgen Habermas, the term 'postsecular' has been adopted in a broad range of intellectual and theoretical traditions and has gained widespread currency. Of pivotal importance in this discourse is the 'secularization myth', so prominent in the West, which has been questioned by recent religious resurgence. This myth connects secularism with progress and modernity on the back of religious backwardness (Jakobsen and Pellegrini, 2008). Secularism is moreover counted among the ideologies that spell danger to democracy in Europe by not sufficiently recognizing the importance of religious and multicultural identities and their implications for active citizenship (Modood, 2007). The postsecular turn seeks to provide a counter-discourse to the myth of secularism by developing a variety of critiques of the myth grounded in discussions on the current political, social, and technological condition in which Europe, in particular, and the Western world more generally, finds itself. What the concept – the postsecular – means and stands for, however, is far from clear. Even though much has been written recently on the postsecular turn or condition, there is no agreement on how to conceptualize the term and connect it to current developments in our societies.

Secularism by any other name

The starting position of this volume is to challenge, as all the contributors in this volume do, the consensus that seems to have emerged in the European public discourse about the privileged link between Christianity and secularism, or faith and reason. Canonized in the dialogue between

Jürgen Habermas and (then) Cardinal Ratzinger in 2004 (Habermas and Ratzinger, 2005), this equation paves the road for a two-layered argument: the exceptional nature of the Christian religion in its relationship to rational thought and therefore the continuity between Christianity and secular critical thinking.

This Habermasian consensus, upheld also by Charles Taylor (2007) among others, rests on the notion that secularism both as an institutional practice – the separation of state from church – and as a philosophical frame is a distillation of Judeo-Christian precepts, notably respect for the law, for the intrinsic worth of the individual person, the autonomy of the self, moral conscience, rationality, and the ethics of love. These values are held by Habermas and Ratzinger as central also to European identity and history and have allowed for the Enlightenment and the ensuing scientific process which has made this continent so important.

In other words, the Christian faith allows for rational thought, based on a teleological or evolutionary vision of the future and on humanist faith in human reason's capacity to self-regulate and steer social progress. This value system defines Humanism as both personal and civilizational ideal in terms of the respect for liberal individualism. It moreover connects both Humanism and secularism to notions of equality and democracy, which lie at the core of European modernity and the emancipatory project of the Enlightenment. It could be argued, then, that the value system of European secular Humanism is intrinsically religious, albeit by opposition and negation. This is what Habermas has in mind when he speaks of the spiritual roots of critical reason and of Western philosophy in general. This line of reasoning leaves all other monotheistic religions, notably Islam, in the singular position of being de-linked from rationality and hence incapable of engendering secularist distinctions. By extension, religions like Islam would have no claim to modernity, emancipation, or human rights. This, as Gellner (1992) and Talal Asad (2003) noted, is not only far from unproblematic politically but also historically false.

The Habermasian claim defines the postsecular turn in the narrowest possible Eurocentric terms and it universalizes a specific brand and historical manifestation of secularism, which is part of the reason why we find it unacceptable. As William Connolly (1999) astutely remarked, this strategy has passed off Western secular systems as achieving absolute moral authority and the social status of a dominant norm.

There are, however, other objectionable aspects to that equation, in that it contains an ambiguous relationship to the project of Western modernization and more specifically to its emancipatory politics. Habermas's position displayed clear signs of postsecular anxiety and it expressed moral panic at the sight of the horrors of the clash of civilizations, on the one hand, and the structural injustices of the global economy, on the other (Borradori, 2003). Even more problematic for Habermas and Ratzinger are the effects of contemporary biotechnological advances. The future of human 'nature' has become the subject of deep concern in the public debate of our globalized times. Habermas coined the term 'postsecular societies' also in order to signal the urgency of a critical and ethical reconsideration of the function of scientific belief systems in the contemporary world. Fear of genetic manipulations, which Habermas (2003) shares with champions of contemporary liberalism like Fukuyama (2002), and a more anarchical-minded thinker like Sloterdijk (2009), implicitly endorses one of the axioms of all monotheistic religions, namely the sacred nature of human life and procreation. This technophobic reaction to our biotechnological progress has led to a return to Kantian moral universalism in critical theory, notably through the work of Martha Nussbaum (1999, 2006), Seyla Benhabib (2002), Nicholas Rose (2001), and others.

Several issues are conflated in this discussion: firstly, there is the legacy of the Enlightenment and the Christian urge to uphold natural law, in opposition to the ravages of technological modernity. Morality becomes mobilized in defence of 'Life' and opposed to technological manipulations. Secondly, the moral and political test case for this belief is the legacy of secularism, which is linked to Christianity by negation. Thirdly, there is the specific issue of the legal and social status of women and LGBT people who have been, together with the anti-slavery and de-colonization movements, the motors of emancipation in modernity (Braidotti, 2008). Last but not least is the acknowledgement that some of the most pertinent critiques of globalization and of advanced capitalism today and of the structural injustices of globalization are voiced by religiously driven social movements. This tendency has intensified in Christianity since the election of Pope Francis, voted 'person of the year' by *Time* magazine in December 2013.

Habermas's postsecular argument, however, displays a topsy-turvy sequence of internally contradictory claims that express deep anxieties about secularism, faith, and the project of Western modernity. Much as the contributors of this volume welcome the ethical aspirations that support these claims, we do not share the Christian exceptionalism of their premises nor the neo-universalism of their ethics. We advocate critical distance both on theoretical and political grounds from the ethnocentrism of this position and also the technophobic fear it expresses (Braidotti, 2002, 2006). The Habermasian claims also mystify the genuine historical achievements of Western emancipatory politics. We would all be better off acknowledging instead that both the modernization process and the emancipation of women and LGBTs are still very much in process in the West and that racism and neo-imperialism are alive and well on the world stage today. Consequently, no simplified dichotomies should be set up between an allegedly progressive Christian tradition and the allegedly backward others, starting with the Muslim.

The counter-consensus expressed in this volume is that the Western secularization model may not be the only or the best one: multiple modernities are actually at stake (Bracke, 2012; Eisenstadt, 2000; Modood, 2007). Therefore, different forms of secularism may be engendered by multiple models of modernity. This allows us to venture the idea that the postsecular condition is diverse, multicultural, and internally differentiated and that no single analysis or blueprint should be taken as the definitive and comprehensive one.

Aims

This volume, therefore, not only builds on the assumption that we need to critique fixed notions of what secularism is but also seeks to bring about the prefix 'post' as a sort of question mark that follows the subsequent central considerations: How does this postsecular critique throw into relief notions of agency in political struggles linked to colonialism, female emancipation, and racism? How does the postsecular challenge existing schemes of political economies, and how may we map out the power structures that make up the European scholarship on the intersection of race, gender, and religion in relation to the political reality of class and social stratification of European societies today? In this context, we would argue that the 'post' in postsecular does not refer to a condition that could be characterized as 'after' secularism in a linear, temporal dimension, but rather to a critical reflection of secularism. In order to provide answers, this volume offers a selection of postsecular discourses and practices through which it seeks to bring attention to the many productive intersections between the political ideas and developments of the postsecular and those in postcolonial and feminist discourse.

Thus, the volume frames the discussion on the postsecular with reference to the idea of globalization in general and more specifically on the many productive intersections between the multiple practices and the complex realities of diasporic conditions and discourse. By approaching the concept in this way, the volume targets specific problems faced by contemporary Europe in terms of the political right-turn it is witnessing. This turn is, for instance, evidenced in the European Parliamentary election in 2009; the rise of neoconservative politics and the financial crisis; and the crisis of multicultural policies in the wake of 9/11 are also paradoxically an expression of the increasingly multicultural and religious space of European nations nowadays. The postsecular condition challenges European political theory, in general, and multiculturalism and feminism, in particular, because it questions the axiom that equates secularism with emancipation. Recent political as well as intellectual developments have seen sexual liberties be appropriated to European national imaginaries. Homophobia and gender violence is represented as belonging to radical Islam only, and thus the new imaginary plays into the hands of the political right that pledge to reinforce the boundaries between us and them – the secular and the religious. It is therefore pivotal that the concept of the postsecular is challenging this binary position, and that the myth of the modern secular individual versus the backwards religious people is exposed. A postsecular approach makes manifest the notion that agency, or political subjectivity, can actually be conveyed through and supported by religious piety and may even involve significant amounts of spirituality.

In terms of gender relations, the undoing of the secular myth has two important corollaries – firstly, that we need to question the axiomatic belief that women's emancipation is directly indexed upon sexual freedom, in keeping with the European liberal tradition of individual rights and self-autonomy. This historically specific model cannot be universalized and more sober accounts are needed of its contingent and hence partial applicability. Most prominent among the questions left unresolved by militant, idealized secularism are: 'How does secularism posit the relationship between equality and difference? And what are we to make of the fact that, both logically and historically, one does not at all guarantee the other?' (Scott, 2007). The second corollary is that political agency need not be critical in the negative sense of oppositional and thus may not be aimed solely or primarily at the production of counter-subjectivities. Subjectivity is rather a process ontology, which involves complex and continuous negotiations with dominant norms and values and hence also multiple forms of accountability (Braidotti, 1992, 2013). Consequently, there exists a necessity to question the 'idealized secular', or the ideology of secularism (Modood, 2007) and its political manipulations by politicians and populists today (Connolly, 1999). This postsecular paradox opens up spaces for new forms of reflection of religion in the public sphere. The concept of the postsecular, thus, brings challenging new perspectives to the discussion about European identity and culture in a globalized world.

The historical route to the postsecular

In order to fully explore the theoretical premises of the postsecular turn it is necessary first to provide its historical background, which can be divided into five overlapping and mutually enriching developments. Firstly, the end of the Cold War has played a major role in the development of the myth of secularism. The subsequent defeat of communism led to the hegemony of a neoliberal discourse that promotes consumerist capitalism as the allegedly most evolved form of human development. Secondly, economic and cultural globalization caused strong movements of resistance in the form of resurgent nationalisms at the macro as well as the micro levels. This led to a resurgence of civilization discourses about Western traditional values which produce, once again, hierarchies of identities, cultures, and even ethnic belongings. In constant fear of the (cultural, ethnic) other, these developments also provoked the rise of a perpetual state of 'new' wars against terror or internal enemies. Finally, a pervasive state of technological mediation has penetrated most aspects of social life, with the convergence between information and biotechnologies as the core issue.

The historical defeat of communism has two major implications for the debate on the postsecular: firstly, the role of the former Eastern European churches – from the Orthodox to the Catholic under double leadership of the Polish trade-union movement *Solidarność* and the Polish-born Pope John Paul II in bringing down the iron curtain. This alone shifts the balance of political power between church and state in former Eastern Europe and contributes to a reappraisal of the political relevance of religiously based activism. Secondly, it brings about serious questioning of the militant atheism of the Marxist tradition. Resting on Hegel's philosophy of history, Karl Marx saw the dismissal of religion by dialectical reason's unfolding upon human history as an inevitable aspect of human progress and emancipation. Nature and religion, need and superstition are part of the oppressive legacy we need to leave behind. Marx supports the working of reason against 'the opium of the masses' as a necessary component of the political project of human liberation. Simone de Beauvoir will follow suit.

After the downfall of communism, neoliberalism reinforced its opportunistic ideology that considers financial success as the sole indicator of the status of development of a society, including of its women. Economic failure is accordingly perceived as a sign of underdevelopment and as a lack of emancipation, as money and individual accumulation alone is taken as the indicator of both freedom and progress. The global celebration of the absolute value of profit as the motor of human and of women's progress implies that even the most basic social democratic principle of solidarity is misconstrued as old-fashioned welfare support and dismissed accordingly. And as the financial crises bring European economies to their knees, the neofascist movements rise.

The emphasis on liberal individualism and capitalism makes neoliberalism profoundly ethnocentric: it takes the form of a contradictory and ethnocentric position, which argues along civilization or ethnic lines (Huntington, 1998). It is complicit with a neoliberal discourse about white supremacy, namely that our women (Western, Christian, mostly white, and raised in the tradition of secular Enlightenment) are already liberated and thus do not need any more social incentives or emancipatory policies. 'Their women', however, (non-Western, non-Christian, mostly not white, and alien to the Enlightenment tradition) are still backwards and need to be targeted for special emancipatory social actions or even more belligerent forms of enforced 'liberation'. Hence the bodies of women, as bearers of authentic ethnic identity, get both sexualized and racialized within a neo-imperial discourse of triumphant Western sovereignty. This simplistic and belligerent position, defended by people as different as Cherie Blair in Britain and Ayaan Hirsi Ali in the Netherlands, to name but a few, reinstates a world view based on colonial lines of demarcation. It fails to see the great grey areas in between the pretentious claim that feminism has unitary goals that have already succeeded in the West and the equally false statement that feminism is non-existent outside this geopolitical region.

One of the recent emblems of this situation is the *burqa*-clad bodies of the Afghan women in defence of whom such an anti-abortionist, conservative, and anti-feminist president as George W. Bush claimed to launch one of his many commercially driven wars of conquest. What cynic would believe the claim that the war was fought to help out the poor oppressed masses of Islamic women? And yet, this is the political discourse that circulates in the global economical world disorder: one in which sexual difference defined as the specificity of women's condition is again the terrain on which power politics is postulated. The 'new' wars of the third millennium are consequently also religious crusades, fought on the principles stated in all the points mentioned above. The so-called 'clash of civilizations' pitches religious 'fundamentalism' as an Eastern problem against secularism as the defining feature of the Western world in a mutually exclusive confrontational discourse.

More complexity is needed in the debate about women's self-determination and feminist agency, especially in view of the impact of technologies – both information and biogenetic – in the making of subjectivity in our globally mediated world (Braidotti, 2006). The lessons imparted by postcolonial and race studies on issues of identity formations and othering are crucial to this discussion and their intersection with feminist approaches absolutely necessary. While technologies may enhance our ability to connect and form new relationships that in turn may support active citizenship and a strong civil society, they are simultaneously enabling anonymous bullying and racial-centric, ethnocentric, and misogynist networks to flourish (Levmore and Nussbaum, 2010). On this score, the European dimension demands attention to which the case of the Norwegian mass murderer, Anders Breivik, testifies. Breivik's international, Islamophobic, online network calls into question the political implication of international, online communities as it 'reveals a subculture of nationalistic and Islamophobic websites' (Brown, 2011). In his infamous manifesto, Breivik linked extensively to scholars on secularism, such as Samuel P. Huntington's clashes of civilizations, and to politicians such as Dutch MP Geert Wilders and Ayaan Hirsi Ali (featuring along with European political icons such as Winston Churchill).

Large parts of the scholarship on secularism are related to the wave of anti-Muslim intolerance that is sweeping across Europe today. This gives rise to a tendency in public discussions on the postsecular condition to concentrate almost exclusively on Islam, making it the most targeted of monotheistic religions, although the case of Breivik has shed light on the complexities of extremism. The focus on Islam accomplishes a double reduction: firstly of the postsecular condition to exclusively religious principles and secondly of the postsecular condition itself to the 'Muslim issue'. This reduction needs to be questioned, especially in a context of a war on terror that results in the militarization of the social space.

By extension this volume rests on the conviction that any unreflective brand of normative secularism in Europe today runs the risk of complicity with anti-Islam racism and xenophobia. The newly forged connection between homosexual lifestyles and anti-Islam is, in particular, clear in the developments of homo-nationalism, as seen in the example of right-wing parties' attachment to gay pride and the homosexual milieu in larger European towns, such as in Copenhagen, Denmark. These developments dovetail the heated debates about freedom of expression and other Western liberties, which are mounted as incorruptible and indisputable ideas and qualities of European democracies and placed in direct opposition to what is perceived as inherently violent and gender segregating practices of Islam. What is needed, therefore, is a more balanced kind of analysis and a more diversified approach that not only includes all the monotheistic religions but also contextualizes them within shifting global power relations and within more complex social dynamics and problems.

Structure of the book

To Jürgen Habermas (2008), the term postsecular society could only apply to affluent, westernized nations, because of the lapse of religious ties in the post-war period. Challenging the secularization myth based in the assumed link between modernity and secularism, Habermas argues that secular citizens must acknowledge and accept religious influence and this is particularly the case, because the identity of Western societies is rooted in Judeo-Christian values (Habermas, 2008). The first contributions on the political implications of the postsecular condition offer three different analyses of how westernized, postsecular societies may cope with their condition.

Tariq Modood approaches the topic of the postsecular by means of the multicultural challenge. Rather than a performed identity or a reawakened Enlightenment critique, the postsecular condition is a necessary way of coping with the arrival and settlement of Muslims and therefore the change of social structures in Western European societies. This, Modood argues, is perhaps a struggle for radical secularism; however, to the 'dominant version' of political secularism this multicultural challenge is a resource.

Anders Berg-Sørensen finds the roots of the secularism myth in the narrative of the European Enlightenment and bases his analyses on the question of how the Enlightenment critique of religion has been reawakened. This perspective draws Berg-Sørensen to connect firmly secularism to democracy and to bring about an analysis of the implications of the reawakening of religious sentiments in the public sphere. Drawing on both the Enlightenment's critique of religion and on critiques levelled against secularism, he argues for shift in discourses from an unreflexive critique of secularism towards a critical secularism.

Following on from Habermas's argument, Ernst van den Hemel in this volume argues that the postsecular identity may be seen as a 'performative construction', for which (neo)conservative politicians in the Netherlands, in particular, have proven gifted. Van den Hemel discusses how postsecular politics rest on a historical construction, which is being enacted through reiterations of religious-cultural values considered to be inherently secular.

Following the work of among others Saba Mahmood, Christoph Baumgartner develops an understanding of 'blasphemy' as violence that makes it possible to better understand the significance and the kind of injury that many believers feel in view of 'blasphemous' acts and artifacts they consider 'blasphemous' or profoundly offensive. Liberal-secularist explanations of why believers feel injured in cases such as the Muhammad cartoon controversy in Denmark do not suffice, Baumgartner argues.

Not only do they not suffice, the liberal-secularist tradition may be used for misconstruing the relationship between human freedom and religious belief, argues William Egginton. Following on from the seminal work on religious agency by Saba Mahmood (2005), Egginton raises the critique of liberal-secular thought's failure to grasp the extent to which religious fundamentalism today may be inspired and fed not by its attachment to an opposing tradition of thought but by the very system of accumulation and exclusion necessitated by capitalism, and at least in part defended by liberal thought.

In a close and complex reading of Alain Badiou's critique of the philosophy of Emmanuelle Levinas, Gregg Lambert explores phenomenological engagements with multiculturalism and neoliberalism. He emphasizes especially the implications of these debates for new understandings of postsecular ethics.

The two following chapters bring together two highly important aspects of the postsecular turn: the role of media in the discourses about religion and secularism in Western societies, and the intersection of religion with other axes of identities, mainly 'race' and ethnicity. Lentin and Titley focus on the association of religion with backwardness in popular media and recent films such as Geert Wilders's *Fitna* and *Innocence of Muslims*. Leurs and Ponzanesi, on the other hand, show how digital media provide ethnic and religious minorities with a space where they can discuss their own experiences, develop their own interpretations of Islam, and discuss how to live in a secular society.

Moreover, Lentin and Titley engage with the argument that 'the postsecular' is often being reduced to the 'Muslim issue'. They argue that in order to widen the terrain of postsecular life, it is not enough to struggle for a more inclusive public sphere; one also has to develop an

Introductory Notes 11

understanding of the racialization of the debates about Islam in Europe. The authors connect this racialization to multiculturalism in Europe and discussions about 'good' and 'bad' diversity.

Leurs and Ponzanesi also counter the idea that the return of religion is a 'Muslim issue' that challenges democracy, secularism, and progress. They show that through digital practices, Moroccan-Dutch youth manage to produce an Islam that is a cool affective marker, not an essentialized category, and is connected in multiple ways to other aspects of their identities (such as ethnicity, nationality, and class).

Klassen argues that even the First Nations in early twentieth century were already postsecular. Despite this different evaluation of the postsecular condition we are in, this author also investigates how religious communities with diverse mentalities relate to the secular. She argues that in order to make a proper analysis of 'postsecular publics' in colonial context, one has to take into account the significance of Christianity regarding norms of communication and comprehension. She envisions that the postsecular could help to reimagine the clash and mixture of mentalities and practices, giving more space to First Nations.

Eisenlohr writes about religious pluralism and how secularism manages this. Contrary to Klassen, the author argues that we have not moved beyond secularism, as the considerable range of policies and practices that are labelled as 'secular' show. He especially emphasizes the importance of the concept in postcolonial contexts. Eisenlohr refers to his fieldwork in India and Mauritius to show the relationship between globalization, religious networks, and secularism.

Midden criticizes the use of a strict secularism/religion binary by some feminists and starts from postsecular critique to develop a feminism that accommodates differences in an affirmative manner. She brings the debates about the postsecular turn together with her empirical research among women in the Netherlands in order to discuss the possibilities of such an inclusive feminism.

Korte, on the other hand, approaches the topic of gender in relation to religion and secularism from a different angle. She starts from the provocative performance of Madonna, staging a crucifixion scene during her *Confessions on a Dance Floor* tour. She shows that it is not the fact that Madonna, as a woman, stands in the place of Jesus Christ that makes it a blasphemous act. It is rather, the particular details of the representation, such as its detached stance towards suffering, that make it problematic. Hence, just as Midden does, Korte deconstructs the rigorous secularism/religion binary and the role of gender in it, but where Midden focuses on the role of feminism, Korte's account analyzes a show that brings together the saint, the idol, and the icon in a remarkable way. This way she manages to account for traditional readings of crucifixion scenes and the role of women in them.

In her postface to the volume, Braidotti strikes an affirmative note by exploring the residual spirituality of critical theory. She argues that this non-theistic faith in the value of critique constitutes one of the main aspects of the postsecular predicament. This is understood in the light of vital materialism and feminist neo-materialism as leading to a reappraisal of the affective roots of the work of critique.

Thus the volume progresses from a political anatomy of the multifaceted crises of secularism in a European contest, through postcolonial perspectives, into a more global reappraisal of the multiple ways in which the 'post' of the postsecular functions. Next to the (too) many reactive meanings of the term as indicating not only a return of religion in the public sphere but also a belligerent and aggressive manipulation of such a 'return' – the volume also points to some affirmative aspects of the same phenomenon. These include ironical replays, subversive and even blasphemous deconstructions, and open, political contestations of a normative vision of the secular. In this respect, the 'post' in the postsecular also marks a positive longing – as in 'going after' – a new, more inclusive, social practice of the secular in the third millennium.

References

Asad, T. (2003). *Formations of the Secular: Christianity, Islam, Modernity*. Stanford, CA: Stanford University Press.
Benhabib, S. (2002). *The Claims of Culture. Equality and Diversity in the Global Era*. Princeton and Oxford: Princeton University Press.
Borradori, G. (2003). *Philosophy in a Time of Terror*. Chicago, IL: The University of Chicago Press.
Bracke, S. (2012). 'Secularization Theories and Islam. How the Narrative of "Pillarization" Frames Muslims and Refigures Dutch Identity in Times of Civilization.' *Journal of Muslims in Europe* 1(1).
Braidotti, R. (1992). 'On the Female Feminist Subject, or: From "She-Self" to "She-Other".' In G. Bock and S. James (eds) *Beyond Equality and Difference. Feminist Politics and Female Subjectivity*, 177–192. London and New York: Routledge.
Braidotti, R. (2002). *Metamorphoses. Towards a Materialist Theory of Becoming*. Cambridge and Malden, MA: Polity Press/Blackwell Publishers Ltd.
Braidotti, R. (2006). *Transpositions: On Nomadic Ethics*. Cambridge: Polity Press.
Braidotti, Rosi (2008). 'Inspite of the Times: The Postsecular Turn in Feminism.' *Theory, Culture & Society* 25(6), 1–24.
Braidotti, R. (2013). *The Posthuman*. Cambridge: Polity Press.

Brown, A. (2011). 'Anders Breivik's spider web of hate.' *The Guardian*, 7 September 2011 http://www.theguardian.com/commentisfree/2011/sep/07/anders-breivik-hatemanifesto [last accessed 20 March 2014].
Connolly, W. (1999). *Why Am I Not a Secularist?* Minneapolis, MN: University of Minnesota Press.
Eisenstadt, S.N. (2000). 'Multiple Modernities.' *Daedalus* 129(1): 1–29.
Fukuyama, F. (2002). *Our Posthuman Future. Consequences of the BioTechnological Revolution*. London: Profile Books.
Gellner, E. (1992). *Postmodernism, Reason and Religion*. London and New York: Routledge.
Habermas, J. (2003). *The Future of Human Nature*. Cambridge: Polity Press.
Habermas, J. (2008). 'Notes on a Postsecular Society.' *New Perspectives Quarterly* 25(4), 17–29.
Habermas, J. and Ratzinger, J. (2005). *The Dialectics of Secularization*. San Francisco, CA: Ignatius Press.
Huntington, S. (1998). *The Clash of Civilizations and the Remaking of World Order*. New York: Simon and Schuster.
Jakobsen, J.R. and Pellegrini, P. (eds) (2008). *Secularisms*. Durham, NC: Duke University Press.
Levmore, S. and Nussbaum, M. (eds) (2010). *The Offensive Internet: Speech, Privacy, and Reputation*. Cambridge, MA: Harvard University Press.
Mahmood, S. (2005). *Politics of Piety*. Princeton, NJ: Princeton University Press.
Modood, T. (2007). *Multiculturalism: A Civic Idea*. Cambridge: Polity Press.
Nussbaum, M. (1999). *Cultivating Humanity: A Classical Defense of Reform in Liberal Education*. Cambridge, MA: Harvard University Press.
Nussbaum, M. (2006). *Frontiers of Justice. Disability, Nationality, Species Membership*. Cambridge, MA: Harvard University Press.
Rose, N. (2001). 'The Politics of Life Itself.' *Theory, Culture & Society* 18(6): 1–30.
Scott, J. (2007). *The Politics of the Veil*. Princeton, NJ: Princeton University Press.
Sloterdijk, P. (2009). 'Rules for the Human Zoo: A Response to the "Letter on Humanism".' *Environment and Planning D: Society and Space* 27: 12–28.
Taylor, C. (2007). *A Secular Age*. Cambridge, MA: The Belknap Press of Harvard University Press.

1
Is There a Crisis of 'Postsecularism' in Western Europe?

Tariq Modood

By secularism or more specifically, political secularism, I mean institutional arrangements such that religious authority and religious reasons for action and political authority and political reasons for action are distinguished; so, political authority does not rest on religious authority and the latter does not dominate political authority. Support for such arrangements can be derived from a religion or a religious authority, and certainly are supported by many religious people.[1] On this very broad conception of political secularism, there is no necessary, absolute separation of religion and political rule, let alone that the state should be hostile to religion, though, of course, such radical views are also amongst those recognizable as political secularism. Many different institutional arrangements and many different political views and ideologies, democratic and anti-democratic, liberal and illiberal, pro-religion and anti-religion, are consistent with this minimal conception of secularism: the non-domination of political authority by religious authority. I take subscription to this idea to be central to modernity and therefore one of the dominant ideas of the twentieth century. I do not mean that everybody in modern societies agrees with this view and, of course, like all ideas, it is not perfectly or purely manifested in any actual case, and people will disagree about the specific cases. Nevertheless, like democracy, political secularism is a hegemonic idea that most people actively and passively support and few argue against in a full-throated way.

An increasing number of academics think that in recent years something highly significant, possibly epochal, has happened to this state of affairs. Established modern societies are producing critics of this taken-for-granted idea in their midst and emergent modern societies do not seem to be smoothly following in the path that led to the historical ascendancy of political secularism. My interest is specifically in Western

Europe. Jürgen Habermas, who has Western Europe very much at the forefront of his mind, has famously announced we are currently witnessing a transition from a secular to a 'postsecular society' in which 'secular citizens' have to express a previously denied respect for 'religious citizens', who should be allowed, even encouraged, to critique aspects of contemporary society and to find solutions to its problems from within their religious views (Habermas, 2006). Instead of treating religion as subrational and a matter of private concern only, religion is once again to be recognized as a legitimate basis of public engagement and political action. Some have gone further and speak of a global crisis. Even quite sober academics speak today of 'a contemporary crisis of secularism' (Scherer, 2010: 4) and that 'today, political secularisms are in crisis in almost every corner of the globe' (Jakelić, 2010: 3). Olivier Roy, in an analysis focused on France writes of 'the crisis of the secular state'(Roy, 2007) and Rajeev Bhargava of the 'crisis of the secular state in Europe' (Bhargava, 2010, 2011).[2]

Of course there is a larger and more specifically sociological thesis about 'desecularization' across the world, about the development of modern economies and institutions without a decline, and indeed by some reversal of an earlier decline in religious belief and practice (Berger, 1999). My interest is limited to the phenomenon of public religion and of how religion is fighting back from its political marginalization. Across the globe, religious groups are protesting against perceived demotion or marginalization in the public space. There is a sense of actual or potential marginality, both culturally and politically, of losing the public space that should rightfully, at least partly, belong to one (Jurgensmeyer, 1994; Marty and Appleby, 1994). This can lead to protest and even anger and an assertive politics. Yet, while in most parts of the world the protestors seek to restore a real, or more probably imagined past – a golden age before the marginalization – this is not the case in Western Europe.[3] More fundamentally, while in the other regions there is a sense that a religious majority has been or is being marginalized, in Western Europe, the group most expressing its sense of marginalization is a minority. So, while the religionist agitation in the US, the Muslim world, and India is about the status and re-empowerment of the religious majority, of making the country in the image of the religious majority, the issue in Europe is about the status of a minority and its right to change the countries that it has recently become part of or is trying to be accepted as part of. In so far as the dominant religion, Christianity, exhibits a new found political assertiveness, it is in reaction to the minority presence and politics and in a context of continuing decline in Christian religiosity and church membership. The majoritarian reaction is sometimes in terms of a sympathetic multiculturalist or multifaith accommodation but all too often, and growingly, in secularist and Christianist oppositional modes. The majority are reacting to the minority, not to the felt constraints of 'secularism' and so the form of the challenge is not a religious resurgence but an ethno-religious multiculturalism – indeed, not postsecularism but secularism, or neo-secularism, is one of the leading majoritarian responses, especially in France.

The accommodation of Muslims in Western Europe

There is no endogenous slowing down in secularization in relation to organized religion, attendance at church services, and traditional Christian belief and practice in Western Europe. For example, to illustrate with the British case, church attendance of at least once a month amongst white people has steadily declined from about 20 per cent in 1983 to about 15 per cent in 2008 and with each younger age cohort (Voas and Crockett, 2005; BRIN, 2011; Kaufmann, Goujon, and Skirbekk, 2013). Which is not to say that religion has disappeared or is about to but for many it has become more in the form of 'belief without belonging' (Davie, 1994) or spirituality (Heelas and Woodhead, 2005) or 'implicit religion' (Bailey, 1997). For example, while belief in a personal God has gone down from over 40 per cent in the middle of the twentieth century to less than 30 per cent by its end, belief in a spirit or life source has remained steady at around 35–40 per cent and belief in the soul has actually increased from less than 60 per cent in the early 1980s to an additional 5–10 per cent today (BRIN, 2011). All these changes, however, are highly compatible with political secularism if not with scientism or other rationalistic philosophies. Whether the decline of traditional religion is being replaced by no religion or new ways of being religious or spiritual, neither is creating a challenge for political secularism. Non-traditional forms of Christian or post-Christian religion in Western Europe are, in the main, not attempting to connect with or reform political institutions and government policies; they are not seeking recognition or political accommodation or political power.[4]

In recent decades, Western Europe has come to share the post-immigration racial and ethnic urban diversity, which has long been a characteristic of the United States.[5] Currently, most of the largest, especially the capital, cities of north-west Europe are about 20–35 per cent non-white (i.e., people of non-European descent, including Turks). Even without further large-scale immigration, being a young, fertile population, these proportions will grow for at least one or two generations more before they stabilize, reaching or exceeding 50 per cent in some cities in the next few decades or sooner. The trend will include some of the larger urban centres of southern Europe. A significant difference between Western Europe and the US, however, is that the majority of non-whites in the countries of Europe are Muslims.[6] With estimates of 12 million to over 17 million Muslims in Western Europe today, the Muslim population in the former EU-15 is only about three to five per cent and is relatively evenly distributed across the larger states (Peach, 2007; Pew Forum, 2010). In the larger cities, the proportion which is Muslim, however, is several times larger and growing at a faster rate than most of the population (Lutz, Skirbekk, and Testa, 2007). In this context, with the riots in the suburbs (*banlieues*) of Paris and elsewhere, the Danish cartoon affair and other issues about offence and freedom of speech, and the proliferating bans on various forms of female Muslim dress just being a few in a series of conflicts focused on minority-majority relations, questions about integration, equality, racism, and Islam, and their relation to terrorism, security, and foreign policy, have become central to European politics.

The issue, then, driving the sense of a crisis of secularism that some sense in Western Europe is the place of religious identities, or identities that are or are perceived to be an ethno-religious identity (like British Asian Muslim or Arab Muslim in France), in the public life of the countries of the region. This multicultural challenge to secularism, is amongst the most profound political and long-term issues to arise from the post-war Western European hunger for labour migrants and the reversal of the population flows of European colonialism. The challenge is far from confined to secularism. It is a broad one: from socio-economic disadvantage and discrimination in the labour markets at one end to a constitutional status or corporate relationship with the state at the other. Moreover, the awareness of this challenge is not due to terrorism, as it began to manifest itself and was perceived before events such as 9/11; nor is it due to the fact that some Muslims, unlike other post-immigration groups, may have been involved in rowdy demonstrations and riots, because some African-Caribbeans were associated with these without raising such profound normative questions. Nor is it due to (Muslim) conservative values, especially in relation to gender and sexuality, though it is related to it.

The core element of the challenge is the primacy given by some muslims to religion as the basis of identity, organization, political representation, normative justification, etc. These matters were thought to be more or less settled (except in a few exceptional cases like Northern Ireland) till some Muslims started to assert themselves as Muslims in the public sphere of various West European countries. Some have thought that primacy could be given to, say, gender, ethnicity, or class; others have thought that primacy should not be given to any one or even a few of these social categories as identity self-concepts, but very few thought that religion should be in the select set (Modood, 2005; Modood, Triandafyllidou, and Zapata-Barrero, 2006).

Multiculturalism

It is not the mere presence of Muslims or Islam that creates a challenge all by itself. It is the presence of Muslims mediated by or in interaction with contemporary values of European states and politics. In particular, we should attend to two key complexes of political ideas, norms and practices which predate and are independent of Muslim immigrant politics but which make available a certain political opportunity structure for Muslims to make claims which create majoritarian and secularist anxieties. Muslims have been able to adapt and utilize these evolving political complexes and this gives a distinctive character to the phenomenon of interest.

The first one of these is not to do with secularism or desecularization or public assertive religious, *per se*, but with claims for accommodation from within Western polities and normative viewpoints in relation to minorities generally. Let us call these debates and activities 'multiculturalism'. These discourses and practices of non-discrimination, rights, equal accommodation, and respect are largely discourses from within Western European normative debates, norms, and laws (though influenced by a larger climate of opinion led particularly by Anglophone, colonial settler, and immigration-based countries such as the US, Canada, and Australia). They are picked up post-immigration and when Muslims or other groups utilize them, the reference is to the status and resources available to other groups in the West, not 'homelands'.[7] The second complex I have in mind is the religion-state linkages and support structures that exist in Western European countries, which I will call 'moderate secularism'.

Multicultural citizenship refers to the presence of ideas, ethos, and politics of 'difference', which allows for the articulation and legitimacy (and illegitimacy) of dealing with certain kinds of claims, in ways that are deemed acceptable and satisfactory. Briefly, I mean three things here (for further details, see Modood, 2007). Firstly, there is the critique of those portrayals of political systems, including contemporary liberal democratic states like those of Western Europe, as consisting of universal norms and rights. The critique is that such norms and rights are inflected by particular historical traditions and national cultures which give distinctive interpretations to ideas such as individual and group, public and private, rights and obligations, and so create a *de facto* second-class citizenship for those who do not identify with that culture or are not privileged within it. Secondly, that despite legal definitions and idealized norms of equality between all individuals, many people see either themselves and/or other citizens not just as individuals or citizens but in terms of membership of groups, such as women, black people, or Muslims. These identities are often imposed upon individuals as markers of social inferiority but equally (and simultaneously) can be forms of self-identity and pride and indeed resistance to inferiorization. Given this, thirdly, the challenge of creating equality between historically privileged and disadvantaged groups within a citizenry is unlikely to be achieved by acting as if group identities no longer exist. In relation to colour racism such pretence is called the pursuit of colour-blind policies and, by analogy, one can speak of gender blindness and Muslim blindness in relation to citizenship equality. It is contended that full civic equality will require not just policies treating all citizens as individuals but, additionally, policies, institutions, and discourses which 'recognize' (Taylor, 1994) that certain group identities are victims of negative treatment, are not going to disappear, and should not be required to disappear. So the best approach is a politics of respect which turns these negative identities into positively valued ones and to remake our sense of common citizenship and nationality to include them. This is my understanding of political multiculturalism based on the ideas of political theorists such as Charles Taylor, Bhikhu Parekh, Iris Young, and Will Kymlicka, though I understand that it is not what many Western European politicians, journalists, and social commentators who are critical of multiculturalism may mean by multiculturalism (Modood, 2007, 2011a). My point is that it is the presence, adaptation, and disputation of these ideas and rhetorics which gives the question of the accommodation of Muslims the character it has, namely a multiculturalist character. The result is that to talk about the integration of Muslims in Western Europe today is to argue about multiculturalism. Indeed, the converse has also become true. To talk about multiculturalism today in Western Europe is to talk about – pro and con – the accommodation of Muslims.

Moderate secularism

It is undeniably true that in terms of vocabulary, concepts, and institutional practices each country in Western Europe is a secular state, but each has its own distinctive take on what this means. Nevertheless, there is a general historical character, which I call moderate secularism, and a lesser strand. The latter is principally manifested in French secularism (*laïcité*), which seeks to create a public space in which religion is virtually banished in the name of reason and emancipation, and religious organizations are monitored by the state through consultative national mechanisms. The main Western European approach, however, sees organized religion as not just a private benefit but a potential public good or national resource, and which the state can in some circumstances assist to realize – even through an 'established' church (Modood, 2010). These public benefits can be direct, such as a contribution to education and social care through autonomous church-based organizations funded by the taxpayer; or indirect, such as the production of attitudes that create economic hope or family stability; and they can have to do with national identity, cultural heritage, ethical voice, and national ceremonies.

Western Europe has been a site of a historical struggle between public churches and political secularists, yet during the nineteenth and especially the twentieth centuries – and especially in Protestant-majority societies – this has not been deeply conflictual and has taken the form of various shifting compromises. The compromises consisted of a successful accommodation of an expanding number of Christian churches within the business and symbolic workings of the state, yet marked by a gradual but decisive weakening of the public and political character of the churches. The 1960s till the end of the century saw a particularly strong movement of opinion and politics in favour of the secularists. In Western Europe, the cultural revolution of the 1960s has been broadly accepted; not only has there been no major, sustained counter-movement but it broadened out from north-western Protestant/secular Europe into Catholic Europe. So, for example, the national system of 'pillarization' in the Netherlands, by which Protestants and Catholics had separate access to some of the state's resources, emerged in the nineteenth century, declined sharply in the middle of the twentieth, and was formally wound up in 1983. The Lutheran Church in Sweden was disestablished in 2000. In the UK, disestablishment of the Church of England was embraced in the early 1990s by the Liberal Democrats (the third political party in the country), by the influential think tank, Institute of Public Policy Research (IPPR) (probably the largest British think tank in the 1990s and a key player in the remaking of the post-Thatcher Labour Party into a governing party), by the left wing of the Labour Party, and the two liberal-left broadsheets (for details, see Modood, 1992: 85 and 1994). Catholic countries – Italy, Spain, Portugal, and Ireland – in the 1980s and 1990s showed rapid signs of the secularization characteristic of Protestant Europe (cf. Davie, 1999: 69–70, 2002: 6–7).

Of course, this has not meant that public religion, even the formal connexions to the state and direct access to governments, disappeared altogether. There has been a trend towards less public recognition, but it has not led to anything like a terminal endpoint, not even in France. Nor, on the other hand, has there been much political challenge from organized religion or political conflict involving religion (Northern Ireland's exceptional character proving the rule). The place of religion in Western Europe has been relatively uncontroversial in the last decades of the twentieth century because religion has not been particularly visible and there has been a general assumption – perhaps shared by many religious people, perhaps even by religious lobbies – that the decreasing public presence of religion is irreversible and better than a political fight to reverse the trend or to take decisive action to take it to its endpoint. Religion did not cease to be public, but because it was not felt to be too challenging or threatening it was noticed less. For example, a political campaign on a religious matter, or led by religious people, was less likely to be reported by the media than, say, an anti-racist or environmentalist protest.

Responding to Muslim assertiveness

This, then, is the context in which non-Christian migrants have been arriving and settling and in which they and the next generation were becoming active members of their societies, including making political claims of equality and accommodation. So, the rising multicultural challenge and the gradual weakening of the political status of Christian churches, in particular the national churches, were taking place at the same time. The intersection of these two trajectories is nicely captured in two policy initiatives in the Netherlands in 1983. In that year in which the national system of 'pillarization' – which had at one time made the country a bi-religious communal state – was formally wound up, a new Minorities Policy (*Nota Minderhedenbeleid*) was announced (see Bader, 2011; Lentin and Titley, 2011: 107–108) that created post-immigration ethnic minorities (*allochtones*) as a mini-pillar, giving them state funding for faith schools, ethno-religious radio and TV broadcasting, and other forms of cultural maintenance (Bader, 2011).

Some of that policy began to be reversed in the 1990s, but looking beyond the Netherlands, the pivotal moment was 1988–1989 and was, quite accidentally, marked by two events. These created national and international storms and set in motion political developments which have not been reversed and offer contrasting ways in which the two Western European secularisms are responding to the Muslim presence. The events were the protests in Britain against the Sir Salman Rushdie's novel, *The Satanic Verses*; and, in France, the decision by a school head teacher to prohibit entry to three girls till they were willing to take off their headscarves in school premises.

The Satanic Verses was not banned in the UK as the protestors demanded and the conduct of some Muslims, especially those threatening the life of the author, certainly shocked and alienated many from the campaign. In that sense, the Muslim campaign clearly failed. In other respects, however, it galvanized many into seeking a democratic multiculturalism that was inclusive of Muslims. A national body was created to represent mainstream Muslim opinion, initially in relation to the novel (UK Action Committee on Islamic Affairs) but later, with some encouragement from both the main national political parties, especially New Labour, it led to a body to lobby on behalf of Muslims in the corridors of power. This new body, the Muslim Council of Britain (MCB) was accepted as a consultee by the New Labour government of 1997 till about the middle of the next decade when it looked for new interlocutors. The MCB was very successful in relation to its founding agenda (Modood, 2011b). By 2001, it had achieved its aim of having Muslim issues and Muslims as a group recognized separately from issues of race and ethnicity; and of being itself accepted by government, media, and civil society as the spokesperson for Muslims. Two additional achieved aims were the state funding of Muslim schools on the same basis as Christian and Jewish schools and getting certain educational and employment policies targeted on the severe disadvantage of the Pakistanis and Bangladeshis (who are nearly all Muslims) as opposed to on minority ethnicity generally. Additionally, it played a decisive role in getting Tony Blair to go against ministerial and civil service advice and insert a religion question into the 2001 UK Census (Sherif, 2011). This meant that the ground was laid for the possible later introduction of policies targeting Muslims to match those targeting groups defined by race or ethnicity – or gender. The MCB had to wait a bit longer to get the legislative protection it sought. Laws against religious discrimination were introduced in 2003, strengthened in 2007 and again in 2010, making them much stronger than anything available in the rest of the European Union (EU). Incitement to religious hatred, the legislation most closely connected to the protests over *The Satanic Verses*, was introduced in 2006, though there is no suggestion that it would have caught that novel. Indeed, the protestors' original demand that the blasphemy law be extended to cover Islam has been made inapplicable, as the blasphemy law was abolished in 2008 – with very little protest from anybody. Moreover, even as the MCB, because of its views on the government's foreign and security policies, fell out of favour, local and national consultations with Muslim groups has continued to grow and probably now exceeds consultations with any Christian body and certainly any minority group. Inevitably, this has caused occasional friction between Christians and Muslims. But on the whole, these developments have taken place not only with the support of the leadership of the Church of England but in a spirit of interfaith respect. (Given how adversarial English intellectual, journalistic, legal, and political culture is, religion in England is oddly fraternal and little effort is expended in proving that the other side is in a state of error and should convert.)

So, that is one path of development from 1988–1989. As can be seen, it was a mobilization of a minority and the extension of minority policies from race to religion in order to accommodate the religious minority. The other development, namely the one arising from the headscarf case (*l'affaire foulard*), was one of top-down state action to prohibit certain minority practices. From the start, the majority of the country – whether it be media, the public intellectuals, the politicians, or public opinion – were supportive of the head teacher who refused to have religious headscarves in school (Bowen, 2007; Scott, 2007). Muslims either did not wish to or lacked the capacity to challenge this dominant view with anything like the publicity, organization, clamour, or international assistance that Muslims in Britain bore to bear on Rushdie's novel.

The Conseil d'État, France's highest administrative court, emphasized freedom of religion as long as the religious symbols were not 'ostentatious' and so ruled that the issue should be treated on a case by case basis (Kastoryano, 2006; see also Bowen, 2007). This quietened things down till they blew up again in 1994 in relation to another state school. On that occasion the Minister of Education forbade the wearing of any ostentatious symbols, which explicitly included the headscarf. The issue would not go away, however, and in 2003 President Chirac appointed a national commission, chaired by Bernard Stasi, to consider the issue. The Stasi Commission recommended the banning of the wearing of conspicuous religious symbols in state schools, and a law to this effect was passed with an overwhelming majority by Parliament in February 2004. A few years later the target of secularist and majoritarian disapproval was the full face veil with just the eyes showing (*niqab*; *burqa*), as favoured by a few hundred Muslim women. This was banned in public places in April 2011. Belgium followed suit in July 2011 and Italy is in the process of doing so (Guardian, 2011). Similar proposals are being discussed by governments and political parties across Western Europe (e.g., the Dutch government [Nikolas, 2011] and the ruling Labour Party in Norway [Larsen and Barstad, 2011]). Even in Britain there is popular support for a ban though the major parties have no truck with it.

While the radical secularist (*laïcité*) trajectory of the banning of some headdress favoured by some Muslim women was taking place, another was simultaneously taking place in countries like France, which is important to note as it does not so easily conform to the common understanding of French *laïcité*. Since 1990, each French government, whether of the left or the right, have set about trying to create a national Muslim council that would be a corporate representative of Muslims in France and the official government consultee. It would be the state's recognition of Islam comparable in some respects to its recognition of the Catholic and Protestant churches, and the Jewish consistory. After at least three abortive attempts by previous interior ministers, Interior Minister Nicolas Sarkozy inaugurated the Conseil Français du Culte Musulman in 2003 (Modood and Kastoryano, 2006: 174–175). Even now, this council has not yet come to be accepted by the majority of Muslims in France and has had little influence on the French media, civil society, or government. Its importance for my argument does not depend on its effectiveness or on whether it has support amongst Muslims in France. I mention it because it exhibits how even a laicist, anti-multiculturalist state, which is supported by most citizens in attacking fundamental religious freedom, is creating institutional linkages to govern Muslims in a way which is *prima facie* contrary to *laïcité*. It is not, however, contrary to the Western Europe tradition of moderate secularism, and France is not alone in following a path comprising of anti-multiculturalist rhetoric – refusal to offer accommodation on specifics,[8] but a willingness to deal with Muslims not just as individual citizens but also as a religious group. Chancellor Merkel's government in Germany assembled a group of Muslims in 2006 in order to hold an *Islamkonfrenz* at the highest level of government and this has been repeated every year. Interestingly, the secularist strand of opinion in Britain, which looks to France as a model, is opposed to the government giving special consultative status to Muslim organizations and sees this as consistent with the older demand for the disestablishment of the Church of England, the removal of bishops from a democratized House of Lords, and a reduction in the number of state-funded faith schools.[9]

Additional responses: Christian values and muscular liberalism

So, two responses have manifested themselves to Muslim action and claims-making: the accommodationist approach – which through dialogue, negotiation, and adaptation has tried to find a space for Muslims within an older, broad racial equality and multiculturalist orientation – and a radical secularist approach. Two other sentiments can also be identified: a Christianist sentiment and an intolerant or 'muscular' liberalism sentiment. By this I do not mean to say that Christians and liberals were not party to the first two approaches. The churches, especially the Church of England, have been actively involved in supporting British multiculturalism and developing interfaith dialogue, networks, and policy coalitions with Muslims and other minorities. Similarly, what I refer to as liberal intolerance overlaps with the secularist intolerance that has already been discussed. What is distinctive about the following two responses to Muslims is that one makes an explicit appeal to Christianity, and the other makes an explicit appeal to the limits of the prized value of toleration.

The reference to Christianity can be quite distant from policy. For example, it seems that the presence and salience of Muslims can be a factor in stimulating a Christian identity. An analysis of the voluntary religion question in the 2001 UK Census shows higher 'Christian' identification in areas near large Muslim populations (Voas and Bruce, 2004). The emergence of a new, sometimes politically assertive, cultural identification with Christianity has been noted in Denmark (Mouritsen, 2006), and in Germany, Chancellor Merkel has recently asserted that '[t]hose who don't accept [Christian values] don't have a place here' (cited in Presseurop, 2010, reported as 'Muslims in her country should adopt Christian values'). Since then, several senior Bavarian politicians have made the link between German nationalism and Christianity even more emphatically (Fekete, 2011: 46). Similar sentiments were voiced in the EU constitution debate and are apparent in the ongoing debate about Turkey as a future EU member (Casanova, 2009). These assertions of Christianity are not necessarily accompanied by any increase in expressions of faith or church attendance, which continue to decline across Europe. What is at work is not the repudiation of a status quo secularism (Casanova, 2009) in favour of Christianity but a response to the challenge of multiculturalism (as Merkel made explicit by asserting that 'multi-kulti' had failed and was not wanted back). Former French President Giscard d'Estaing, who chaired the Convention on the Future of Europe, the body which drafted the (abortive) EU constitution, expresses nicely the assertiveness I speak of: 'I never go to Church, but Europe is a Christian continent.'[10]

Such political views, however, are also being expressed by Christian organizations, especially by the Catholic Church. Early in his papacy, Pope Benedict XVI, in a speech at the Bavarian Catholic University at Regensburg, suggested that while reason was central to Christian divinity, this was not the case with the God of Islam, which licenced conversion by the sword and was deeply antithetical to the European tradition of rationality.[11] It has been argued that Pope John Paul II 'looked at the essential cleavage in the world as being between religion and unbelief. Devout Christians, Muslims, and Buddhists had more in common with each other than with atheists' (Caldwell, 2009: 151). Pope Benedict, the same author contends, 'thinks that, within societies, believers and unbelievers exist in symbiosis. Secular Westerners, he implies, have a lot in common with their religious fellows' (Caldwell, 2009: 151). The suggestion is that secularists and Christians in Europe have more in common with each other than they do with Muslims. That many secularists do not share Pope Benedict's view is evident from the fact that the proposed clause about Christianity was absent from the final draft of the abortive EU constitution. Moreover, it is indicative of the place of Christianity in Europe relative to radical secularism, that it emerged as a third, not a first or second, trend. That is to say, it joined a debate in which the running had been mainly made by an accommodationist multiculturalism and an exclusionist secularism allied with nationalism. Yet, while there is little sign of a Christian right in Europe of the kind that is strong in the US, there is, to some degree, a reinforcing or renewing of a sense that Europe is 'secular Christian', analogous to the term 'secular Jew' to describe someone of Jewish descent who has a sense of Jewish identity but is not religiously practising and may even be an atheist.

A fourth trend focuses on Muslims' conservative or illiberal moral values and practices. These are likely to centre on issues of gender and sexuality, and so this trend overlaps with that which has led to legal restrictions on the wearing of the headscarf and the face veil but is worth identifying separately, as it goes much wider and can be independent of questions of religion-state relations. It is alleged that the state needs to take special action against Muslims because, for example, their attitudes to, but not only, gender equality and sexual orientation equality are less than and threatening to reverse what has been achieved in Western countries. This argument is found across the region and across the political and intellectual spectrum but is particularly strong in the Netherlands. Pim Fortuyn's call, for example, at the turn of this century, for a halt to Muslim immigration because of their views on sex and personal freedom achieved considerable electoral success (Economist, 2002). The Dutch government produced a video to be shown to prospective Muslim immigrants which included a close-up of a topless woman on a beach and gay men kissing in a park to assist in the process of assessing applicants for entry into the country (Monshipouri, 2010: 51). In neighbouring Denmark, the newspaper *Jyllands-Posten* famously published satirical and irreverent cartoons of the Prophet Muhammad to, according to its cultural editor, assist Muslims to be acculturalized into Danish public culture (Levey and Modood, 2009: 227).[12] Ayaan Hirsi Ali, a former Dutch MP of Somali Muslim origin, became an international figure through her argument that the subordination of women was a core feature of orthodox Islam. The position I am referring to could be said to be a form of liberal perfectionism; that is to say, the view, in contrast to a Rawlsian neutralism, that it is the business of a liberal state to produce liberal individuals and promote a liberal way of life (Mouritsen and Olsen, 2012), perhaps what Charles Taylor once called, liberalism as 'a fighting creed' or what Prime Minister Cameron has called 'muscular liberalism'. Its actual political dynamic has been to create and lead popular anti-Muslim hostility as in the form of Geert Wilders's comparison of the Qur'an with *Mein Kampf* and campaign to ban the former as long as the latter is banned. His campaign against the 'Islamization of Europe' has many echoes across Western Europe and not just across the Netherlands, where the Party for Freedom he founded in 2005 became the third-largest party in the 2010 elections and a negotiating partner in the formation of a government.

Islamophobia

In relation to the topic of this article, this 'muscular liberalism' is perhaps squarely with the radical secularism of the *hijab* and *burqa* bans (that is how it has been interpreted by Christian Joppke, 2009),[13] but I mention it separately as it is intellectually distinct and, more importantly, because it helps to bring out that the dynamic which political secularism – and indeed liberalism – is being subjected to and is being tested on is the presence of Muslims and anti-Muslim hostility from various intellectual and political directions. Another example of this broad anti-Muslim coalition is the majority that voted in a referendum to ban the building of minarets in Switzerland in 2009. It has been analysed as including those whose primary motivation is women's rights to those 'who simply feel that Islam is "foreign"', who may have no problems with Muslims per se but who are not ready to accept 'Islam's acquiring of visibility in public spaces' (Mayer, 2009: 6) and generally did not vote 'out of a desire to oppress anybody, but because they are themselves feeling threatened by what they see as an Islam invasion' (Mayer, 2009: 8). So, prejudiced or fearful perceptions of Islam are capable of uniting a wide range of opinion into a majority, including those who have no strong views about church-state arrangements, as indeed has been apparent from the very beginning that Muslim claims became public controversies.

It means that the current challenge to secularism in Western Europe is being debated not just in terms of the wider issues of integration and multiculturalism but also in terms of a hostility to Muslims and Islam based on stereotypes and scare stories in the media that are best understood as a specific form of cultural racism that has come to be called Islamophobia (Meer and Modood, 2010; Sayyid and Vakil, 2010) and is largely unrelated to questions of secularism. A meta-analysis of opinion polls between 1998 and 2006 in Britain concluded that 'between one in five and one in four Britons now exhibits a strong dislike of, and prejudice against, Islam and Muslims' (Field, 2007: 465). A Pew survey in 2008 confirmed the higher figure and found its equivalent in France to be nearly double (38 per cent) and just over 50 per cent in Germany (Pew Research Center, 2008). These views are growing, are finding expression in the rise of extreme right-wing parties, and even in terrorism, as happened in Oslo and the island of Utøya in July 2011 (Bangstad, 2011). This, to put it mildly, is not a favourable context for accommodating Muslims and underscores the point that the so-called crisis of secularism is really about the presence and integration of Muslims, which, of course, partly depends upon how some Muslims behave (e.g., acts of terrorism or declarations of disloyalty to the country).

So, looking at the four trends and the wider Islamophobic climate of opinion, it looks as if the radical secularist trend and the Christianist trend could unite through a cultural nationalism or a cultural Europeanism animated by an Islamophobia. I hope not, I would like to think that the spectre of a populist, right-wing nationalism, not to mention racism, will make enough people rally round a moderate secularism, which they will recognize has to be pluralized. But either way, what this analysis suggests is that the real choice is between a pluralist, multi-faith nationality or Europeanism and a monoculturalist nationalism or Europeanism. Or, to put it another way, the crisis of secularism is best understood within a framework of multiculturalism. Of course, multiculturalism currently has few advocates at the moment and the term is highly damaged.[14] Yet, the repeated declarations from the senior politicians of the region that 'multiculturalism is dead' (Fekete, 2011) are a reaction to the continuing potency of multiculturalism which renders obsolete liberal takes on assimilation and integration with new forms of public gender and public ethnicity, and now public religion. Muslims are late joiners of this movement, but when they did so, it slowly becomes apparent that the secularist status quo, with certain residual privileges for Christians, is untenable as it stands. We can call this the challenge of integration rather than multiculturalism, as long as it is understood that we are not just talking about an integration into the day-to-day life of a society but also into its institutional architecture, grand narratives, and macro-symbolic sense of itself (Modood, 2012). If these issues were dead, we would not be having a debate about the role of public religion or coming up with proposals for dialogue with Muslims and the accommodation of Islam. The dynamic for change is not directly to do with the historic religion nor the historic secularism of Western Europe; rather the novelty, which then has implications for Christians and secularists, and to which they are reacting, is the appearance of an assertive multiculturalism which cannot be contained within a matrix of individual rights, conscience, religious freedom, and so on. If any of these were different the problems would be other than they are – just as today we look at issues to do with, say, women or homosexuality not simply in terms of rights but in a political environment influenced by feminism and gay liberation, within a socio-political-intellectual culture in which the 'assertion of positive difference' or 'identity' is a shaping and forceful presence. It does not mean everybody is a feminist now, but a heightened consciousness of gender and gender equality creates a certain gender-equality sensibility. Similarly, my claim is that a multiculturalist sensibility today is present in Western Europe and yet it is not comfortable with extending itself to accommodate Muslims nor able to find reasons for not extending to Muslims without self-contradiction.

Conclusion

Political secularism has been destabilized. In particular, the historical flow from a moderate to radical secularism and the expectation of its continuation has been jolted. This is not because of any Christian desecularization or a 'return of the repressed'. Rather, the jolt is created by the triple contingency of the arrival and settlement of a significant number of Muslims; a multiculturalist sensibility which respects 'difference'; and a moderate secularism, namely that the historical compromises between the state and a church or churches in relation to public recognition and accommodation are still in place to some extent. To speak of a 'crisis of secularism' is highly exaggerated, especially in relation to the state. It is true that the challenge is much greater for *laïcité* or radical secularism as an ideology. As many social and political theorists are sympathetic to this ideology, and in any case, being more sensitive to abstract ideas, they are less able to see the actually existing secularism of Western Europe, with the exception of France, is not the radical variant. They, thus, mistakenly project the incompatibility between their ideas and the accommodation of Muslims onto the Western European states. Indeed, as applied to Western Europe 'crisis of secularism' is not only exaggerated but misleading. As I hope I have shown, the problem is more defined by issues of post-immigration integration than by the religion-state relation per se. The 'crisis of secularism' is really the challenge of multiculturalism. Far from this entailing the end of secularism as we know it, moderate secularism offers some of the resources for accommodating Muslims. Political secularists should think pragmatically and institutionally on how to achieve this; namely, how to multiculturalize moderate secularism, and avoid exacerbating the crisis and limiting the room for manoeuvre, by pressing for further, radical secularism.

Notes

1. This paper was first published as 'Is There a Crisis of Secularism in Western Europe?' in *Sociology of Religion* Summer 2012, 73(2), 109–129, doi:10.1093/socrel/srs029. 'Render unto Caesar the things which are Caesar's, and unto God the things that are God's' is, of course, a political view, or about politics, based on the authority of St Matthew's Gospel.
2. Bhargava does not believe the crisis is confined to Europe; see also Zucca (2009).
3. Peter Berger expressly mentions 'Europe, west of what used to be called the Iron Curtain' as an exception to his desecularization thesis (1999: 9). This is a good geographic approximation of what I mean by Western Europe.
4. It may be the case that some government policies are seeking to delegate certain welfare responsibilities, but that is not based on rethinking secularism or Christianity but on wishing to limit the scale of the state for revenue or other reasons.
5. Of course, the presence of black people in the US as a whole is a consequence not of immigration but slavery, but the urban racial and ethnic mix is due to internal migration as well as to many waves of immigration.
6. The UK, where Muslims form about a third of non-whites or ethnic minorities, is one of the exceptions.

7. Though new discourses of Islam emerge that develop these concepts and see the ideals of some contemporary Western publics (e.g., feminists, multiculturalists, anti-imperialists, etc.) as ideals within Islam, too, that have regrettably been obscured in the past (see, e.g., Safi, 2003).
8. Sometimes refusal at a national level is accompanied by local compromises (Bowen, 2010).
9. See National Secular Society and the British Humanist Association websites; for similar views amongst centre-left Christians, see the website of the think tank, Ekklesia.
10. More recently, Prime Minister Cameron, who has confessed to not being a steadfast believer, made a major speech arguing that Britons should not be shy of asserting that Britain is a Christian country (http://www.number10.gov.uk/news/king-james-bible). While many secularists protested, the speech was welcomed by the chair of the Mosque and Community Affairs of the Muslim Council of Britain, Sheikh Ibrahim Mogra (http://www.bbc.co.uk/news/uk-16231223).
11. November 2006, http://www.zenit.org/article-16955?l=english.
12. Even though he, or at least his newspaper, took a different view of an anti-Christian cartoon earlier (Fouché, 2006).
13. 'Perfectionist liberalism is not intolerant *per se*... Intolerance (and conflict with traditional liberal pluralism) enters at the point where officially promoted ideals of good liberal citizenship come to be seen as so important, so threatened, and so much in conflict with specific *un-civic* (religious) practices and dispositions, concentrated in defined and targetable out-groups, that attempts to change, penalize or even outlaw them become legitimate' (Mouritsen and Olsen, 2012).
14. Which does not mean subscription to the thesis that multiculturalism is in retreat. Firstly, analysis of policies in 21 countries shows that whilst the growth of multicultural policies between 1980 and 2000 was modest, far from halting or retreating continued to progress between 2000-2010, with only three countries having a lower score in 2010 than 2000 (MCP Index: http://www.queensu.ca/mcp/immigrant/table/Immigrant_Minorities_Table_2.pdf). An alternative index of fourteen countries confirms this "consolidation at moderate levels of multicultural policies, albeit with important cross-national variation in both directions" (Koopmans 2013: 8). Secondly, much of the anti-multiculturalism cannot be justified within the terms of assimilation and individual integration (Modood, 2011).

References

Bader, V. (2011). 'Associational Governance of Ethno-Religious Diversity in Europe. The Dutch Case.' In R. Smith (ed.) *Citizenship, Borders, and Human Needs*, 273–297. Philadelphia, PA: Penn State University.

Bailey, E.I. (1997). *Implicit Religion in Contemporary Society*. Kampen and Weinheim, Germany: Kok Pharos.

Bangstad, S. (2011). 'Norway: Terror and Islamophobia in the Mirror.' *Open Democracy*. Online source, available at http://www.opendemocracy.net/sindrebangstad/norway-terror-andislamophobia inmirror [last accessed 12 October 2011].

Berger, P.L. (1999). *The Desecularization of the World: Resurgent Religion and World Politics*. Washington, DC: Ethics and Public Policy Center.
Bhargava, R. (2010). 'States, Religious Diversity, and the Crisis of Secularism.' In *Hedgehog Review*. Online source, available at http://www.opendemocracy.net/rajeev bhargava/states-religious-diversity-and-crisis-of-secularism-0 [last accessed 22 August, 2014]
Bhargava, R. (2011). 'States, Religious Diversity and the Crisis of Secularism.' In *Open Democracy*. Online source, available at net/rajeev bhargava/states-religious-diversity-and-crisis-of-secularism-0 [last accessed 22 August, 2014].
Bowen, J. R. (2007). 'Why the French Don't Like Headscarves: Islam, the State, and Public Space.' *European Review* 15(3), 397–400.
Bowen, J. R. (2010). *Can Islam be French? Pluralism and Pragmatism in a Secularist State*. Princeton, NJ: Princeton University Press.
BRIN (2011). 'Religious Affiliation and Church Attendance in Britain, 1983–2008.' *British Religion in Numbers*. Online source, available at http://www.brin.ac.uk/figures/#AffiliationAttendance [last accessed 12 October 2011].
Caldwell, C. (2009). *Reflections on the Revolution in Europe : Immigration, Islam and the West*. London: Allen Lane.
Casanova, J. (2009). 'Immigration and the New Religious Pluralism: a European Union United States Comparison.' In G.B. Levey and T. Modood (eds) *Secularism, Religion and Multicultural Citizenship*, 139–163. Cambridge: Cambridge University Press.
Davie, G. (1994). *Religion in Britain since 1945: Believing without Belonging*. Oxford: Blackwell Publishers.
Davie, G. (1999). 'Europe: the Exception That Proves the Rule.' In P.L. Berger (ed.) *The Desecularization of the World*, 65–84. Washington, DC: Ethics and Public Policy Center.
Davie, G. (2002). *Europe: The Exceptional Case: Parameters of Faith in the Modern World*. London: Darton Longman & Todd.
Economist. (2002). 'A Wind of Change in the Netherlands – and across Europe.' *The Economist*. 16 May 2002.
Fekete, L. (2011). 'Understanding the European-wide Assault on Multiculturalism.' In H. Mahamdallie (ed.) *Defending Multiculturalism*, 38–52. London: Bookmarks.
Field, C. (2007). 'Islamophobia in Contemporary Britain: the Evidence of the Opinion Polls, 1988–2006.' *Islam and Christian-Muslim Relations* 18, 447–477.
Fouché, G. (2006). 'Danish Paper Rejected Jesus Cartoons.' *The Guardian*. 6 February.
Guardian. (2011). 'Italy Approves Draft Law to Ban Burqa.' *The Guardian*. 3 August 2011.
Habermas, J. (2006). Religion in the Public Sphere. *European Journal of Philosophy* 14(1), 1–25.
Heelas, P. and Woodhead, L. (2005). *The Spiritual Revolution: Why Religion Is Giving Way to Spirituality*. Malden, MA: Wiley-Blackwell.
Jakelić, S. (2010). 'Secularism: A Bibliographic Essay.' *The Hedgehog Review*. Online source, available at http://www.iasc-culture.org/THR/THR_article_2010_Fall_Jakelic.php [last accessed 22 August 2014]
Joppke, C. (2009). *Veil: The Mirror of Identity*. Cambridge: Polity.
Jurgensmeyer, M. (1994). *Religious Nationalism Confronts the Secular State*. Oxford: Oxford University Press.

Kastoryano, R. (2006). 'French Secularism and Islam: France's Headscarf Affair.' In T. Modood, A. Triandafyllidou, and R. Zapata-Barrero (eds) *Multiculturalism, Muslims and Citizenship*, 57–69. London & New York: Routledge.

Kaufmann, E., Goujon, A., and Skirbekk, V. (2012). 'The End of Secularization in Europe? A Socio-Demographic Perspective.' *Sociology of Religion* 73(1), 69–91.

Koopmans, R. (2013). 'Multiculturalism and Immigration: A Contested Field in Cross-National Comparison.' *Annual Review of Sociology* 39, July.

Larsen, C.J. and Barstad, S. (2011). 'Ap-nei til Hijab i Domstolene.' *Aftenposten*. 10 April.

Lentin, A. and Titley, G. (2011). *The Crizes of Multiculturalism: Racism in a Neoliberal Age*. London: Zed Books.

Levey, G.B. and Modood, T. (2009). 'Liberal Democracy, Multicultural Citizenship, and the Danish Cartoon Affair.' In G.B. Levey and T. Modood (eds) *Secularism, Religion and Multicultural Citizenship*, 216–242. Cambridge: Cambridge University Press.

Lutz, W., Skirbekk, V., and Testa, M.R. (2007). 'The Low-Fertility Trap Hypothesis: Forces That May Lead to Further Postponement and Fewer Births in Europe.' *IIASA REPRINT*. Online source, available at http://paper.blog.bbiq.jp/Lutz_et_al_2006.pdf [last accessed 7 October 2011].

Marty, M.E. and Appleby, R.S. (1994). *Fundamentalisms Observed*. Chicago: University of Chicago Press.

Mayer, J.-F. (2009). 'Analysis: A Majority of Swiss Voters Decide to Ban the Building of New Minarets.' *Religioscope Institute*. Online source, available at http://religion.info/english/articles/article_455.shtml [last accessed 7 October 2011].

Meer, N. and Modood, T. (2010). 'The Racialization of Muslims.' In S. Sayyid and A. Vakil (eds) *Thinking Through Islamophobia: Global Perspectives*, 69–84. London and New York: Hurst and Columbia University Press.

Modood, T. (1992). *Not Easy Being British: Colour, Culture and Citizenship*. Stoke-on Trent, UK: Runnymede Trust and Trentham.

Modood, T. (1994). 'Establishment, Multiculturalism and British Citizenship.' *Political Quarterly* 65(1), 53–73.

Modood, T. (2005). *Multicultural Politics: Racism, Ethnicity and Muslims in Britain*. Edinburgh: Edinburgh University Press.

Modood, T. (2007). *Multiculturalism. A Civic Idea* (second edition, 2013), Cambridge: Polity.

Modood, T. (2010). Moderate Secularism, Religion as Identity and Respect for Religion. *The Political Quarterly* 81(1), 4–14.

Modood, T. (2011a). 'Multiculturalism and Integration: Struggling with Confusions.' In H. Mahamdallie (ed.) *Defending Multiculturalism*, 61–76. London: Bookmarks.

Modood, T. (2011b). *Still Not Easy Being British: Struggles for a Multicultural Citizenship*. Stoke-on-Trent, UK: Trentham.

Modood, T. (2012). Differenz und Integration. *Forschungsjournal Soziale Bewegungen* 25(1), 5–20.

Modood, T. and Kastoryano, R. (2006). 'Secularism and the Accommodation of Muslims in Europe.' In T. Modood, A. Triandafyllidou, and R. Zapato Barrero (eds) *Multiculturalism, Muslims and Citizenship: a European Approach*, 162–178. London: Routledge.

Modood, T., Triandafyllidou, A., and Zapata-Barrero, R. (2006). *Multiculturalism, Muslims and Citizenship: A European Approach.* London: Routledge.
Monshipouri, M. (2010). 'The War on Terror and Muslims in the West.' In J. Cesari (ed.) *Muslims in the West after 9/11: Religion, Politics and Law,* 45–66. London: Routledge.
Mouritsen, P. (2006). 'The Particular Universalism of a Nordic Civic Nation: Common Values, State Religion and Islam in Danish Political Culture. In T. Modood, A. Triandafyllidou, and R. Zapata-Barrero (eds) *Multiculturalism, Muslims and Citizenship: A European Approach.* London: Routledge.
Mouritsen, P. and Olsen, T.V. (2012). 'Liberalism and the Diminishing Space of Tolerance.' In J. Dobbernack and T. Modood (eds) *Hard to Accept. Perspectives on Intolerance, Toleration and Respect.* Basingstoke, UK: Palgrave Macmillan.
Nikolas, K. (2011). 'The Netherlands to Pass Burka Ban.' *Digital Journal.* Online source, available at http://digitaljournal.com/article/311630 [last accessed 10 October 2011].
Peach, C. (2007). 'Muslim Population of Europe: A Brief Overview of Demographic Trends and Socioeconomic Integration, with Particular Reference to Britain.' In *Muslim Integration: Challenging Conventional Wisdom in Europe and the United States.* Washington, DC: Center for Strategic and International Studies.
Pew Forum. (2010). 'Muslim Networks and Movements in Western Europe.' Online source, available at http://pewresearch.org/pubs/1731/muslim-networks movements Western-europe [last accessed 4 February 2011].
Pew Research Center. (2008). 'Unfavorable Views of Jews and Muslims on the Increas in Europe.' *Pew Research Center.* Online source, available at http://pewglobal.org/2008/09/17/unfavorable-views-of-jews-and-muslims-on-the increase-in-europe [last accessed 7 October 2011].
Presseurop. (2010). 'Mutti Merkel Handbags Multikulti.' *Presseurop.* Online source, available at http://www.presseurop.eu/en/content/article/364091-mutti-merkel handbags-multikulti [last accessed 28 March 2011].
Roy, O. (2007). *Secularism Confronts Islam.* New York: Columbia University Press.
Safi, O. (2003). *Progressive Muslims: On Justice, Gender and Pluralism.* Oxford: Oneworld.
Sayyid, S. and Vakil, A. (eds). (2010). *Thinking through Islamophobia.* London: Hurst.
Scherer, M. (2010). 'Landmarks in the Critical Study of Secularism.' *The Immanent Frame.* Online source, available at http://blogs.ssrc.org/tif/2010/11/12/landmarks secularism/ [last accessed 10 October 2011].
Scott, J.W. (2007). *The Politics of the Veil.* Princeton, NJ: Princeton University Press.
Sherif, J. (2011). 'A Census Chronicle: Reflections on the Campaign for a Religion Question in the 2001 Census for England and Wales.' *Journal of Beliefs & Values* 32(1), 1–18.
Taylor, C. (1994). 'The Politics of Recognition.' In A. Gutmann (ed.) *Multiculturalism and 'The Politics of Recognition': An Essay,* 25–73. Princeton, NJ: Princeton University Press.
Voas, D. and Bruce, S. (2004). 'Research Note: The 2001 Census and Christian Identification in Britain.' *Journal of Contemporary Religion* 19(1), 23–28.
Voas, D. and Crockett, A. (2005). 'Religion in Britain: Neither Believing nor Belonging.' *Sociology* 39(1), 11–28.
Zucca, L. (2009). 'The Crisis of the Secular State – A Reply to Professor Sajó.' *International Journal of Constitutional Law* 7(3), 494–514.

2
Reawakening Enlightenment? Contesting Religion and Politics in European Public Discourse

Anders Berg-Sørensen

Introduction

Free speech has become a battle point between religious and secular political movements in twenty-first century European public discourse. Consider a few highly contested recent cases: the movie *Submission* and the murder of its director Theo van Gogh in November 2004; the twelve cartoons depicting the Prophet Muhammad published in the Danish daily newspaper *Jyllands-Posten* in September 2005 and the subsequent death threats, impassioned demonstrations, burning of flags and embassies in Muslim countries; the debate on the Qur'an critical movie *Fitna* released in March 2008 by Dutch right-wing politician Geert Wilders, founder of the Party for Freedom fighting against immigration; the debate on boycotting the UN Durban Review Conference in April 2009 because of restrictions of free speech for reasons of blasphemy and the violent reactions against the recently released YouTube movie *Innocence of Muslims* in September 2012. And the list goes on.

Engaging in such cases, European politicians and intellectuals are debating the constitutive values of European democracies, such as freedom of speech vis-à-vis self-censorship; equal worth and dignity irrespective of religion, ethnicity, sex, and gender; human rights and the protection of minorities within minorities, especially women and homosexuals; toleration and its limits; religious fanaticism, terrorism, and violence; and security and public order. Within these debates, a strong stance is forwarded that the constitutive values of European democracies inherited from the Enlightenment – in the present case (*in casu*), the political ideal of freedom of speech – are non-negotiable irrespective of economic, social, and political consequences. And the crucial role of Enlightenment discourse for European societies – emphasizing the separation of religion and politics, equal civil rights and liberties, religious toleration and mutual respect – is framed in opposition to the darkened minds of the religious peoples demanding to be treated specially *as* religious people. Hence, the Enlightenment seems to be reawakened in terms of a reiteration of the Enlightenment critique of religion and the eventual abuse of power in the name of religion.

Such cases seem to provide evidence of religion having become more visible in the public sphere and having come to play an increasing role in political life in European democratic regimes. As indicated above, however, the challenge of religion in democratic politics has been met by counter-reactions criticizing the increasing role of religion in the public sphere and political life. The political doctrine of secularism plays a special role in this reawakening of the Enlightenment heritage in the encounter with religious forces. The political doctrine of secularism claims the separation of religion and politics and, thus, constitutes the guidelines for regulating religious people. So that which could be labelled *the secularist movement* in European public discourse emphasizes the political ideals of the Enlightenment, especially the separation of religion and politics and the equal civil rights and liberties, such as the individual freedoms of conscience and of expression as crucial pillars in a democratic society that has the use of reason as modus operandi. Furthermore, the secularist movement points out the dangers of the irrational passions of religion urging religious movements into anger and violence as well as focusing on the totalitarian dangers of mixing religion and politics into political religions and totalitarian politics in radical Islam and Christian fundamentalism with reference to the twentieth-century European experiences with totalitarianism. In other words, the secularist movement reawakens the Enlightenment critique of religion and the eventual abuse of power in the name of religion while at the same time highlighting various dimensions of the Enlightenment heritage.

However, the political doctrine of secularism is met with the critique that, in regulating religion in the name of secularism by separating religion and politics, the political ideals of secularism become undermined. The secular regulation of religions represents a use of power that, paradoxically, could be characterized 'political-theological'; in regulating religion, the secular state operates as a political-theological authority that transgresses the border between public and private and imposes norms of how to behave and reflect on oneself as religious people living in a democratic regime. Thus, the Enlightenment critique of the use and abuse of power is turned upside down and directed against the use of power in the name of secularism.

Engaging these insights, the aim of this chapter is to (a) reconstruct the contestation of the Enlightenment heritage in European public discourse with focus on the Enlightenment critique of religion and (b) discuss the implications hereof for the democratic ideals regarding liberty and equality, tolerance, neutrality, and impartiality. The primary focus will be on *the secularist movement*, taking the point of view that even within this 'movement' there are various conceptions of secularism. In other words, secularism is held to be a contested concept. This refers to the principles of strict separation of religion and politics justified by the use of secular or public reasoning but also implies various concrete institutions and policies regulating the religion-politics relationship, reiterating various contextual political traditions and cultures. The meaning of secularism is ambiguous and, as such, also subject to democratic negotiations drawing the line between religion and politics and creating conceptions of legitimate and illegitimate points of view in democratic governance rather than constituting the necessary presupposition of democracy.

From this point of view, the chapter will end up sketching what is called a *critical secularism* articulated in accordance with the Enlightenment critique of religion as well as including some of the insights from the *critique of secularism*. In other words, it seems plausible to talk about a shift from critique of secularism *to* critical secularism.

Enlightenment critique of religion vs. religious critique of Enlightenment

The reiteration of the Enlightenment critique of religion often constitutes a simple opposition between religion and Enlightenment. The same is the case with the reactions against the Enlightenment from various religious angles. In other words, the one part represents the counterpart as either a 'fundamentalist' religion or 'fundamentalist' Enlightenment. However, the question is whether this religion-Enlightenment opposition, as articulated in European public discourse, provides an adequate picture of the present religion-politics debate and whether this is a fruitful and plausible approach to the problems at stake.

For instance, Jonathan Israel, Enlightenment scholar and author of the three-volume *opus magnum* on European Enlightenment – *Radical Enlightenment* (2001), *Enlightenment Contested* (2006), and *Democratic*

Enlightenment (2011) – conceives the Dutch liberal politician of Somali origins and author of the film manuscript to *Submission*, Ayaan Hirsi Ali, as 'an heir to Spinoza'[1] and, thus, the tradition of radical Enlightenment. Baruch Spinoza (1632–1677), author of the infamous *Theological-Political Treatise* (published anonymously and banned in 1670), represents the heretic taking all of the burdens of the inquisitor on his shoulders. He was excommunicated at age 23 from his Sephardic Jewish community because of his heretic thoughts and writings questioning the authority of religions. Jonathan Israel describes the radical Enlightenment tradition of Spinoza as an 'overthrow of 'superstition', kingship, 'priestcraft', and 'institutionalized social hierarchy', replaced 'by democracy, equality, and individual liberty' (Israel, 2006: 41). In that sense, Israel emphasizes the opposition between religion and Enlightenment and what he conceives as the associated overthrow of absolutist regimes' religious-authorized abuse of power by democratically legitimate powers with reference to the political ideals of the Enlightenment. Israel emphasizes the ideals of freedom and equality within the frame of a democratic regime of rule of law.

In his sketch of the European Enlightenment traditions, Israel distinguishes between the radical Enlightenment of, among others, Spinoza versus the moderate Enlightenment of Locke and Voltaire. The radical Enlightenment was an uncompromised defence of the general Enlightenment ideals and values, whereas, according to Israel, the moderate Enlightenment was intertwined with the absolutist political regimes and religious institutions and denominations of the day. Thus, the moderate Enlightenment compromised their own ideals. The picture Israel draws adds more details to the religion-Enlightenment opposition while at the same time reproducing this opposition framed as a distinction between radical and moderate Enlightenment. This is reflected in the polemic exchange between Pascal Bruckner, Ian Buruma, and Timothy Garton Ash (among others) that took place in the early spring of 2007 (Ash, 2007; Bruckner, 2007; Buruma, 2007).

The focal point in this exchange was the influence of Ayaan Hirsi Ali on the contemporary European debate on religion and politics, especially Islam, on the basis of Buruma's book, *Murder in Amsterdam* (Buruma, 2006). Bruckner framed this in terms of either *pro* or *contra* Ayaan Hirsi Ali and, thus, either for or against the Enlightenment critique of religion and the universal values of human rights inherited from the Enlightenment. Buruma and Ash, on the one hand, expressed their admiration for Hirsi Ali's defence of democracy and individual freedom but, on the other, criticized her monolithic view on Islam. From both angles, the crucial question became whether and how an Enlightened European Islam could be possible, and they constituted conceptual chains between the Enlightenment tradition and critique of religion, Biblical criticism and the possibility of critical interpretations of the Qur'an, human rights, liberty and equality, democracy, and toleration. In that sense, the various dimensions of the Enlightenment critique of religion were revitalized. However, these points of view were also forwarded as fierce attacks on the other parts in the polemic, especially framed as an opposition between the principle of secularism giving priority to the French model of secularism (laïcité) and the principle of multiculturalism in accordance with British, Canadian, and Dutch models.

But what is at stake in this debate? Irrespective of their substantial disagreement and polemic tone, Bruckner, Buruma, and Ash defend the protection of individual rights and liberties against the use and abuse of power, either by religious or political authorities, and they encourage constitutive values, such as dignity and equality, freedom and self-determination, democracy and rule of law, tolerance and mutual respect, as crucial for the future European political communities. However, they disagree on how to fulfil these ideals, the various models of secularism and the implied rights and liberties, and how to understand and interpret these models. This reflects their attitudes towards various interpretations of the Enlightenment ideals and values. For instance, is free speech considered a non-negotiable fundamental pillar of a democratic regime, not to be questioned at all? Or is it a fundamental pillar in which the interpretations of its meaning in application are open for deliberation and contestation? In that sense, their respective interpretations of the various models of secularism constitute the frame of their different approaches to the actual problems of religion and politics.

Secularism is therefore the focal point in the rest of this paper, understood as a political doctrine taking over the heritage of the Enlightenment critique of religion and the Enlightenment political ideals and values.[2] Furthermore, the disagreement over the interpretation of the various models of secularism points towards the potential insight to be found in the present European debates on religion and politics.

Secularism and its critics

In the dominant discourses, secularism constitutes the lens through which the religion-politics relationship is conceived (cf., e.g. Audi, 2011a, 2011b; Habermas, 2006; Taylor, 1998). Secularism forms a vocabulary and scheme of thought claiming the separation of religion and politics as *institutional arrangement* and *individual reason*: Political institutions are to be *organized* in such a manner that they are independent and free of religion, and this organization of the political realm is *justified* by the use of secular or public reason. In other words, organizing a neutral political realm and taking impartial political decisions based on commonly accessible reasons requires the translation of religious beliefs and convictions into a common political language and, thus, not taking them into consideration. The dominant discourses of secularism, in terms of the institutional arrangement and individual reason, separate religion and politics for the purpose of the Enlightenment ideals of liberty and tolerance, equality and impartiality, neutrality, and universality.

As mentioned above, however, secularism is a contested concept, and it seems more plausible to refer to secularism *in the plural* than *in the singular*. The understanding of secularism in the plural focuses on the various dimensions in which secularism operates, especially the interaction between institutionalization and identification within concrete political contexts. A further part of this multi-dimensional understanding of secularism is that the discourses of secularism operate as various forms of power ranging from abstract principles to concretely embodied points of identification.

Furthermore, the political doctrine of secularism is caught up in various paradoxes: the ambition of universality reflects the particular norms of political communities, political institutions, or political strategies; the ambition of inclusion in the name of liberty and equality, neutrality and impartiality, and by the use of ethical reasoning, excludes at the same time the perspectives that challenge the dominant interpretation of these norms and, thus, undermines the very norms themselves.

Talal Asad's critique and other critiques of secularism point out how discourses of secularism paradoxically operate by *political-theologizing* as a specific form of power (cf. Anidjar, 2006; Asad, 2006, 2008; Hurd, 2008; Mahmood, 2006). A reading of the headscarf debates in, for example, Denmark and France underlines this idea at first glance. In both Denmark and France, it is possible to identify a politics of secularism operating as a political-theological authority mixing up religion and politics, political theology, and secularism. In the Danish case, a religious secularism in terms of a Danish Lutheran secularism (Berg-Sørensen, 2010b), while in France, a principled secularism with reference to the absolute sovereignty of the French state based on the principle of secularism (*laïcité*).

Let us return to Asad in order to understand his approach better. In analysing the French headscarf affair as a case in which the French principle of secularism *(laïcité)* was rearticulated as an authoritative point of reference for regulating the Muslim citizenry, Asad inscribes this principle in the history of the French state and its characteristics from absolutism, that is, the absolute power of the sovereign state:

> I want to suggest that the French secular state today abides in a sense by the *cuius regio eius religio* principle, even though it disclaims any religious allegiance and governs a largely irreligious society. In my view, it is not the commitment to or interdiction of a particular religion that is most significant in this principle but the installation of a single absolute power – the sovereign state – drawn from a single abstract source and facing a single political task: the worldly care of its population regardless of its beliefs. (Asad, 2006: 499)

Based on this understanding of the absolutist heritage still playing a role in the contemporary French state, Asad includes the conception of sovereignty formulated by Carl Schmitt: 'Sovereign is he who decides on the exception' (Schmitt, 2005: 5).

It is claimed that the Republic treats all religions equally. But this does not preclude its taking certain decisions that affect religion, although religion may never intervene in matters of state. This asymmetry is, I suggest, a measure of sovereign power.

Schmitt pointed out that sovereignty is the ability to define the exception. *Laïcité* is made up of exceptions, and it is the function of sovereignty to identify and justify them – to forestall thereby the Republic's 'disintegration'. But in view of the famous doctrine that France is 'la République une et indivisible', it is not entirely clear how the fear of 'disintegration' relates to the singular, invisible state as opposed to those many persons (officials and citizens) who *represent* it (Asad, 2006: 504–505). And he continues: 'I want to suggest that *that* very exercise of power to identify and deal with the exception is what subsumes the differences within a unity and confirms Republican sovereignty in the Schmittian sense' (Asad, 2006: 507).

In the contested reception of Schmitt's political theology, two crucial elements are pointed out: his notion of sovereignty and the state of exception just mentioned and his conceptual sociology – 'all significant concepts of the modern theory of the state are secularized theological concepts' (Schmitt, 2005: 36). The latter expresses the Schmittian understanding of the permanence of the theologico-political. In his terms, there is a structural analogy between, on the one hand, ancient and medieval theological concepts and, on the other, modern political concepts emphasizing both the theological origins of political concepts and the theologico-political horizon of politics. This leads to the first crucial element of Schmitt's political theology: his notion of sovereignty. The sovereign is the one who decides that there is state of exception and makes decisions within this state of exception. The sovereign is both outside and inside this situation of choice; both higher than and involved in as sovereign power. Sovereignty is a boundary concept, both operating at the boundary and setting boundaries. In that sense, sovereignty is a theologico-political concept constitutive of modern politics and the decision of the sovereign is the political act *par excellence* setting the relationship between friend and enemy.

According to Asad, the French state operates continuously as a sovereign that defines exceptions that could threaten the order, unity, and security of the Republic. In other words, the French state acts out of fear by defining such threats, *in casu* by defining religious symbols as threats to the French public order. This emphasizes the point that the French state acts by political-theologizing in the sense that, in the headscarf ban, *the state* defines religion in order to operate within the borders between religion and politics and the permitted spaces of religion and politics, respectively. Furthermore, this understanding of the proper relationship between religion and politics is imposed on the religious citizens: how they are to understand themselves in order to be recognized as proper citizens able to make autonomous decisions and free to choose their own ways of living and visions of a good life. At this point, Asad adds Foucault's conception of governmentality to the Schmittian understanding of the sovereign use of power that imposes a proper self-understanding on the citizens: they are to be autonomous in order to be considered legitimate and, thus, the French state governs the citizens 'by letting them govern themselves' (Asad, 2006: 521–522).

Asad's analysis of how the French principle of secularism operates as an exercise of power by political-theologizing in the concrete case – defining the proper relationship between religion and politics, the separate spheres of religion and politics based on a specific understanding of religion articulated by the state representatives – provides crucial insights into the power mechanisms of political secular principles. The question is, however, whether the Schmittian conception of political theology and sovereignty is the only available perspective on these mechanisms and whether it is the most plausible.

First of all, Asad's analysis of the French prohibition of religious signs and symbols in public schools, *in casu* the Muslim headscarf (*hijab*), reflects the tendency in European countries to propose legislation prohibiting headscarves in various public institutions on the basis of a stereotypical understanding of the meaning of the headscarf (i.e., the suppression of Muslim women by a patriarchal religion and culture in conflict with the secular ideals of liberty and equality). And the analysis points out the paradox that the secular state itself suppresses these religious women and their religion because it does not listen to their voices and include other possible meanings that could challenge the stereotypical understanding in deliberating and negotiating the legislation. I follow Asad so far.

With reference to the Schmittian conception of political theology and sovereignty, Asad draws a picture of the secular state as a united and indivisible entity that gives priority to security issues masked as national interest and acts out of fear against what are conceived as threats to the public order. This is a picture of the secular state that Asad has reiterated in other recent analyses, as in his analysis of the challenges that Egypt meets after the democratic revolution in 2011–2012 (Asad, 2012). However, by adopting this Schmittian conception of political theology and sovereignty, Asad draws a picture of the secular state that has some weaknesses, analytically and normatively. Asad has become so overly focused on security issues that he only understands one possible motive for political decisions and actions (i.e., fear) and therefore fails to pay sufficient attention to the institutional complexity of a secular state and the cultural pluralism of a secular society.

This critique of Asad's image of the secular state and, thus, secularism could be framed otherwise. One could claim that he – because of the Schmittian conception of political theology and sovereignty – has become too prejudiced in his conception of the secular state and secularism which has closed a potential openness towards other conceptions and understandings. According to Asad, secularism is *per definition* hostile towards religion, and it expresses this hostility by sovereign acts of power out of fear and for reasons of security (cf. Asad, 2011, 2012). Thus, in Asad's vocabulary, the secular state and secularism have per definition a negative sense. The consequence of this normative prejudice is that this negative sense of secularism is attached to Christianity, democracy, and the nation-state *per se* because they are associated with secularism and the secular state. However, these normative prejudices block for his analytical programme of enquiring about various concrete modes of secular formations and interactions between the secular and the religious and the involved power mechanisms in, for example, a democratic rule of power.

Asad seems to recognize the potential plurality of perspectives at play in the regulation of religion and politics in a democratic regime and, thus, the 'varieties of secularism' (Asad, 2006: 526). However, he does not draw the consequences in his analysis of the French headscarf affair and general conception of the secular state, sticking to the Schmittian conception of political theology and sovereignty. This has implications for his conception of democracy in a plural society. Asad distinguishes between 'a democratic ethos' and 'a representative democracy' as two distinct and separate forms of democracy (Asad, 2011: 672). The democratic ethos includes the plurality of perspectives involved in democratic deliberation, negotiation, and contestation, while the representative democracy, according to Asad, is driven by the sovereign use of power out of fear in order to protect the national interest. Because of this narrow-minded conception of representative democracy along the lines of the Schmittian conceptions of political theology and sovereignty, Asad is unable to see any possible interactions between his two forms of democracy. Thus, he neglects the democratic potentials of the plurality of perspectives in the representative democratic institutions and processes. In the case of the French headscarf affair, he presents the Muslims only as victims of the secular state, neglecting their democratic potentials as ordinary citizens raising their democratic voices of disagreement at the same time as they actually accepted the decisions made in the representative democratic institutions; an acceptance that recognized the democratic process as continually ongoing deliberation, negotiation, and contestation and, thus, the possibility of another decision at some time in the future.

Asad's reference to Schmitt's political theology reflects the vital role that the German interwar dialogue on political theology plays in the contemporary political thinking of religion and politics. Asad emphasizes how the secular state acts as a sovereign in the regulation of religious subjects, understood as public enemies. Paradoxically, the secular state acts as a theological authority that subjectivates religious people. However, this conception of political theology has been criticized by those who pay attention to the normative restrictions on the sovereign use of power, which points to other aspects of the interwar dialogues on political theology and their revitalization in the contemporary debate (cf. Berg-Sørensen, 2010a).

These debates in contemporary political theory on the relationship between theology and political theory emphasize the processes of reflecting and setting the boundaries between religion and politics; and especially the various forms of interchange and interdependence between the theological and religious spheres, on the one hand, and the political sphere, on the other. A point of view that is common among the various perspectives is the focus on the paradoxical situation that when secular political theory repudiates theology and excludes the religious sphere from politics, it reproduces the authority that theology and religion formerly had, in a negative or positive sense. In other words, it is impossible not to include theological imaginations in thinking of a secular political order that is supposed to be independent of religion. Furthermore, the debates point out the circumstance that it is not that simple to establish an exclusively secular normative point of view for justifying political obligations and restrictions in the use of power without also including ethical points of view forwarded by various theological doctrines. In the present postsecular situation, Jürgen Habermas and others argue that the secular state must take theology seriously, both as a distinct form of knowledge – that is, as an academic discipline – and as a religious authority constitutive of religious communities. This represents a necessary shift in the secularist self-understanding of the state in order to live up to the secular, democratic ideals of liberty and toleration, equality and impartiality, neutrality, and universality.

In that sense, the debates addressing the boundaries between religion and politics point out the critical potential of theology and political theology in respect of the blind spots of secular political theory and secular political regimes. In general, it is a critique of liberal democracy and its focus on formal procedures, rights, and liberties. At the same time, the various perspectives reflect upon the societal disintegrative aspects of religious communities and the democratic dangers of political theologies for modern democratic societies. Thus, the contemporary debate on various conceptions of political theology adds an analytical vigilance towards the masking of power exercises in political processes regulating the citizenry.

However, this raises some questions regarding Asad's application of Schmittian political theology and the associated conception of sovereignty in his analysis of the discursive power of secularism: Has the secular use of power by political-theologizing the absolute character ascribed by Asad? Or would it be more productive to focus on the relational and contingent character of the various secular powers and the ambiguity and contestation at play in the interpretation and application of various traditions and cultures of secularism? This insight, empirical as well as theoretical, might call for other conceptions of political theology in order to better understand the various political processes of regulating the citizenry by principles of secularism.

Enlightenment critique and critical secularism in a postsecular age

If Enlightenment critique of religion is about criticizing the use and abuse of power in the name of religion and the institutional and cultural conditions making this exercise of power possible, one could claim that the multi-dimensional approach sketched in the last section is a further development of the Enlightenment critique of religion reflecting the political ideals of Enlightenment. However, this approach is a critique of power *in concreto* rather than a critique of religion *per se*. It gives priority to the political in so far as the political constitutes the conditions for the exercise of power and, thus, is articulated within the frame of secularism granting priority to politics over religion, but secularism in a postsecular age in which the religious and political spheres are mixed and in interaction and transformation rather than upholding a distinct opposition between secularism and religion or political theology (cf., e.g. Lilla, 2007).

Think of Jürgen Habermas's work on the postsecular society, where he reconsiders a secular awareness of the moral, social, and political influence of religions and associates this awareness with a contested but 'critical overcoming of ... a narrow secularist consciousness' (Habermas, 2006: 16). This means that there is no teleological societal evolution towards a secular society. This is reflected in attitudes towards religious people. Take a step further and relate this postsecular sensitivity to the point forwarded that secularism – as a contested and contestable concept – is also subject to democratic negotiations drawing the line between religion and politics and creating conceptions of legitimate and illegitimate points of view in democratic governing (cf. Freeden, 1996, 2004, 2005). Within this frame of the democratic implications of conceiving secularism a contested and contestable concept, one could include the reflections of Rogers M. Smith on the contested and contestable character of 'stories of peoplehood', writing: 'I seek to check their dangers while also energizing politics by calling for a politics of contestation among multiple stories of peoplehood, both more particularistic and more universalistic' (Smith, 2003: 15). The postsecular sensitivity implies an openness towards the plural forces that energize politics and, thus, emphasizes the democratic gain by committed contestation without neglecting the violent dangers of political struggles. If one presumes that articulations of secularisms are 'stories of peoplehood', then they could operate as ongoing reflections regarding the politics–religion distinction that imply an awareness of the contingency and the fallibility of one's own perspective. In other words, we have – potentially – to do with various secularisms taking the postsecular condition seriously in their own modesty (cf., e.g. Gorski et al., 2012; De Vries, 2006).

Thus, this chapter presents an *alternative secularism* rather than an *alternative to secularism* (cf. Bhargava, 2006). Going through the crucial insights from the *critique of secularism* – especially the focus on the multi-dimensional exercise of power – the chapter takes the stance of what could be called *critical secularism*. A critical secularism creates a movement backwards and forwards between the contextual analyses of *secularisms* and the normative dimensions of *secularism* reflecting the Enlightenment political ideals (cf. Laborde, 2008). The final section sketches some vague ideas about the future of secularism in a postsecular age under the label of *critical secularism*. Crucial is the multi-dimensional use of power that the critique of secularism has pointed out. However, in order to understand this multi-dimensional use of power *in concreto*, the Schmittian notion of political theology emphasizing the creation of oppositions between friend and enemy, between the secular and the religious, with an evaluative point taken from the perspective of the religious subject, seem to reduce the plurality of possible conceptions of political theology and narrows down the scope of political and democratic potentials. The critique of secularism brings crucial insights to the fore but ends up in an either-or deadlock of simple oppositions that it aimed at dissolving itself.

What is to be brought back in is the contestation among a plurality of perspectives on the relationship between religion and politics, such as the various perspectives of secularism (cf. Connolly, 1999, 2005). The contestation includes moments of critique: both critique of the other perspectives in the interpretation and application of secular principles of liberty and equality and critique of one's own perspective in terms of an awareness of its fallibility. In that sense, the critical vigilance of a critical secularism adopts the point of view that everything can be questioned and subjected to deliberation and contestation, whether interpretations of political principles, organizations of political institutions, ideas and values taken for granted in a religious or national culture and tradition, or values enhanced with deep existential meaning by the ordinary citizens. The crucial point is that such critical vigilance goes both ways and includes both the other and oneself.

Thus, a critical secularism pursues the political ideals of the Enlightenment – liberty and equality, tolerance, and impartiality. They constitute the political vision of a critical secularism. At the same time, a critical secularism adopts the Enlightenment critique of religion – not a critique of religion *as such*, but a critical vigilance towards the *concrete* use and abuse of power in the name of religion – and it extends this critical insight to the eventual use and abuse of power in the name of secularism by pointing out the various dimensions of the exercise of power from formal institutions and regulations to informal points of identification, self-reflection and -understanding, and embodied experiences and dispositions. In other words, a *critical* secularism is a *self-critical* secularism. From this point of view, a critical secularism gives priority to the political over the religious; the political in the specific sense of an ongoing democratic contestation and negotiation between a plurality of perspectives and points of view on deep existential matters as well as common affairs.

This emphasis on the relationship between plural democracy and critical secularism brings us back to the question of separation. It has been claimed that the separation of religion and politics is impossible with reference to all of the historical and current examples in which religious and political institutions are intertwined, even in states without an established church. However, these factual references do not necessarily undermine the political vision of secularism – that a separation of religion and politics in terms of institutions provides better conditions for a plural democratic society giving all plural perspectives equal weight and freedom – rather, they indicate that there is still a long way to go and that realizing the political ideals of secularism in contemporary society requires hard work.

The reason why it makes sense to give priority to the political over the religious and claim a separation of religion and politics at the institutional level is, then, that it is more likely that secularism as an institutional arrangement will provide an equal weight and freedom to all citizens, irrespective of religious, philosophical, and metaphysical belonging, than an established relationship between religious and political institutions, which will give priority to majority cultures and embedded national traditions and institutions. The institutional separation, therefore, forms the basis of democratic political processes in a plural society, where various perspectives are engaged in common endeavours. The institutional separation does not necessarily imply a demand on the mode of reasoning and justifying political decisions as in the dominant political doctrine of secularism; rather, it involves processes of contestation and negotiation between the various perspectives.

The approach emphasizes the actual political thinking in terms of diverse narrative strategies and the points of identification involved in the concrete political processes (cf. Freeden, 2005, 2008) rather than understanding democracy in terms of rational reconstructions of universal premises for collective decision-making and presupposing the separation of religion and politics in legitimate democratic reasoning by requiring the translation of religious points of view and convictions into a supposed universal political language as assumed in the dominant normative political theory. Normatively, one focuses on the democratic negotiations reflecting principles of equal basic rights and liberties but involved in various political processes reflecting and reiterating different contextual institutional and cultural characteristics. In other words, it outlines the normative implications not in terms of established criteria for collective decision-making but as the social imaginations and forces involved in the political decision-making processes, where plural perspectives and reasoning are encountering each other in deliberation, negotiation, and contestation.

Secularism is a contested concept. Even the normative principles of secularism are open for different interpretations in the ongoing political processes. The conflicts of interpretation cannot be settled by moral philosophical justification. Within this frame, the religion-politics relationship is subject to continuous democratic negotiations between diverse perspectives and reasoning and, thus, as an ambiguous and unstable relationship the categories of secular and religious could be mixed up in the processes of governing and authorizing the use of power. In that sense, a critical secularism contributes with a critical edge for understanding the establishment of closing rather than opening tendencies in the production of normative criteria and principles for regulating religion and politics (cf. Keenan, 2003).

The key question regarding the normative implications for democracy of a critical secularism is, then, whether the political processes are kept open and give space to diverse narrative strategies and points of identification that constitute the actual societies over which collective decisions are made or whether they are dominated by a single narrative strategy reducing the field of political deliberation, negotiation, and contestation with reference to an unambiguous authoritative set of vocabularies and institutions, including the political use of simple oppositions such as the clash of civilizations thesis or the religious-secular divide. Thus, the focal point of the democratic question is the tension between closing and opening tendencies and the degrees of contestation, critique, and self-critique in the political processes. This is where a critical secularism can begin.

Notes

An earlier version of this chapter has been presented at the Political Theory Seminar at the Department of Political Science, University of Pennsylvania, October 2012; in the Political Theory Group at the Annual Meeting of the Danish Political Science Association, October 2012; and in the Political Theory Seminar at the Department of Political Science, University of Copenhagen, November 2012. I would like to thank the participants for their comments and questions, especially Signe Blaabjerg Christoffersen, Hans Boas Dabelsteen, Torben Bech Dyrberg, Jeffrey E. Green, Nancy Hirschmann, Lis Højgaard, Carsten Bagge Laustsen, Anne Norton, Tore Vincents Olsen, Christian F. Rostbøll, Rogers M. Smith, and Lars Tønder. I would also like to thank the editors of this volume for their valuable comments and constructive criticism.

1. Quote from Buruma (2006: 24).
2. The notion of secularism is to be distinguished from secularization. Secularism is a political doctrine claiming the separation of religion and politics from the point of view of political ideals of liberty and toleration, equality and impartiality, neutrality and universality, whereas secularization refers to historical and social processes of rationalization, social differentiation, privatization of religion, and the decline of religious faith (cf. Asad, 2003; Casanova, 2006; Norris and Inglehart, 2004). However, some point towards the implicit normative goal of secularism framing the theories of secularization, so even a clear-cut distinction like the one just made hides the normative ideals implicit in secularization theories (Asad, 2003; Jakobsen and Pellegrini, 2008).

References

Anidjar, G. (2006). 'Secularism.' *Critical Inquiry* 33(1), 52–77.
Asad, T. (2003). *Formations of the Secular: Christianity, Islam, Modernity*. Stanford, CA: Stanford University Press.
Asad, T. (2006). 'Trying to Understand French Secularism.' In H. De Vries and L.E. Sullivan (eds) *Political Theologies: Public Religions in a Postsecular World*, 494–526. New York: Fordham University Press.
Asad, T. (2008). 'Reflections on Blasphemy and Secular Criticism.' In H. De Vries (ed.) *Religion: Beyond a Concept*, 580–609. New York: Fordham University Press.
Asad, T. (2011). 'Thinking about the Secular Body, Pain, and Liberal Politics.' *Cultural Anthropology* 26(4), 657–675.
Asad, T. (2012). 'Fear and the Ruptured State: Reflections on Egypt after Mubarak.' *Social Research* 79(2), 271–298.
Ash, T.G. (2007). 'Better Pascal Than Bruckner.' Online source, available at www.signandsights.com [last accessed 16 August 16 2007].
Audi, R. (2011a). *Rationality and Religious Commitment*. Oxford: Oxford University Press.
Audi, R. (2011b). *Democratic Authority and the Separation of Church and State*. Oxford: Oxford University Press.
Berg-Sørensen, A. (2006a). 'Politicising Religions.' *Political Theory* 34(6), 800–806.

Berg-Sørensen, A. (2006b). 'Cultural Governance, Democratic Iterations and the Question of Secularism: The French Head Scarf Affair.' *Nordic Journal of Religion and Society* 19(2), 57–74.
Berg-Sørensen, A. (2010a). 'Theology.' In M. Bevir (ed.) *Encyclopedia of Political Theory*. Thousand Oaks, CA: Sage.
Berg-Sørensen, A. (2010b). 'The Politics of Lutheran Secularism: Reiterating Secularism in the Wake of the Cartoon Crisis.' In L. Christoffersen, H.R. Iversen, H. Petersen, and M. Warburg (eds) *Religion in the 21st Century: Challenges and Transformations*, 207–214. Farnham, UK: Ashgate.
Berg-Sørensen, A. (2013). *Contesting Secularism*. Farnham, UK: Ashgate.
Bhargava, R. (2006). 'Political Secularism.' In J.S. Dryzek, B. Honig, and A. Phillips (eds) *The Oxford Handbook of Political Theory*, 636–655. Oxford: Oxford University Press.
Bruckner, P. (2007). 'Enlightenment Fundamentalism or Racism of the Anti-Racists?' Online source, available at www.signandsights.com [last accessed 16 August 2007].
Buruma, I. (2006). *Murder in Amsterdam: The Death of Theo van Gogh and the Limits of Tolerance*. New York: Penguin Press.
Buruma, I. (2007). 'Freedom Cannot Be Decreed.' Online source, available at www.signandsights.com [last accessed 16 August 2007].
Casanova, J. (2006). 'Secularization Revisited: A Reply to Talal Asad.' In D. Scott and C. Hirschkind (eds) *Powers of the Secular Modern: Talal Asad and His Interlocutors*, 12–30. Stanford, CA: Stanford University Press.
Connolly, W.E. (1999). *Why I Am Not a Secularist*. Minneapolis, MN: The University of Minnesota Press.
Connolly, W.E. (2005). *Pluralism*. Durham, NC: Duke University Press.
De Vries, H. (2006). 'Introduction: Before, Around, and Beyond the Theologico-Political.' In H. De Vries and L.E. Sullivan (eds) *Political Theologies: Public Religions in a Post-Secular World*, 1–88. New York: Fordham University Press.
Freeden, M. (1996). *Ideologies and Political Theory: A Conceptual Approach*. Oxford: Oxford University Press.
Freeden, M. (2004). 'Essential Contestability and Effective Contestability.' *Journal of Political Ideologies* 9(1), 3–11.
Freeden, M. (2005). 'What Should the 'Political' in Political Theory Explore?' *Journal of Political Philosophy* 13(2), 113–134.
Freeden, M. (2008). 'Thinking Politically and Thinking about Politics: Language, Interpretation, and Ideology.' In D. Leopold and M. Stears (eds) *Political Theory: Methods and Approaches*, 196–215. Oxford: Oxford University Press.
Gorski, P.S., Kim, D.K., Torpey, J., and VanAntwerpen, J. (eds) (2012). *The Post-Secular in Question: Religion in Contemporary Society*. New York: New York University Press.
Habermas, J. (2006). 'Religion in the Public Sphere.' *European Journal of Philosophy* 14(1), 1–25.
Hurd, E.S. (2008). *The Politics of Secularism in International Relations*. Princeton, NJ: Princeton University Press.
Israel, J.I. (2001). *Radical Enlightenment: Philosophy and the Making of Modernity 1650–1750*. Oxford: Oxford University Press.
Israel, J.I. (2006). *Enlightenment Contested: Philosophy, Modernity, and the Emancipation of Man 1670–1752*. Oxford: Oxford University Press.

Israel, J.I. (2011). *Democratic Enlightenment: Philosophy, Revolution, and Human Rights 1750–1790*. Oxford: Oxford University Press.
Jakobsen, J.R. and Pellegrini, A. (eds) (2008). *Secularisms*. Durham, NC: Duke University Press.
Keenan, A. (2003). *Democracy in Question: Democratic Openness in a Time of Political Closure*. Stanford, CA: Stanford University Press.
Laborde, C. (2008). *Critical Republicanism: The Hijab Controversy and Political Philosophy*. Oxford: Oxford University Press.
Lilla, M. (2007). *The Stillborn God: Religion, Politics, and the Modern West*. New York: Knopf.
Mahmood, S. (2006). 'Secularism, Hermeneutics, and Empire: The Politics of Islamic Reformation.' *Public Culture* 18(2), 323–347.
Norris, P. and Inglehart, R. (2004). *Sacred and Secular: Religion and Politics Worldwide*. Cambridge: Cambridge University Press.
Schmitt, C. (2005). *Political Theology: Four Chapters on the Concept of Sovereignty*, G. Schwab (trans.). Chicago: The University of Chicago Press.
Smith, R.M. (2003). *Stories of Peoplehood: The Politics and Morals of Political Membership*. Cambridge: Cambridge University Press.
Taylor, C. (1998). 'Modes of Secularism.' In R. Bhargava (ed.) *Secularism and Its Critics*, 31–53. Oxford: Oxford University Press.
Taylor, C. (2007). *A Secular Age*. Cambridge, MA: The Belknap Press of Harvard University Press.

3
(Pro)claiming Tradition: The 'Judeo-Christian' Roots of Dutch Society and the Rise of Conservative Nationalism

Ernst van den Hemel

From burgeoning EU scepticism in Great Britain,[1] to criticism of Islam and multiculturalism in Belgium,[2] Germany,[3] France,[4] and the Netherlands, the appeal to 'Judeo-Christian' roots of Western societies has been part of the rise of conservative nationalisms all over Europe. If the 'postsecular' at its very basis indeed signals a renewed place for religion in political debates, conservative nationalists have proven to be more effective postsecularists than their counterparts. By discussing uses of the phrase Judeo-Christian in Dutch political debates, this article aims to investigate the successful mixture between neoconservatism and the postsecular invocation of religious roots that, as I will argue, plays an important role in the current transformation of Dutch society. I will conclude by suggesting a number of vistas for research that can contribute to the debate surrounding the religious roots of Dutch identity.

It is an undeniable fact that the Netherlands is undergoing fundamental changes. The change of a tolerant progressive country to a country that has been at the forefront of a turn to the right in European politics is beginning to hit home, slowly but surely changing the international image of the Netherlands. This 'turn to the right' in Dutch politics has been often debated (cf., for instance, Buruma, 2007). Less often, however, do we find discussions of how the rise of populist rightwing politics, and its infamous hardliner stance on Islam, has, from the very start, been connected to a reappraisal of religious identity of Dutch society. As I will show, classical Dutch values such as tolerance, secularism, gay rights, and feminism have been reframed as secular, yet

Judeo-Christian accomplishments are perceived to be in need of protection from threats – most notably, the threat that is Islam.

Let us take a look at the simultaneous start of the tumultuous integration debate as well as of invocation of Judeo-Christian roots as the basis of Dutch society. I choose to take as the beginning 1991, when the leader of the Dutch liberal party, Frits Bolkestein, stated the following in his lecture entitled 'De integratie van minderheden' (*The integration of minorities*):

> Rationalism, humanism and Christianity have, after a long history that includes many black pages, brought forth a number of fundamentally important political principles, like the separation of Church and State, freedom of speech, tolerance and non-discrimination. (Bolkestein, 1992)[5]

Bolkestein continues by stating that these universal values have shaped Dutch culture, whereas other cultures, most notably 'Islamic culture' do not contain these values and are therefore inherently less compatible with Dutch society. Bolkestein states that, as a result, conceptualizations of Dutch culture as open and tolerant to all should be re-evaluated. In Bolkestein's analysis, 'multiculturalists' have entertained the dream that these universal values could 'accommodate everyone'; reality in Dutch society, however, 'has proven otherwise'. Bolkestein states that if the Netherlands wants to remain the liberal, tolerant country it has become, a harder, more combative stance needs to be taken up. Which means: tougher rules concerning integration, less immigration (predominantly less immigration from 'Islamic countries'), and a renewed emphasis on national identity of which Judeo-Christianity is an integral part.

This article can be seen as the beginning of the infamous integration debate that has drastically changed the Dutch political landscape, and it can be seen as a precursor to a conservative turn in many Western European countries. It is worth pointing out that, for Bolkestein, emphasis on a tougher stance on immigration and Islam is inherently connected to an affirmation of the religious identity and religious past of the Netherlands, and, by extension, the West. In his argumentation, Bolkestein repeats the mainstream narrative of secularization: Christianity (I will speak of the disappearance of the 'Judeo' part of the expression below) has led to liberal values as freedom of speech, tolerance, and non-discrimination. It is also not surprising in this respect that Bolkestein mentions humanism and rationalism as rising up out of Christianity. Yet, at the same time, Bolkestein states that the traditional *telos* of this myth, an all-inclusive multiculturalist community, is now in urgent need of redefinition: for Bolkestein, the presence of a large number of immigrants that do not subscribe to these basic values makes clear that these values should be defended and grounded in a particular religious identity. Speaking as a politician from a liberal party, this entailed a change of important dogmas of liberalism: neutrality of religion being the most important point of contention. The lecture of Bolkestein functions as an early example of a particular political practice that would be copied by Pim Fortuyn, Geert Wilders, and a host of neoconservative and liberal thinkers. This essay, I suggest using the adjective 'postsecular' to describe this strategy.

The term 'postsecular', as the articles in this volume outline, is not a concept that can be easily defined.[6] It has been used to characterize a period, a mode of doing politics, as well as a mode of criticizing the role of religion in contemporary political debates (cf. Beckford, 2012). Yet, at the very basis, most scholars agree that the term is connected to the realization that the theory of secularization is no longer a valid way to describe developments concerning religion in the Western world. The eventual withdrawal of religion from the public sphere and its unavoidable decline in influence were once popular elements of the secularization thesis, but now one would be hard-pressed to find scholars willing to defend it. Instead religion returned to the agenda in more ways than one. Critics of secularism have pointed out that, for instance, even the universal agenda characteristic of the secularization thesis might be the continuation of Protestantism under a different header (Asad, 1993; Mahmood, 2005). This, however, does not mean that the term 'postsecular' contains a clear critical agenda, nor that it is even clear how one should proceed after the secularization thesis has shown itself to be flawed. For instance, an influential phrasing of this predicament is offered by Jürgen Habermas in his 2008 lecture 'Notes on a Postsecular Society':

> How should we see ourselves as members of a postsecular society and what must we reciprocally expect from one another in order to ensure that in firmly entrenched nation states, social relations remain civil despite the growth of a plurality of cultures and religious world views? (Habermas, 2008: 21)

Even though his attempt is to re-evaluate secularism's normative claims and to include morals that arise from religious traditions as potentially valuable contributions to an inclusive public sphere, Habermas's conceptualization of the postsecular has been criticized by those who point out that his use of the notion nonetheless retains quite a lot of the normative dimensions of secularism, and perhaps is not quite able to reflect upon its own assumptions, with a potential bias as the result (cf., for instance, Jansen, 2011). Take the following quote, where 'egalitarian universalism', an important ingredient of a civil and inclusive public sphere, is explicitly connected to Judaic and Christian roots:

> Egalitarian universalism, from which sprang the ideas of freedom and social solidarity, of an autonomous conduct of life and emancipation, of the individual morality of conscience, human rights and democracy, is the direct heir of the Judaic ethic of justice and the Christian ethic of love. This legacy, substantially unchanged, has been the object of critical appropriation and reinterpretation. To this day, there is no alternative to it. And in light of the current challenges of a postnational constellation, we continue to draw on the substances of this heritage. Everything else is just idle postmodern talk. (Habermas, 2006: 150–151)

One could wonder whether the connection between egalitarian universalism and a Judaic and Christian ethic does not pose severe challenges to Habermas's conceptualization of the postsecular public sphere.

To return to the question of defining the postsecular: As De Vries and Sullivan have argued, postsecularism should perhaps not merely be seen as 'an attempt at historical periodization (following upon equally unfortunate designations such as the 'postmodern,' the 'post-historical,' or the 'post-human') but merely as a topical indicator for – well, a problem' (De Vries and Sullivan, 2006: 2).

If the postsecular 'problem' is defined as the challenge to shape political communities in a time when secular values have lost their neutrality, and religion once again takes on an important role, the conservative nationalists I will discuss have found a successful though not less problematic answer in their unequivocal proclamation that the foundation of the secular West lies in its Judeo-Christian roots.

For, as I will show in what follows, it is interesting that many of the academic criticisms levelled against the notion of the postsecular (it would be exclusionary, too much focused on the West, too much connected to secular ideals, and closed off to other conceptualizations of the public sphere, to name but a few arguments), are acknowledged by contemporary conservatives: the politicians and thinkers that I will analyse in this article explicitly affirm that secularism is rooted in a biased take on religion, and they simply affirm that the specific religious roots of secular values imply an exclusion of Islam from the public sphere. In short, a lot of the criticism involved in the notion of post-secularism is simply, yet very productively, embraced by conservative nationalists all over Europe.

Before assessing the varied use of the appeals on Judeo-Christian roots, it is worth summing up a number of their core characteristics. First of all, these claims are, historically speaking, not very detailed: references to a religious past are seldom combined with historical evidence for, say, the connection between Judeo-Christian influences and liberal values (Spruyt being an exception). References to a shared theological unity or to confessional identity remain largely absent.[7] Personal faith or religious experiences are usually fully absent from these discussions. Nonetheless, as varied, vague, and paradoxical as they may be, the appeals on Judeo-Christian roots nonetheless share a number of aspects: First of all, the appeals are predominantly aimed at the articulation of a national identity that arose out of a religious past. Secondly, this identity is characterized by values traditionally associated with secularism, such as the separation of church and state, freedom of expression, gay rights, and feminism. Thirdly, the varied appeals to this religiously informed secular identity share the sentiment that this identity has come under threat from Islam and multiculturalists. As a result, the secular values of Judeo-Christian Dutch society are perceived to be in need of resolute defence. Finally, it is worth mentioning that the appeals are not connected to an idealization of an actual existing past. The twentieth century, with its pillarization, for instance, that has been claimed by Abraham Kuyper as the Calvinist origin of Dutch constitutional freedom and tolerance, does not function as a model (Kuyper, 2008). The proponents of Judeo-Christian Dutch identity do not propose a return to pillarized society.[8]

Progressive critics of this turn in Dutch politics have often pointed at the incoherent, incorrect historical foundation for this appeal. Furthermore, politicians who have gained electoral success by appealing to the religious foundation of Dutch secular society have been criticized as either employing a form of nostalgia to the past or as coyly introducing a form of populist politics solely aimed at the 'gut' of the electorate. Nonetheless, as I will attempt to show, these appeals are symptomatic for a mode of doing politics that needs to be taken more seriously. This particular appeal to religious roots of Dutch society problematizes the old divide between secular, progressive politics, on the one hand, and conservative, confessional politics, on the other.

This can be illustrated by election results: In spite of the returned emphasis on religious roots and the supposed return of religion, Christian-Democratic parties are in steady decline. But, at the same time, this does not seem to be connected to ongoing secularization of politics either. As a study by Grotenhuis and others of the results of the main Dutch Christian-Democratic party CDA has shown, the decimation of seats of the CDA is not connected to a simultaneous decline in numbers of religious voters (Grotenhuis et al., 2012). Grotenhuis et al. claim that church-going voters did not leave the CDA because of a demise of the role of religion in politics. Rather, Grotenhuis suggests, the simultaneous rise of political parties that have claimed to embody Judeo-Christian values might point to voters believing that Judeo-Christian values are upheld more effectively by the New Right than by classical confessional parties. The decline in votes for CDA is contemporary to the rise of votes for parties that explicitly claim to defend Judeo-Christian values of Dutch society. The decline of Christian-Democratic politics and the rise of New Right appeals to Judeo-Christian values could therefore be seen as part of a change in the way religion functions in politics: as the decline of the CDA showed, voters moved from confession-based politics to postsecular politics. Without wanting to delve deep into details of voter behaviour, this example illustrates the point that the perceived return to Judeo-Christian roots is of a different, more complex nature than the narratives of a return of traditional confessional politics allow.

'Judeo-Christian roots': history and rise

It is important to realize that this particular use of the term Judeo-Christian, denoting a combination of religious history with universal secular values, is relatively recent. It is only at the end of the twentieth century that this use of the term arises. Before delving further into the specifics of its contemporary use in the Netherlands, it is worthwhile to briefly recap some of the major moments in the history of the term (see also Wallet, 2012).

The first explicitly political use, that I am aware of, was in the work of Voltaire who used it to extend his critique of religion to all Abrahamic religions. In his *Dictionnaire Philosophique*, Voltaire wrote of '*du fanatisme judéo-chretien*', in which the typical Judeo-Christian fanatic is described as follows: 'he who experiences ecstasy, visions, he who mistakes dreams for reality and his imagination for prophesy, this person is a novice fanatic, who before long will be ready to kill for his love of God'[9] (Pomeau and Le Roy Ladurie, 1994: 97). The Judeo-Christian tradition, being a theology of revelation has a penchant for fanaticism and religiously motivated violence. Voltaire's deism is meant to be a replacement for this tradition, removing its belief in supernatural events and replacing it with a tolerant, rational religion, untroubled by a God who is now conceptualized as someone who does not interfere in earthly affairs (Toscano, 2010). Incidentally, without wanting to take a stand in the debate whether Voltaire was an anti-Semitic writer, the 'Judeo' in Judeo-Christian is consistently used by Voltaire to identify the worst of the two forces: 'The Jews had God Himself for master; see what has happened to them on that account: nearly always have they been beaten and slaves, and today do you not find that they cut a pretty figure?' (Pomeau and Le Roy Ladurie, 1994: 97).

Friedrich Nietzsche equally used the term to criticize the limitation of the individual in Abrahamic religions. He used the term in his *Anti-Christ* (1895) in a way that strongly linked the phrase 'Judeo-Christian' to slave morality: '*ressentiment* morality...this is the Judeo-Christian morality through and through' (Nietzsche, 2008: 21). For Nietzsche, then, the term Judeo-Christian meant the shared history of sacrificing the individual to a transcendental authority. Judeo-Christian furthermore testifies to the illegitimate fusion of philosophy with theology, as well as a departure from the natural state of affairs. Also, again without wanting to participate in the debate whether or not Nietzsche was an antisemitic author, it is worthwhile to point out that also for Nietzsche the 'Judeo' part of the term usually is seen as even worse than the 'Christian'. Or, as Nietzsche states, 'the Christian is only a Jew of a 'more liberal' persuasion' (2008: 44).

But the term did not function as a positive adjective also in circles less hostile to monotheism: In an influential Hegelian theological school in the nineteenth century (the Tübingen school), the term was used to indicate a phase in the early history of Christianity, where elements of Judaic religion and early Christianity were still connected. It frequently had an overtone of impurity, of transition from a state of impure tribalism to pure, universal Christian belief. Ferdinand Christian Baur, for instance, emphasized in 1836 that in early Christianity, a conflict existed between Pauline universal Christianity, and Petrinist 'Judeo-Christianity' that wanted to ground Christianity in a particular identity (Baur, 1836). In this stage the 'Judeo' in Judeo-Christian was associated with an old-fashioned clinging to a tribal past that blocked the development of a universal religion. Judeo-Christian was the moniker of an imperfect moment in a dialectical development that moved towards purification and towards the end of history (Silk, 1984).

As these examples show, the hyphen connecting Judeo and Christian was generally not seen as a positive thing, and tended to tie the term to a flaw in history, where Judaism denoted the lowest and most reproachable part of the equation.

The term received positive connotations in its use in the United States in the 1930s, when it was used to mobilize the American population against fascist antisemitism in the 1930s (Healan Gaston, 2012). Dwight D. Eisenhower stated in 1941: 'Our form of government has no sense unless it is founded in a deeply felt religious faith, and I don't care what it is. With us of course it is the Judeo-Christian concept but it must be a religion that all men are created equal' (Silk, 1984: 65). The term was used to rally a population against an enemy (fascism), by binding together previously disparate elements in a community (Jews and Christians) whose values are based on a notion of equality. Furthermore, in Eisenhower's statement, it was proclaimed that religion is a necessary background for a government that safeguards equality. Eisenhower, furthermore, moves away from actual theology, and moves towards a broad religious inspiration for political order that Robert Bellah has named 'post-traditionalist civil religion' (Bellah, 1991). This use was continued in the era of the Cold War, where the term was used to denote a mixture of democracy, liberalism, and capitalism bundled up with reference to multi-denominational devout faith and American traditionalism. Here the Judeo-Christian heritage was used as a term that identified the 'us' versus 'the enemy' (i.e., communism), in order to 'deny the atheistic and materialistic concepts of communism with its attendant subservience of the individual' (Domke and Coe, 2008: 15). This was an important moment in forging the alliance between conservative thinkers and evangelical Christians that can still be seen in the Republican party today: the electoral victory of Ronald Reagan was largely made possible by the alliance between conservatives and evangelical Christians who found common ground in the shared project of fighting godless communists and liberal licentiousness, while retaining a connection to the modern life of the average American individual (Corey, 2011; Steinfels, 1980).

Finally, in the transition from the Cold War era to the 'End of History', as exemplified in the works of Wilders (2007b), Huntington (2004) and Francis Fukuyama (2007), the term started to denote a shared set of values that set the modern secular West over and against non-secular and non-modern Islam. In his famous essay 'The Clash of Civilizations?' published in 1993, Huntington quotes Bernard Lewis approvingly:

We are facing a meed and a movement far transcending the level of issues and policies and the governments that pursue them. This is no less than a clash of civilizations – the perhaps irrational but surely historic reaction of an ancient rival against our Judeo-Christian heritage, our secular present, and the worldwide expansion of both. (Huntington, 1993: 32)

This final stage of the term arises in the 1990s. The clash of civilizations rhetoric came to a climax in the aftermath of 9/11. Currently the emphasis on 'Judeo-Christian heritage' still most often means a conservative affirmation of secular, Western values, and, more specifically, the exclusion of intolerant Islam.

In short, the term Judeo-Christian as a positive, shared, cultural framework expressing the religious background of secular values should be seen as a relatively recent invention. In this sense, current use stands in contrast with the political history of the term, where Judeo-Christianity was frequently seen as an obstacle on the way to universal ideals. However, a sense of continuation of history can be identified as well. All throughout its history, the term Judeo-Christian, far from neutrally describing a set of religious-cultural affinities, or historical facticity, has been a fighting term – a term *explicitly* used to divide as much as to identify, to attack as much as to defend. I emphasize 'explicitly' because, in the eyes of its propagators, the politics of use of the term seems to be more important than its historical accuracy. Having made this historical detour, we can now zoom in on this politics of use, by focusing on the Dutch context.

Dutch Judeo-Christian roots

In Dutch political debates, starting at the end of the 1990s and peaking halfway through the first frequently decade of this millennium, the Judeo-Christian roots of Dutch society are invoked to defend secular, liberal values against the threat of intolerant non-secular Islam, and to make a claim that the particular identity of the Netherlands should not be subsumed under either multiculturalist relativism or supranational EU bureaucracy. To take perhaps the most controversial example: In 2004, the successful populist right-wing politician Geert Wilders offered his reaction to the news that in the (then) newly appointed cabinet two functionaries with Islamic backgrounds would be installed:

> I want us to affirm the *Leitkultur* of the Netherlands in article 1 of the constitution (*that now expresses equality and outlaws discrimination,*

evdh). Our dominant values are based on the Jewish, Christian and humanist tradition. We should be proud of that, because these values express the foundations of who we are. And, in this way we can affirm what we don't want. We should not want a different culture, Islamic culture, to rule over us. (Wilders, 2011)[10]

The interviewer continues by asking whether this is similar to what the Christian-Democrat-led cabinet proposes: Isn't this appeal similar to the classic Christian-Democratic emphasis on morality and shared values? Wilders replies by explicitly rejecting the 'sphere sovereignty', a classical concept in pillarization theory, where every group in society has a certain autonomy in their own 'sphere'. In Wilders's view, this theory places insufficient emphasis on the shared cultural identity that should bind different groups together in Dutch society:

> The Christian-Democrats got their 'sphere sovereignty': all notions of communality have been institutionalized by this government. They think the family is important, so they create a ministry for Youth and Family Affairs. The word 'together' is mentioned about 10.000 times in the coalition agreement of this government, but that doesn't say a single thing about what really binds people. We should launch a debate about our cultural identity, but that is ignored completely by (prime-minister) Balkenende. (Wilders, 2011)[11]

This interview is exemplary for many of the uses of the term 'Judeo-Christian roots' in Dutch political debates: it signifies an emphasis on the identity of a community, an identity that is under threat and that should be reclaimed by defiantly insisting on its superiority. It furthermore breaches with hitherto commonly accepted means of giving these roots a voice in the Christian-Democratic tradition. As such, it is a break with what is perceived to be a failure, across the board, to address and nurture this shared background.

In 2002, populist pioneer Pim Fortuyn had appealed in a similar sense to the irreducible connection of secular values to their Judeo-Christian roots:

> Problems concentrate around all those fellow-citizens that originate from areas that are culturally very different from us. In general we can say that Islamic cultures are very different from areas that are culturally speaking Judeo-Christian.... Problems concerning integration and mutual acceptance are centered on the relation between the

dominant Judeo-Christian humanistic culture on the one hand and Islamic culture on the other. I consciously speak in the broad terminology of culture rather than of religion. One can leave a religion, as we can see happening massively in our country, a culture however, one cannot leave behind. (Fortuyn, 2002a: 83)[12]

It becomes clear that one needs to subscribe to a number of Judeo-Christian values in order to participate in this debate in the public sphere. Furthermore, it is clear that what is at stake here for Wilders, Fortuyn, and Bolkestein is a culturalized notion of religion. To quote Frits Bolkestein (1992):

> The shared myth [of Christianity] is gone. And now the question is whether we can function without that myth. ... we can say: 'hurray! We are no longer Christian!' but I wonder whether that attitude will be sufficient. I'm afraid not. Some intellectuals converted to Catholicism for that reason. For me that would be too artificial, because I am not a religious person, but culturally speaking, I am most certainly Christian.[13]

Frequently, these appeals have been criticized as mere populist rhetoric, aimed at the gut of the electorate and violating historical accuracy and decency in the process. I suggest that these appeals should not be seen as irrational (or historically incorrect) politics but as part of a conservative rhetorical practice that simultaneously:

- Aims to articulate that which underlies the core values of Dutch culture (universal secular values);
- Emphasizes the serious threat to this culture (presence and influence of 'Islam' in the Netherlands);
- Launches a criticism of the universal appeal of secular values and argues against its neutrality; and
- Presents a need to insist on the non-neutrality of these values (by insisting on the specific Judeo-Christian roots of these values).

Intriguingly, there is a historical specificity here. This means that the entire liberal tradition, including tolerance and openness, should now be defended in a conservative manner as being part of a single identity. As Paul Cliteur, a leading liberal thinker in the Netherlands has quipped: 'to be a liberal nowadays, you have to return to the roots, that means, you have to be conservative' (Standaard, 2004),[14] or, in the words of conservative author and former ideologue of Geert Wilders, Bart Jan Spruyt (2005): 'conservatism is needed to prevent liberalism from killing itself'.[15]

In this sense, classical progressive values can be connected to the conservative emphasis on the protection of a national religious identity. Both Fortuyn as well as Wilders explicitly connect feminism, gay rights, tolerance, and anti-fascism to the Judeo-Christian tradition, whereas Islam is perceived to be a sexist, homophobe,[16] intolerant form of 'desert-fascism'. For these reasons, Wilders has launched a campaign to ban the '*Mein Kampf* of Islam', the Koran, in 2007.[17] For a convincing analysis of this change in the status of progressive ideals, see Paul Mepschens and Jan Willem Duyvendak's analysis of the culturalization of citizenship and the way in which homosexuality has been adopted as a conservative nationalist value (Duyvendak and Mepschen, 2012). In their analysis, they have shown how gay rights have been used to argue for the superiority of Dutch national identity ('homo-nationalism'). Similar analysis could be made regarding feminism, the critique of fascism, and a number of other progressive ideals. Thus, paradoxically, values usually associated with a secular outlook, or even an anti-religious attitude can be presented as 'proof' of the superiority of Judeo-Christian culture.

On the one hand, this seems quite a paradoxical statement: secular values are claimed as religious in origin, and gay rights are a Judeo-Christian invention. Yet, if we see the appeal on Judeo-Christian roots as a rhetorical tool, a linguistic act meant to invoke more than to describe, we might find a new way of analysing this phenomenon. As I will show, the use of the rhetorical invocation of a religious ground of identity should be seen as a conservative strategy.[18] All along the history of conservatism, a mode of invocation can be identified that is quite suitable to analyse the contemporary predicament. An illustration of its rhetorical mode is useful to understand how such conservative proclamations provide a rhetorical foundation for national identity.

(Pro)claiming tradition

As I have showed above, Samuel P. Huntington's 'The Clash of Civilizations?' marked an important innovative moment in the history of the term Judeo-Christian. Yet Huntington's article is also a classical example of what Huntington himself would call conservative rhetoric. In his *Conservatism as Ideology* (1957), the same Huntington traces the roots of conservatism to the affirmation that conservatism is above all: 'the rationalization of existing institutions in terms of history, God, nature, and man' (Huntington, 1957). Moreover, as Huntington emphasizes, the conservative appeal to history is a fighting history:

> The conservative ideology is the product of intense ideological and social conflict. It appears only when the challengers to the established institutions reject the fundamentals of the ideational theory in terms of which those institutions have been molded and created. (Huntington, 1957: 458)

This is, for Huntington, not so much connected to a certain position in the division between left-wing and right-wing politics, but rather to a mode of defence of what has been accomplished:

> Just as aristocrats were the conservatives in Prussia in 1820 and slave owners were the conservatives in the South in 1850, so the liberals must be the conservatives in America today. Historically, American liberals have been idealists, pressing forward toward the goals of greater freedom, social equality, and more meaningful democracy. The articulate exposition of a liberal ideology was necessary to convert others to liberal ideas and to reform existing institutions continuously along liberal lines. Today, however, the greatest need is not so much the creation of more liberal institutions as the successful defense of those which already exist. This defense requires American liberals to lay aside their liberal ideology and to accept the values of conservatism for the duration of the threat. (Huntington, 1957: 472–473)

In short, what Huntington saw as the pinnacle of conservatism is the grounding of a community by appealing to its foundations in times of struggle. Huntington emphasizes that its lack of ideological coherence is in fact a strong point of conservatism. The coherence of the conservative tradition should be sought in its capacity to defend universal values from attack.

This status of the appeal to tradition as an active construction in the present has led some commentators to accuse conservatives of telling the populace 'noble lies', of twisting the truth in order to mobilize populations into believing in a threat. This, for instance, has been an influential discussion concerning criticism of the work of the influential conservative philosopher Leo Strauss as well. As many authors have explicitly stated with regards to the rise of the neoconservative movement in the United States, 'Leo Strauss gave the ideological impetus to the Bush years: his noble lies enabled people to believe in a notion of community and a notion of an enemy' (Drury, 2005: xxiv). The notion 'noble lie' stems from Plato's *Republic* (414b–414c) where Socrates proposes to tell the citizens of the 'ideal city' a 'noble myth': the first part is the 'myth of autochthony', that the people have an intrinsic connection to the place they were born. The second part is the 'myth of the metals', stating that the Gods mixed in valuable methods when each type of citizen was made, rendering them beautiful and valuable. In this way, the ideal society can be strengthened by a myth that is not true, but nonetheless 'in the service of justice and truth'. It is the apparent embrace of Strauss of the 'noble lie' that is often used to criticize Straussian influence for portraying a false image of identity to the populace in order to manipulate public order. That makes people believe their birthplace is worth more than the birthplaces of others. Specifically, Strauss is accused of 'regarding religion merely as a political tool intended for the masses but not for the superior few' (Drury, 2004).

Written from a need to criticize the rise of neoconservatism in the Bush years, this view of Strauss and of conservative politics in general can be called biased, to say the least. Commentators have engaged in a fierce debate over the accuracy of Drury's claims (Minowitz, 2009). Leaving that debate aside for the moment, allow me to point out that the description of conservative appeals to religion as a 'noble lie', does not reach the core of what I have outlined above as the rhetorical mode characteristic of the conservative tradition: first of all, the word 'lie' implies the existence of truth. Whereas, it is might be more characteristic of Strauss's philosophy that 'truth' is not at stake in politics. For Strauss does not so much endorse telling noble lies; rather, he exposes and uses the rhetorical dimension underlying all constructions of identity. In a more astute and less partisan close reading of Strauss's appeals to tradition, John G. Gunnell emphasizes the rhetorical dimension of the conservative emphasis on tradition:

> In one place, Strauss argues that 'only because public speech demands a mixture of seriousness and playfulness, can a true Platonist present the serious teaching, the philosophical teaching, in a historical and hence, playful garb.' My concern is not to conjecture about Strauss's true teaching, but to note the rhetorical function of the myth of the tradition and the instrumental tasks served by this kind of argument. In Strauss's case, the account of the tradition may be employed as a correlate to a philosophical argument, or as a surrogate when discursive argument is inadequate, much as Plato employs mythohistorical tales in his dialogues. (Gunnell, 1978: 133)

Rather than as a 'noble lie', Gunnell sees Strauss's emphasis on tradition and history as a 'dramaturgical account':

> Strauss's explication of the tradition of political philosophy is not a research conclusion but a dramaturgical account of the corruption of modernity designed to lend authority to his assertions about the crisis of our time. It is an epic history, complete with epic formulae. (Gunnell, 1978: 131)

Gunnell also stresses the particularly creative dimension of such a theory:

> The 'tradition' is a retrospective analytical construction which produces a rationalized version of the past. It is a virtual tradition calculated to evoke a particular image of our collective public psyche and the political conditions of our age, if not the human condition itself. It professes to tell us who we are and how we have arrived at our present situation.... What emerges is a historical drama, but the import of any substantive version depends initially on the audience's predisposition to accept the tradition as a reality. (Gunnell, 1978: 132)

A similar approach as Gunnell's to the conservative rise in Dutch political debates would be fruitful. For the conservative invocation of tradition, as the grounding of identity in something else than rational, enlightened truth can be seen as an inherent part of Dutch public debates as well. Prominent conservative thinker Andreas Kinneging in his 'Het Conservatisme: Kritiek van de Verlichting en de Moderniteit' places himself squarely in the tradition of conservatism, and writes approvingly of the role of religion as a foundation beyond (scientific) reason:

> In general, we can say that the Christian intellectual tradition is an indispensable source of knowledge and science, even if most of what is expressed in this tradition cannot be proven scientifically. (Kinneging, 2000)[19]

For Kinneging, the conservative appeal to tradition, which is also a construction of that tradition, is not an accurate, scientific description of what binds a community. As any introductory textbook to anthropology will affirm, it is through the invocation of identity and that which it excludes, that this identity is formulated. Bart Jan Spruyt, director of the Edmund Burke foundation and co-author of the first political programme for Geert Wilders's Partij voor de Vrijheid (Party for Freedom, or PVV), describes the need to find opposition to Judeo-Christian values in order to rediscover Dutch national identity. He references Carl Schmitt and states that more so than describing what Dutch society is, by proclaiming Dutch Judeo-Culture to be superior, 'we' will find out what Dutch society has been all along:

> Let's hope that Schmitt was right when he stated that the enemy is 'the figure of our own question' and that in this confrontation we rediscover our own identity. (Spruyt, 2005: 63)[20]

This incomplete sketch of the role of the appeal on religion in conservative thought serves to illustrate an important point: the appeal to Judeo-Christian roots should be seen as a performative-linguistic act, an invocation rather than a description, that has as its goal the simultaneous defence and construction of a community that is perceived to be under threat, by appealing to a tradition that cannot be grasped in rational, objective terms.

Progressive critics

Critics of the turn to the right in the Netherlands have had difficulty in interacting with this mode of doing politics. Frequently, the role of appeals to the religious dimension of Dutch society is misunderstood to be either historically erroneous or old-fashioned. One telling example is Rob Riemen, who in his *De Eeuwige Terugkeer van het Fascisme* (*The Eternal Return of Fascism*) decries twenty-first century appeals to Judeo-Christian norms as 'the exact inverse of Judeo-Christian and humanist traditions': 'What the PVV offers us in reality is diametrically opposed to the Judeo-Christian and humanist traditions' (Riemen, 2010: 45).[21] Riemen states that the Christian tradition, known for its 'profound reflection', 'high cultural values', and 'respect for the individual', is taken hostage by 'thugs' that promote thoughtless and ruthless power struggles. Interestingly enough, Riemen's book reads like a reaffirmation of Judeo-Christian-secular values over and against the populist fascists. The main narrative that drives the postsecular appeal to religious roots, that religious values are needed to safeguard to liberal values, is implicitly repeated here, but in a more elitist sense. The people have merely been tricked into believing that hatred for Islam is part of Dutch culture, whereas, *in reality*, Judeo-Christian culture is characterized by tolerance and inclusivity. The question of the limits of tolerance, which fuels the debate, is largely avoided.

A second reaction to the rise of conservative nationalism has been to decry its appeals to Judeo-Christian norms as a return to confessional politics. Jos de Mul has argued that, on the contrary, values like liberalism, secularism, and tolerance have been created not because of, but in opposition to, the Judeo-Christian tradition, and that any return to these religious roots necessarily means a regress in development. We see here a conceptualization of religion as diametrically opposed to secular values (De Mul, 2011). De Mul does not address the driving force behind these appeals to religious roots: the goal of these appeals, as we have seen, is mostly to offer a foundation for these secular values because they are perceived to be under threat. Again, secular values are presented as much better than religious values, as a result, the question of the perceived threat to the same secular values is largely ignored.

These two reactions to appeals to Judeo-Christian roots are symptomatic for the way in which progressive commentators fail to address the core of, let alone offer an alternative to, the conservative performative. This is problematic for a number of reasons: unqualified appeals to the value of secular values are successfully taken up in narratives that equate religion with the genesis and protection of these secular values. As a result, the grounding of these values – the main drive behind conservative postsecular thought – remains largely undisputed. By missing the point that what is at stake is an immanent construction of identity, the 'debate' about national identity is doomed to continue on two separate tracks: one side invokes identity in a manner that addresses itself to those who share the feeling that ground is lacking, whereas the other side speaks in terms of historical accuracy and an outdated separation between secular objectivity and religious dogmatism.

It is interesting that many of the academic criticisms levelled against the notion of postsecularism (it would be exclusionary, too much focused on the West, too much connected to secular ideals, and closed off to other conceptualizations of the public sphere, to name but a few arguments raised against conceptualizations of the postsecular), are actively embraced by contemporary conservatives: the politicians and thinkers mentioned above affirm explicitly that secularism is, in fact, based on a biased take on religion; they simply affirm that this religious-secular identity is a way to exclude Islam. In short, a lot of the criticism levelled against the notion of postsecularism is actively embraced by its proponents. Thus, like Hans Joas, De Vries, and Sullivan have argued, postsecularism perhaps should not be seen as a historical periodization, but 'a change in mindset of those who, previously, felt justified in considering religions to be moribund'. It is from this realization that many of the previously secular politicians have embraced Judeo-Christian values as a foundation for an identity they have presented as being under attack. And as the poor quality of the Dutch debate testifies, an answer to this postsecular mode of doing politics has not yet been found.

At the moment of writing, Geert Wilders's PVV is the largest in the polls. If the recent polls are something to go by, the debates concerning religion, secularism, and national identity will not fade away anytime soon. Those who want to participate in this continuous recreation of religious identity, have the task to catch up and learn to understand postsecular politics. I will therefore conclude with some reflections on some possible reactions to these conservative appeals on religion in the public debate.

Conclusion: the postsecular demand

There exists a large gap between the political use of religion, which is successful and effective, and the academic study of religion, which, in this particular moment, institutionally speaking, is dwindling and struggling to find its role in society. As Theology faculties in the Netherlands make the transition to faculties of Religious Studies, the volatile religious climate poses an urgent challenge to scholars of religion. What is the relevance of the study of religion in a time and a society that makes religion into a central controversy? What role does the study of Judaism or Christianity play in times when culturalized versions of these belief systems play an important role in reframing Dutch culture? Some thoughts on how the study of religion can become not just a relevant contribution to but perhaps also an antidote to a volatile and divisive political climate:

Criticism alone might not be enough. As an impressive volume by Talal Asad, Wendy Brown, Judith Butler, and Saba Mahmood has eloquently investigated, the critical subject might be a position tied in close with secular notions of individuality (Asad et al., 2009). In what I have attempted to describe above, many a Dutch commentator has attempted to criticize the appeals to Judeo-Christian roots as historically inaccurate, or as nothing more than populism aimed at the unintelligent masses who, if they would only listen, would distance themselves immediately from this agenda the moment they found out the truth. This runs the risk of missing the central performative character of conservative rhetoric (and, perhaps, of constructions of communities in general). A pitfall of this reaction to the rise of conservative postsecular rhetoric is elitism, where historical accuracy is divorced from, instead of reconnected with, the way in which the past is mobilized in political debates. Instead, perhaps an answer lies in affirming counter-histories and counter-identities.

Colonialism, for instance, is largely left out of the equation as a characteristic of Judeo-Christian culture. On the contrary, most authors mentioned above display an allergy for what is perceived to be politically correct feelings of guilt towards the colonial past. Emphasizing the constructive role of religious practices that blur the boundaries between white Judeo-Christianity and its others both in history and in contemporary practices can provide a firm basis for restaging the performative. James Kennedy and Markha Valenta, as well as Peter van der Veer, have, for instance, emphasized that the Netherlands were, during the colonial occupation of what is now called Indonesia, the largest Islamic country on earth (Kennedy and Valenta, 2006). A rewriting of Dutch history that takes this seriously, an Islamo-Judeo-Christian history, perhaps, would therefore be an important start.

A similar case can be made for the 'Judeo' in Judeo-Christianity: this is, as we have seen, a recent invention: before the Second World War, one would be hard-pressed to find a description of Western culture as Judeo-Christian, meant in a positive sense. Furthermore, in all of the invocations seen above there seems to be no actual connection to Judaic traditions. This leads to intriguing paradoxes; for instance, Geert Wilders, whilst pushing for a ban on ritual slaughter out of defence of Judeo-Christian values, enabled the outlawing of kosher food as well (Valenta, 2012). Also, there is hardly any reference to the centuries of antisemitism that is also part of religious history ('Islamic fascism', or 'Islamic antisemitism', has taken over that role). The result is a rather one-sided inclusion of Jewish influence in the constitution of Dutch national identity that can just as well be called an exclusion. The westernization (which in fact is a colonization) of Judaism can be countered by stressing not just the fact that for centuries the Jewish tradition was Christianity's other (as is shown by the antisemitic overtones in the history of the term Judeo-Christian), but also by stressing affinities between traditions and geographical locations.

The claim that progressive values such as gay rights are part of an explicitly Western, secular-religious framework threatens to equate emancipation with Western practices. In the work of Saba Mahmood, as in the work of Rosi Braidotti and Joan Scott, a case is made for a redefinition of feminism: these new forms of feminism would have the challenge to be able to incorporate religious practices as emancipatory practices as well and to avoid the pitfall of equating feminism with secular critique (Mahmood, 2005; Braidotti, 2008; Scott 2009). These sort of emancipatory acts that do not fit the Judeo-Christian-secular model of emancipation, whether in history or in the present, need to be recognized as politically relevant.

Finally, the almost complete absence of faith in the appeals to Judeo-Christian roots creates the potential for actual religious experiences to return and disrupt the 'culturalization' of religion. Faith, as well as religion in general, instead of its secular definition as a pietistic internal affair, and the culturalized definition described above, can be reconceptualized as a politically relevant act with consequences for the implicit history symbolized by the culturalization of Judeo-Christian roots. But, in order for this debate to take off, the (pro) claiming of tradition and national identity needs to happen on more fronts than just the conservative, nationalist, postsecular one. Old separations between disciplines, institutions, and modes of identifications are in dire need of reassessment. In spite of all its ambiguity, postsecular scholarship will have an important role to play in the Netherlands.

Notes

1. See the following excerpts from a speech by EU-sceptic Nigel Farage, in which Nigel Farage moves seamlessly from 'Judeo-Christian values' to 'all the good Christianity has done over the ages', note how the 'Judeo' is increasingly absent from these reflections: http://www.youtube.com/watch?v=ME4lHJVU1iE.
2. See the reflection by Bart de Wever, contemporary nationalist politician in Belgium on the link between Judeo-Christian roots and the outlawing of polygamy: http://www.standaard.be/artikel/detail.aspx?artikelid=343NSB0H&s=1.
3. See conservative author Robert Spaemann's appeal to reinstate the ban on blasphemy to protect the specifically Judeo-Christian roots of German society: http://www.faz.net/aktuell/feuilleton/debatten/robert-spaemann-zur-blasphemie-debatte-beleidigung-gottes-oder-der-glaeubigen-11831612.html.
4. See Sarkozy's appeal to Judeo-Christian roots in France in February 2012: http://www.lefigaro.fr/politique/2012/02/10/01002-20120210ARTFIG00586-nicolas-sarkozy-mes-valeurs-pour-la-france.php.
5. 'Na een lange geschiedenis met tal van zwarte bladzijden hebben rationalisme, humanisme en christendom een aantal fundamentele politieke beginselen voortgebracht, zoals de scheiding van kerk en staat, de vrijheid van meningsuiting, de verdraagzaamheid en de non-discriminatie' (Bolkestein, 2005).

6. James Beckford, for instance, identifies six main clusters of definitions of postsecularism, and proceeds to offer a convincing critique of all six of them (Beckford, 2012). See also Veith Bader's article in which he criticizes the use of postsecularism for, amongst other reasons, failing to offer a 'sound basis for normative debates' (Bader, 2012).
7. Leading to sometimes paradoxical results: in 2010 and 2011, a debate ensued in the Dutch Parliament and Senate following a law that would outlaw ritual slaughter. Geert Wilders's PVV, a strong proponent of defending Judeo-Christian Dutch identity strongly supported the ban, leading to the paradoxical situation that a ritual practice characteristic of a religion central to Dutch society was banned by those claiming to defend its interests, see Valenta (2012).
8. For a discussion of the contemporary status of pillarization, see Kennedy and Valenta (2006).
9. 'Celui qui a des extases, des visions, qui prend des songes pour des réalités, et ses imaginations pour des prophéties, est un fanatique novice qui donne de grandes espérances: il pourra bientôt tuer pour l'amour de Dieu' (Pomeau and Le Roy Ladurie, 1994).
10. 'Ik wil dat we de Leitkultur in Nederland in artikel 1 van de Grondwet gaan vastleggen. Onze dominante waarden zijn gebaseerd op de joodse, humanistische en christelijke traditie. Daar moeten we trots op zijn, want daarin ligt besloten wie wij zijn. Bovendien kunnen wij daarmee vastleggen wat wij niet willen. We moeten niet willen dat een andere cultuur, de islamitische, gaat overheersen.'
11. 'De christen-democraten hebben hun soevereiniteit in eigen kring gekregen: alle gemeenschapszin is in het regeerakkoord geïnstitutionaliseerd. We vinden het gezin belangrijk, dús komt er een minister voor Jeugd en Gezin. Het woord 'samen' komt 10.000 keer voor in het regeerakkoord, maar dat zegt niets over de verbanden tussen mensen. We moeten het debat gaan voeren over onze culturele identiteit, maar dat negeert Balkenende volledig' (Wilders, 2011). Translation mine.
12. De problemen concentreren zich op al die medeburgers die komen uit cultuurgebieden die ver tot zeer ver af staan van de onze. Meer in het algemeen kan worden gesteld dat de islamitische culturen ver af staan van de joods-christelijk humanistische cultuurgebieden. ... De problemen inzake integratie en wederzijdse acceptatie spitsen zich toe op de relatie van de dominante joods-christelijk humanistische cultuur enerzijds en de islamitische cultuur anderzijds. Ik spreek hier uitdrukkelijk in de veel bredere termen van cultuur dan van godsdienst. Een godsdienst kan men verlaten, zoals in ons land op grote schaal gebeurt, een cultuur kan men echter niet verlaten (Fortuyn, 2002: 83).
13. 'Maar dat bezielend verband, of zoals sommigen het noemen de gedeelde mythe, is er niet meer. En nu is de vraag, of we ook zonder dit verband goed kunnen functioneren. Er zijn velen die menen dat de Grondwet een bezielend verband kan geven. Maar zelf heb ik het stiekeme gevoel dat dit niet voldoende is. We kunnen wel zeggen: 'hiep hoi, we zijn geen christenen meer'. Maar houdt dat op de lange duur? Hoe staan we er over vijftig tot tachtig jaar voor? Sommige intellectuelen zijn om die reden katholiek geworden. Voor mij zou dat kunstmatig zijn, omdat ik niet godsdienstig ben. Maar ik zou me zeker een cultuurchristen willen noemen. ... ' Bolkestein (1992).

14. 'om liberaal te zijn moet je tegenwoordig terug naar de wortels. Dus conservatief zijn' (Standaard, 2004).
15. 'Het conservatisme is nodig om het liberalisme voor zelfmoord te behoeden' (Spruyt, 2005).
16. Cf. Fortuyn (2002): 'I don't want to have to do the emancipation of gays and women all over again.'
17. For details see 'Genoeg is genoeg: verbied de Koran' ('Enough is enough: Outlaw the Koran') in *Volkskrant*, 8 August 2007 (Wilders, 2007).
18. For a detailed analysis on the historical connection between the turn to the right in the Netherlands and both Dutch and American think tanks, see Oudenampsen (2013).
19. 'In het algemeen geldt dat de klassieke en christelijke intellectuele traditie een onmisbare bron is van kennis en wetenschap, ook al kan het meeste wat in die traditie wordt verwoord niet worden 'bewezen' volgens de criteria van de moderne natuurwetenschap' (Kinneging, 2000).
20. 'Laten we hopen dat Schmitt gelijk had toen hij zei dat de vijand "onze eigen vraag als gestalte" is, en dat wij in deze confrontatie onze identiteit weer herontdekken' (Spruyt, 2005: 63). Translation mine.
21. 'Wat ons echter daadwerkelijk wordt aangeboden door de Partij van de Vrijheid, is het schaamteloze tegendeel van de joods-christelijke en humanistische radities' (Riemen, 2010: 45). Translation mine.

References

Asad, T. (1993). *Genealogies of Religion: Discipline and Reasons of Power in Christianity and Islam*. Baltimore, MD: Johns Hopkins University Press.
Asad, T., Brown, W., Butler, J., and Mahmood, S. (2009). *Is Critique Secular? Blasphemy, Injury, and Free Speech*. Berkeley, CA: Townsend Center for the Humanities.
Bader, V. (2012). 'Postsecularism or Liberal-Democratic Constitutionalism?' *Erasmus Law Review* 5(1), 5–26.
Baur, F.C. (1836). 'Über Zweck und Veranlassung des Römerbriefs und die Damit Zusammenhängenden Verhältnisse der Römischer Gemeinde.' *Tübinger Zeitschrift für Theologie* 3, 59–178.
Beckford, J.A. (2012). 'SSSR Presidential Address Public Religions and the postsecular: Critical Reflections.' *Journal for the Scientific Study of Religion* 51(1), 1–19.
Bellah, R. (1991). *Beyond Belief: Essays on Religion in a Post-Traditionalist World*. Berkeley, CA: University of California Press.
Bolkestein, F. (1992). 'De Integratie Van Minderheden.' In *Woorden Hebben Hun Betekenis*. Amsterdam: Prometheus.
Bolkestein, F. (2009). 'Frits Bolkestein vreest Europa zonder Christendom.' *Nederlands Dagblad* 23 May.
Bracke, S. (2012). 'Secularization Theories and Islam. How the Narrative of 'Pillarization' Frames Muslims and Refigures Dutch Identity in Times of Civilization.' *Journal of Muslim in Europe* 1(1).
Braidotti, R. (2008). 'In Spite of the Times: The Postsecular Turn in Feminism.' *Theory, Culture & Society* 25(6), 1–24.

Buruma, I. (2007). *Murder in Amsterdam: Liberal Europe, Islam and the Limits of Tolerance*. London: Penguin.
Cliteur, P. (2004). 'Het Nieuwe Conservatisme van Paul Cliteur.' *De Standaard*. 20 March.
Corey, Robin (2011). *The Reactionary Mind: Conservatism from Edmund Burke to Sarah Palin*. Oxford University Press.
De Mul, J. (2011). *Paniek in de Polder: Polytiek en Populisme in Nederland*. Zoetermeer, Belgium: Klement.
Domke, D. and Coe, K. (2008). *The God Strategy: How Religion Became a Political Weapon in America*. Oxford: Oxford University Press.
Drury, S.B. (2004). 'Leo Strauss and the Grand Inquisitor.' *Free Inquiry Magazine* 23(4).
Drury, S.B. (2005). *The Political Ideas of Leo Strauss*. New York: St. Martin's Press.
Duyvendak, J.W. and Mepschen, P. (2012). 'European Sexual Nationalisms: The Culturalization of Citizenship and the Sexual Politics of Belonging and Exclusion.' CLOSER. Online source, available at http://religionresearch.org/martijn/2012/12/30/sexual-nationalisms culturalization-of citizenship/ [last accessed December 2012].
Fortuyn, P. (2002a). *De Verweesde Samenleving. Een Religieus-sociologisch Traktaat*. Uithoorn, Netherlands: Karakter
Fortuyn, P. (2002b). 'Pim Fortuyn Op Herhaling: "De Islam Is Een Achterlijke Cultuur".' *VK*, 2 August 2000 http://www.volkskrant.nl/vk/nl/2824/Politiek/article/detail/611698/2002/02/09/De islam-is-een-achterlijke-cultuur.dhtml.
Fukuyama, F. (2007). 'The Challenges of Positive Freedom.' *New Perspectives Quarterly* 24(2), 53–56.
Grotenhuis, M. te, Meer, T. van der, Eisinga, R., and Pelzer, B. (2012). 'In Hoeverre Bepalen Ontkerkelijking en Gewijzigd Stemgedrag onder Kerkleden het Aantal CDA Kamerzetels?' *Christen-Democratische Verkenningen* 3, 135–144.
Gunnell, J.G. (1978). 'The Myth of the Tradition.' *The American Political Science Review* 72(1), 122–134.
Habermas, J. (2006). *Time of Transitions*. Cambridge: Polity.
Habermas, Jürgen (2008). 'Secularism's Crisis of Faith: Notes on Post-Secular Society'. *New Perspectives Quarterly* 25, 17–29.
Healan Gaston, K. (2012). 'Interpreting Judeo-Christianity in America.' *Relegere: Studies in Religion and Reception* 2(2), 291–304.
Huntington, S.P. (1957). 'Conservatism as an Ideology.' *The American Political Science Review* 51(2), 454–473.
Huntington, S.P. (1993). 'The Clash of Civilizations?' *Foreign Affairs* 72(3), 22–49.
Jansen, Y. (2011). 'Postsecularism, Piety and Fanaticism: Reflections on Jurgen Habermas and Saba Mahmood's Critiques of Secularism.' *Philosophy Social Criticism* 37(9), 977–998.
Kennedy, J. and Valenta, M. (2006). 'Religious Pluralism and the Dutch State: Reflections on the Future of Article 23.' In W.B.H.J van de Donk, A.P. Jonkers, G.J. Kronjee, and R.J.J.M. Plum (eds) *Geloof in Het Publieke Domein: Verkenning van Een Dubbele Transformatie*. Amsterdam: Amsterdam University Press.
Kinneging, A. (2000). 'Het Conservatisme. Kritiek van Verlichting en Moderniteit.' *Philosophia Reformata* LXV, 126–153.

Kuyper, A. (2008). *Lectures on Calvinism: The Stone Lectures of 1898*. Peabody, MA: Hendrickson Publishers.
Mahmood, S. (2005). *Politics of Piety: The Islamic Revival and the Feminist Subject (New in Paper)*. Princeton, NJ: Princeton University Press.
Minowitz, P. (2009). *Straussophobia: Defending Leo Strauss and Straussians Against Shadia Drury and Other Accusers*. Lanham, MD: Lexington Books.
Nietzsche, F. (2008). *The Anti-Christ*. Radford, VA: Wilder Publications.
Oudenampsen, M. (2013). 'Postprogressive Politics: On the Reception of Neoconservatism in the Netherlands.' *Krisis* 1, available at http://www.academia.edu/3256524/Postprogressive_politics_on_the_reception_of_noconservatism_in_the_Netherlands.
Pomeau, R. and Le Roy Ladurie, E. (eds) (1994). *Dictionnaire de la Pensée de Voltaire par Lui-même*. Brussels: Editions Complexe.
Robin, C. (2011). *The Reactionary Mind: Conservatism from Edmund Burke to Sarah Palin*. Oxford: Oxford University Press.
Riemen, R. (2010). *De Eeuwige Terugkeer van het Fascisme*. Amsterdam: Atlas Contact.
Santaniello, W. (1994). *Nietzsche, God, and the Jews: His Critique of Judeo Christianity in Relation to the Nazi Myth*. New York: SUNY Press.
Scott, J.W. (2009). 'Sexularism.' Ursula Hirschmann Annual Lecture on Gender and Europe, Robert Schuman Centre for Advanced Lectures.
Silk, M. (1984). 'Notes on the Judeo-Christian Tradition in America.' *American Quarterly* 36(1), 65–85.
Spruyt, B.J. (2005). *Boekenweekessay 2005: De Toekomst van de Stad*. Zoetermeer, Belgium: Boekencentrum.
Standaard. (2004). 'Het Nieuwe Conservatisme van Paul Cliteur.' *De Standaard*. 20 March 2004.
Steinfels, P. (1980). *Neo-conservatices: The Men Who Are Changing America's Politics*. New York: Simon and Schuster.
Toscano, A. (2010). *Fanaticism: On the Uses of an Idea*. London: Verso.
Valenta, M. (2012). *Pluralist Democracy or Scientist Monocracy? Debating Ritual Slaughter*. SSRN Scholarly Paper. Rochester, NY: Social Science Research Network.
Valk, G. (2011). 'Het Koninkrijk van Allah Zal Er Nooit Komen.' *NRC*, 12 March.
Vries, Hent De and Lawrence Eugene Sullivan (2006). *Political Theologies: Public Religions in a Post-Secular World*. Fordham University Press.
Wallet, B. (2012). 'Zin En Onzin Van De "Joods-christelijke Traditie".' *Christen Democratische Verkenningen* 2, 100–109.
Wilders, G. (2007). 'Genoeg Is Genoeg: Verbied de Koran.' *VK*, 8 August 2007, available at http://www.volkskrant.nl/vk/nl/2686/Binnenland/article/detail/870859/2007/08/08/G noeg-is-genoeg-verbied-de-Koran.dhtml.
Wilders, Geert (2007). "Wilders Spreekt: Ik Capituleer Niet." *HP/De Tijd*, December.

4
Re-examining an Ethics of Citizenship in Postsecular Societies

Christoph Baumgartner

Jürgen Habermas is, without any doubt, one of the most influential, albeit not undisputed, authors in the debate about 'postsecularity', 'postsecularism', 'the postsecular', 'postsecular societies', and so forth. Unlike many other authors who use these concepts to describe and explain the continuing presence of religion in contemporary 'modern' societies (see Beckford, 2012), the core of Habermas's notion of the postsecular society is *normative*. It includes an ethics of citizenship that aims at making it possible that all citizens can participate as equals in democratic procedures, including public political debate about matters of common interest, and hence in co-determining the development of their society. This contribution critically examines Habermas's proposal of an ethics of citizenship in postsecular societies in view of the question whether it is able to adequately deal with problems that arise in public controversies about particular verbal and non-verbal acts of expression, namely acts which are understood by their authors as contributions to public debate, which are experienced by numerous believers as denigration of their religion, and as offence to their religious sensibilities. Controversies about such acts offer especially interesting possibilities for an investigation of normative dimensions of the notion of the postsecular and postsecular societies, respectively. For what is at stake, here, is not only the demand of religious people that they themselves should be allowed to practise their religion (like in the case of debates about ritual slaughter or the wearing of religious clothing). Rather, the controversies that I am interested in concern the formal and informal rules that structure the public sphere common to all members of society, whether religious or not (see March, 2012: 320), and the discursive space that is essential for the legitimate exercise and control of democratic politics. Accordingly, this chapter aims to contribute both to the debate about postsecularism and to the broader political philosophical task of developing an ethics of citizenship in democratic and pluralistic societies. The concrete example that will serve as the background of my analysis of Habermas's position is the public controversy about the so-called Muhammad cartoons, published first in 2005 by Danish newspaper *Jyllands-Posten*, and – importantly – about public protests against it. I will argue that Habermas's understanding of an ethics of citizenship in postsecular societies is too limited to be able to adequately deal with the various obstacles that can prevent people from participating as equals in public political debate. As I will show, the main reason for this is that Habermas focuses strongly, albeit not exclusively, on epistemic attitudes that are situated on a cognitive level, while important obstacles to participation in public political debate are related to emotional, and cultural elements. I will suggest that political philosophy must go beyond Habermas's ethics of citizenship in postsecular societies, in order to be able to grasp and possibly dismantle elements that can effectively exclude citizens from public political debate.

Habermas's ethics of democratic citizenship in postsecular societies

Like other authors who address the notion of the postsecular and postsecular societies, respectively, Habermas unfolds his considerations about postsecular societies against the background of the failure of the secularization thesis. The theoretic angle, however, from which Habermas approaches the topic, differs significantly from that of, for instance, sociologists of religion who describe developments in the religious landscape of particular societies. His considerations are part of a larger political philosophical project that aims to answer the question of how we should understand ourselves as members of democratic societies where religion plays an important role in the lives of many citizens, and what we can, or must, reciprocally expect from another in order to make it possible that all citizens can participate as equals in social interactions, including public political debate.[1] More specifically, Habermas aims to provide a solution of a problem that results from the claim that, according to the model of deliberative democracy, political decisions can only be taken to be legitimate if they can be justified by reasons that all citizens can equally accept. Reasons that depend on religious authorities such as sacred texts or instructions of religious dignitaries do not count as acceptable in that sense. Because of this, religious citizens cannot directly contribute with their religiously based convictions to democratic debate but are supposed to 'translate' them into what counts as 'secular' or 'public' reasons which are independent of any reference to religion. This, however, means that religious citizens are 'encumbered with an asymmetrical burden' (Habermas, 2006: 11), since they may make (valid) contributions to public political debate only if they translate their 'religious language' into 'public reasons', whereas secular citizens are not required to make comparable efforts. Even more, for some people it can be impossible to translate their religious views into a language of secular reasons since this would require them to undertake an 'artificial division [between 'religious' and 'secular' convictions] within their own minds' (Habermas, 2006: 8) which would not be possible without jeopardizing their identity as pious persons. To require believers to pay such a price for the possibility to make use of their right to political participation, however, is morally problematic: 'a state cannot encumber its citizens, whom it guarantees freedom of religious expression, with duties that are incompatible with pursuing a devout life – it cannot expect something impossible of them' (Habermas, 2006: 7).

To solve this problem of an undue asymmetrical burden, Habermas restricts the 'translation proviso' to the realm of institutionalized practices of deliberation and decision-making in political bodies such as the parliament. In the '"wild life" of the political public sphere', however, religious citizens should be allowed to couch their contributions in religious language. Furthermore, and for the context of this chapter especially importantly, Habermas construes the task of translating religious contributions into a 'generally accessible language' as a collaborative task: Both religious and non-religious citizens must likewise participate in this task, and 'secular citizens must open their minds to the possible truth content of those presentations and enter into dialogues from which religious reasons then might well emerge in the transformed guise of generally accessible arguments' (Habermas, 2006: 11). This has a number of normative implications that concern the cognitive or epistemic attitudes that both religious and non-religious citizens of postsecular societies need to develop.

Religious citizens, on the one hand, must develop epistemic attitudes that enable them to constructively cope with challenges and cognitive dissonances that could arise from the fact that their religion is faced with pluralism, the emergence of modern science, and profane morality and law. Regarding the latter, Habermas points out, fundamental normative principles such as the separation of religion and state and, related to this, the secular legitimation of politics must be supported from within the view of the respective religious traditions and communities. In this regard, Habermas speaks of a 'modernization of religious consciousness' that results from a 'learning process' that must be undertaken from within religious traditions themselves (Habermas, 2006: 14).[2]

Non-religious, or 'secular' citizens, on the other hand, are required to develop comparable epistemic attitudes in the context of a postsecular society: They must self-reflectively transcend a secularist self-understanding of modernity that encounters religion with 'sparing indifference' and that understands religious traditions as 'archaic relics of pre-modern societies' (Habermas, 2006: 15). In other words, secular citizens must develop an epistemic stance that prepares them to take religious contributions to public political debate seriously and even to actively help to investigate whether such contributions include moral intuitions that can be expressed in secular language and justified by reasons that are accessible for all.

This specific ethics of democratic citizenship is the core of Habermas's notion of postsecularism and postsecular societies, respectively. Accordingly, the decisive feature of a postsecular society is not so much a return or a revitalization of religions in the public sphere, et cetera, but rather 'that it is *epistemically adjusted* to the continued existence of religious communities' (Habermas, 2006: 15, italics in original) which requires a change in mentality that is cognitively exacting for both religious and non-religious citizens. To be 'postsecular' in that sense is not so much a 'fact' (like the 'return' and continuing presence of public religion is said to be) but rather a political ethical requirement, because neither a widespread secularist mentality including a more or less blunt rejection of religion as 'backward' or 'anti-democratic', nor 'fundamentalist' attitudes of a large number of religious citizens are compatible with deliberative democracy and the ideal of equality of participation in public political debate (Habermas, 2008: 27). This requirement, however, does not primarily concern institutions of society (such as the law), but mental attitudes and, especially, cognitive capacities of citizens which is why Michele Dillon points out that 'it seems [Habermas] really intends to talk about a postsecular Zeitgeist' rather than about a postsecular society (Dillon, 2012: 257). The ethics of citizenship of which the postsecular Zeitgeist is a part, is construed almost exclusively in cognitive terms by Habermas; other elements, such as culturally predominant imaginaries, embodied emotions and frameworks for perception and interpretation that are applied more or less unconsciously, are largely, but not entirely, ignored. There are some small traces that can be understood as acknowledgement of the influence that not purely cognitive elements can exercise on the process of public debate, in general, and the inclusion of convictions of 'religious citizens' in this process, in particular. The above-mentioned requirement that 'the secular citizens must open their minds to the possible truth content' of contributions that are made in religious language (Habermas, 2006: 11) could be understood as indication that Habermas does not completely overlook such not purely cognitive aspects. However, this does not alter the fact that his ethics of citizenship in postsecular societies is construed primarily in terms of 'cognitive burdens' and an 'epistemic adjustment' of society and its citizens respectively to the presence of religion.

Conditions of participating in public political debate

As was already mentioned above, the main purpose of an ethics of citizenship in postsecular societies is to make it possible that all citizens can participate as equals in democratic procedures, including public political debate. Clearly, open public debate is important for democratic societies since legitimate democratic power is constituted and controlled by the people. Matters of common interest need to be publicly discussed and all members of society, certainly those who are affected by a certain matter or political decision, must be able to fully participate in public debate about it.

Concern for an open public debate in pluralistic democratic societies was also the frame into which the editors of *Jyllands-Posten* placed the publication of the Muhammad cartoons. According to Flemming Rose, cultural editor of *Jyllands-Posten*, the reason to commission and publish the cartoons was what he perceived as an increasing self-censorship among authors, artists, and translators which was, according to Rose, caused by fears and feelings of intimidation in dealing with issues related to Islam (Klausen, 2009: 13–20; Rose, 2006). Such self-censorship motivated by fear, Rose argued, was incompatible with political democratic debate, and the goal of the publication of the cartoons 'was simply to push back self-imposed limits on expression that seemed to be closing in tighter' (Rose, 2006). In other words, the stated aim of *Jyllands-Posten* was to further public debate in democratic societies about issues such as freedom of expression, freedom of religion, cultural and religious diversity, but also about possible relations between Islam and violence.

But what does it mean for public debate to be 'open' in the normatively relevant sense mentioned at the beginning of this section? To be able to function as democratic political forum, public debate must be open in a twofold sense. First, it is necessary that *all matters* that are considered of common interest can be publicly discussed. Second, *everyone who is affected* by a certain matter or political decision must be able to contribute to public debate about it. These formal requirements are grasped by the right to freedom of expression, including the right to access to mass media. There are, however, also informal preconditions. As a form of public communication, political democratic debate is always dependent on what Bernhard Peters calls 'public culture' that consists of stocks of shared knowledge, norms, values and conventions, rituals, symbols, and so forth, which build contexts of meaning, dispositions for attentiveness, and components for frameworks within which certain events and decisions are interpreted or justified (see Peters, 2008: 69–76, 219–221). On the basis of a public culture, it becomes possible for different people to understand statements, events, or decisions, to evaluate and weigh them, and to communicate about them in a broader public. In that sense, public culture is 'the quintessence of facilitative and restrictive conditions of communication within a community. Public culture works like a sluice, opening and closing communicative opportunity.' (Wessler and Wingert, 2008: 5). For the interest of this chapter it is especially important that certain components of public culture concern the respective community or society itself. These 'collective self-images' (Peters, 2008) refer, for example, to the history and the current state of the respective community and to cultural, historical, or political achievements. Furthermore, they include criteria that are used to ascribe group membership to certain people and to exclude others; they are linked with (mostly positive) self-evaluations and ideals, on the one hand, and with 'contrasting images of other groups' and 'definitions of the relations to other collectivities (as friendly or hostile and so on)' (Peters, 2008: 72), on the other hand. In democratic societies, 'public culture' includes normative assumptions that predetermine 'how citizens interpret their civic bonds in practice, who they regard as competent citizens, who they regard as incompetent, how much unity and how much diversity they think a democratic polity needs or can endure' (Brink, 2007: 354). Such 'informal conceptions of democratic life' (Brink, 2007) are usually rooted in dominant traditions and often represent and reproduce social power relations. They strongly influence the way in which citizens who are differently situated within the informal power relations of society think of themselves and of others in view of democratic citizenship. Accordingly, they influence the dominant 'grammar' of public debate and determine who is recognized as competent and 'respectable' contributor and what passes for a valuable contribution. This is especially important in the case of public political debate as a specific form of communication where people do not merely want to tell others their views but put in normative, political claims, for instance concerning free speech, self-censorship and the relation between particular religions and violence (like *Jyllands-Posten* did) or regarding the proper public treatment of what religious believers consider sacred (like many protestors against the publication of the Muhammad cartoons did). In doing so, contributors claim the authority of somebody who is, as member of a democratic society and on a par with others, legitimately engaged in the process of self-government and in the ongoing process of developing and (re)shaping of society and its formal and informal institutions. This distinguishes public political debate from other forms of public communication that do not share the normative significance for democratic politics. In order to succeed, the specific authority of the speaker as having a say in matters concerning the society in question must be recognized by other participants of the debate. Otherwise, the person may be able to make use of her right to freedom of expression; she may be able to use media to convey her claims and arguments. Nevertheless, without being recognized as somebody who has a say in matters concerning the development of society, the person cannot succeed to fully participate as peer in public political debate.[3] It is this latter aspect of a specific authority that needs to be recognized by others in order to be able to fully and effectively participate as equal in public debate that is especially interesting in the analysis of, for instance, the controversy about the Muhammad cartoons in light of the notion of the postsecular.

Debating Muhammad cartoons – construing debaters[4]

Almost immediately after the publication, the cartoons became an object of intense public debate. The editors of *Jyllands-Posten* received moderate support, and the cartoons were republished on the Internet and by newspapers in various countries. There was, however, also harsh criticism of the publication of cartoons, which partially was staged for political and economic reasons not, or not directly, related to the cartoons. It cannot be doubted, however, that many Muslims experienced the cartoons as moral insult, offence to their religious sensibilities, or as expressions of hostility against Islam (see Klausen, 2009; Mahmood, 2009; Levey and

Modood, 2009). Many Muslims voiced their discontent in newspapers, talk shows, and in public protests in countries almost all over the world. In Europe, on which I will focus here, protestors predominantly reacted moderately and expressed their protest in, for example, petitions to political representatives and passionate but peaceful demonstrations. In countries of the Middle East, the Caucasus region, South and Southeast Asia, and Africa, however, imams and political representatives mobilized demonstrations that partly turned into riots and violent acts, such as attacks on Danish embassies and death threats against cartoonists and editors. The protests, in turn, were followed by reactions of (amongst others) journalists, intellectuals, and politicians, and this is the part of the controversy that I am especially interested in. Although the debate about the different kinds of protests against the publication of the Muhammad cartoons was very heterogeneous and often disordered, I suggest distinguishing three types of reactions to the protests: qualified solidarity, assimilationist critique, and exclusive rejection. I do not claim that it is possible to capture the details of the entire controversy by means of this classification, but it is sufficient to yield insights that can be used for a re-examination of Habermas's ethics of citizenship in postsecular societies.

Qualified solidarity. Throughout the debate, Muslims who objected to the publication of the cartoons received solidarity from members of other religions, as well as from non-religious people. Sympathetic reactions that followed the protests usually pointed out that freedom of expression does not include the right to intentionally offend religious sensibilities, but rather a responsibility to treat the deeply held religious beliefs of others respectfully. Such views were advocated, for example, by the Nordic Bishops' Conference of the Catholic Church which declared that they deplored the publication of the cartoons, describing them as an 'attack on religion' that caused hurt among Muslims. The Nordic Bishops' Conference pointed out that they 'welcome free and open discussion which searches the truth but in a context and climate of mutual respect and knowledge about what one is speaking of' (Conferentia Episcopalis Scandiae, 2006). Similarly, representatives of the United Nations, the European Union, and the Islamic Conference jointly stated that they shared 'anguish' of the Muslim world at the Muhammad cartoons, claiming that '[i]n all societies there is a need to show sensitivity and responsibility in treating issues of special significance for the adherents of any particular faith, even by those who do not share the belief in question' (United Nations Department of Public Information, 2006). The solidarity with protesting Muslims was *qualified*, however, since tighter legal restrictions on freedom of expression did not find much support, and violent reactions to the cartoons were condemned virtually unanimously in the public debate of Western societies. The essential message was that critique and public debate must be possible, but that *Jyllands-Posten* went overboard by publishing depictions that were bound to be profoundly offensive to a religious minority in Denmark.

Assimilationist critique. Reactions to protests against the cartoons that are in accordance with this type of critique point out that, since one man's orthodoxy is another man's blasphemy, in democratic and pluralistic societies, all citizens will encounter practices, statements, and images that are, in one way or another, offensive to them. However, it was said, all citizens of pluralistic societies need to be able to cope with such acts and objects constructively. Against this background, protests against the Muhammad cartoons were construed as proof that many Muslims were hyper-susceptible to religious offence which again was seen as evidence that they take their religion 'too seriously', and that they were not yet enlightened or properly integrated in democratic culture (see Rostboll, 2009: 626). Such 'religious squeamishness', however, needs to be abandoned according to proponents of this type of critique, since otherwise believers will not be able to function as competent citizens of democratic and pluralistic societies. In this context, acts and events like the publication of the Muhammad cartoons were understood to be provocative, but valuable contributions, not only because they point to possibly problematic aspects of particular ideologies but also because they can unsettle the (religious) self-understanding of believers. This can lead to a deconstruction of religious identities that are in conflict with fundamental principles and practices of democratic and pluralistic societies. Thus, according to this view, religiously offensive acts such as the publication of the Muhammad cartoons can have a cathartic and integrative effect.

This take on the publication of the cartoons and protests against it concurs with the views of Carsten Juste, Editor in Chief of *Jyllands-Posten*. Juste explained why the cartoons were published by claiming that Muslims who publicly represent Islam in Denmark were voices from 'a dark and violent middle age' and beset by a 'sickly oversensitivity' to critique (Klausen, 2009: 13). Others joined in the course of the debate, notably Flemming Rose who pointed to the Danish tradition of satire that deals with, amongst other things, the royal family and other public figures. Rose argued that the cartoonists treated Islam in the same manner that they treat other religions. In so doing, he claimed, they treated Muslims in Denmark 'as equals', and 'they made a point: We are integrating you into the Danish tradition of satire because you are part of our society, not strangers. The cartoons are including, rather than excluding, Muslims' (Rose, 2006). As witness for his position Flemming Rose refers to the Somali-born former Dutch politician Ayaan Hirsi Ali who stated that the cartoons had sped up the integration of Muslims into European societies by 300 years.

Exclusive rejection. This third type of critique is closely related to the second, and the two often blend into each other. Reactions to protests against religiously offensive acts that are in accordance with this view take any opposition against the cartoons to be evidence not only of an ostensible need for Muslims to 'modernize' their religious consciousness and to better integrate into democratic culture but also as expression of *anti*-democratic attitudes and values. Proponents of this view interpreted the predominantly peaceful protests of European Muslims in light of the relatively few violent protests in Europe and the much fiercer and violent reactions of Muslims, for example, in Lebanon and Syria. Samuel P. Huntington's thesis of a 'clash of civilizations' and of 'bloody borders of Islam' (Huntington, 1996) was used as hermeneutic framework here. 'From this perspective', Jytte Klausen points out, 'the protests were represented as entirely predictable results of the atavistic opposition of Muslims to Europe's secular values' (Klausen, 2009: 10).

The tendency to construe opposition against the cartoons as evidence of an ostensible clash of civilizations and a fundamental incompatibility of liberal democracy and Islam was identified in an analysis of the media treatment of the debate about the cartoons in Denmark and France that was carried out by social scientists Carolina Boe and Peter Hervik (Boe and Hervik, 2008). Their analysis shows that protesting Muslims were not only construed as not being sufficiently offence-resilient and in need of a reconstruction of their (religious) identity but were also construed as fiercely *opposing* liberal democracy and its normative foundations. This is remarkable inasmuch as the vast majority of Muslims and other opponents of the cartoons used perfectly legitimate means to express their discontent, including writing letters to the editor, demonstrating, or suing newspapers that had published the cartoons (Boe and Hervik, 2008: 214). Nevertheless, various influential contributors to the debate conflated different forms of protest, both violent and non-violent, and interpreted them all as an apparent threat of an anti-democratic religious totalitarianism. One of several examples thereof is Ayaan

Hirsi Ali's speech 'The Right to Offend' that she delivered in Berlin in February 2006. In that speech, Hirsi Ali claims that the publication of the cartoons:

> has... revealed the presence of a considerable minority in Europe who do not understand or will not accept the workings of liberal democracy. These people – many of whom hold European citizenship have campaigned for censorship, for boycotts, for violence, and for new laws to ban 'Islamophobia'. (Hirsi Ali, 2006)

Hirsi Ali mentions ordinary means of civic participation in public debate and democratic processes and the campaigns for violence, in the same breath, and she seems to link all forms of protest against the cartoons to anti-democratic attitudes. Other contributions were even more explicit and harsher in their use of rhetoric of war in the description of the controversy about the Muhammad cartoons. Boe and Hervik's media analysis shows that Islam was often strikingly compared to totalitarianism and fascism (Boe and Hervik, 2008: 219–221). Furthermore, in both French and Danish media coverage of the cartoon controversy, references to Nazi Germany in the 1930s were used in order to compare resistance against Nazism with a battle against 'Islamism' which is – according to many voices in the debate – to be fought today (Boe and Hervik, 2008: 219). Boe and Hervik also show that public debate about the cartoon controversy hardly allowed for any differentiated positions to be adopted. Rather, the discussion seems to have followed the motto: 'You are either with us, or against us'. The attitude of many participants in the controversy was not the attitude of an open debate about the ongoing development of society, but rather of strict opposition or even of conflict and struggle. Again, Hirsi Ali's February 2006 speech provides an example of her blaming those people who did not unreservedly support the editors of the newspapers which (re)published the cartoons.

> Shame on those papers and TV channels who lacked the courage to show their readers the caricatures in The Cartoon Affair. These intellectuals live off free speech but they accept censorship. They hide their mediocrity of mind behind noble-sounding terms such as 'responsibility' and 'sensitivity'. Shame on those politicians who stated that publishing and re-publishing the drawings was 'unnecessary', 'insensitive', 'disrespectful' and 'wrong'. (Hirsi Ali, 2006)

A critical re-examination of Habermas's ethics of citizenship in postsecular societies

What does this analysis of parts of the Muhammad cartoons controversy mean for Jürgen Habermas's ethics of citizenship in postsecular societies? Is his proposal able to achieve what it aims to achieve: to enable all citizens, whether religious or not, to participate as equals in public political debate about matters of common interest?

The brief sketch of different types of responses to protests against the publication of the Muhammad cartoons shows that the process of translating religious convictions into a seemingly generally accessible language and 'secular reasons', which is the core of Habermas's proposal, seems not to have been of major importance here. The only claim of protesting Muslims that was based on particular religious beliefs was the argument that the cartoons were wrong because images of Muhammad were generally forbidden, a view that is contested in Islamic tradition itself (see Naef, 2007). This argument, however, did not feature prominently in the protests of believers. Much more important were arguments related to profound offence or social marginalization and denigration, all of which were usually couched in 'secular' terms. In light of this, Habermas's strong focus on *epistemic* attitudes and strictly deliberative forms of public debate appears surprising and rather unfruitful. A brief re-reading of the three types of responses to protests against the Muhammad cartoons in light of Habermas's notion of the postsecular (and the other way round) promises to yield insights that could be used for a possible future revision of an ethics of citizenship in postsecular societies.

In the case of the first type of response, qualified solidarity, it is important to recognize that those people who expressed solidarity with profoundly offended Muslims were willing to imagine something, and take it seriously, that they themselves did not experience, namely a specific kind of moral insult that is related to a particular religious subjectivity, as Saba Mahmood has shown. Mahmood points out that, for certain pious Muslims, religion is experienced as habituated embodied practice, and a devout Muslim's relation to Muhammad a relationship of intimacy and similitude (Mahmood, 2009: 72). Such people experience the kind of moral injury brought about by the publication of the Muhammad cartoons as profound offence which emanates 'from the perception that one's being, grounded as it is in a relationship of dependency with the Prophet, has been shaken' (Mahmood, 2009: 78). The implied notion of religion differs from the understanding of religion and proper religious subjectivity that was dominant in the cartoon controversy and that is prominent in Habermas's writings: a 'modern concept of religion...as a set of propositions in a set of beliefs to which the individual gives assent' (Mahmood, 2009: 72); a liberal 'Protestant' notion of religion. As a result, the insult that constituted the main problem of the cartoons in the eyes of a group of devout Muslims remained to a large extent unintelligible for other members of society. Against this background, the 'openness' of non-Muslim citizens who expressed their solidarity with protesting Muslims does not simply go without saying, since (if the solidarity was based on an empathic understanding of the insult that some Muslims suffered) it presupposes the ability to conceive a form of religious subjectivity that differs from what is predominantly conceived as 'modern', without at the same time (dis)qualifying these believers as anti-modern or religious fundamentalists, and without denying them the status of equal members of society. This could be understood as being in accordance with Habermas's claim that secular citizens must open their minds to the possible 'truth content' of contributions that are in one way or the other related to the religion of some of their fellow citizens. However, a process of *translation* of 'religious language' into 'generally accessible arguments' in Habermas's sense seems not to be involved here, at least not prominently.

The core of the second type of response to the protests, assimilationist critique, is that Muslims who protest against the Muhammad cartoons are seen as not yet being competent democratic citizens because of their ostensible hyper-susceptibility to religious offence. To a certain extent, this seems to be in line with Habermas's claim that in postsecular societies religious citizens need to develop epistemic attitudes that enable them to constructively deal with the challenges that can result from encounters with other religions or non-religious world views (see Habermas, 2006: 14). But Habermas's position seems not to be able to empathically deal with the moral insult that, according to Saba Mahmood's analysis, devout Muslims feel in view of, for instance, the Muhammad cartoons. But is this a problem? Mahmood is able to describe and explain the religious subjectivity of a certain group of devout Muslims and the special kind of moral insult that can result from encounters with images such as the Muhammad cartoons. Her analysis does not show, however, that such believers have a right that others refrain from treating their religion as if it was 'modern' in the above-mentioned sense: a set of beliefs which one accepts or rejects (and Mahmood does not claim such a right). Religions are always public in the sense that they also 'produce doctrines beliefs, practices, institutions, symbols and discourses that others experience as part of *their* social world', and because of this 'offense or injury may simply be a double-effect of persons expressing themselves about how they experience that world.' (March, 2012: 336). In light of this, a claim that 'non-Protestant' forms of religious subjectivity should be protected from injurious speech is, ironically 'nothing other than a demand that other citizens treat their own beliefs in 'Protestant' terms – that is, as beliefs that must only be privately assented to and not manifested in public through conduct and speech' (March, 2012: 337).

So it seems that we encounter the problem that in certain situations the 'burdens' that are connected with one's being a member of a liberal and pluralistic society are almost necessarily distributed unevenly for people with different religious subjectivities. People who understand their religion not primarily in terms of propositions and beliefs but as embodied practices can be especially susceptible to painful experiences in public debate about matters that are directly or indirectly related to what is sacred to them, and an essential part of their identity. Jürgen Habermas tries to deal with this by stating that in postsecular societies religious people must develop epistemic attitudes that allow them to constructively deal with pluralism (see above). This comes close to the claim that religious people are required to transform their religious subjectivity in a way that it accords with a liberal 'Protestant' type of religion. Habermas seems to feel uneasy with this when he rejects the view that the required epistemic attitude of religious citizens could result 'from drill and forced adaptation' which would, as he points out, contradict the self-understanding of the constitutional state. 'Learning processes can be fostered, but not morally or legally stipulated' (Habermas, 2008: 28; see also Habermas, 2006: 14). He tries to solve this problem by construing the transformation of religions as result of a 'learning process' and of 'arduous work of hermeneutic self-reflection' that 'must be undertaken from within religious traditions' (Habermas, 2006: 14), and assimilationist critique ascribes to 'provocative' acts, such as the publication of the Muhammad cartoons, a special constructive potential to initiate such transformations and 'learning processes'. This, however, does not take away the fact that a possible transformation of religious subjectivities is far from being independent from social and political circumstances, which always include formal and informal relations of power. 'Obviously', Andrew F. March points out, 'liberalism is not indifferent to that transformation; it prefers religions that do not oppose it to religions that do, and liberal terms of social cooperation are more accommodating of some kinds of religious community than others' (March, 2012: 337). What is important, however, in view of public debates such as the Muhammad cartoons controversy about religiously offensive acts, is that one cannot conclude from this that people who do experience particular acts or objects as religiously offensive, and express this – for instance in the form of public protests and symbolic acts such as the burning of copies of newspapers – lack cognitive or emotional competencies that are – ostensibly – necessary in order to function as competent democratic citizen. To do so, and hence to construe religious people who bring their concerns and injuries into public political debate as insufficiently integrated into democratic societies, effectively means that a specific form of religion and religious subjectivity, respectively, becomes a necessary condition for participation in public debate. This, however, comes close to an informal but powerful discrimination against certain forms of religion and to an informal exclusion of some devout believers from public debate. They are, as it were, communicatively disabled because others deny them the competency and the authority to participate in the ongoing development of their society. This communicative disablement is especially strong in the case of the third type of response to protests against the cartoons, exclusive rejection, where sometimes fierce but peaceful protests are mixed up with violent riots and understood and publicly described as anti-democratic attitudes.

In terms of Habermas's ethics of citizenship in postsecular societies, the roots of this problem of communicative disablement could be ascribed to a failure of secular citizens to develop an epistemic attitude that enables them to take seriously contributions of religious citizens, and to be open to the possibility that claims that are – at first sight – connected to or even based on religion, are valuable contributions to the public political debate about the future of society. However, this does not address the core of the problem that is at stake here. Habermas's almost exclusive focus on cognitive aspects of more comprehensive mentalities, and on deliberative forms of public debate, is not able to adequately deal with communicative distortions that are caused by visceral and emotional aspects rather than by problems of translating religious truth claims into 'secular' reasons. In the case of 'exclusive rejection' and partly also in the case of 'assimilationist critique', religious people who publicly voiced their protests against what they experienced as denigration of their religion were rendered mute, as it were, not because they couched their contributions in religious language but because they were construed as lacking the requisite competence and authority to participate as equals in public debate. This can be understood with reference to the concept of public culture. As I pointed out above, public culture makes possible forms of public communication by providing stocks of shared of knowledge, norms, values, conventions, and so forth. In the case of public political debate, informal conceptions of democratic life can be seen as part of public culture. Together with 'collective self-images' of established groups, the informal conceptions of democratic life predetermine who is considered a legitimate contributor to public debate about the current state of affairs and the future development of society. In the case of 'exclusive rejection', believers who protested against the publication of the Muhammad cartoons were publicly construed as opposing important elements of public culture and dominant informal conceptions of democratic life. Not only their contributions but also the believers themselves, and even their religion as such, were described as being 'foreign' or even a threat to democracy. In light of violent riots and harsh statements of religious and political leaders outside of Europe, which were an undeniable part of the controversy and strongly influenced the media coverage of it, religion, more specifically Islam, was used as a marker that made the process of 'othering' possible. There is a threat that such constellations result in a 'closure' of public debate: participants are informally excluded by denying them the requisite competence and authority, or because the speakers are suspected of questionable motives and false consciousness (see Peters, 2008: 115).

Conclusion

The above considerations show that Habermas's ethics of citizenship in postsecular societies has strengths but also important limitations. It cannot solve important problems that can make it hard or even impossible for believers to participate as equals in public political debate, and to be recognized in their authority to participate as equal in processes that determine the future development of society. One of the reasons of these limitations of Habermas's ethics of citizenship in postsecular societies is Habermas's strong focus on deliberative dimensions of public debate and the related cognitive aspects; in particular, the problem of how to justify political decisions in democratic and pluralistic societies without encumbering believers with an extra and undue burden. This is an important problem, and Habermas's proposal for its solution has been very influential. However, the analysis of parts of the public debate about the Muhammad cartoons shows that, at least in the case of this controversy, believers were not excluded from public debate because they used 'religious language'. The problem was also not that 'secular' citizens refused to take part in processes of translation, primarily because there was no need to translate 'religious' into 'generally accessible' language. Rather, the factors that could have prevented some believers from participating on a par with others in public debate were related to specific constellations where non-cognitive aspects played an important role. An ethics of citizenship in postsecular societies must deal with this, and include, for example, the powerful influence of 'public culture' and dominant informal conceptions of democratic life in analyses and theory development. Such elements of 'informal politics of society' (Scanlon, 2003) are especially effective and much harder to control than formal rules concerning the legitimacy of specific validity claims. In light of this, one important requirement of a revised ethics of citizenship in postsecular societies will be that all citizens will primarily be listened to and addressed as somebody who has a say in matters concerning the development of society – not as a member of a specific community or group – for instance, a religion, a cultural, or an ethnic group (see Brink, 2007: 365). A further important requirement is that 'pre-rational' elements that underlie public debate, and influence it significantly, such as public culture and informal conceptions of democratic life are submitted to constant critical reflection and possibly revision. Here I see an important collaborative task for both religious and non-religious citizens.

An important conclusion that postsecular political philosophy can draw from the analysis that is offered by this chapter is that an ethics of citizenship that aims at enabling all citizens to participate as equals in public debate must not limit its focus on cognitive or epistemic requirement as Habermas does. Public political debate is not a purely 'rational' or 'cognitive' endeavour but permeated by bodily and cultural influences that co-determine who is recognized as a competent and 'respectable' contributor and what passes for a valuable contribution. The felicity conditions of the very specific act that 'contributing as fully recognized citizen to public political debate' is can be disturbed by influences from all of the different elements, be it cognitive, emotional, or cultural. Accordingly, an ethics of citizenship in postsecular societies must address all of these elements in order to be able to identify and dismantle obstacles that prevent people from exercising their right to participate as equals in public political debate about matters of common interest, including matters concerning the formal and informal rules that structure the public sphere common to all members of society, whether religious or not.

Notes

1. The following sketch of Habermas's position is primarily based on Habermas (2006) and Habermas (2008).
2. Habermas made this point in an earlier contribution as well: If conflicts of loyalty are not to simmer, the necessary role differentiation between members of one's own religious community and co-citizens of the larger society needs to be justified convincingly from one's internal viewpoint. Religious membership is in tune with its secular counterpart only if (from the internal point of view of each) the corresponding norms and values are not only different from each other but if the one set of norms can consistently be derived from the other. If differentiation of both memberships is to go beyond a mere *modus vivendi*, then the modernization of religious consciousness must not be limited to some cognitively undiscerning attempt to ensure that the religious ethos conforms to externally imposed laws of the secular society. It calls instead for developing the normative principles of the secular order from within the view of a respective religious tradition and community (Habermas, 2004: 12).
3. This dependence of particular forms of communication on the recognition of speaker's authority is well investigated in philosophy of language. Mary Kate McGowan, for instance, distinguishes between purely communicative speech acts such as telling, on the one side, and speech acts that she calls 'communication-plus', on the other. For 'telling' it is essential (and sufficient) that the hearer recognizes the speaker's intention; as soon as the addressee recognizes my intention to tell him or her (p), I have succeeded in telling him or her (p). This is different in the case of 'communicative-plus'-speech acts: Such speech acts can only succeed if the speaker has a specific authority that is recognized by the addressee. McGowan illustrates this by means of the example of an order: '[S]uppose that I try to order my boss to give me a raise. Although the boss recognizes that my (misguided) intention to order her to give me a raise, I nevertheless fail to do so exactly because I lack the requisite authority' (McGowan, 2009: 193).
4. This section follows, partly in wording, Baumgartner (2013).

References

Baumgartner, C. (2013). 'Secular Critique of Protests against Religiously Offensive Acts. A Threat Against Democracy?' In G. Buijs, T. Sunier, and P. Versteeg (eds) *Risky Liaisons? Democracy and Religion: Reflections and Case Studies*, 112–127. Amsterdam: VU University Press.

Beckford, J.A. (2012). 'Public Religions and the Postsecular: Critical Reflections.' *Journal for the Scientific Study of Religion* 51(1), 1–19.

Boe, C. and Hervik, P. (2008). 'Integration through Insult?' In E. Eide, R. Kunelius and A. Phillips (eds) *Transnational Media Events. The Mohammed Cartoons and the Imagined Clash of Civilizations*, 213–234. Gothenburg, Sweden: Nordicom.

Brink, B. van den (2007). 'Imagining Civic Relations in the Moment of their Breakdown: A Crisis of Civic Integrity in the Netherlands.' In A.S. Laden and

D. Owen (eds) *Multiculturalism and Political Theory*, 350–373. Cambridge: Cambridge University Press.

Conferentia Episcopalis Scandiae (2006). 'The Nordic Bishops' Conference Deplores the Publication of Cartoon Drawings of the Prophet Mohammed.' 2 February. Retrieved from http://www.katolsk.no/nyheter/2006/02/02-0003.gif.

Dillon, M. (2012). 'Jürgen Habermas and the Postsecular Appropriation of Religion: A Sociological Critique.' In P.S. Gorski, D.K. Kim, J. Torpey, and J. VanAntwerpen (eds) *The Postsecular in Question. Religion in Contemporary Society*, 249–278. New York: New York University Press.

Habermas, J. (2004). 'Religious Tolerance – The Pacemaker for Cultural Rights.' *Philosophy* 79(1), 5–18.

Habermas, J. (2006). 'Religion in the Public Sphere.' *European Journal of Philosophy* 14(1), 1–25.

Habermas, J. (2008). 'Notes on Postsecular Society.' *New Perspectives Quarterly* 25(4), 17–29.

Hirsi Ali, A. (2006). 'The Right to Offend.' Speech delivered in Berlin, 9 February 2006. *NRC Handelsblad*, 10 February 2006. Retrieved from http://www.nrc.nl/opinie/article1654061.ece/The_Right_to_Offend.

Huntington, S. (1996). *The Clash of Civilizations and the Remaking of World Order*. New York: Simon & Schuster.

Klausen, J. (2009). *The Cartoons That Shook the World*. New Haven and London: Yale University Press.

Levey, G.B. and Modood, T. (2009). 'Liberal Democracy, Multicultural Citizenship and the Danish Cartoon Affair.' In G.B. Levey and T. Modood (eds) *Secularism, Religion and Multicultural Citizenship*, 216–242. Cambridge: Cambridge University Press.

Mahmood, S. (2009). 'Religious Reason and Secular Affect: An Incommensurable Divide?' In T. Asad, W. Brown, J. Butler, and S. Mahmood (eds) *Is Critique Secular? Blasphemy, Injury, and Free Speech*, 64–100. Berkeley, Los Angeles, London: University of California Press.

March, A. (2012). 'Speech and the Sacred: Does the Defense of Free Speech Rest on a Mistake about Religion?' *Political Theory* 40(3), 319–346.

McGowan, M.K. (2009). 'On Silencing and Sexual Refusal.' *The Journal of Political Philosophy* 17(4), 487–494.

Naef, S. (2007). *Bilder und Bilderverbot im Islam. Vom Koran bis zum Karikaturenstreit*. München: Verlag C.H. Beck.

Peters, P. (2008). *Public Deliberation and Public Culture. The Writings of Bernhard Peters 1993–2005*. Edited by H. Wessler. New York: Palgrave MacMillan.

Rose, F. (2006). 'Why I Published Those Cartoons.' *Washington Post*. 19 February. Retrieved from http://www.washingtonpost.com/wp-dyn/content/article/2006/02/17/AR2006021702499.html.

Rostboll, C.F. (2009). 'Autonomy, Respect and Arrogance in the Danish Cartoon Controversy.' *Political Theory* 37(5), 623–648.

Scanlon, T. (2003). *The Difficulty of Tolerance. Essays in Political Philosophy*. Cambridge and New York: Cambridge University Press.

United Nations Department of Public Information, Secretary General SG/2105. (2006). 'Joint UN, European Union, Islamic Conference Statement Shares

"Anguish" of Muslim World at Muhammad Caricatures, but Condemns Violent Response.' Retrieved from http://www.un.org/News/Press/docs/2006/sg2105.doc.htm.
Wessler, H. and Wingert, L. (2008). 'Study of the Public Sphere. Bernhard Peters' Interest and Contribution.' In B. Peters (author) and H. Wessler (ed.) *Public Deliberation and Public Culture. The Writings of Bernhard Peters 1993–2005*, 1–13. New York: Palgrave Macmillan.

5
The Eradication of Transcendence
William Egginton

From the comfortable vantage of the metropolis, religion today recalls the bumptious, somewhat embarrassing relative one wishes would not show up just when the other guests are arriving. And that's only the charitably culturalist view. For the avidly secular, true believers are a medieval remnant infecting a potentially pacific modernity with intolerant ignorance and deadly brutality. From the urban West, we look down on the backwardness of our own backyards while looking aghast at the slaughter abroad, and we blame it all on a credulity that we find oddly out of place in modern, mainstream life.

Modern intellectual and cultural history provides a narrative to explain our discomfort. Secularization describes the process whereby the modern metropolis cast off the shrouds of irrational beliefs and learned to base knowledge on evidence and politics on consensus around commonly shared goals. Religious beliefs, which are resistant to evidence and shared only by the select, were seen as inherently incompatible with a rational public sphere and were relegated to the private sphere, where, it was hoped by some, they could quietly wither away.

That this has not happened, that not only on distant shores but in the heart of metropolitan modernity religion has again reared its ugly head has provoked myriad attempts to explain what Jürgen Habermas called 'a sweeping desecularization' (Habermas, 2005: 12). As others, including Janet Jakobsen and Ann Pellegrini (2008) have argued, the 'secularization myth' is itself suspect, and serves the interests of a very specific version of modernity. In what follows, I concur with these authors by criticizing the manifestation of the secularization myth inherent in the view that Western modernity has liberated itself from political theology. In so doing, I will largely focus my arguments on the position of Mark Lilla, an intellectual historian at Columbia University, whose work regularly appears in highbrow popular outlets like *The New York Review of Books*, who has articulated to my mind one of the strongest versions of the secularization myth. Lilla's 2007 book, *The Stillborn God: Religion, Politics, and the Modern West*, was notably dissimilar to some of its more raucous cousins published during roughly the same period: books by the so-called new atheists, including Sam Harris, Christopher Hitchens, and Richard Dawkins. Unlike those authors, Lilla did not so much inveigh against the evils of religion as paint in detail the intellectual history that made possible what Charles Taylor referred to as *A Secular Age* (2007) while simultaneously cautioning his readers about the fragility of that tradition and the need to protect it against a renascent irrationalist past.

While rigorous in its recounting of the history of Western political philosophy, Lilla's book rehearses a profound misconception concerning the relationship of human freedom and religious belief. By focusing on the alternative liberalism offers to political theology, Lilla's history paints over how liberal political thought often served as a quiet handmaiden to the interest of a new and rising economic and political elite. Defending *carte blanche* 'the great tradition' of liberal thought against the threatening tide of religious fervour, as he calls for, Lilla fails to grasp the extent to which religious fundamentalism today may be inspired and fed not by its attachment to another great tradition of thought but by the system of accumulation and exclusion necessitated by capitalism and at least in part defended by liberal thought.

Lilla credits the Western liberal tradition as having created the unprecedented possibility of a notion of sovereignty not based on theology. And indeed the authors he cites took part in a culture-wide movement to eradicate any notion of a transcendental support from theories of political sovereignty. What he does not stress, however, is how the same authors often reveal how the essential finitude of the human condition necessitates transcendental reference points in the construction of political models. By attempting to eradicate or otherwise disregard this minimal degree of transcendence, the liberal tradition's basic notion of the self ultimately naturalizes a political economy based on property, competition, and accumulation.

The real divide, then, is not between the great traditions of political theology, on the one hand, and secular liberalism, on the other; rather, it is between discourses that attempt to reduce or channel the human urge to transcendence to serve the interests of political and economic elites, and those – very much in the minority but in no way limited to the four-hundred-year history of the modern West – that seek to remind us again and again that the baseline realities framed by the cultural elite of any time are not the only options; that politics and economics are, like culture, grounded neither in God or science but only in the shifting sands of human finitude.

Religion and the legitimization of liberalism

'The twilight of the idols has been postponed' (Lilla, 2007: 4). Thus begins Lilla's defence of the Western liberal tradition against the re-emergence of political theologies the world over. Western liberalism has been taken by surprise, he argues, in part because liberal democracies have been so successful in 'creating an environment where public conflict over competing revelations is virtually unthinkable today' (Lilla, 2007: 4). A major reason for this complacency is that we have been separated from our own 'long theological tradition of political thought by a revolution in thinking that began roughly four centuries ago. We live, so to speak, on the other shore. When we observe civilizations on the opposite bank, we are puzzled, since we only have a distant memory of what it was like to think as they do' (Lilla, 2007: 4). The purpose of his book is to reacquaint us with that other side of the bank, to make us appreciate the 'fragility of our world' (Lilla, 2007: 6), and ostensibly to be 'clear about those alternatives, choose between them, and live with the consequence of our choice' (Lilla, 2007: 13).

A powerful, even clarion call; and yet an enormous question seems left for the begging: is it really so clear who 'we' are on this shore, staring across the waters at other traditions, distant in either time or culture from us? Is it really the case that on this, 'our' side, 'public conflict over competing revelations is virtually unthinkable today'? Or should not such a claim, upon reflection and any given night's election-year coverage, provoke astonishment and the question, 'which shore was it that you happen to live on'? That the shore in Mark Lilla's case is the Morningside Heights neighbourhood around Columbia University may explain a lot, for in the extra-academic environment of today's religious and political debates, both global and domestic, a shore devoid of such conflict would be hard, indeed, to come upon.

The reason Mark Lilla's shore seems so comfortable in its freedom from revelation is that its intellectual foundation was, from its origins, adopted as the justificatory pedestal for a mode of organizing both knowledge and wealth that has proven enormously adept at reproducing itself, even as it has served the interests of elites whose economic, political, and cultural distance from the masses excluded from such privilege grows to extraordinary proportions. When Lilla writes, 'The novelty of modern political philosophy was to have relinquished such comprehensive claims by disengaging thought about the human political realm from theological speculation about what might lie beyond it' (Lilla, 2007: 7), he gets that much right; but that is only part of the story. To the extent that modern political philosophy engaged in a project of removing the question of 'what might lie beyond it' from the human political realm, it effectively acted to ground politics on a particular understanding of the individual as a propertied, accumulating force, and then to universalize that assumption.

Lilla's own pantheon of heroes of the great separation begins with Hobbes and Locke in the seventeenth century, and the Scottish thinker David Hume in the eighteenth century. In the time that passed between them the basic principle that politics should and can be organized without regard to theology had been accepted, such that Lilla can write of Hume, 'his Christian readers abhorred his religious views and rejected his skepticism, but when it came to politics they were already adapting themselves intellectually to the principles of the great separation he practiced' (Lilla, 2007: 102–103). Indeed, the 'art of intellectual separation' developed by Hobbes, Locke, and Hume is the model for the political philosophy Lilla wishes to defend. The 'crossing' to our shore was complicated, in his words, by both lingering Christian political theology and a sort of deviation into religious anthropology by later Enlightenment thinkers like Rousseau and Kant; but it was given its greatest drive by these former thinkers. Hume's eradication of transcendence informs not only his religious skepticism; it is integral to his epistemology and ethics as well. At the same time, though, Hume's thought consistently if inadvertently acknowledges the operativity of human finitude in politics, and hence the very source of the transcendence he seeks to eradicate. Moreover, the form of his argumentation reveals that his idea of human subjectivity is motivated less by a rejection of religious doctrine than by a legitimization of the basic assumptions underlying economic liberalism.

In his *Enquiry Concerning the Principles of Morals* (1998), Hume tried to articulate a theory of morals that dispensed with transcendent principles by undermining what we could call the epistemological privilege of subjectivity. It is not a coincidence that Hume can be counted along with Spinoza and Leibniz as one of Gilles Deleuze's philosophical heroes, and was the subject of his dissertation and first book, *Empiricism and Subjectivity* (1991). In that book, Deleuze reads Hume as having laid the groundwork for a radical empiricism that will enable the thinking of subjectivity without recourse to any transcendental terms. As he puts it, 'Empirical subjectivity is constituted in the mind under the influence of the principles affecting it; the mind therefore does not have the characteristics of a preexisting subject' (Deleuze, 1991: 29). For Deleuze, Hume's subject is radically immanent, built upon the sedimentation of impressions and associations, and thus harbouring no bedrock of independence from the natural or social world, and requiring no point of transcendence outside that world.

After announcing in his introduction that philosophers have been divided on the question of whether the principles of morality have been drawn from reason or sentiment – that is, from abstract and universal rules or from shared feelings in favour of virtue and in aversion to vice – Hume announces that the origins of morality can indeed be found, but only through applying the methodologies proven by natural philosophy, that is, to 'hearken to no arguments but those which are derived from experience' (Hume, 1998: 77). By observing how people, in fact, act, in other words, Hume proposes to define adequately the principles of morality. By the middle of his enquiry, experience has taught him enough to claim that selfless action is an irreducible aspect of human behaviour, universally admired and esteemed, and that 'no better system will ever, for the future, be invented, in order to account for the origin of the benevolent from the selfish affections, and to reduce all the various emotions of the human mind to a perfect simplicity' (Hume, 1998: 166). Morals need not be derived from either self-interest or any transcendental principle, because the presumption of the exclusive dominance of self-interest in human motivation was wrong in the first place; rather, 'it appears, that a tendency to public good, and to the promoting of peace, harmony, and order in society, does always, by affecting the benevolent principles of our frame, engage us on the side of the social virtues' (Hume, 1998: 117).

Relying on experience thus leads Hume to posit the existence in the human animal of 'the benevolent principles of our frame', a conclusion that can indeed be called on to support the Deleuzian idea of a subjectivity built on immanent terms. Yes, there are principles at stake, but these principles are derived from the observation of human behaviour; there is no recourse to anything outside the expected Humean toolkit of habit, convention, and association. It's no big mystery that humans act altruistically; the only mystery is why we assumed this wasn't part of human nature in the first place. No transcendent principle is required where no apparent barrier requires it.

This deflationary argument undercuts any *a priori* idea of justice, for instance, for we see that 'the rules of equity or justice depend entirely on the particular state or condition, in which men are placed, and owe their origin and existence to that UTILITY, which results to the public from their strict and regular observance' (Hume, 1998: 86). This observation leads us inexorably to the conclusion that removing or reversing such a state or condition utterly obviates the need for a concept like justice, such that 'by rendering justice totally useless, you thereby totally destroy its essence, and suspend its obligation upon mankind' (Hume, 1998: 86). The radical nature of this argument should not be underestimated. If a foundational moral principle like justice can be shown to be derived merely from context-dependent social utility such that the removal or reversal of contingent conditions would destroy its essence and suspend its obligatory force, then much of Hume's argument against the transcendence of moral principles has been validated. And if moral principles are immanent to human behaviour and derive merely from the sedimentation of useful rules and conventions, then the very idea that some barrier might challenge interpersonal communications and thus require transcendent principles begins to lose force. Moreover, the solid grounding of morals on existing human mores is, ultimately, profoundly conservative. Contestatory gesture, or a politics that would question the very legitimacy of established mores, would appear to be excluded; utopian projects based on a rejection of the status quo disappear from the realm of theoretical possibilities.

As powerful as his case appears, though, the very argumentative strategy Hume uses ultimately undermines his position. In order to make his case for the context-dependent status of moral principles, Hume deploys a series of thought experiments intended to illustrate contexts in which principles would cease to make sense because their social utility would vanish. It is worth quoting one at length:

> Again; suppose, that, though the necessities of the human race continue the same as at present, yet the mind is so enlarged, and so replete with friendship and generosity, that every man has the utmost tenderness for every man, and feels no more concern for his own interest than for that of his fellows: It seems evident, that the USE of justice would, in this case, be suspended by such an extensive benevolence, nor would the divisions and barriers of property and obligation have ever been thought of. Why would I bind another, by a deed or promise, to do me any good office, when I know that he is already prompted, by the strongest inclination, to seek my happiness, and would, of himself, perform the desired service; except the hurt, he thereby receives, be greater than the benefit accruing to

me? In which case, he knows, that, from my innate humanity and friendship, I should be the first to oppose myself to his imprudent generosity. Why raise land-marks between my neighbor's field and mine, when my heart has made no division between our interests; but shares all his joys and sorrows with the same force and vivacity as if originally my own? (Hume, 1998: 84)

Hume is perfectly aware that the picture he draws is fanciful, but he claims this fiction to be a mere matter of degree, not kind, citing in his favour the closeness of families and the alliance of interests between married couples. But is it not now clear where the slight of hand has taken place? The picture Hume paints is not simply an exaggerated idyll of brotherly community; it is literally inhuman. No matter how close our relations and how great our love for one another, human experience remains, in a fundamental sense, defined by the fact that I *cannot* share my neighbour's joys and sorrows with the same force and vivacity he does, that I cannot know what ultimately prompts him, that my heart always recognizes some division between my own and others' interests. This picture, in other words, is already an affective fantasy projection motivated by the more profound and existential experience of human finitude that is the ground zero of subjectivity.

That finitude both limits human possibilities of knowledge and opens human possibilities of imagination. A politics based on the reduction of essential opacity treats itself and its consequences as the only possibilities for right action. It naturalizes the current state of relations, implicitly claiming that state to be related to (because grounded in) a natural human condition – one in which, for instance, there is no division between human interests. But of course there are divisions, and violent ones at that. The property owner's perspective espoused by Hume is thus built into the very foundations of the liberal tradition, and its apparent emancipation from political theology masks an, at times, even greater (because more clandestine) servitude to the interests of capital.

This is an insight that did not escape one of the earliest and greatest defenders of liberal capital. Adam Smith begins his *Theory of Moral Sentiments*, published some ten years after Hume's book, by noting that, 'As we have no immediate experience of what other men feel, we can form no idea of the manner in which they are affected, but by conceiving what we ourselves should feel in the like situation' (Smith, 2009: 13). Our senses, as he continues, are incapable of feeling what another man feels, as 'they never did, and never can, carry us beyond our own person, and it is by the imagination only that we can form any conception of what are his sensations' (Smith, 2009: 13). Smith's concern is that, without a 'source for the fellow-feeling of the misery of others' (Smith, 2009: 14), there can be no basis for community, governance, or propriety of action. Understanding the mechanism for this fellow-feeling, therefore, becomes one of the key issues for political and moral theory.

Smith finds this mechanism in sympathy, and while he acknowledges that it is based in bodily affect and that discrete affects have a capacity for direct transmission, he distinguishes sympathy as relying on the mediation of the subject's imagination of himself in the place of another[1]:

> Even our sympathy with the grief or joy of another, before we are informed of the cause of either, is always extremely imperfect. General lamentations, which express nothing but the anguish of the sufferer, create rather a curiosity to inquire into his situation, along with some disposition to sympathize with him, than any actual sympathy that is very sensible. The first question that we ask is, What has befallen you? Till this be answered, though we are uneasy both from the vague idea of his misfortune, and still more from torturing ourselves with conjectures about what it may be, yet our fellow-feeling is not very considerable. (Smith, 2009: 16)

If our fellow-feeling or sympathy for another depends on the mediation of our understanding of his situation, and specifically in the form of imagining ourselves in that situation, the corollary of this mediation is that our own sense of morality and ability to distinguish right from wrong is irreducibly subjective. I make judgements concerning the morality of my own conduct, in other words, only in so far as I can externalize myself and view my actions as if I were another. As Smith puts it, 'we either approve or disapprove of our own conduct, according as we feel that, when we place ourselves in the situation of another man, and view it, as it were, with his eyes and from his station, we either can or cannot entirely enter into and sympathize with the sentiments and motives which influenced it' (Smith, 2009: 133). We imagine ourselves as others in order to form the fellow-feeling that motivates selfless action, just as we internalize the perspective of others in order to judge our own conduct.[2] But this projection of the self, out of its own circumstances into those of another, is a transcendence of the self-born of the inescapable transcendence of others. Among the very founding texts of liberalism, in other words, commingled with attempts to found politics on something other than theology, we see an implicit and at times explicit recognition that politics cannot be self-contained or immanently grounded; politics must, it seems, include within its very justification an unoccupied space. It is only the discourse justifying politics that strives to fill that space and does so either with the explicit will of revealed religion or the surreptitious interests of the powerful.

Theology and unframed politics

For Lilla, the time of the 'Great Separation' is unique in human history: 'before Rousseau, whenever Christian theologians disputed these matters [theological truth claims] they took their assertions to be absolutely true on the basis of reason and revelation, independent of man' (Lilla, 2007: 123–124). But this assertion ignores a vital streak of theological thought running from Plotinus through Augustine, Maimonides, and even Aquinas, and whose indelible imprint made its way into Kant and Hegel's thought via Luther. Maimonides only gets passing mention in Lilla's treatment, specifically as an example of how Jewish theology lay down 'strict rules for judging prophets' (Lilla, 2007: 69). But, from the neo-Platonists and himself, Maimonides inherited, developed, and passed on to theologians and philosophers who followed him a powerfully critical attitude toward humanity's capacity for understanding the will of God. Maimonides wrote his *Guide for the Perplexed* to 'enlighten a religious man' who is 'lost in perplexity and anxiety; because his 'moral and religious duties' have come into conflict with 'his philosophical studies'. The religious man is convinced of the truths he learns through science, and thus 'finds it difficult to accept as correct the teaching based on the literal interpretation of the Law'. Maimonides solves the problem by insisting that the Torah and the Midrashim be interpreted based on an understanding of words as having multiple meanings. In other words, because we believe scripture to be the language of God as opposed to a human language, we fail to make scripture compatible with human reason. The religious man errs when he assumes the language of the Torah to be a truly divine language, for which every word would signify exactly one aspect of the world. No language can have that status. And this critique is formulated precisely in the discourse of theology. When language is deployed pragmatically in everyday contexts it seldom encounters its inherent limitations. Buttressed by context, words disregard their homonymic limitations and seem to do a fine job of more or less unambiguously designating objects of cognition. The totality of being, past and present, however, could never be an object of cognition. Cognition, perception, and descriptions are activities that take place in space and time and have no ability to make judgements outside space and time.

For a theologian such as Maimonides, 'God' names an ungraspable totality, a creative force untamable by the human intellect. 'The Torah speaks according to the language of man', he quotes, 'that is to say, expressions, which can easily be comprehended and understood by all, are applied to the Creator. Hence the description of God by attributes implying corporeality, in order to express His existence; because the multitude of people do not easily conceive existence unless in connection with a body' (Maimonides, n.d.). He clarifies by adding that most people would not deny God the ability to move, but they would justifiably ridicule the idea of the Creator sitting down for a nice plate of pasta and a glass of Chianti. 'In fact', Maimonides points out, 'it makes no difference whether we ascribe to God eating and drinking or locomotion; but according to human modes of expression, that is to say, according to common notions, eating and drinking would be an imperfection in God, while motion would not, in spite of the fact that the necessity of locomotion is the result of some want' (Maimonides, n.d.).

Assertive secularists and religious fundamentalists succumb to the same error – that of assuming that human knowledge and the sort of knowledge God would have are of the same nature.

> A doubt has been raised, however, of whether His thought includes the infinite... Philosophers... have decided that the object of knowledge cannot be a non-existing thing, and that it cannot comprise that which is infinite. Since, therefore, God's knowledge does not admit of any increase, it is impossible that he should know any transient thing. (Maimonides, n.d.)

By applying the same logic to static things we end up asserting that God is an idiot. How did we get to this point? Merely because we assumed that God knows things in a way similar to how we know things: 'The cause of the error of all these schools is their belief that God's knowledge is like ours' (Maimonides, n.d.).

In the context of Christian theology, no Church father is more central to Catholic doctrine than Saint Thomas Aquinas, and yet key to Aquinas's concept of faith is how it differs from matters of the intellect, that is, how it differs from our view of knowledge. For Aquinas, faith is certain; but it is vital to note how he contrasts the supposed certainty of faith with that of knowledge. In the *Summa Theologica*, he considers and rejects three challenges to the claim that faith may have a greater certainty than the intellectual virtues. The first of these is the most important: while scientific knowledge can be certain about its object, faith often suffers from doubt, and as doubt is to certainty as blackness is to whiteness, scientific knowledge must be more certain than faith. Aquinas's response speaks volumes about his conception of the relation between faith and knowledge: 'This doubt is not on the part of the cause of faith, but on our part, in so far as we do not fully grasp matters of faith with our intellect. ... Matters of faith are above the human intellect, while the above three virtues [wisdom, science, and the understanding] are not' (Aquinas, n.d.). Faith, that is to say, can be certain only in those areas of life not subject to our intellect, areas where we cannot obtain knowledge by dialogue, measurement, or analysis. In the heart of scholastic Christian doctrine, in other words, centuries before Kant was to famously impose 'limits on knowledge in order to make room for faith', Saint Thomas Aquinas had already separated the two.

If Hume, Hobbes, and Locke are the heroes of Lilla's story, Jean Jacques Rousseau and Immanuel Kant have a more ambivalent role to play. Powerful Enlightenment thinkers themselves, their move to understand the religious impulse instead of reject it outright leads them ultimately to inject into modernity a dangerous toleration for the other shore. As Lilla puts it, 'Kant was a philosopher, not a theologian, but the concepts and vocabulary he developed for analyzing the sources and implications of religious belief came very close to theology – so close that contemporary German theologians immediately seized on his work as a means of legitimating a new kind of language for discussing the divine nexus' (Lilla, 2007: 112). Because of the crucial nature of German thought, in particular to the development of political theory in the nineteenth century, this deviation as represented by Rousseau and especially Kant takes on a special importance: 'It is no exaggeration to say that, together, Rousseau and Kant caused the major rift between Anglo-American and continental European approaches to modern political thought. ... We still live with the consequences of that rift today' (Lilla, 2007: 113).

For Lilla, Kant's reading of Rousseau's *Emile* inflects his thought from the outset; while the majority of Kant's writings lead one to believe that he shared Locke's more limited hope for a basic toleration between religions as the condition for civil government, Kant's 'argument about the sources and nature of moral religion, so different from those of Locke and the deists, forced him onto a different path when it came to the ultimate value of the Christian churches' (Lilla, 2007: 155). While it is true that Kant ultimately defends Christianity as 'the true universal church', I would argue that the deference to religion in his writing is not symptomatic of a deviation; rather, the room Kant famously made for faith at the very core of his philosophy bears witness to an awareness in his thought, extending and building on that of prior generations of philosophers and theologians, that human knowledge is of essence limited when it comes to the ability to understand the entirety of existence. Kant's religious anthropology in other words, does not force him onto a different path so much as corroborate a philosophical position that is essential to his thought, and that we see operational in the very core of the response to Hume and Leibniz that inspire his *Critique of Pure Reason*.

According to Gottfried Leibniz, were two things to be alike in every possible way, they would not in fact be two things but one thing. For Kant, this principle bespoke Leibniz's failure to distinguish between appearances and how things are in themselves. If the principle of the identity of indiscernibles were valid, Kant argued, it could be so only for an entirely intellectual world independent of space, and time, the forms of intuition through which we come to know the world. Appearances, in contrast, need space and time to be manifest and thus must be discernible from one another even while the identity of their referent remained the same. We must, in other words, be capable of discerning self-identical objects in space and time in order to perceive them as objects in the first place.

For Leibniz, then, the world is identical to *the idea* of the world, or what we could call its code. For any self-identical entity there is a specific code, and the repetition of that code would entail the repetition of all its possible attributes and would thus result in its exact reproduction. Leibniz's theory is thus based on the belief that the world is equivalent to its information, which was why he engaged in the popular seventeenth-century project for the creation of a perfect, rational language. The search for the perfect language – and the conviction underlying it that the world could indeed be the expression of a single language or master code – is an old one, indeed, and had been primarily the work of theologians hoping to discover trace back the language of God. By adopting this search to his purposes, Leibniz was translating into a scientific framework religious and philosophical convictions that dated from the earliest foundations of Western culture.

While the ideology underlying the idea of the world as a kind of code was often religious, it would be wrong to believe that the resistance to this idea sprung from a scepticism toward religious belief. In fact, belief in the underlying code of the world has informed secular thought as profoundly as it has informed religious thought. Equally true, however, is how real possibilities of resistance to this notion of the world as code have developed from a tradition of scepticism *within* theology of the idea that creation is reducible to a kind of knowledge even, in principle, accessible to human beings.

Although both Leibniz and Kant were religious in that their philosophies assumed the existence of God, they also each represent one possible path for secular humanism. For the Leibnizian approach, everything we sense is reducible to a code, an underlying language that, when unlocked, can give us access to the universe as it really is. Once the code is understood, secrets as impenetrable as the consciousness of another human being will be opened to us. Scepticism toward such an objectifying view of human being is what differentiates the Kantian from the Leibnizian path. For Kant, when we make observations of the world, we can only do so in time and space, but that we do so tells us nothing about the world as it really is, independent of those observations.

For Kant, God functions what he calls as a regulative ideal, a supplement to our thought necessary for arriving at truths about the world and for governing our actions. But aside from believing in God in this way, Kant insists that we can no more know God's will than we can know the universe as it is itself. By believing in God in this way and not believing that we can know his will, Kant argues that we accomplish something quite vital. Beliefs about metaphysical truths that we hold strictly separate from our actual knowledge about the world can free us to pursue science and politics unimpeded by dogma and fanaticism. Concomitantly, decoupling belief in from any requirement for demonstrable evidence can allow for tolerance between faiths and, eventually, even peace among nations. None of this is to say that Kant's own prejudice toward Christianity, and his even more troubling prejudice against Jews, is either defensible morally or unimportant for intellectual history. The point is rather to insist that Kant's recuperation in philosophical form of the transcendental dimension of human experience was, in a sense, logically prior to his religious anthropology and not the other way around. Thus, while it may be the case, as Lilla argues, that Kant's thought laid the groundwork for a 'new, and thoroughly modern, political theology' (Lilla, 2007: 140), the core of his philosophical contribution lies elsewhere, and contributes to a philosophical scepticism toward totalizing discourses that may aid in undermining both religious fundamentalisms as well as those forms of thought that seek to exclude from the field of consideration all real alternatives to those political and economic models that undergird the existing modern world system.

110 William Egginton

Democracy and hermeneutic theology

Marx's assessment of the political value of religion was famously unambiguous. But more recent critical thought has been less inclined to dismiss religious practice and belief wholesale as the opiate of the masses. The postmodern turn in theology has notable progressive affinities, and openly leftist and, in some cases, self-proclaimed communist thinkers have publically espoused a return to theological question or even aspects of specific religious traditions.[3] It is not my aim to review these various positions here; rather, in this concluding section I will propose an argument, based on the previous critique of the dialogic assumptions of Lilla's defence of secularism, for how and why contemporary leftist thought finds a real basis for solidarity with at least a certain kind of religious belief.

In their important recent book *Hermeneutic Communism* (2011), Gianni Vattimo and Santiago Zabala lay the groundwork for both a thoroughgoing critique of and potentially resistance to what they term 'framed democracy'. According to Vattimo and Zabala, scientific rationalism, along with philosophical realism, are forms of thought complicit with the maintenance of power by entrenched elites. As they write,

> A politics of description does not impose power in order to dominate as a philosophy; rather, it is functional for the continued existence of a society of dominion, which pursues truth in the form of imposition (violence), conservation (realism), and triumph (history). These metaphysically framed political systems hold that society must direct itself according to truth (the existing paradigm), that is, in favor of the strong against the weak. Only the strong determine truth, because they are the only ones that have the tools to know, practice, and impose it. (Vattimo and Zabala, 2011: 12)

The political form that society of dominion has assumed in the contemporary Western world is, of course, liberal democracy. But the elites who benefit from the status quo are at pains to ensure that democracy such as it is continues to support and sustain the system of privileges that flow to them. Hence, the evolution of democracies in the modern Western world, seat to the majority of the world's multinational corporations, into often highly unrepresentative oligarchies where access to the upper echelons of power is limited to a class defined by its extreme and increasing wealth. The institutions and individuals complicit in this system and its privileges then play an active role in assuring that democracy does not become more democratic than its current manifestation; alternatives are excluded from the framework that defines adequately functioning formal democracy.

Certainly secularists are correct when they decry religious fundamentalists as being a threat to democracy. Any discourse that determines in advance the nature of truth and who has access to that truth is by definition a threat to democracy. But what is often masked by the stand-off between secularism and its 'irrationalist' opponents is how the unquestioned nature of secularism's own framing of truth claims, while complicit with framed democracy, is in fact also a threat to unframed democracy, or what Derrida called the 'democracy to come'. This is why the communism of Vattimo and Zabala's title is at once hermeneutic and limited to the status of a Kantian regulative idea. It is hermeneutic because, as the authors write, hermeneutics is the very essence of politics:

> If politics, as Hannah Arendt explained, is not exclusively conflicting assertions of truth, claims to recognition, and power relations but rather the action necessary to create a public realm in which individuals coexist freely while protecting the private space necessary for their development, then hermeneutics is also political. It relies on a plurality of individual developments, that is, active interpretations. A philosophy that relies on a plurality of interpretations must avoid not only any metaphysical claims to universal values, which would restrict personal developments, but also that passive conservative nature that characterizes descriptive philosophies in favor of action. (Vattimo and Zabala, 2011: 77)

Hermeneutics is what happens externally and prior to metaphysical framing; it is the container to the contained of framed democracy; and it is what must be suppressed in order both for metaphysics and framed democracy to establish their implicit claims to exclusive validity.

Communism is, then, the name for a democracy unframed, unleashed from the constraints of prior metaphysical assumptions. In no way, then, can this communism be related to the violent impositions of power that assumed its mantle in the twentieth century. Communism from a hermeneutic perspective can only ever be an incomplete, utopian project. It is the very realization of hermeneutics in the political sphere, the attempt to hold open the excluded spaces and populations of framed democracy, so as to permit a modicum of ferment to undermine their self-certain truths. As the authors write,

While we cannot imagine a world where communism is completed, neither can we renounce this ideal as a regulative and inspiring principle for our concrete decisions.... Kant's lesson of practical reason also has this meaning: the union between virtue and happiness is not only the end that gives meaning to moral actions but also something impossible to carry out in the world. Nevertheless, this impossibility does not remove the obligation toward the categorical imperative. In sum, communism is utopia or, as Benjamin would have it, a 'weak messianic power, a power on which the past has a claim'. (Vattimo and Zabala, 2011: 117)

The real threat to democracy is not the return of political theology; political theology never really left us to begin with. It merely changed its shape as sovereignty evolved through its several 'passages' on the route from God to what Hardt and Negri (2000) called 'Empire'. And in a similar vein, Kant's foray into religious anthropology was not a deviation; his recognition of the ineradicable nature of the transcendental dimension in human life was perhaps his key insight. The interpretation of God as regulative idea was thus not a holdover allowing an unfortunately remnant of unreason in his otherwise secular system; it was the anchor stone to an edifice of thought that recognized the dangers of fanaticism in all its forms. Making the goal and beacon of our politics 'something impossible in this world' means not shutting the door on a democracy that would be possible in this world but that we don't yet recognize. In the same way, valuing and even promoting tolerant and pluralistic religious belief and practice is a means of remaining attentive to other ways of knowing that may not even have been discovered yet but that risk elimination under the presumptive knowledge of secularism and its acceptable forms of truth.

Notes

1. As Fonna Forman-Barzilai puts it, 'Sympathy [for Smith] was a social practice through which individuals who share physical space participate together in an ordinary exchange of approbation and shame, and through repetitive interactions over time learn to become 'social' – learn to adjust their passions to a 'pitch' commensurate with living in a society with others' (Forman-Barzilai, 2010: 12–13).
2. As Marie Martin puts it, 'Morality cannot be reduced to individual sentiment, but must always refer, at least implicitly, to the sentiments of others' (Martin, 1990: 112).

The Eradication of Transcendence 113

3. Some examples of the trend would include Gianni Vattimo, Slavoj Žižek, Jeffrey Robbins, John D. Caputo, Hent De Vries, Alain Badiou, and Carmelo Dotolo, among many others.

References

Aquinas, T. (no date). 'Summa Theologica – Christian Classics Ethereal Library.' Online source, available at http://www.ccel.org/ccel/aquinas/summa.toc.html [last accessed 2 May 2012].
Badiou, A. (2003). *Saint Paul: The Foundation of Universalism.* Stanford, CA: Stanford University Press.
Caputo, J.D. and Scanlon, M.J. (1999). *God, the Gift, and Postmodernism.* Bloomington, IN: Indiana University Press.
Davis, C., Milbank, J., and Žižek, S. (2005). *Theology and the Political: The New Debate.* Durham, NC: Duke University Press.
Dawkins, R. (2006). *The God Delusion.* London: Bantam.
Deleuze, G. (1991). *Empiricism and Subjectivity: An Essay on Hume's Theory of Human Nature.* New York: Columbia University Press.
Derrida, J. (2005). *Rogues: Two Essays on Reason.* Stanford, CA: Stanford University Press.
De Vries, H. (2002). *Religion and Violence: Philosophical Perspectives from Kant to Derrida.* Baltimore, MD: Johns Hopkins University Press.
Dotolo, C. (2006). *The Christian Revelation: Word, Event, and Mystery.* Aurora, CO: Davies Group.
Forman-Barzilai, F. (2010). *Adam Smith and the Circles of Sympathy: Cosmopolitanism and Moral Theory.* Cambridge: Cambridge University Press.
Habermas, J. (2005). 'Religion in the Public Sphere.' Online source, available at the Holberg Prize website http://www.holbergprisen.no/images/materiell/2005_symposium_habermas.p f#ameddest=habermas [last accessed 20 November 2012].
Hardt, M. and Negri, A. (2000). *Empire.* Cambridge, MA: Harvard University Press.
Harris, S. (2004). *The End of Faith.* New York: Norton.
Hitchens, C. (2007). *God Is Not Great: How Religion Poisons Everything.* New York: Twelve.
Hume, D. (1998). Trans. by T.L. Beauchamp, *An Enquiry Concerning the Principles of Morals.* Oxford: Oxford University Press.
Jakobsen, J.R. and Pellegrini, A. (eds) (2008). *Secularisms.* Durham, NC: Duke University Press.
Kant, I. (1998). P. Guyer and A.W. Wood (eds) *Critique of Pure Reason.* Cambridge: Cambridge University Press.
Leibniz, G.W. (1898). Trans. by R. Latta,'Monadology.' Online source, available at http://philosophy.eserver.org/leibniz-monadology.txt [last accessed 2 May 2012].
Lilla, M. (2007). *The Stillborn God: Religion, Politics, and the Modern West.* New York: Knopf.
Maimonides, M. (no date). 'Guide for the Perplexed.' *Internet Sacred Text Archive Home.* Online source, available at http://www.sacredtexts.com/jud/gfp/index.htm [last accessed 2 May 2012].

Martin, M.A. (1990). 'Utility and Morality: Adam Smith's Critique of Hume.' *Hume Studies* 16(2), 107–120.
Smith, A. (2009). *The Theory of Moral Sentiments.* New York: Cosimo.
Taylor, C. (2007). *A Secular Age.* Cambridge, MA: Harvard University Press.
Vattimo, G. (2010). *Christianity, Truth, and Weakening Faith: A Dialogue.* New York: Columbia University Press.
Vattimo, G. and Zabala, S. (2011). *Hermeneutic Communism: From Heidegger to Marx.* New York: Columbia University Press.
Žižek, S. (2000). *The Fragile Absolute, or, Why Is the Christian Legacy Worth Fighting For?* London: Verso.

6
The Unprecedented Return of Saint Paul in Contemporary Philosophy

Gregg Lambert

The conceptual relationship between crisis (*krisis*) and critique (*krinein*) in post-Kantian philosophy, pronounced most forcefully by Husserl in the opening lectures of *The Crisis of European Sciences and Transcendental Phenomenology*, is well known to most readers of contemporary philosophy. 'The difficulty that has plagued human psychology', Husserl writes, '[and] not just in our time but for centuries – its own peculiar 'crisis' –...leads [us] back to *the enigma of subjectivity* itself and thus is inseparably bound to the *enigma of psychological subject matter and method*' (Husserl, 1970). The question I will turn to in this discussion is whether the contemporary crisis announced under the term of the 'postsecular', referring in this sense to the decline of scientific method and the return of something akin to a 'faith position' expressed by certain contemporary philosophies, is remarkably different than the earlier crisis between the humanistic disciplines – including modern philosophy (*Geisteswissenschaften*) – and the positivistic sciences announced by Husserl in 1936 and, even earlier, the crisis between faith and reason during the period of the Enlightenment? In taking up this question – What's this postsecular crisis all about? – I will turn to examine the writings of the contemporary French philosopher Alain Badiou around the somewhat emblematic figure of Saint Paul.

My argument will be that 'the return of Paul' on the contemporary scene, spurred on by the recent readings of the Pauline figure by Agamben and Badiou (and by Žižek, to a lesser degree), represents a postsecular (i.e., post-scientific) response to the perceived crisis of philosophical subjectivity that has emerged alongside the decline of what has gone under the name of 'Critical Theory' (or simply 'theory') in

North America and elsewhere (in short, the anti-humanistic traditions of primarily German and French philosophy). What I am defining as 'postsecular,' in this moment, occurs when the subject of philosophy is grounded in something resembling a 'form of faith' and no longer on a scientific principle of reason, which has been reduced in the postmodern period to being merely one 'fable' among others (i.e., ideology). This does not mean that all philosophy thereby becomes religious, or nostalgically assumes a pious stance with regard to the world (even though this has certainly happened), but rather concerns the manner in which philosophy assumes a subjective form of certainty concerning its own truth claims in contradistinction to the truth procedures of the other sciences.

First, let us recall Heidegger's earlier claim that philosophy is not opposed to theology but rather to faith as 'a subjective form of existence' (Heidegger, 1998: 41). This is because, for Heidegger, philosophy is 'factically ever changing,' whereas he understands religious faith as the inward or subjective form of existence that is characterized by something like permanent conviction, or belief (*pistis*). In other words, the philosopher's convictions are historically ever changing because philosophers constantly change their minds about philosophy's own truth procedures, to employ Badiou's term, and this is especially evident in the case of the procedures invented by earlier philosophers, which undergo constant revision. By contrast, for Heidegger, the form of existence defined by faith is founded upon a set of firm convictions that are impervious (at the very least, resistant and sometimes openly hostile) to a complete 'transformation of mind' (*metanoia*) that appears as the historical condition of philosophy's ever-changing appearance, since such a change would also necessarily imply the destruction of the subject (of faith), that is, the subjective core of a belief system. Therefore, to change one's faith entails something more radical than a mere change in opinion, since the truth of propositions may change over time but do not require the complete 'destruction' of the subject (*subiectum*) that underlies them. It is for this reason that Heidegger claims that faith is the 'mortal enemy' (*todfeind*) of the form of existence that is called philosophy.[1]

In the contemporary moment, however, it appears that it is the factically ever-changing nature of truth claims that now appear as the entire problem of philosophy's own subjective form of existence and authority, especially in light of the ever-changing, multiple, and shifting identities belonging to globalized societies (to paraphrase a refrain often made by Žižek). Today philosophy appears bereft of the power to brand its own truth claims with the stamp of the Real that was formerly provided by its earlier claim to the idea of Reason, or by adherence to a form of scientific method, as in the case of the phenomenology. Even in the so-called postmodern period, the appeal to a Structuralist method, or to the 'logic of the Signifier,' still assumed the epistemological form of a 'Science of the Subject,' especially in psychoanalysis and Althusserian Marxism. It is in this context, perhaps, that we might regard a contemporary philosopher like Badiou who resolves to transform the subjective form of philosophy by exchanging the principle of reason for a firmer foundation of faith (or what I would as a postsecular form of 'conviction,' which is not religious in principle). For Badiou, moreover, this gesture represents the 'heroic' effort to vindicate the militant subjectivity of Marxist-Leninist critique against competing truth procedures, especially those that have been formulated most successfully in Europe and the United States in the contemporary period by feminist and minority critiques under the banner of what he will call a Levinasian 'ethics of difference', which I will return to discuss below (Badiou, 1993).

But first, why Paul? In other words, how does Pauline Christianity provide a foundation for the new Universalism proclaimed by an atheist and Marxist philosopher like Badiou? Although this might appear somewhat paradoxical, at first glance, the answer will be found in the implicit parallelism between the 'Christ-event' proclaimed by Paul in 1 CE and the truth event of Marx proclaimed by Badiou, which can only be understood by subtracting, as a condition of this claim, any reference to an historical reality or 'objective aggregate' of facts. Some of these facts would include, as the editors of this volume have already commented, the role played by former Eastern European churches in the historical defeat of Communism and the subsequent reappraisal of religious activism, in addition to 'the serious questioning of the militant atheism of the previous Marxist tradition' (Badiou, 1993: xx). To this I would only add the global consequences that both precipitated and followed the collapse of the Soviet Union: the political bankruptcy and gradual 'senilization' of any remaining Marxist-Leninist or Maoist regimes, which only appear as what Althusser called 'survivals' (*survivants*) in a world increasingly ruled by neoliberal principles of 'governmentality' (Foucault).

In the context of Badiou's own argument, given the parallelism that he finds between our contemporary world and the world of the first century (CE), the truth procedure invented by Paul to establish the subjective foundation of a Universalist identity (i.e., an identity without any 'identitarian characteristics') in response to his own political and cultural situation, may provide the necessary strategy to guarantee the survival of his own 'critical' position in contemporary neoliberal society, especially in view of the role played by the United States in his cosmic allegory. 'Paul's unprecedented gesture,' Badiou writes, 'consists in subtracting truth from the communitarian grasp, be it that of a people, a city, an empire, a territory, or a social class' (Badiou, 2003: 5). Likewise, in order to avoid being defeated on the basis of 'mere facts', our contemporary militant philosopher must first devise a method of subtracting his own truth procedure from any current historical circumstances in establishing its claim of proof, or certainty, since it is faith (or rather, 'conviction') and not reason that also grasps the nature of the truth event as a subjective form of existence, 'an event whose only "proof" lies in its having been declared by a subject' (Badiou, 2003: 5).

What, then, is the so-called truth procedure invented by Paul that Badiou reduces, on the one hand, to an 'unprecedented gesture' (a pure act without foundation in previous tradition) and, on the other hand, to a 'pure element of Saying' (*pointe de fable*)? Certainly, Paul's original gesture consists in subtracting the entire narrative of the historical Jesus of Nazareth (including the narrative of the life of Jesus given in the gospels, as well as everything that Jesus said) and in reducing the 'Christ-event' to one pointed Saying: 'Jesus is resurrected!'[2] Of course, this 'pure element of Saying' cannot be understood philosophically as a proposition, as Badiou rightly observes, but rather in the strongest sense as a proclamation of *faith in the event* (which would not be accurately captured as 'belief' in the usual sense accorded to the Greek word *pistis*). At the same time, as a self-proclaimed atheist, Badiou does not merely seek to repeat the content of Paul's original statement either, since the reality of the resurrected Christ is declared to be a 'fiction,' according to the secondary meaning of *fabula*, as he defines it, a residue that still clings to the pure element of Saying and is mediated by the Imaginary (Badiou, 2003: 5). Stripped of its 'fabulous content', therefore, and 'unburdened by all the imaginary that surrounds it', what is retained is only the pure element of the Saying itself. Although the form of this faith is certainly 'religious' (and it is philosophical only in its own unique 'fable'), it is consciously a religious form stripped of its religious 'fable' (i.e., its fiction, or genre, is form of Saying), one in which 'conviction' replaces 'faith' (*pistis*), the subject of militant conviction replaces the subject of love (*agape*, or charity), and the subjective form of 'certainty' replaces 'hope' (*elpis*) (Badiou, 2003: 5).

What exactly is this element? Again, it is the unprecedented and heterogeneous nature of the 'truth event' first introduced by Paul as both a form of thought but also the act of declaring the truth of this thought, which is violently posed against two other world views that Paul is in a struggle to extricate the meaning of a Christian form of existence: the Greek and the Jewish moral universes. As early Christian scholar Wayne A. Meeks writes: 'The novelty of the proclamation [Saying, *pointe de fable*], which violates or at least transcends expectations based on either reason or on Jewish traditions (1 Cor. 1:18–25), *permits it to serve as a warrant for innovation*' (Meeks, 1983: 180, emphasis mine).

In this regard, Badiou is completely accurate in his reading of the meaning of the statement 'Jesus is resurrected!' as a radical departure from both moral and philosophical systems that renders the subjective element of a distinctively Christian 'life' (*zoe*), one that is 'indifferent' (in a word) to the former determinations of the flesh (*sarx*) under Jewish law, and the natural predisposition of things and persons to come or 'to return to their own place' according to Greek wisdom. The event proclaimed by Paul could never exist in either universe, which becomes the basis for the heterogeneity of the Christian form of existence as a new determination of life *(zoe)*, no longer predicated on the previous ethnological and cultural characteristics of kinship and class. As Meeks writes, 'In particular, Paul uses the paradox of the Messiah's crucifixion explicitly to support the union of Jew and gentile and the abolition of the distinction between them, by bringing to an end the boundary setting function of the Torah' (Meeks, 1983: 180).

In his own argument, Badiou employs the Pauline 'paradox' as the foundation for a new form of Universalism, defined as a militant subjective form of a '[radical] indifference that tolerates differences' (Badiou, 2003). In other words, he uses the 'unprecedented gesture' of Paul in the form of a precedent (as one also says in legal jurisprudence) to found his own gesture on another fable – the revolutionary fable of the truth event first proclaimed by Marx. It is around this point, however, that the explicit parallelism that Badiou seeks to establish between the heroic (and fanatical) subject of Paul, who proclaims the truth event of the resurrected Christ, and the subject of 'he who proclaims the pure event' (i.e., the subject of Badiou himself?) becomes overtly contrived, which is one reason why Badiou elides in his account the second part of the Pauline saying: 'Christ is Lord' (meaning also that all Christians are to be understood as 'slaves to Christ').

I have already established above the two senses of the 'fable' by which Badiou determines the 'Christ-event' of St Paul as an allegorical means of addressing the situation of crisis in contemporary philosophy. Of course, allegory is a type of fable often employed in moral philosophy, which Badiou's own discourse unquestioningly is. How we know it is allegorical is explicitly stated in the 'situation' to which this discourse is addressed, when Badiou writes that Paul's original discourse speaks directly *to us* from out of the same conditions as the Roman Empire's period of increasing despotism and militarism, which is represented *in our time* by the United States:

> By transplanting Paul, along with all his statements, into our century, one sees them encountering there a real society every bit as criminal and corrupt, but infinitely more supple and resistant, than that of the Roman Empire. (Badiou, 2003: 5)

Moreover, in his own allegorical identification with the figure of St Paul, Badiou also might also appear to us today as 'heroic', 'fanatical', or even as a 'zealot'. Simply put, Paul was also a self-defined zealot for Christ in the same manner that Badiou remains a zealot for Lenin and Mao, and particularly against those who would declare this conviction to be a 'folly', given the evidence against this system of belief and the disappearance of the peoples that marked its historical existence. However, it is only in the peculiar sense of heroism employed by Badiou to describe his own 'situation' vis-à-vis that of Paul that the saying 'Jesus is resurrected!' is given its true meaning as allegory.

Returning now to Badiou's appropriation of the original Pauline argument that 'there is no distinction between Greek and Jew,' *this argument is only valid if we also fully accept the following claim as a condition*: that the 'new type of subject' proclaimed by Badiou ('for him who considers that the real is pure event') fulfils and, at the same time, 'cancels out' the reality of all ethnic and cultural identity in the same manner that, as in the argument of Paul, Christ came to fulfil and thereby to satisfy the laws of the Torah, bringing them to closure through the inauguration of a new subject for whom the continued recognition of ethnic and cultural differences would now have an anachronistic and 'backward' meaning (Badiou, 2003: 57).[3] In other words,

> To declare the nondifference between Greek and Jew establishes Christianity's potential universality; to found the subject as division, rather than the perpetuation of a tradition, renders the subjective element adequate to this universality by terminating the predicative particularity of cultural subjects. There is no doubt that universalism, and hence the existence of any truth whatsoever, *requires the destitution of established differences* and the initiation of a subject divided in

itself by the challenge of having nothing but the vanished event to face up to. (Badiou, 2003: 57–58, emphasis mine)

It is only upon assuming the full reality of this event, or this universal 'subjective void', that the subject is capable of 'radical indifference' in the face of which all identities will henceforth appear as fictions, opinions of culture and tradition, and including the very phenomenal appearance of racial and sexual characteristics, which are henceforth regarded as the fictive projections of the Imaginary. Here, in many other statements, Badiou actually reveals himself to be gnostic in his attitude; thus, the cancellation of reality of cultural, racial, and sexual difference is based on a prior denial of the reality of this world, which is ruled by chaos and by demons. Here, it is crucial to note that for Badiou, as for Paul, the greatest evil is belief in multiple identities, which poses the greatest threat to the potential universality of the Subject. Multiple identities are the little 'daemons' that rule in chaos; as Paul says, 'one cannot drink from the cup of Christ and the cup of demons at the same time' (that is, without contamination). It is around this final point that Badiou's identification of Levinas as the founder of a neoliberal 'ethics of difference' also becomes somewhat contrived, if not a form of calculated subreption.

But secondly, why Levinas? In other words, why does Levinas's ethical philosophy appears as the object of Badiou's most fervent critiques from 1993 onward, as the real antagonist and opponent, in an almost identical manner as the one who Paul calls 'the Teacher' in the letter to the Galatians, whom he accuses of preaching 'a fraudulent gospel' (Meeks, 1983: 176)? In answering this question, first, as Badiou says often of the relation Nietzsche-Paul, I will say of the relation Badiou-Levinas: that the latter is more like a rival than a real enemy. The most critical difference between their philosophical systems only appears in a statement at the end of *Saint Paul*, where Badiou declares 'that in order for people to be gripped by truth, it is imperative that universality not present itself under the aspect of particularity' (Badiou, 2003: 99). This argument is made even more explicit in the passage that follows and provides the very basis for the rhetorical strategy all along:

> Against universalism conceived as the production of the Same, it has recently been claimed that the latter found its emblem, if not its culmination in the death camps, where everyone, having been reduced to a body on the verge of death, was absolutely equal to everyone else. This 'argument' is fraudulent. (Badiou, 2003: 109)

Of course, Badiou's criticisms of this clichéd understanding of Christian universalism as being entirely responsible for the Holocaust and for the reduction of all political life to 'bare life' are correct; in particular, the camps were responsible for introducing completely new and exorbitant differences between absolute death and bare life into our 'civilization' as actual, and not merely possible, forms of social and political existence – and in the sense that they continue to remain a real possibility for our political forms today and in the future (that is, unless one believes that genocide is no longer possible as a political weapon). Secondly, the Pauline formula of Christian universalism (based on the fusion of community through love) cannot be reduced to Nazi 'exceptionalism'. based on the exclusion and extermination of difference from a community understood as a 'closed substance, continuously driven to verify its own closure, both in and outside itself, through carnage' (Badiou, 2003: 11). Nevertheless, the implication that the ethical thought of Levinas, as perhaps the most systematic contemporary critique of 'the production of the Same', is the origin of this point of view is also a type of fraud, or at the very least, a false testimony perpetrated by Badiou himself. Strategically, as I noted above, it constitutes a form of 'subreption', which, according to an older usage, is the deliberate misstatement of facts in order to gain an ecclesiastical advantage.

First, let us again recall that according to the etymology of the word that exists in both Jewish and Greek systems, a fable is 'saying' (*logos, legein*); however, for Levinas, the pure element of 'Saying' (*Dire*) is expressed in a manner that cannot be reduced to 'the said' (*le dit*), and thus also remains heterogeneous to every attempt to totalize its sense within an order of nature or reason. It is in this sense of heterogeneity that is already accorded to the pure element of the 'truth event', as we have seen, that Badiou perceives the ethical fable of Levinas as the most powerful rival to his own fable under the name of Paul:

> *For Paul*, the Christ-event is heterogenous to the law, pure excess over every prescription, grace without concept or appropriate rite. The real can no more be what the elective exception becomes literalized in stone as timeless law (Jewish discourse), than what comes or returns to its place (Greek discourse) ... *For him* who considers that the real is pure event, Jewish and Greek discourses no longer present, *as they continue to do in the work of Levinas, the paradigm of a major difference in thought*. This is the driving force behind Paul's universalist conviction:

that 'ethnic' or cultural difference, of which the opposition between Greek and Jew is in his time and in the empire as a whole, the prototype, is no longer significant with regard to the real, or to the new object that sets out a new discourse. *No real distinguishes the first two discourses any longer, and their distinction collapses into rhetoric.* (Badiou, 2003: 57)

In the above passage I have underlined the surreptitious replacing of the subject in the statement, '*For him* who considers that the real is pure event,' which no longer refers to Paul, nor even to the 'Christ-event' which is merely a fable but again to the subject of the pure universal event of the Real without mediation. Here, we find the philosophy of Levinas defined as 'the paradigm of a major difference in thought' – that is, the ethical foundation for the ideology of the 'right to difference' and what Badiou refers to as the 'contemporary catechism of goodwill with regard to "other cultures" (i.e., multi-culturalism)' (Badiou, 1993: 20).[4] To put it crudely, in the manner of Badiou, Levinas's ethical philosophy is responsible for what in the United States has gone under the name of 'identity politics', and in France from the early 1990s onward, for the political appeals based on the recognition of the rights of immigrant groups and other social minorities.

According to the terms of Badiou's own argument, however, we would need to affirm that Levinas's ethical philosophy has actually been successful in overturning the Greek *logos* by supplanting ontological difference with ethical difference, thereby introducing a new position of 'critique' into the contemporary philosophical genre. For Levinas, as we know, difference is incarnated in 'the face', which is anterior to the self-reflexive identity of the Ego with the other, either as the coexistence of two terms in a 'logical unity', or in the form of a 'transcendental apperception' of an ultimate intentionality. Therefore, ethical difference can only be phrased in the accusative mode, which is derived from intersubjective space that is primordially asymmetrical; it is only in this manner that difference is introduced as severely restricting the Ego's own freedom and self-presence, thereby making possible the two poles of obsession (*eros*) and nihilation (*abaddon*). However, in order to understand Badiou's claim that a Levinasian conception of difference as 'the paradigm of a major difference in thought,' we would first need to translate the above concepts into the form of a truth procedure that would illustrate the concept of difference enacted by all forms of 'identitarian politics' today. Accordingly, the concept of difference is enacted or produced by something like the following truth procedure:

1. Difference is introduced from the 'position' of an other who is determined in the pure element of Saying, in the epiphany of a face, and whose 'position' expresses the essential asymmetry and exteriority of all social relations;
2. Difference is expressed in the form of an accusative that is addressed to the sovereign and atemporal position of the 'I', thereby making this Subject 'responsible to' the very condition of exteriority and alterity of the other (often described by Levinas in terms of privation of being or poverty); and
3. The Saying (*le Dire*) of Difference becomes the formal occasion of a truth procedure and the 'conversion' of the other into another subject (in the act of self-nomination), and thus, all subsequent truth procedures belonging to the name of the particular difference (*le dit*) become the basis for the positive construction of both subjective knowledge and social being (*conatus*).

Although this very schematic portrayal of a common truth procedure can be easily recognized in many critical identity claims (of ethnic minorities, for example, or in the history of feminist critique), we should immediately recall Badiou's admission that this schema 'is strikingly distant from Levinas' actual conception of things.' In point of fact, Levinas would regard the third step in the truth procedure outlined above as merely another instance of 'the return into the Same', whereby 'one signifies the other and is signified by it', and the one and the other become the coexistence of two terms in the same theme, despite their actual difference. For example, this often occurs when identity enters in as a third term (e.g., a name) that mediates the one and the other in a common theme, immersing the co-implication of different subjective and temporal instances 'in a collective representation, a common ideal, or a common action' (Levinas, 1978: 95).

From his earliest work, *Existence and Existents* (1947), Levinas does argue that the space of thought cannot be separated, to be considered in isolation, or even appear as the epiphenomenal distance from social space (as in writing), inasmuch as characteristic of alterity that conditions the appearance of thought is first introduced by the relationship to others. In other words, the Ego as subject cannot endow itself with its own alterity, its own temporal nothingness, that is, with the scintillating alteration of presence and absence that first gives to the Ego the freedom to pull back from its engagement with the world without being able withdraw completely. *It is the original alterity of the other that first creates this freedom and temporality as a possibility of existence, even though this freedom can only exist in relation to the world of others.* Otherwise, Levinas asks, '[h]ow could time arise in a solitary subject?'

> The solitary subject cannot deny itself; it does not possess nothingness.... This alterity comes to me only from the other. Therefore, is not sociality something more than the source of our representation of time: is it not time itself?... The dialectic of time is the very dialectic of the relationship with the other, that is, a dialogue which has to be studied in terms other than those of the solitary subject. The dialectic of the social relationship will furnish us with a set of concepts of a new kind. And the nothingness necessary to time, which the subject cannot produce, comes from the social relationship. (Levinas, 1978: 93–94)

In this passage we might find, in much plainer terms, the entire trajectory of Levinas's subsequent project, as well as a much clearer justification for the precedence of the 'ethical relation' over the ontological, according to a statement that appears later on that 'ethics precedes ontology'. It is this rich formulation, which unfortunately has been taken up in the most threadbare and philosophically naïve manner by many contemporary readers of Levinas, that will provide the basis of Badiou's accusation that it has become the 'major paradigm of difference in thought' for ethnic and cultural expressions of particularism.

At this point, I will make two preliminary remarks that run contrary to Badiou's own conception of all things 'Levinasian'. First, at least at this stage of the phenomenological argument, there is little to suggest that Levinas is attempting to erect a purely religious understanding of ethics in place of a Greek and philosophical system, much less that the origin of this understanding must be located in Jewish law. Second, there is even less evidence to suggest that what Badiou labels as a ideological and culturalist assumption of multiculturalism, identity politics, or of an ethical particularism that refuses to tolerate real differences and seeks to suppress them under a neoliberal form of universalism. Perhaps one could argue that both the primacy of a theological representation of 'the Other' and of the characteristics of Jewish exceptionalism become features of his later works, which depart from an earlier phenomenological understanding of these as themes. For Levinas, who was Jewish, the concept of a pre-original anteriority of 'the Other' could be called 'religious', that is, 'if the term itself did not also carry the risk of becoming theological' (Levinas, 1972: 80–81). However, in the earlier work, Levinas already defines this anteriority strictly in terms of the dialectic of the social relationship (which is equally a dialectic of temporality); at this point, it is only the social relationship that 'will furnish us with a set of concepts of a new kind' (Levinas, 1978: 94).

In fact, Levinas would define the representations of theology among the 'hypostases of the Ego', which fundamentally distort and cover over the initial asymmetrical character of all social relations (for example, between the child and the parent, or between genders, which becomes the focus of the subsequent work of *Totality and Infinity*). In both the earlier and the later works, in his analysis of the relationships brought about by Eros as a 'pathos of distance in proximity' where the asymmetrical nature of this duality of beings is maintained, Levinas will also locate the primary asymmetrical relationship between the enemy and the friend as key political concepts in which the asymmetrical formations belonging to racism and ethnocentrism will be determined as well. Thus, in the same but opposite measure that the failure of communication in love constitutes the presence of the other *qua* other as an object of obsession and desire, equally the failure of communication in hostility and warfare constitutes the presence of the stranger *qua* enemy as the object of impersonal hatred and derision. In both subjective states, the other appears as the one who holds me hostage and persecutes me, and in the case of the latter, the Ego can only hope to escape by fusing its own being with the anonymous and impersonal power of the collective, the group, the nation, the people, or the race. 'To this collectivity of comrades', Levinas writes early on, 'we contrast the I-you collectivity which precedes it. It is not participation in a third term – intermediate person, truth, dogma, work, profession, interest, dwelling, or meal; that is, it is not communion' (Levinas, 1978: 95).

Here, given the explicit reference to the common 'meal' and 'communion' in this passage, that is, the Christian and subsequently modern notions of 'participation in the common' *(metaxia)*, I must return now to provide some historical context for these criticisms by supplying their direct object. The primary object of Levinas's critique in *Existence and Existents* is Heidegger's analytic of Dasein with the emphasis upon the solitary states of *ek-static* temporality in the experiences of boredom, anxiety, and dread – that is, the existential states of nothingness and nihilation of being that Levinas argues are neither primordial, nor even 'ontological' forms of negation and nothingness.

Again, this would presuppose that the solitary subject, subtracted from all social space or intersubjective relations would be capable of giving to itself the form of alterity (i.e., non-being), which is to say, the subjective form of time itself.

Our relationship with others is the source of our own internal consciousness of time, and it is the presence of others that is responsible for introducing the nothingness from which the dynamism of the 'I' (the Subject) appears in the very exigency of the present to return; although the Ego is fundamentally passive in relation to this dynamism and this exigency, and the solitary subject can only 'dream, perchance, sleep, to shuffle off its mortal coils'. In the simplest terms, without any hint of spiritualism or divinity, it is the particular alterity of the other that first gives to the Ego the possibility of non-being, both the origin and the limit of its inalienable freedom as a subject, which, contrary to an entire tradition of philosophy, the subject cannot give to itself – not even in the form of a transcendental subjectivity of the non-I, of a System or Structure, or of History. (Thus, if there is any particularism in other, it cannot be embodied in a subject or identity.) It is the concrete presence of others that first 'positions' the subject, but it is also the non-identity of the other with the Ego that first gives the subject the 'freedom to withdraw from others'; however, as we have already seen, even the hope in community is only a temporal withdrawal and forgetting of this primordial 'position'. Thus, paradoxically, the idea of fusion that informs the 'we' of collectivity around a common object, a work, or a third term, is always in danger of forgetting and potentially betraying the social relation to others, later defined by Levinas in terms of passivity (which is not simply passive), vulnerability (which is not merely emotional), and responsibility (which is not only moral).

In some ways, Levinas's priority of the relationship to the other as primary form of alterity (of the splitting of the subject and the Ego) shares many of the same principles as the psychoanalytic critique of the subject, and I would only recall the prominence given to both paternity and gender in the subsequent studies as the primary forms of intersubjectivity. More rigorously understood, therefore, the statement that ethics precedes ontology must be understood as follows. 'Intersubjective space is initially asymmetrical', Levinas writes:

> The exteriority of the other is not an effect of space, which keeps separate what conceptually is identical, nor is there some difference in the concepts which would manifest itself through spatial exteriority. It is

precisely inasmuch as it is irreducible to these two notions of exteriority that social exteriority is an original form of exteriority that takes us beyond the categories of unity and multiplicity which are valid for things [i.e., the primacy of social exteriority takes us beyond ontology], that is, are valid in the world of an isolated subject, a solitary mind. Intersubjectivity is not simply the application of the category of multiplicity to the domain the mind [i.e., 'the One-All' and, ironically, here we have a good approximation of the principle thesis of Badiou's ontology]. It is brought about by Eros, where in the proximity of another the distance is wholly maintained, a distance whose pathos is made up of this proximity and this duality of beings. (Levinas, 1978: 95)

In the above statement we are given the explicit connection between ontology, the solitary subject (or *cogito*) and a world deprived or forgetful of others. Consequently, ontology is a world without others, and can only exist from the perspective of a solitary subject of the philosopher who manages (even only temporarily or through creating a 'fable') to withdraw from the world that is populated by other people, or to dream of the 'fusion of egos' in the communion of community. As an aside, is not Badiou our most solitary philosopher today as well?

Finally, Levinas was writing these arguments between 1940 and 1945 while he was a prisoner in the German concentration camp at Hannover; during the same period, several members of his family were being exterminated in concentration camps in his native Lithuania. Given this historical political context, his rejection of the Heideggerian analytic of Dasein, but particularly his severe criticism of the *Mitsein-andersein* formulation in *Being and Time* ('a collectivity of the *with*, and *around* truth' in an authentic form) are telling. Here, we must ask, what would be the implicit relationship that is drawn between the existential and solitary moods that are privileged in the earlier Heidegger, and the *Mitsein-andersein* privilege of the authentic community of the German people (*volk*) that belong to the same period of the philosopher's work and biography? Extending Levinas's critique of the solitary subject who cannot give nothingness to itself, from out of its own substance, can a people (or a race) give to itself its own creative nothingness, which in turn, will give birth to its unity in an ideal future? If only by implication, Levinas suggests that this is only possible through a violent denial of the primordial relationship to 'others', by a frenzied pathos for the creation of a 'proximity in distance', by an Eros borne from the ideal of fusion that belonged to National Socialism at this moment.

To conclude, it is obvious that, according to Marxist dogma, there is only one authentic species (*Geshlecht*) of social relationships that determine the asymmetrical organization of intersubjective social space, that is, prior to and in 'the final instance' of all other forms of asymmetry: the class relationship. In view of this 'authentic' social form of asymmetry, all other species of inequality (between genders, ethnic groups, minorities), as well as the different subjects of human rights, are fraudulent and 'imaginary' projections of false consciousness produced by the ideological machines controlled by the masters. (In this regard, Badiou, like Žižek, is extremely Orthodox in his understanding of the priority of class struggles and a politics based on the 'non-recognition' of any other form of social inequality as 'authentic'). However, perhaps the faith in the existence of 'authentic class', or of an 'authentic community' (a fraternity of comrades, or brothers and sisters in Christ), who can rightfully claim the name of the universal, should yet again be placed into question. The notion of an authentic community or people bears the special status of a secular myth of modernity, one that was born alongside the more archaic myths of nation and race, which are like its shadows and populist forms. But again, Levinas's critique of the 'authentic form' of this collectivity that can only be found in the solitary subject may have a renewed value for us today. Does not this 'I-you' collectivity return again in the political dyad of the friend-enemy couple, which continues to un-found any potential universalism of the collectivity of the 'we'?

Returning now to our contemporary moment and to Badiou, his most explicit criticism comes in *Ethics* (1993), written several years before the work on *Saint Paul*, where Badiou states: 'To put it crudely: Levinas' enterprise serves to remind us, with extraordinary insistence, that every effort to turn ethics into the principle of thought and action is essentially religious' (Badiou, 1993: 23). Here, we are given a stark alternative between religious ethics and militant philosophy, which in some ways recalls Heidegger's somewhat 'fundamentalist' viewpoint concerning the absolute hostility between faith and reason. As for Badiou, I suspect that it is the apparent success of Levinas's ethical principle of turning thought into a virulent form of active differentiation that poses the greatest problem for his own position of 'anti-philosophy': how to combine the principle of thought and action in a pure element of Saying that is not merely determined as the introduction of another subjective production of difference in the worldly proliferation of alterities. As he discovers in the unprecedented gesture of St Paul, it is only by laying claim to the position of the Universal itself, and casting off all forms of relative difference, that this principle can be attained. Or, as he resolves several years later in the conclusion of *Saint Paul*:

> This is why, as Paul testifies in exemplary fashion, universalism, which is an absolute (nonrelative) subjective production, indistinguishes saying and doing, thought and power. *Thought becomes universal only in addressing itself to all others, and it effectuates itself as power through this address.* But the moment all, including the solitary militant, are counted according to the universal, it follows that what takes place is the subsumption of the Other to the Same. ... *The production of equality and the casting off, in thought, of differences are the material signs of the universal.* (Badiou, 2003: 109, my emphasis)

Nevertheless, I don't think we can immediately accept this final claim that the cancellation of all differences that is first proposed in thought would be, in itself, sufficient to produce the material signs of equality among all others. (This is merely another hypostasis of thought and action in the philosophy of the Subject.) More critical, however, is the claim that thought can address itself to all others, and then 'effectuating itself with power from this address.' In fact, only Christian universalism could allow us to imagine such a thought, the unprecedented gesture of addressing 'all of Humanity,' but in order to 'effectuate[s] itself as power through this address', it needed an 'apparatus' (*dispositive*) that the Roman Empire later provided. This is something, by the way, that could never have been imagined by Paul out of his own time but which permanently remains as a precedent in our own.

Notes

1. 'This peculiar relationship does not exclude but includes the fact that *faith*, as a specific possibility of existence, is in its innermost core the mortal enemy [*todfeind*] of the *form of existence* that is an essential part of *philosophy* and that is factually ever-changing' (Heidegger, 1998: 53).
2. 'In this regard, it is to its element of fabulation [*point de fable* – although I prefer to translate this phrase according to the Latin sense of *fabula* as a form of 'saying'] alone that Paul reduces the Christian narrative, with the strength of one who knows that in holding fast to this point as real, one is unburdened of all the imaginary that surrounds it' (Badiou, 2003: 5).
3. 'Paul declared that for gentile Christians now to wish to be 'under the Law' would not be a step forward but backward, equivalent to a return to Paganism (Gal. 4:8–11). It would not be an act of obedience to God's will, but of disobedience toward the new order established by the Messiah's coming and crucifixion' (Meeks, 1983: 176).

4. Although, in the very same breath, Badiou will also admit that the popular conceptions of 'the ethics of difference' do not fit with Levinas's 'actual conception of things' (Badiou, 1993: 20).

References

Badiou, A. (1993). Trans. by P. Hallward. *Ethics: An Essay on the Understanding of Evil*. London: Verso.
Badiou, A. (2003). Trans. by R. Brassier. *Saint Paul: The Foundation of Universalism*. Palo Alto, CA: Stanford University Press.
Heidegger, M. (1998). 'Phenomenology and Theology.' In W. McNeill (ed.) *Pathmarks* 41. Cambridge: Cambridge University Press.
Husserl, E. (1970). Trans. by D. Carr. *The Crisis of European Sciences and Transcendental Phenomenology*. Evanston, IL: Northwestern University Press.
Levinas, E. (1978). Trans. by Alphonos Lingis. *Existence and Existents*. The Hague: Martinus Nijhoff.
Levinas, E. (1972). *Humanisme de l'autre homme*. Paris: Fata Morgana.
Meeks, W.A. (1983). *The First Urban Christians: The Social World of the Apostle Paul*. New Haven, CT: Yale University Press.

7
More Proof, If Proof Were Needed: Spectacles of Secular Insistence, Multicultural Failure, and the Contemporary Laundering of Racism

Alana Lentin and Gavan Titley

Introduction

Innocence of Muslims is a trailer in search of its film, featuring actors in search of their roles, directed by a propagandist sought by the FBI. It did eventually find its audiences, active audiences that could, in many instances, act on it without having seen it. If this kind of reaction is usually held up as evidence of censorious ignorance, in this instance it was merely adequate to the form, as the globally circulated trailer was conceived with relatively firm expectations of its viewers and witnesses. Posted on YouTube during July 2012 by Nakoula Basseley Nakoula – an Egyptian-American Coptic Christian who used the pseudonym 'Sam Bacile' – what has become known as the *Innocence of Muslims* exists for the vast majority of its audience as a 14-minute pastiche, *The Real Life of Muhammad*, a 'trailer' for an unverified full-length movie called *The Innocence of Bin Laden* allegedly screened in Hollywood during June 2012.

The – now indignant and litigious – actors starring in the production believed they were featuring in a low-budget film called *Desert Warrior*, a swords-and-tattered-sandals affair following the early Egyptian adventures of a character called 'Master George'. In post-production Master George became the Prophet Muhammad, who in this interpretation noisily courts the charge of blasphemy by having sex with children, talking to donkeys, and murdering random Christians (Bradshaw, 2012). Following the concerted online promotion of an Arabic-dubbed version in August 2012, the next month saw the gradual irruption of protests and riots 'in the Arab world' and in Muslim-majority nations, and ultimately mistaken assumptions that it triggered the lethal attack on the US ambassador to Libya, Christopher Stevens, on 13 September.

Writing in *The Guardian* following the attack, Ghaith Abdul-Ahad (2012) noted that the protests owed much to 'the organizational skills of the Salafis...wrong-footed by the Arab Spring.' The strategic affinity between provocative fire-starters and the enthusiastically inflamed was consummated, as Rebecca MacKinnon and Ethan Zuckerman argue, in 'a targeted attack designed to exploit the predispositions of our media systems' (MacKinnon and Zuckerman, 2012: 17). The desire to intervene in the revolutionary conditions in Egypt certainly informed Nakoula's actions, and that of the blogger Morris Sadek – founder of the small National American Coptic Assembly – who was influential in circulating the Arabic version subsequently presented by Sheikh Khaled Abdullah on the Egyptian satellite channel *al Nas* (and remediated as a 'US-sponsored production'). This strategy was broadly acknowledged in initial, critical discussions that focused on the paucity of censorial responses to the politics of digital provocation. For MacKinnon and Zuckerman, the producers of the video are 'essentially trolls', seeking to:

> ...Provide Middle Eastern Muslims with evidence that Americans misunderstand and disrespect Islam so badly that hundreds of people are willing to get together and make a film insulting the Prophet. The ensuing protests play to the American commercial media's focus on the sudden and violent reactions, at the expense of processes that may be more important but are hard to portray visually: the authoring of a Libyan constitution, peaceful elections in Egypt. (MacKinnon and Zuckerman, 2012: 18–19)

For their imagined 'Western viewer', at least, the provocative intent of the video is obvious, and the answer to this provocation, according to Meredith Tax, is not 'censorship' of the video by Google and YouTube but rational restraint; 'The film was designed to insult, but nobody forces people to go crazy when their religion is insulted' (Tax, 2012). However, this is to mis-recognize the preferred *audiences* for the video, and to assume that the question of free expression transcends the structure of provocation. In early September, the Pro Deutschland

Citizen's Movement announced plans to hold a screening of the video in Berlin, weeks after they had demonstrated at several Berlin mosques brandishing copies of the *Jyllands-Posten* Muhammad cartoons. Responding to criticisms that they sought to 'recklessly pour oil on the fire', the movement's leader, Manfred Rouhs, argued that 'for us, it's a question of art and freedom of expression' (Dowling, 2012). While the appropriative defence of liberal principles by actors from determinedly anti-liberal traditions has limited public credibility, the French magazine *Charlie Hebdo* pursued Rouh's question towards a familiar set of answers by publishing a series of cartoons of Muhammad, including images of the 'Prophet naked'. According to Editor-in-Chief Gérard Biard, the publication of the cartoons was to satirize 'the silly film', and because

> The decision to publish the images was in keeping with France's proud history of secularism. There is only one reason [for the cartoons] – it was the news of the week. We have the silly movie, the silly film, about the Prophet Muhammad and we have the burning of the American embassy in Libya. We are a satirical, political magazine, we publish in France which is a *laïc* [secular] nation and...we are against all religions. The cartoons' publication is not in itself a violence-provoking act. (Khazan, 2012)

But, what kind of act is it? In the networked 'comment cultures' (Lovink, 2011) activated by the act of publication, it was widely interpreted as proposing normative questions of the limits of freedom of expression and, concomitantly, the 'right to offend' in defence of the secular. It is through this second-order shift that the full structure of provocation is realized. John Durham Peters (2006, 2009) argues that debates about freedom of speech are recursive; the substantive issue in question is frequently subsumed to abstract(ed) debates about the remit and status of the first principles invoked. This recursivity is frequently structured around a 'threefold cast of characters' initiated by the protagonist who breaks a taboo, who is subsequently defended – in principle if not motivation – by champions of the open society, who come to regard the subjects that have 'taken offence' as '...deficient in comparison with the evident open-mindedness of those who tolerate transgression' (Peters, 2009: 276). 'Nobody forces people to go crazy when their religion is insulted'; if the first-order issue is that of the mediated provocation, it is the second-order issue of the deficiency of the insulted that – at least since the Danish Cartoon affair – garners most attention, and serves to enact dramas of secular resistance to the 'non-European' responses of European Muslims.

This recurrent triangulation is of structural centrality to the circulation of *Innocence of Muslims*, the latest in a referential chain of intensive, often globally mediated events that invite the postsecular publics that are the subject of this book to align themselves in familiar patterns on a well-marked terrain. The strategy of provoking 'the offended' seeks a vision of an achieved state of publicness threatened by this surplus of emotional investment; the state of being secular that is widely accepted as 'common sense' in Western nation-states (Jakobsen and Pellegrini, 2008). If secularization theses, as Charles Taylor (2007) argues, circulate as 'subtraction stories', these mediated events seek to foreground and foreclose on the uninvited addition, an irruptive backwardness that is always, in these set pieces, Muslim. 'There is no right not to be offended'; each 'transgressive' communicative act thus also claims the status of moral advance, holding and demarcating the civilizational line, but also offering the promise of an unsentimental education to the backward, an opportunity for them to embrace, however painfully, progress.

For this reason, the politically orchestrated, diffused *free speech events* of the last years have become central generators of public discourse on the postsecular, and critical to the 'reduction of the postsecular condition to the "Muslim issue"' (Braidotti, 2008). The political motility of these events, and the ways in which they seek to engage postsecular publics, are discussed in this chapter. Anatomizing these public spectacles, we argue, is central to addressing the central point made by Jakobsen and Pellegrini, who, in arguing for the need to interrupt the binary rhetoric of progressive secular and backward religiosity, contend that '...challenging the ways in which the secularization narrative is told are thus more than academic exercises in terminological precision. The ways in which the terms secularism and religion frame contemporary debates mean that possibilities for moving out of these impasses are obscured' (Jakobsen and Pellegrini, 2008).

Moving out of this framing impasse involves recognizing that the reduction of the postsecular debate to the 'Muslim issue' depends on the occlusion of the politics of race in putatively post-racial polities. We agree with Rosi Braidotti that 'this reduction of the postsecular condition to the "Muslim issue", in the context of a war on terror that results in the militarization of the social space, means that any unreflective brand of normative secularism runs the risk of complicity with anti-Islam racism and xenophobia' (Braidotti, 2008). However we would go beyond 'complicity' to insist that countering this reductive understanding of the postsecular requires a reckoning with a mode of racialization invested in constructing and legitimizing a categorical difference between race and religion.

The embedding of the secular in a narrative of modern achievement imperilled by religious backwardness maps onto this, and provides lines of racial ordering despite the purported move beyond into post-racial times. In combining an insistence on racialization within post-racial polities with an analysis of how postsecular publics are invited to rehearse familiar, recursive scripts, we seek to illustrate the multiple forms of aversion directed at those held to problematically repopulate the space of subtraction. The 'secular', projected and territorialized as a property of European public space, provides a terrain for the post-racial sorting and ordering into what we have termed 'good' versus 'bad diversity' (Lentin and Titley, 2011: 161–192). Transcending the binary of secular/religion, we argue, depends on recognizing that this ordering produces racialized divisions in that race acts not only to determine acceptability, visibility, and citizenship but also to fix those deemed unacceptable, as less-than citizens, and as immutable subjects, unwilling and incapable of change.

To show this, the chapter first discusses the post-racial idea and its relevance for an understanding of postsecularism in an era characterized by the opposition to multiculturalism, a mythical return to 'national values', and the barely veiled assimilatory logic of the insistence on 'integration' in Europe, and increasingly Canada and Australia. If we accept, as Barnor Hesse (2011) argues, that, rather than being a recent political development of the post-Obama era, the idea that the West is post-race is foundational to modern racism, we can better understand how some arguments against religiosity can counter claims of racism while remaining anchored in raciological logics (Gilroy, 2002). Secondly, we uncover the ways in which the backlash against multiculturalism is intrinsically post-racial in that it is predicated on a separation from race and culture – and by extension religion – which establishes it as non- or anti-racist.

Lastly, we examine the ways in which spectacles of secular insistence, and their amplification and translation across times and spaces of communication, act to cement the post-racial formations that the opposition of secularism/Islam rely upon. A narrow-gauge focus on the putative threats posed by recalcitrant 'migrant' minorities to secularism risks extending the 'reverse racism' claims of backlash politics (Hewitt, 2012) by locating the primary source of racism among the 'illiberal minorities' permitted to challenge the settled ways of secular life in postcolonial Europe. Through such spectacles, the post-racial elision of power relations between Western hosts and perennial guests is deepened.

Postracial common sense

The motto of the Stop the Islamization of Europe (SIOE) movement is 'Racism is the lowest form of stupidity, but Islamophobia is the height of common sense'. Such a construction hints at an awareness of how the trace of race is always immanent in its disavowal, yet it also summarizes the legitimation of a new hierarchy of belonging, hiding in plain sight. 'The whole apparatus of race', as Peter Wade argues, 'has always been as much about culture as it has about nature, shifting between these two domains' (Wade, 2010: 45). Yet, as the considerable literature on so-called culturalist or 'new' racism indicates, this 'differentialist' racism involves a disavowal of race as tied to quasi-scientific categorization and phenotypical difference, while instead pressing cultural and religious signs into service as racial signifiers (Balibar and Wallerstein, 1991; Taguieff, 1989; Stolcke, 1995). A particular form of rationalist critique of religion furthers this; if religious faith is regarded as an intellectual commitment that can be rescinded, how can criticism of religion be racist when racism is of the body and of the past?

The SIOE slogan signals the centrality of post-racial certainty as an organizing principle of a new racial formation. However, it is important to recognize that this has always been a feature of the elucidation of modern racisms, and establishing this helps understand why it is articulated so emphatically in contemporary debates. In constructing an argument on 'The Postracial Horizon', Barnor Hesse proposes that the idea that racism has been substantively resolved is made possible only by a narrow understanding of racism 'as a concept with a particular history of emergence and a particular logic of indicting race' (Hesse, 2011: 157). Discussing the early European anti-racist writing of the interwar years, in particular Huxley and Haddon's (1935) *We Europeans*, Hesse notes that while the authors were concerned with the way in which the pseudo-biology of racism was polluting science with illiberal (Nazi) ideology (Hesse, 2011: 158), it nevertheless takes for granted the 'naturalization of the colonial or racially segregated world' (Hesse, 2011). That is, the colonial rule by Europeans of a majority of the world's population, through oppressive structures – and subjugating and exploitative arrangements – was understood as separate to the problem of racism.

What Hesse is claiming, therefore, is that far from being a new phenomenon, often associated with the twenty-first century and, more particularly, with the election of Barack Obama, racism has always been post-racial. The silence about race (Lentin, 2004) has always been written into racism. Furthermore, the post-racial was given voice in part by those who sought to undo racism. By foreclosing on the colonial as what must 'remain unspeakable' in relation to race (Hesse, 2011: 158), anti-racists such as Huxley, but more importantly, Western nation-states after the dismantling of fascist regimes in Europe and racial segregation in southern US states, repeatedly reproduced racial formations (Omi and Winant, 1994). This narrative of the progressive expunging of racism allowed for the contours of state anti-racism to be defined according to a view of racism that saw it as inherently pathological, and thus implicitly in contravention of Western values. Anti-racist discourses that problematized this by insisting on the racial nature of colonial rule and the persistence of colonial logics in postcolonial arrangements – especially in countries with large numbers of postcolonial immigrants, or in settler colonial societies – could thus be positioned as in opposition to this dominant mode of anti-racism. The French *politologue* Pierre-André Taguieff, for example, drew a line between anti-racism as a universalist cause, and the 'communitarian' third-worldism of Frantz Fanon and those who insisted on a critique of colonial arrangements and their enduring significance.

The postracial crisis of multiculturalism

The dominant association of post-racialism with the context of post-civil rights racial politics in the US contrasts with a general disregard for the concept in discussions of Europe. However, by adopting the approach established by Hesse, we can see that its fundamental dialogic importance to racism means that it has wider purchase. The European variant of post-racialism – echoed in Canada and Australia – is predominantly articulated through the notion that multiculturalism, imagined as a coherent if not totalizing social experiment, has been, as German Chancellor Angela Merkel put it in 2011, an 'utter failure'.

As we argued in *The Crises of Multiculturalism* (2011), the blanket denunciation of multiculturalism by political leaders and public commentators has become something of a political orthodoxy in the post-9/11 era. Contrary to these imagined projects of experimental failure, there is no history of coherent multicultural policy in any European country.

Multicultural policies rarely amounted to what Goldberg (2009) terms 'prescriptive multiculturalism' in any European context, but rather to a patchwork of initiatives that frequently depended on a reified, culturalist view of 'minority ethnic communities' – a view that still prevails in discourses of multicultural backlash.

Rather, as Stuart Hall has noted, multiculturalism is a 'maddeningly spongy and imprecise discursive field', and it is precisely this capaciousness that has allowed multiculturalism to become a central signifier of discontent and aversion in diverse, postcolonial migration societies. Multiculturalism, therefore, can be approached analytically as a mobilizing metaphor and discursive assemblage that facilitates and orders debate on questions of race, legitimacy, and belonging in societies that are now experienced through what Velayutham and Wise (2009) call 'everyday multiculturalism'.

The rhetoric of multicultural crisis is avowedly post-racial; it is predicated upon a silencing of the racial, and on a recognition that the official universal commitment to anti-racism involves no radical implications. Thus those who rally against an amorphous multiculturalism frequently do so in the name of 'anti-racism'. Ben Pitcher (2009) illustrates this when, in his analysis of the 2005 British general election campaign, he recalls the Conservative slogan 'Are You Thinking What We Are Thinking?' – the subtext beneath a large faux handwritten billboard that reads, 'It's not racist to impose limits on immigration.' As Pitcher argues, this argument can proceed only once its non-racist intention has been spelled out:

> The public disavowal of racism points to the success of what might be termed a language war over racial reference. As with the impact of feminism on public debate, any direct approach to the question of race must be channelled through a public discourse that explicitly signals the illegitimacy of racist beliefs and practices. (Pitcher, 2009)

The non-racism of much anti-multiculturalist discourse is achieved by reinforcing the separation made between race and culture. Reflecting the identification made in the 1980s and 1990s of a new, culturalist or differentialist racism (Barker, 1981; Taguieff, 1991; Stolcke, 1995), the contemporary emphasis on 'problematic' cultures is carefully predicated on a rejection of racism, where race is reduced to the pseudo-science of the differences of 'colour, hair and bone' (Du Bois, 1897). Thus, for example, Christopher Caldwell, in his widely publicized book *Reflections* on the Revolution In Europe: Can Europe Be the Same with Different People In It? (2009) is careful to deflect the charge of racism in relation to Spanish policies preferring immigration from Latin America, instead turning to religion as a natural basis for exclusion:

> [This policy is] not racist. Spain is less concerned that its immigrants be white than they have similarities of worldview with the people already established there, starting with knowing what the inside of a church looks like. (Caldwell, 2009: 52)

Of course, this simplistic divide between race and culture denies the fact that both biological and cultural reasons – and most often a combination – have always served as justifications for racist dispossession (Young, 2005). Whether a person is attacked on the grounds of biology or culture may be largely irrelevant to the experience of 'discrimination and insult' (Du Bois, 1940). However, as Hesse explains, because race had become so intertwined with a notion of racism shaped by associations with European Nazism and the North American colour line, this division can be readily sustained. In fact, the wholesale opposition of race to culture was already in place, allowing recent backlashes to multiculturalism to be mapped onto it, thus lending weight to their non-racism.

The 'crisis of multiculturalism' is post-racial, therefore, in that, while publicly denouncing racism, it proceeds to rehearse the dynamics of race as a technology of power and hierarchy. The assault on multiculturalism frequently depends on fixing problematic populations as culturally immutable and determined, a fixity which functionally reproduces the absoluteness of racial categorization while holding out the promise of integration, if only they (could) change. Yet, it is this putative refusal to change that informs a related dimension of the post-racial – the frequent invocation of 'reverse racism' that accompanies much of this discourse. In this sense, the opposition to a strategically inflated multiculturalism mirrors right-of-centre US post-racialism more directly. The texture of this 'racism' is particularly revealing if juxtaposed with Hesse's argument about the foundational silence about race. If racism, as Hesse argues, was a European discussion of a European problem, and one which progressed in denial of the colonial context in which it was nevertheless being theorized, it is unsurprising that 'anti-white racism' has emerged as a non-ironic term today. In the context of the failure of experimental and excessively generous multicultural experiments, racism can be held to 'cut both ways' and directed by non-whites at those hosts who strove to accommodate them. In some contexts, France, in particular, this 'reverse racism' has been given the unequivocal name of 'anti-white racism'. The French conservative, Jean-François Copé, who triggered a debate on 'anti-white racism' in France during his campaign for the leadership of Nicolas Sarkozy's UMP party in 2012, writes,

> I know I am breaking a taboo by using the term 'anti-white racism' but I do it on purpose, because it is the truth being experienced by some of our fellow citizens and remaining silent only serves to aggravate their trauma. (Copé, 2012)[1]

The 'trauma' elucidated by Copé includes being called 'Gaullois' by those *banlieusards* who now oppose white people for simply having 'a different religion, a different skin colour, or a different ethnic origin' (Copé, 2012). Copé's rhetorical commitments to the need for greater 'diversity' in media and politics – the official anti-racist position – can without a problem sit alongside his proclamation of anti-white racism. Post-racial anti-multiculturalism is, therefore, constructed through a presentation of racism as universal – something unfortunately experienced by everyone, depending on circumstance. In a suburb where there is a large presence of North Africans, for example, it is to be expected, following Copé's logic, that whites will be the victims of racist trauma. Thus anti-racism can be extended to include those who would defend an embattled white majority from attack by those still constituted as immigrants. In an aligned example, Arun Kundnani's study of the English Defence League, (EDL) shows that their defence of a 'way of life' against Muslim 'extremism' allows them to position themselves as post-racial freedom fighters – even appropriating the anti-racist slogan 'Black and White, Unite and Fight' (Kundnani, 2012).

These reconfigurations of the terrain of racism, always intrinsic and necessary for racial formation, are politically dissociated from the civilizational oppositions constructed between secularism and minority religious identities. Yet, the purported 'crisis of multiculturalism' centres Islam and the presence of Muslims as definitive of the problem for Europe. The presence of Islam in Europe recalls the failure of colonialism to completely conquer racial, cultural, or religious difference. The disciplinary appeal to the purported universality of the secular follows a similar logic to racism's quest to construct an ideal of universal man (*sic*) as a standard against which to assess all non-moderns (Balibar, 1994). Yet, the foundational *postness* of race obscures this from view, thus cleansing Islamophobia of the taint of racism.

Fixing the fixed notion: spectacles of secular insistence

For this reason, we contend that a fixed notion of the secular is bound up in processes of racialization; it fixes the modern secular individual as against backwards religious people and collectivities. If racism, as Les Back argues, is a 'scavenger ideology', the alacrity with which anti-Muslim networks have appropriated the defence of the secular on the post-multicultural ideological terrain is hardly surprising. In a survey of the transnational anti-Muslim ideoscape, Liz Fekete (2012) describes an overlapping series of conspiracy theories, from 'Internet-focused counter-jihadist activists at one end and neoconservative and cultural conservative columnists, commentators and politicians at the other' (Fekete, 2012: 30). While broadly unified by visions of creeping Islamification facilitated by the elite weakness of relativist multiculturalism, Fekete notes that a key point of differentiation is between those who disseminate deliberate conspiracy theories, and those who locate the irruption of Muslim excess in the naïve elitism and political paralysis of the 'liberal left'. Understood not only as a religion but also as a totalitarian political and cultural system, any fragment of evidence of Islamic backwardness is given up as further proof of the global nature of this totalizing drive and integral threat.

Sharing Geert Wilders's conviction that Islam is a 'cult', Muslims are constructed as theological automatons. Thus, over and above association with terrorism, their very presence is held to signify a 'new stage in an old war'; any cultural manifestation of presence, from minarets to headscarves, can be cast as evidence of ideological, cultural, religious, and even demographic conflict. The implacable differentialism of 'new racism' (Barker, 1981) is here extended through an idealist focus on the problem of religion. The subject can theoretically repudiate religion. However, as Fekete points out, 'those who see an Islamic conspiracy...suggest that Muslims who do not signal their Muslimness...are merely posing as modern, progressive and westernized. They are in fact camouflaged, and this makes them the more dangerous' (Fekete, 2012: 35). Echoing the anti-Semitic fear of the assimilated Jew (Arendt, 1966), it illustrates how 'racial historicism' shades into and depends on the 'naturalist racism' it strategically denies – 'cultural difference', in this frame, is so set and irremediable as to make no meaningful difference (see Goldberg, 1993).

Freedom of speech, gender equality, and sexual freedom provide a transparently strategic vocabulary for marking out the irreducible problem of the Muslim in Europe, and this marking out posits a civilizational hierarchy that has no need to appeal to pathologized racism. While the appropriation of these discourses by conventionally anti-immigrant and right-wing groups is widely recognized, what has been termed 'muscular liberalism' has staked out its claims on the same post-multicultural terrain that, we argue, is generative of racism, postrace. Adam Tebble (2006) has traced a shift towards what he terms 'identity liberalism', defined in explicit opposition to relativist multiculturalism, and advocating national cultures of shared values, compulsory forms of immigrant assimilation, and a duty of the state to protect liberal culture, up to and including the exclusion of non-liberal forms of life in defence of democracy.

Identity liberalism's claim to distinctiveness is not based on a singular national ethnos threatened by incompatible cultures but instead on a vision of the defence of liberal principles and ways of life – the national identity of liberal polities – against illiberal forces, and against the threat of regressive cultures to both the liberal polity and the individual rights of minorities. Thus, for identity liberals, 'multiculturalism as a response to diversity does not represent the equalization of cultural expression but rather the death of the very culture that permitted multiculturalism in the first place' (Tebble, 2006: 481). Identity liberalism depends on the reductive culturalism discussed earlier, for as Anne Philips notes, '...in the debates around multiculturalism, to allow for the *relevance* of culture without making culture a *determinant* of action' is held to lapse into a hapless relativism (Philips, 2007: 130–131; italics in original). This clarifies how identity liberalism is not an ontological rejection of multiculturalism, but a re-composition of its foundational assumptions – the problem is not culture but cultural excess of the wrong kind. Tebble's formulation is persuasive as it captures the rise of a liberal *identity politics* but one based on a narrative of past failures: identity politics is something *they* do, and that was indulged to dangerous excess. These illiberal others are racialized not, as with right-wing Islamophobia, on the basis of the insurmountability of cultural difference but because of their perceived refusal to surmount it. Race, Angela Mitropolous argues, now 'marks the boundary of that which is considered not to be amenable to will; that which lies beyond or without will, that which is deemed to be neither responsive to liberalism's "good will" nor capable of assuming its inclination' (Mitropolous, 2008: 1). Identity liberalism, then, provides a transnationalist modality that inscribes 'already achieved' freedoms as the core values of the enlightened nation, and Europe, and the secular, as a space of freedom achieved, cannot be beholden to bad will. It is here that the refrain that 'religion can never mean race' is at its most potent. To insist, in this political conjuncture, on religious, and specifically Muslim, presence in secular space is to reject liberalism's 'good will', which can only be done in 'bad faith', or on account of the 'deficiency' noted by John Durham Peters (2009). Jeff Sparrow makes a similar point in analysing the 'weaponization' of the so-called New Atheism post-9/11:

> If religion is an intellectual doctrine and nothing more than that, the persistence with which so many cling to God faith becomes explicable only in terms of their congenital inability to reason. Or to put it another way, if religion is purely and simply a fairy tale, then ipso facto those who cling to it are little better than children. (Sparrow, 2012)

European postracialism is primarily articulated not through a rejection of cultural difference but of cultural excess. It is announced through an embrace of diversity, where diversity is understood as that which racism rejects. But where there is diversity – tolerated, accepted and celebrated – there is also that which is *not* diversity, or bad diversity. The terrain of racism under neoliberal and securitarian logics foregrounds the subject who is autonomous and non-conflictual, who constitutes good diversity to be cultivated. However 'bad diversity', like the headscarf, for example – the expression of the problem of wrong freedom or bad choice – has come to embody the opposition to identitarian liberalism. This 'piece of cloth' is emblematic of the risky, excessive communitarianism of the failed, multiculturalist past. Naming, managing, and disciplining 'bad diversity' is thus central to the postracial articulation of the common, transcendent values that mark 'us' out as different.

Where diversity is acknowledged as a good, current 'race relations' paradigms aim to govern that which is surplus, seeking 'to avoid postracial disorder by managing the impact of "dangerous ethnic emotions"' (Kyriakides and Torres, 2012). In the spectacle of secular insistence, any reaction to provocation which does not replicate the idealized rational restraint invoked by Meredith Tax (2012) risks being cast as evidence of precisely this kind of dangerous ethnic emotion, bad diversity, unamenable to good will, out of place in the public sphere. As this brief summary of political trajectories suggests, the racialization of Muslims in and through the fixity of the secular is predicated on disciplining the excess and the surplus, that which refuses the new 'integration line' of the post-multicultural moment. Identifying these ideological formations does not in and of itself explain their public formation. It is here that a consideration of spectacles of secular insistence is useful, as they seek to animate the problem of bad diversity in a transnational media space by inviting active audiences to rehearse principled, postracial exclusions. The general intent of the circulation of *Innocence of Muslims* (*IoM*) was to provoke violent reactions to blasphemous provocation, but also to stir echoes, to reprise antecedent events that foregrounded the Muslim problem through recursive debates on freedom of speech, the scope of the secular, and in defence of the modern.

According to Cindy Lee Garcia, a Californian actress who played a *IoM* character who gives her daughter in marriage, 'Sam Bacile' wanted her daughter to look as if she was seven years old, rather than ten, to heighten the outrage when 'Master George' had sex with her. This refinement was apparently rejected on the film set, but 'Is your Muhammad a child molester?' is the altered line that Garcia's character eventually utters. The discourse of child molestation focuses on Aisha, the third, and youngest, of Muhammad's wives, and has become a staple dimension of right-wing provocation. As the case of Lars Hedegaard of the Danish Free Press Society – who been prosecuted in Denmark for drawing on this trope to assert that 'Girls in Muslim families are raped by their uncles, their cousins or their fathers' – indicates, this fixation seeks to further suture gender politics to Islamophobic justification, but not only. The accusation of paedophilia seeks to posit a taboo that must be broken, and thus broken, must be defended in principle as a question of free speech and as an instructive, secular assault on the charge of blasphemy.

The template for spectacles of insistence such as that created by the diffusion of *IoM* is the global currency of the *Jyllands-Posten* cartoon 'crisis' of 2005–2006. Given the polysemy of the cartoon form, and the decontextualization and reframing of the cartoons in bewildering syntagmatic chains across time and space (see Klausen, 2009), no dominant framework can be applied to their knotted interpretations. However, as Peter Hervik argues, the 'collective memory' of the affair in Denmark is as an assault on the Danish expression of the core Western value of free expression, rather than as an event generated as an explicit contribution to 'culture war' in an intensely nationalist context, globalized by the actions of both Danish imams and the ideologues associated with the paper:

> The debate in Danish news is marred by the repeated assertion that 'freedom of speech is a Danish freedom' and foreign events such as demonstrations...are not examples of freedom of expression. The

moral anger of some Danes is tremendous when it comes to the foreign reactions, but when it comes to the cartoon publications, the right to publish is the first thing evoked. Hence the debate suggests that the free speech response is not much more than a reflection of the powerful, hegemonic dichotomization of a positive 'us' and a negative 'them' in Danish society. (Hervik, 2009: 70)

Similarly, Ferruh Yilmaz illustrates how the 'timeless ontological categories' of Muslims and the West were naturalized through the globalized recursive focus on freedom of speech and the question of blasphemy and the normative demand that journalists adopt some form of principled position on the scope of free expression. Reproducing these timeless categories, Yilmaz argues, effects a 'hegemonic displacement' by eliding the political conditions in Denmark and by collapsing the dynamic globalization of an event into the static civilizational terms preferred by its protagonists:

> To bring back politics to the center of the discourse, we need to ask much simpler questions: who initiates these crises around Muslims and Islam? What are their politics, and what are the socio-political implications of these crises? A discussion of such questions will reveal that there are certain political and ideological sources that push certain issues onto the agenda and force us to be drawn into principled discussions about those issues rather than the politics of the debate. (Yilmaz, 2011)

The productive potential of this abstraction explains why the cartoons remain such a potent signifier, from their hypertextual rehearsal in *Fitna*, Geert Wilders's freedom-of-speech roadshow, to the framing of the prohibition of campaign posters in Lausanne during the minaret construction referendum in Switzerland in 2009 as the latest instalment in multiculturalism's betrayal of secularism and free expression (see Titley, 2012: 52–53). Research on the conduct of 'integration debates' in different Western European sites points to how international events frame domestic discussions, particularly 'terrorist events abroad and fears that "imported" Islamic fundamentalist and "illiberal, intolerant" movements will take root in "modern western" Europe, increasingly frame the domestic news in reporting of issues related to the Muslim community' (Fekete, 2009: 23).

Spectacles of insistence go to work because the networked and instantaneous dynamics of mediation draw on heavily culturalized images and indexicalities, translating headline issues from context to context. This ensures that disparate Muslim populations must always negotiate the public positioning of their 'community' in relation to evidence of the Muslim 'issue' or 'problem' from elsewhere. Yasmin Ibrahim (2007) has argued that the post-9/11 period has involved the production of a 'referential archive' of associations and images that '...creates an intertextuality which constantly weaves events as new memories crafting a new temporality to gauge and locate Islam' (Ibrahim, 2007: 49), a process she terms *disorientalism*:

> Since 9/11 the narrative of Islam has put the focus on Muslim communities in the West. Unlike the Islamic revolution in Iran in the late 1970s and 1980s, this 'reimagining' of Islam, narrated as posing a clear and present danger to civilisation, has placed Muslim communities in the West under relentless scrutiny. The Muslim intellectual debates and responses emanating from the communities are often seen as being externalized from the conditions of modernity or its incumbent reflexivity. The constant need to respond to events associated with Islam renders immense pressure on these communities to negotiate the sustained moral and social stigmatization in narrating Islam. (Ibrahim, 2007: 48)

In other words, they are asked to become and to perform as referents for the 'timeless ontological categories' of Muslims and the West, in the West, ensuring that the second-order question of their reactions, and their deficiencies, remains at the heart of principled debates about 'our' guiding values.

Conclusion

In his essay on the 'weaponization' of atheism, Jeff Sparrow notes that 'Anti-Muslim writers commonly declare that Islam needs its own reformation. But that's a charge that should really be levelled at atheism' (Sparrow, 2012). Regardless of the specific charge, Sparrow is correct that a movement that has settled into 'a crude nineteenth-century positivism' requires a resurgence of political antagonism, opening a critical space capable of untangling 'new' atheism's investments in and affinities with neo-imperial rationality. In this chapter, we are arguing for a similar disruption of the terms of the opposition between progressive secularism and backward religiosity by insisting on the racializing dividend of this opposition in contemporary European societies, a dividend deepened and extended by the postracial certainty upon which the disavowal of multiculturalism, as the central axis of raceless racism, relies.

The centrality of race to modern political formations is scarcely acknowledged, and race is broadly neglected in discussions of secularism and modernity (see Taylor, 2007). This neglect must be addressed if, as we have argued, hollowing out the 'race' in racism requires its replacement with other malleable domains of differentiation and hierarchy, with religion being primary. Just as there is nothing novel, bar updated referents, about culturalist attitudes to problematic difference, so, too, the framing of particular world views, practices, and identities as incompatible with Western ideas and ideals is foundational to raciological thinking. The 'scavenger-like' adaptability of racism is neglected in analyses that decentre race as analytically critical to understanding how debates on the boundaries of the secular play out politically in contemporary Europe. The significance of understanding this is underlined in a recent article by the spokesperson of the French decolonial organization, the *Mouvement des indigènes de la République*, Houria Bouteldja. She reflects on her involvement in a debate on gay marriage during a television chat show:

> I will tell you straight up, this debate doesn't concern me. It doesn't concern me because my words are particular and they are situated. A certain number of positions are expressed on this set and in France when this issue is discussed: you're either on the right or on the left, progressive or reactionary. I don't fit within that frame at all. I am outside of all of that because my words are situated somewhere else politically. I am situated in the history of postcolonial immigration and in the working-class neighbourhoods.

Bouteldja's point is assuredly not – as the Islamophobic frame would assume – that those of immigrant backgrounds, many of them Muslim, are neither homosexual themselves or favourable to gay equality. Rather, it is 'not a priority issue' for her as a political spokesperson because 'people are dealing with things that are more important and urgent', yet the condition of her entry to mainstream debate is to occupy preordained roles as a Muslim. But furthermore, she claims that a decolonial position cannot advocate for a universalist framing of the struggle for gay rights because to do so would erase both the complicity of that struggle with racializing and neocolonialist politics today (see Long, 2007), and the role played by colonialism in erasing 'the history of sexual practices in Islamic lands, including homo-eroticism'. The homophobia existent in France's 'immigrant neighbourhoods' is not a function of Islam but a result of the fact that 'imperialism in all its forms turns the indigène into a savage.' For Bouteldja, individual acts of homophobic aggression should neither be excused nor denied, but like Yilmaz, she is arguing against the constant displacement onto headline civilizational terms, the recursive move that evacuates the situated and the political. That is, it is fruitless to attempt to explain contemporary social conflicts over gender and sexuality, or indeed class, labour, or political representation, as if they were wholly unconnected to the history of how what Hesse terms 'raceocracy' has served to create not only material but ideational hierarchies that continue to divide (Burtenshaw, 2013). If the 'postsecular' has been reduced to the 'Muslim issue', securing a wider terrain for considerations of postsecular life and subjectivities requires not just calling for a more open and inclusive public terrain but understanding the work of racialization in effecting and extending this stubborn reduction. As a contribution to this, we argue not only for a focus on the postracial, but also for taking seriously those events and spectacles that invite postsecular publics to take principled positions in relation to an abstract 'secular', projected and territorialized as an exclusive property of European public space.

Note

1. See Copé (2012); translation authors' own.

References

Abdul-Ahad, G. (2012). 'Anti-Western Violence Gripping the Arab World Has Little to Do with a Film.' *The Guardian*, 14 September.
Arendt, H. (1966). *The Origins of Totalitarianism*. New York: Harcourt Brace.
Arun Kundnani (2012). Twenty-first Century Crusaders, *Critical Muslim* (3), June 2012. http://criticalmuslim.com/issues/03
Back, L. (2006). 'The Problem of the Immigration Line: State Racism and Bare Life.' In A. Lentin and R. Lentin (eds) *Race and State*. Newcastle: Cambridge Scholars Press.
Balibar, E. and Wallerstein, I. (1991). *Race, Nation, Class: Ambiguous Identities*. London: Verso.
Barker, M. (1981). *The New Racism: Conservatives and the Ideology of the Tribe*. London: Junction Books.
Bolt, N. (2012). *The Violent Image: Insurgent Propaganda and the New Revolutionaries*. London: Hurst & Co.
Bowen, J. (2011). 'Europeans against Multiculturalism.' *The Boston Review*. July/August.
Bradshaw, P. (2012). 'A Dark Demonstration of the Power of Film.' *The Guardian*, film blog retrieved from http://www.guardian.co.uk/film/filmblog/2012/sep/17/innocence of-muslims demonstration-film [last accessed 10 February 2013].
Braidotti, R. (2008). 'In Spite of the Times: The Postsecular Turn in Feminism.' *Theory Culture & Society* 25(6), 1–24.
Burtenshaw, Ronán (2012). An Interview With Dr Barnor Hesse – Part 1. In: *Irish Left Review*, 24.10.2012. http://www.irishleftreview.org/2012/10/24/raceocracy/.
Carr, M. (2006). 'You Are Now Entering Eurabia.' *Race & Class* 48(1), 1–22.

Caldwell, C. (2009). *Reflections on the Revolution in Europe: Can Europe be the Same with Different People in It?* London: Doubleday.
Copé, J.-F. (2012). 'Copé dénonce l'existence d'un "racisme anti-Blanc".' *Le Figaro*, 26 September 2012. Retrieved from http://www.lefigaro.fr/politique/2012/09/26/01002-20120926ARTFIG00428-cope-denonce-l-existence-d-un-racisme-anti-blanc.php [last accessed 10 August 2014].
Dowling, S. (2012). 'Far-right German Group Plans to Show Anti-Islamic Film.' *The Guardian.* 16 September.
Durham Peters, J. (2005). *Courting the Abyss: Free Speech and the Liberal Tradition.* Chicago, IL: University of Chicago Press.
Du Bois, W. E. Burghardt (1897). *The Conservation of Races.* The American Negro Academy Occasional Papers, No.2. Washington, D.C.: Published by the Academy, p. 75.
Du Bois, W. E. Burghardt (1940). 'The Concept of Race', in *Dusk of Dawn*, p. 59.
Etienne Balibar (1994). *Masses, Classes, Ideas: Studies on Politics and Philosophy Before and After Marx.* New York: Routledge.
Fekete, L. (2009). *A Suitable Enemy: Racism, Migration and Islamophobia in Europe.* London: Pluto Press.
Fekete, L. (2012). 'The Muslim Conspiracy Theory and the Oslo Massacre.' *Race & Class* 53(30), 30–47.
Fleras, A. (2009). *The Politics of Multiculturalism.* Basingstoke, UK: Palgrave Macmillan.
Gilroy, Paul (2002). *Against Race: Imagining Political Culture Beyond the Colour Line.* Harvard University Press.
Goldberg, D.T. (1993). *Racist Culture: Philosophy and the Politics of Meaning.* Wiley-Blackwell.
Goldberg, D.T. (2009). *The Threat of Race: Reflections on Racial Neoliberalism.* Oxford: Wiley Blackwell.
Grillo, R. (2007). 'An Excess of Alterity? Debating Difference in a Multicultural Society.' *Ethnic and Racial Studies* 30(6), 979–998.
Guild, E., Groenendijk, K. and Carrera, S. (eds) (2009). *Illiberal States: Immigration, Citizenship and Integration in the EU.* Farnham, UK: Ashgate.
Hervik, P. (2009). 'Original Spin and its Side Effects: Freedom of Speech As Danish News Management', in A. Philips, R. Kunelius, and E. Eide (eds).
Hesse, B. (2011). 'Self-fulfilling Prophecy: The Post-Racial Horizon.' *South Atlantic Quarterly*, Winter 110(1), 155–178.
Hewitt, R. (2012). 'Multiculturalism.' *Acta Sociologica* 55(3), 289–293.
Ibrahim, Y. (2007). '9/11 as a New Temporal Base for Islam: The Narrative and Temporal Framing for Islam in Crisis.' *Contemporary Islam* 1(1), 37–51.
Isin, E.F. (2004). 'The Neurotic Citizen.' *Citizenship Studies* 8(3), 217–235.
Jakobsen, J.R. and Pellegrini, A. (2008). 'Times Like These.' In J.R. Jakobsen and A. Pellegrini (eds) *Secularisms.* Durham, NC: Duke University Press.
Khazan, Olga (2014). ' Charlie Hebdo cartoons spark debate over free speech and Islamophobia.' *The Washington Post*, 9/19/2012 http://www.washingtonpost.com/blogs/worldviews/post/charlie-hebdo-cartoons-spark-debate-over-free-speech-and-islamophobia/2012/09/19/4b3ba988-026b-11e2-9b24-ff730c7f6312_blog.html (last accessed 17 August 2014)
Klausen, J. (2009). *The Cartoons that Shook the World.* Yale University Press.
Kyriakides, C. and Torres, R.D. (2012). *Race Defaced: Paradigms of Pessimism, Politics of Possibility.* Stanford, CA: Stanford University Press.

Lentin, A. (2004). *Racism & Anti-Racism in Europe*. London: Pluto Press.
Lentin, A. and Titley, G. (2011). *The Crises of Multiculturalism: Racism in a Neoliberal Age*. London: Zed Books.
Lovink, G. (2011). *Networks Without a Cause*. Cambridge: Polity.
MacKinnon, R. and Zuckerman, E. (2012). 'Don't Feed the Trolls.' *Index on Censorship* 41(4), 14–22.
Mitropoulos, A. (2008). 'The Materialisation of Race in Multi-Culture.' *Darkmatter*. Retrieved from www.darkmatter101.org/site [last accessed 2 February 2013].
Omi, M. and Winant, H. (1994). *Racial Formation in the United States*. London: Routledge.
Peters, John Durham (2009). 'Afterword: In Quest of Even Better Heresies.' in A. Philips, R. Kunelius, and E. Eide (eds) *Transnational Media Events: The Mohammed Cartoons and the Imagined Clash of Civilizations*. Gothenburg: Nordicom.
Phillips, A. (2007). *Multiculturalism without Culture*. Princeton University Press.
Phillips, A. and Saharso, S. (2008). 'The Rights of Women and the Crisis of Multiculturalism.' *Ethnicities* 8(3), 2–12.
Pitcher, B. (2009). *The Politics of Multiculturalism: Race and Racism in Contemporary Britain*. Palgrave Macmillan.
Scott Long (2009). 'Unbearable Witness: How Western Activists (mis)recognize Sexuality in Iran.' *Contemporary Politics* 15(1), 119–136.
Seymour, R. (2012). '2083: Breivik's 21st Century Fascist Manifesto.' In E. Humphrys, G. Rundle, and T. Tietze (eds) *On Utøya: Anders Breivik, Right Terror, Racism and Europe*. London: Elguta Press.
Sparrow, J. (2012). 'The weaponization of Atheism', *Counterpunch*, April 9. http://www.counterpunch.org/2012/04/09/the-weaponization-of-atheism/ (last accessed 17 August 2014)
Stolcke, V. (1995). 'Talking Culture: New Boundaries, New Rhetorics of Exclusion in Europe.' *Current Anthropology* 36(1), 1–24.
Taguieff, P. (1989). *La Force du Prejugé: Essai sur le Racisme et ses Doubles*. Paris: La Découverte.
Tax, M. (2012). 'The Politics of Provocation.' *Open Democracy*. 18 September, retrieved from http://www.opendemocracy.net/5050/meredith-tax/politics-of-provocation [last accessed 2 February 2013].
Taylor, C. (2007). *A Secular Age*. Boston: Harvard University Press.
Tebble, A.J. (2006). 'Exclusion for Democracy.' *Political Theory* 34(4), 463–489.
Titley, G. (2012). 'Exclusion through Openness? A Tentative Anatomy of the Ritual of Migration Debates.' CollEgium, *Journal of the Helsinki Collegium for Advanced Studies* 11.
Wade, P. (2010). 'The Presence and Absence of Race.' *Patterns of Prejudice* 44(1), 43–60.
Walton, S.J. (2012). 'Anti-feminism and Misogyny in Breivik's "Manifesto".' *NORA – Nordic Journal of Feminist and Gender Research* 20(1), 4–11.
Wise, A. and S. Velayutham (eds) (2009). *Everyday Multiculturalism*. Palgrave Macmillan.
Yilmaz, F. (2011). 'The Politics of the Danish Cartoons Affair: Hegemonic Intervention by the Extreme Right.' *Communication Studies* 62(1), 5–22.
Young, Robert (1995). *Colonial Desire. Hybridity in Theory, Culture, and Race*. London: Routledge.

8
Remediating Religion as Everyday Practice: Postsecularism, Postcolonialism, and Digital Culture

Koen Leurs and Sandra Ponzanesi

Introduction: postsecular and postcolonial engagements

This essay focuses on instances of religion in everyday online practices as expressed by migrant youth (i.e., Moroccan-Dutch youth in the Netherlands). We explore, in particular, how the engagement with digital practices, such as participation in social network sites like Hyves and Facebook and online discussion forums such as www.Marokko.nl, offer specific instances of the postsecular condition that deserve further scrutiny. The digital realm offers, in fact, medium-specific modalities for creating counter-publics – locations of appropriation and contestation of the dictums imposed by so-called secular society on migrant groups and their faiths and beliefs – but also an arena for alternative affective networks, through which religion is embedded and incorporated in everyday personal needs.

In order to do so, we take into account how the reawakened interest in the role of religion, or spirituality, in society at large has taken a radicalized turn after the events of 9/11, creating a racialization of religion (Balibar, 1991) which often leads to singling out Muslim groups as outside of the frame of modernity. In response to this, migrant groups construct strategies and tactics to react and subvert these wider phenomena from safe/intimate digital spaces. For this purpose, an exploration of the entanglement of the 'postsecular' with the 'postcolonial' is timely as the two terms share a prefix which contests both the secular and the colonial as common requisites for the condition of modernity.[1]

Despite this connection, postcolonial critique has been reluctant to engage with the recent postsecular turn, based possibly on Said's heritage of secular humanism, which has been hugely influential for postcolonial studies. In his introduction to *The World, the Text and the Critic*, Said explains his notion of 'Secular Criticism' (Said, 1983) as inherently linked to his notion of humanism. In the conclusion to the same book, within the chapter titled 'Religious Criticism', he positions the return of religion as a result of 'exhaustion, consolation, disappointment' among intellectuals (Said, 1983: 291). In his world view, Said does not take *per se* religion as his target, nor attempts to bypass religion as irrelevant within postcolonial societies. He rather calls for a challenge to fundamentalist dogmas in all societies and cultures. Criticism can be secular only if it takes nothing as sacred, and submits to no certainties. As Robbins writes, 'this credo reinstates in the vocabulary of the sacred and the secular what Said elsewhere put into a geographical figure: the sacred is being at home, the secular is being in exile' (Robbins, 2012,: 118–119).

Elaborating on Robbins's understanding of Said's secularism Aamir Mufti argues that Said most often opposes the term secular not to religion *per se* but to nationalism. Secular implies, for Said, a critique of nationalism that is enunciated not from an elite but from a minority position. As Mufti further writes, 'Said's use of the word *secular* is therefore catachrestic, in the sense that Spivak has given to the term – that is, it is a meaningful and productive *mis*use. It is an invitation to rethink, from within the postcolonial present, the narrative of progress that underlies the very notion of secularization' (Mufti, 1998: 107).[2]

Therefore, if we extrapolate from this, we intend the postsecular as another challenge to the legitimizing and normative narrative of Western modernity, one that contests the 'secularization myth' as a prerequisite for democracy and progress. Though these 'posts' (postsecular and postcolonial) can never be seen as interchangeable, they signal a deconstructive manoeuvre which contests fixed notions of political subjectivities and affective belonging.

Digital postsecularism

In this chapter we want to explore, therefore, the notion of postsecularism as one of the many disjunctions and differences in the global cultural economy which signal the need for a renewed understanding of the relation between migration, technology, and religious belonging. Appadurai explains how previous thoughts of separate centre-periphery models and push and pull (in terms of migration theory) do not correspond to the movements of cultural expression. For this we need to take into account diasporic movements and the new circulation of goods, people, media, ideas, and money in order to make sense of the tensions between cultural homogenization and cultural heterogenization, and how locations, identities, and imaginaries are constantly on the move (Appadurai, 1996).

Though the relation between religion and media (both old and new media) has received attention in recent studies (Couldry, 2003; Højsgaard and Warburg, 2005; Hoover, 1988, 2006; Mitchell and Marriage, 2003; Morgan, 2008; Nynäs, Lassander, and Utriainen, 2012; Stolow, 2010), the link to (new) media studies, and the way in which 'religion' manifests itself and is reconfigured online, has not been sufficiently elaborated upon, especially in the combination between theoretical and empirical approaches. In her recent *Digital Religion* (2012), Heidi Campbell argues, for example, that different religious communities negotiate complex relationships with new media technologies in light of their history and beliefs. This requires the further exploration of the nexus between postcolonial studies and new media studies, in order to address the racialization of religions as new forms of cultural and political exclusion along with emerging critiques of multi-layered digital inequalities (Huggan, 2010; Nayar, 2010; Nakamura and Chow-White, 2012; Gajjala, Yartey, and Birzescu, 2013). For this purpose the link between the postsecular debate, postcolonialism, and digital culture in Europe, and in particular the Netherlands, is explored, focusing on how religion, or religious practices, are lived, articulated, and performed online, responding to public debates as well as to intimate needs.

Europe, the geographical context of our study, can be understood as being coterminous with Christianity, its later project of secularization, up to the contemporary question of European Identity in relation to the EU expansion and consolidation. These questions culminate in anxieties regarding the integration of post-communist Eastern Europe, secular Turkey and its predominant Muslim populations, and also in particular the frictions with European Muslim youth, mostly descendants of guest workers from Morocco and Turkey (Baban and Keyman, 2008). In the contemporary European urban centres, the dividing lines between religion and the secular are increasingly blurred (Beaumont and Baker, 2011). In particular, the returning of postsecular frictions with Muslim populations are largely played out in the digital sphere, including the controversies surrounding Theo van Gogh's 2004 *Submission*, the Danish Muhammad cartoons in 2005, Geert Wilders's 2008 *Fitna*, and Nakoula Bassely Nakoula's 2012 *Innocence of Muslims*, and recent controversies across Europe over YouTube videos and Facebook pages supporting Islamic State (IS) violence in Iraq (Vis, Zoonen, and Mihelj, 2011). This chapter focuses on the discursive participation of young, urban, Muslim migrants in digital culture as this provides an uncharted entry point to explore the complex trajectories of European metropolitan postsecularism and postcolonialism (Salvatore, 2004). By examining digital practices of Moroccan-Dutch young people our aim is to investigate how the 'postsecular' is enacted and experienced from different positionalities and medium specificities. This chapter explores how issues of religion are surfacing and being negotiated online by Moroccan-Dutch migrant youth between 12 and 18 years old. In particular, we draw upon survey findings, qualitative in-depth interviews, and ethnography, and demonstrate how this data speaks back to new media, postcolonial, and postsecular thinking. We specifically approach digital practices from two analytic angles: the public sphere where collective counter-publics are created in order to respond to the racialization of religion in the public domain, and the individual realm through the creation of intimate and affective belongings that create identity networks.

The first angle concerns the online formation of safe collective spaces, or digital 'subaltern counterpublics' (Fraser, 1990: 67). Nancy Fraser developed this notion in extension of Jürgen Habermas's ideal-type of the 'bourgeois public sphere'. In Habermas's view, society resolved around a singular, all-embracing public sphere. Fraser rightly noted this conceptualization does not meet the demands to capture the reality of contemporary stratified societies. Rather, she recognizes that a multiplicity of competing publics provide arenas for subordinated groups. By circulating 'counter-discourses' these people can engage in 'discursive contestation' (Fraser, 1990: 62). Online discussion forums provide subordinated groups with particular counter-publics; away from the mainstream they can be seen as safe 'hush harbors' where hegemonies can be scrutinized and group cohesion can be fostered (Byrne, 2008: 17). In particular, we argue Moroccan-Dutch youth appropriate forum discussion pages as counter-publics through which they forge relations and establish their own shared space to counteract, subvert, or engage with dominant spheres of state-based secular culture, defiant public media reports, and parental versus peer expectations with its imposition of dictums and norms about proper religious behaviour.

The second angle is dedicated to the analysis of religion as being part of affective belongings and emotional networks. Digital everyday experiences illustrate the workings of affective belongings. The affective encounter of bodies with digital artifacts shifts attention from understanding processes of symbolic meaning making towards apprehending digital practices as sparking emotions, feelings, and experiences that matter to the individual user (Karatzogianni and Kuntsman, 2012). Online, religion is not something exceptional and visible only in the public sphere (where it gets attacked) but is also intimate, private, and personal, subject to multiple interpretations and tied to multiple other belongings. In particular, we unpack the postsecular notion of 'cool Islam' (Boubekeur, 2005; Gazzah, 2009; Meyer, 2011), which captures how religiosity is infused with youth culture. By combining Islam cultural signs with fashion, life styles, and music, religion is re-appropriated to counter stereotypes and negotiate multiple affective belongings that often steer away from either identity politics or the embracing of a delocalized brand of global youth. Migrant youth digital practices show how religion is a cultural and affective marker that is used both to affirm diversity while practising inclusion. It connects the intimate with the political through several forms of negotiations which are shown through forms of self-profiling. In particular, we take the practice of hyperlinking as an entry point to address the intersection between affectivity and digital media experiences that span local, national, and transnational contexts.

Postcolonial and postsecular readings of religious practices online allows to detect how the postsecular condition is not a new label, or particularly expresses the revival of religion and religiosity among Muslim migrant youth as distinctive form of identification, but a public and private everyday practice that is deeply embedded in digital affordances and networks (Lynch, 2010; Meyer, 2011).

Moroccan-Dutch youths in the Netherlands: society and academy

Moroccan-Dutch youths have become the primary locus of fear over ethnic and religious otherness in the Netherlands. Consisting of 355,883 people, those of Moroccan-Dutch descent make up some 2.1 per cent of the total Dutch population of 16.6 million. Of this group, 47 per cent migrated to the Netherlands from the 1960s onwards as guest workers, while the second and third generations, who were born in the Netherlands after their parents had migrated, amount to 53 per cent (CBS, 2011). The majority of guest workers who arrived in the Netherlands originate from the northern Morocco Rif area, where people mostly identify as Berber in contrast with French- and Arab-speakers in Morocco's urban areas (Gazzah, 2009: 403–404).

Moroccan-Dutch young people receive a lot of attention in media reporting, governmental policymaking, and scholarly research. They are systematically stigmatized and made hypervisible by right-wing journalists and politicians, who frame them as anti-citizens that pose a threat to secular Dutch society. Time and time again, politicians such as anti-Islamic Member of Parliament Geert Wilders and fellow members of his Freedom Party (PVV) argue that the Netherlands has to strongly respond strongly to the so-called 'Moroccan problem' it is facing. Simultaneously, parental expectations experienced by Moroccan-Dutch youth born in the Netherlands may differ from Dutch (youth) cultural expectations.

Gender is of central concern in these processes as boys and girls relate differently to both Dutch society and Islam. Their position about Islam also differs in the public debates in the Netherlands. The stereotypical positions, racisms, and expectations they face are not the same (Farris and Jong, 2013). While boys are dominantly framed in mainstream news media as criminals or Islamic extremists, they are believed to achieve greater autonomy from their parents during adolescence (Pels and Haan, 2003). Two prejudiced discourses can be recognized to discipline Muslim girls in the Netherlands: secular (neo)Orientalist representations of backwardness and oppression by Muslim men and conservative Islamist discourses that criticize Western women as sex objects (Piela, 2012). Thus, young Moroccan-Dutch people have to carve out a path between notions of European secularity and gendered Dutch stereotypes, but also sometimes stringent views of their parents and the wider (Islamic) community (Brouwer, 2006).

In studies on the Moroccan-Dutch community, the focus has predominantly been on juvenile delinquency, mental health problems, reliance on social security benefits, discrimination in the labour market, and early school leaving (i.e., Jong, 2007; Crul and Heering, 2008; Farris and Jong, 2013). In studies of Internet use and religion, the focus is also often on excesses such as Islamic radicalization (i.e., Stekelenburg, Oegema, and Klandermans, 2011). These issues are undeniably important, but focusing on them singles out a narrow slice of their experiences. Things are going well for the majority of Moroccan-Dutch youths, but their realities remain largely invisible in contemporary debates. This chapter aims to provide greater insight in everyday realities of Moroccan-Dutch youths by considering their digital negotiation with multiple publics, taking into account how postcolonial issues intersect with notions of postsecularim.

Methodological framework

The fieldwork was conducted in the context of Wired Up, a collaborative, international research project operating at the interface of the humanities and social sciences, aimed at understanding the multifarious implications of digital media use among young migrants. By combining large-scale questionnaires with in-depth interviews and virtual ethnographies, we join differently located and situated but complimentary perspectives.

From early spring to late fall 2010, a survey sample of 1408 secondary school students was established among seven schools in the Netherlands through a collective effort of data collection. This article principally considers data from 344 Moroccan-Dutch students – 181 girls and 163 boys – who participated in the questionnaire. On average they are 14.5 years old and, when prompted, 98.5 per cent describe themselves as Muslim. Three-quarters (76.2 per cent) of these young people speak Dutch at home with their parents, both in combination with a Berber language (66.9 per cent) and with Moroccan-Arabic (52.6 per cent).

From all survey participants, 30 Moroccan-Dutch young people aged 12–16 were invited to join the second phase of the study that consisted of face-to-face in-depth interviews. In order to include 17- and 18-year-olds, 13 Moroccan-Dutch youths were contacted using snowballing methods in three cities. In sum, in-depth interviews were carried out with a group of 43 Moroccan-Dutch individuals, 21 girls and 22 boys between 12 and 18 years old. Their average age was 15 years. Except for four informants who have migrated themselves at a young age, the majority of the interviewees were born in the Netherlands from parents who had migrated to the Netherlands as guest workers. Interviews took place in winter 2010 and spring 2011, but additional conversations for the present chapter were held during winter 2012.

In the third and final phase, digital media texts, images, and videos circulating in online message boards, instant messaging, social networking sites, and video-sharing platforms such as YouTube were gathered through virtual ethnography, a form of online participant-observation. The informants found these four Internet applications most important and spent most of their time there. The ethnography included continued correspondence with informants both face-to-face as well as mediated via Internet applications such as instant messenger and social networking sites such as Facebook and its Dutch counterpart Hyves (Leurs, 2012).

Case study 1: Message boards as subaltern counter-publics

> It is a sort of support. As a process of feeding [your emotions], by sort of reacting to each other. You'll have everyone who backs you up. It's like everyone is on the same side. You kind of become more sure of yourself. You just know, yes, look we are not the only ones who think this way and so on. Thus you can express your opinion and just put everything up and you hear that others are similar to you.
>
> – Ilham, 13 years old

The first case study explores how Internet applications are used by Moroccan-Dutch youth as safe arenas to form counter-publics and exert agency. During our interview, Ilham eloquently described the emotional support she receives from being able to secure speaking power on the online discussion forum Marokko.nl. Message boards, also known as Internet discussion forums, are digital spaces where users can engage in conversations by publicly posting messages in response to each other. Seizing the opportunity to speak for herself and hearing others appreciate her voice, Ilham self-consciously claims membership within a group of people of her choice. Virginie Mamadouh observed that online message boards seems to hold a specific appeal: 'young Dutch Moroccans are more likely to discuss and dispute Moroccan and Dutch traditions in the safe encounter of quasi-anonymous forums than in face-to-face contacts with relatives, peers or teachers' (Mamadouh, 2001: 271). This section elaborates how online discussion forums such as Marokko.nl can be used to construct 'subaltern counter-publics', which Nancy Fraser defined as 'parallel discursive arenas where members of subordinated social groups invent and circulate counter discourses to formulate oppositional interpretations of their identities, interests, and needs' (Fraser, 1990: 67). Online forums allow for the proliferation of new, oppositional, and/or alternative voices in the digital public domain, countering mainstream definitions of secularism and integration.

Although message boards are, in principle, publicly accessible to all Internet users, the informants perceive Marokko.nl as a welcoming space to publish and read alternative voices. The site, in their view, operates under the radar. For instance 14-year-old Senna states, 'I don't know, I think that half of the [Dutch] people does not even know that it exists'. Message boards' perceived hidden character, tucked away from the mainstream, has been acknowledged as a main reason minority groups become attracted to them. Dara Byrne describes message boards that 'fly well below the mainstream radar', frequented by minorities such as AsianAvenue.com, MiGente.com, and BlackPlanet.com with the postcolonial term 'hush harbors', a notion used to describe spaces in which slaves gathered away from supervision from their white masters (2008). As a space to negotiate unequal power relations, Vorris Nunley notes that historically 'African Americans have utilized camouflaged locations, hidden sites, and enclosed places as emancipatory cells where they can come in from the wilderness, untie their tongues, speak the unspoken, and sing their own songs to their own selves in their own communities' (Nunley, 2004: 223). In parallel, the hushedness of Internet forums, Byrne writes, is appreciated among ethnic minorities for developing 'group cohesion' and a shared sense of belonging. Because the right of access is based on foregrounding a shared ethnicity, dedicated discussion forums are 'relatively free of *mass* participation by ethnic outsiders' (Byrne, 2008: 17). More specifically, we focus in this section on how online forums are taken up among the informants as counter-publics to (re)articulate their positionality at the crossroads of gender, ethnicity, and religion. In our conversation, Ilham explained she receives emotional support to both negotiate the sometimes stringent religious expectations of her parents as well as the Dutch stereotypical representation of Moroccan-Dutch youth. The multiple roles online message boards play in the lives of these young people are explored: first attention is given to the ways in which generation-specific religious and gendered dictums are negotiated, while secondly the use of these forums to contest Dutch societal stereotypes is discussed. In this way, theoretical discussion on postsecularism is grounded in everyday practices and affinity networks.

Negotiating religious dictums

> I was born and raised here in the Netherlands. But my father emigrated to the Netherlands together with my grandfather when he was 18 years old. He has taken Moroccan customs to the Netherlands and he uses them here. I think the habits of my parents are just very old-fashioned, even though they do try to learn the customs of the Netherlands. My parents were raised much stricter in terms of religion. My parents do teach me many things about our belief, but most of the time I go on and look up things about Islam myself. This is different from what they did: listening to the stories of their parents and copying those.
>
> – Meryam, 15 years old

During our interview, 15-year-old Meryam spoke about *Handboek voor Moslimvrouwen* (*Handbook for Muslim Women*), a book that she had in her handbag. She shared that she liked to keep a book like that with her at all times: 'I read those, because it gives you a lot of rules and how you can do your best to become a good Muslim woman'. These books give her something to hold on to, offering guidance in making everyday decisions. For similar purposes, she turns to Marokko.nl to read about personal stories that people have shared. The book, she notes, was bought 'at the mosque and it gives you rules to abide by'. However, she says 'on the Internet, you can learn much more. In the mosque you have to listen to an imam who exposes you to topics you might not want to learn or that you know already'. While 'on Marokko.nl, I type "Islam" and many different pages appear. And I look at those'. Meryam described how she 'noses around' in discussions on Islam. The tension between Meryam being given meanings by authorities such as the imam and her parents and taking the opportunity to articulate personal religious interpretations herself lies at the heart of this section on the negotiation of religious dictums. Online, the specificity of Moroccan-Dutchness emerges as the informants publicly negotiate postsecular positionalities at the crossroads of age, gender, ethnicity, religion, generation, and youth culture.

Bibi (16 years old) said she feels at home on the forum because there, she says, she can experience 'that proper Moroccan atmosphere'. Such remarks resonate feelings among informants that message boards can be seen as a digital counterpart to the mosque. Another example is shared by Soufian (13 years old): 'I find it very important to go to the mosque, because there I feel I am among likeminded people', while on Marokko.nl users also congregate with like-minded peers. She continues, 'it is your own circle' and 'the people there are like you, that's nice'. Inas, a 13-year-old girl, explains that online 'you have the feeling you get nearer to each other, you feel connected'.

As a distinct invocation of a counter-public sphere our informants report to engage in religious meaning-making activities. Sixteen-year-old Ilana states that in the rubric 'Islam and me', 'many things about Islam are discussed, also the rules of Islam'. Sahar, a 14-year-old girl, also participates in the discussions in this rubric and adds that people exchange ideas 'about things you should and you should not do'. Negotiating sometimes-strict Muslim demands with Dutch liberal youth culture, informants told us that many young users discuss whether certain things are '*halal*' (allowed in Islam) or '*haram*' (forbidden in Islam). For example, as Ferran, a 14-year-old boy, says: 'whether you may have a boyfriend and so on'.

Moroccan-Dutch girls are sometimes seen as gatekeepers 'to maintaining the family honour', and Pels and De Haan recognize 'they still face the most restrictions, and they spend much of their leisure time with female family members and friends in domestic settings' (Pels and Haan, 2003: 52–61). Especially Moroccan-Dutch girls confess they feel less restricted on discussion forums and, because of that, dare to bring up personal experiences they struggle with and cannot share elsewhere. During the interviews, it became apparent that online discussion forums are considered a safe space to speak about gendered taboo issues that might transgress the limits of dominant community standards. Bibi (16 years old) reports that she turned to Marokko.nl to discuss issues of intercourse and sexuality in the context of marriage, stating she would rather turn to the online community instead of bringing it up with her parents:

> [Y]ou don't dare to go to your parents, because you find it really embarrassing. Yes, for example about sex or something, and marriage, and then they say, 'Yes' because with the Muslim faith when you have the first day you are not to oppose your husband and just do 'it'. And [with] these things I'm definitely not going to my parents 'Mom, dad, listen, is that the case'. Yes it is *hchouma* you know, I am shy to tell my parents about these things.

Having a space to discuss issues that are difficult to broach in conversations with parents is of the utmost importance. This enables Moroccan-Dutch girls to express themselves and discuss behaviour that is not possible in their usual social-cultural spheres. Not everyone appreciates bottom-up interpretations of what is *haram* or *halal*. Some see disadvantages in online performances of religion, as Nevra, a 16-year-old girl, critiques that 'you now see that people who are engaged with their faith, they actually make a personal version of their faith. They do things that they are not allowed to do, because many people do it [and share their actions online], they say, they can also do it'. Inas, a 13-year-old participant, also voiced her scepticism about online discussions on Islam: 'I do not try to find too many things about it'. She chooses to uphold her own conceptions about Islam: 'those are my own opinions. And no one should change them'. Nonetheless, these forum discussions remain popular.

In her study on online discussion forum use, Lenie Brouwer found that Moroccan-Dutch girls in their message board participation 'demonstrate counterviews towards the dominant western image of Muslim women as well as to their own communities' (Brouwer, 2006). The remarks informants made resonate her argument: participating in online forums, Moroccan-Dutch girls turn to message boards to engage with topics such as health, meeting new friends, intimacy, romantic relationships, and sexuality (Leurs, Midden, and Ponzanesi, 2012). Girls report to experience a greater sense of freedom to discuss the sometimes-stringent social-cultural codes of socialization of their parents and wider community. In this way, religious dictums from the community as well as expectations and requests from the hosting society about gender agency and freedom are appropriated and abrogated in specific personal ways. By doing so, normative ideas about emancipation as a secularizing process are deconstructed.

Countering stereotypes

Users appreciate discussion sites such as Marokko.nl because they can communicate with their own circle of people and share or hear alternative voices regarding Moroccan communities in the Netherlands. The existence of this religious-ethnic-minority communication platform to some extent reflects the need for this group to have a mediated voice and counter-public of their own. This corner of the Internet is often used to discuss and reframe dominant images circulating in news media. Thirteen-year-old Salima describes Dutch news media as follows: 'they speak about Moroccans very often. If it would be a Turk or someone else, then it is not immediately news or so, but when there are Moroccans involved, it is immediately like: all right, these are Moroccans, instantly on the news'. Ideally, national news media reflect the broad dynamics of a society, including the multicultural dimension of that society, however in the Netherlands, ethnic minorities feel as though coverage is skewed (D'Haenens et al., 2004: 69). Fourteen-year-old Senna remarks that, 'on Marokko.nl you also get news, news is discussed, it is more about Moroccan news and so on. That you do not find in *de Telegraaf* [a popular sensationalist Dutch newspaper]'. Sixteen-year-old Nevra finds 'there is often negative talk about Moroccan youths', while 'different stories' can be shared on Internet forums.

Interviewees especially emphasized the heated debates over controversial Dutch anti-Islamic Member of Parliament Geert Wilders on Marokko.nl. They have a sense that Wilders can say whatever he likes, while everything Moroccan-Dutch young people say is put under the microscope. On the forum, interviewees feel more secure and confident to speak out than they might feel elsewhere. In the words of Bibi (16 years old):

> The main topic mainly concerns Geert Wilders and so on. He of all people can say things about Muslims. While we for instance cannot talk about the Jews, because then we are the racists. About those things, we say 'Why is he allowed to do it,' and to be honest, everyone thinks he is a retard, a dog; we do not like him at all.

Fifteen-year-old Inzaf maintains that message boards such as Marokko.nl help Moroccan-Dutch youths to cope with negative positions ascribed. Site members share a number of ideas that also bond them together. They all refute the polarizing brought forth by Wilders and the PVV:

> We speak about various Moroccan things, but we agree about one thing. For instance about Geert Wilders, all of Marokko.nl agrees that he is no good, or that he lost his mind. On Hyves it would be different; everyone would have a different opinion. You have very few people who have a totally different opinion. Everyone would think something like, 'yeah if I see him on the streets, I will shoot him dead', and then you have few people who would say something like 'No why? He is not doing anything wrong?'

Marokko.nl is considered as a safe space of one's own where people agree upon a shared set of assumptions. Perpetuating the stereotypical frames of extremism, at first glance the statement by Inzaf demonstrates how forum contributors are complicit in perpetuating the othering of the Moroccan-Dutch community as a whole. However, the statement is only a polemic mimicry of extremism, as it is to be read in the context of cultural repertoires of street language and hip-hop youth culture. Her way of expressing her feelings about the debate in the Netherlands can therefore be interpreted as a 'diss', a strong carnivalesque polemic, instead of an actual death wish. For Mikhail Bakhtin, the carnivalesque refers to 'peculiar folk humor that always existed and has never merged with the official culture of the ruling classes' (Bakhtin, 1965: 474), which may include 'ridicule of officialdom, inversion of hierarchy, violations of decorum and proportion' (Brandist, 2001). The carnivalesque is a theatrical form of parody that can offer resistance to hegemonic forms. The controversial song 'Hirsi Ali Diss' by the Moroccan-Dutch rappers DHC from The Hague is another example of carnivalesque ridicule. In the song, Somalian-Dutch prominent Islam critic Hirsi Ali was similarly dismissed: 'We are busy preparing for your liquidation / Bomba action, against Hirsi Ali / That is my reaction for the unrest she is making / Talking on TV about *integration*' (lyrics to 'Hirsi Ali Dis', 2004). In this song, coarse language of the street, assertive dissing, and the demand for respect come together in a reaction on the Dutch debate on integration. Verbally threatening Hirsi Ali in the song is DHC's way of forming a response to being mistreated (Koning, 2005). In the global, linguistic flows of hip-hop youth culture, 'the-violence-as-verbal metaphor' is a significant example of a particular politics of language (Newman, 2009: 200).

Similarly, Inzaf's statement is a part of such a verbal duel expressed as a culmination of feelings of discrimination, injustice, and subordination. Inzaf shows how deep the feeling of being disrespected by anti-Islamic Dutch people runs among Moroccan-Dutch youths. Symptomatic of the social injustice inflicted on the Moroccan-Dutch community, they reveal a great deal about their perception of Dutch political and societal centres of power. As Soufian shared: 'I think that non-believers, not all of them, are very much discriminating in their thinking and talking about my belief, and that makes me very sad', adding 'we live in a multicultural society and I am of the opinion you should accept every human being as he or she is and treat his [or her] religion with respect'. However, maintaining contact and discussing intersecting matters of religiosity, gender, and ethnicity cannot be seen in isolation from other prominent digital activities such as publishing personal affective belongingness to various communities on social networking sites. The postsecular notion of disengagement with Eurocentric master narratives gets grounded and interwoven with multiple positionalities.

Islam and other affective belongingness

The second case concerns the personal, affective side of digital Muslim manifestations on profile pages. When prompted, 98.5 per cent of the Moroccan-Dutch youth who participated in our survey described themselves as Muslim. The question arises how they understand and circulate their Muslimness, especially in connection with other affective youth-cultural belongings. Affect is a translation from the Latin term *affectus* which can be understood as 'passion', 'emotion', and 'desire'. We consider the cultural politics of affectivity as theorized by Sarah Ahmed. She argued that emotions are doings that should not only be considered as mental states but also as 'social and cultural practices' (Ahmed, 2004: 9). Her focus is on how emotions arise from the contact of people with material objects. Affectivity may cement personal attachments to groups of people, things, or ideas. Exploring affectivity and digital practices, for example, Lena Karlsson noted that the affective pleasures of women's diary blog reading stem from their search for various forms of 'recognition' and shifting alliances of 'sameness' along the lines of gender, age, and race/ethnicity (Karlsson, 2007: 138). Below, we unravel how religion is digitally remediated, showing how the personal 'Islamic touch' revives religion by absorbing it in a cool youth-cultural endeavour that links the everyday needs of a growing multicultural youth generation.

'An Islamic touch'

Among Moroccan-Dutch young people, both online and offline, 'Islam is used to give music, fashion, food, style or cultural imagery in general an Islamic touch' (Gazzah, 2009: 413). Islamic street-wear and the presence of Muslim rappers allows for the performance of a contemporary urban-based 'cool Islam' (Boubekeur, 2005; Meyer, 2011). In this second case study, we propose how an 'Islamic touch', as digitally published, must be understood in its relationship with multiple networks of affective belongingness, including youth culture.

In our questionnaire, we asked respondents which subcultural affiliations they would include on their personal social networking profile page (see Figure 8.1). Roughly half of the respondents reports to publish affiliations with a Muslim subculture and one-fifth see themselves as urban and hip hop. Gender differences become apparent; girls affiliate themselves more with dance music and being trendy and fashionable while boys see themselves more as sporty. As described in the previous section, religious positions are negotiated on Internet forums. It can be noted that defining oneself by expressing 'I am Muslim' for many Moroccan-Dutch youths has become a more positive way to articulate one's individual identity as opposed to an ascribed ethnic identity such as 'you are allochthonous'[3] or 'you are a c**t-Moroccan'. However, next to hip hop, urban, and the like, Moroccan-Dutch young people chose to be 'Muslim online' (Buitelaar, 2008: 244–247).

During the interviews, informants expanded on religious elements they incorporated in their self-presentations. Underlining ethnic proudness and wearing the headscarf as an important identity marker, 13-year-old Inas describes her construction of a personal profile page as follows: 'it's like, I'm wearing a headscarf. When I post a photo of me wearing a headscarf, you can so to say see that I have an Islamic background. And with my name and so on'. Furthermore, interviewees report to highlight their attachment to Islam by including religious acclimations such as

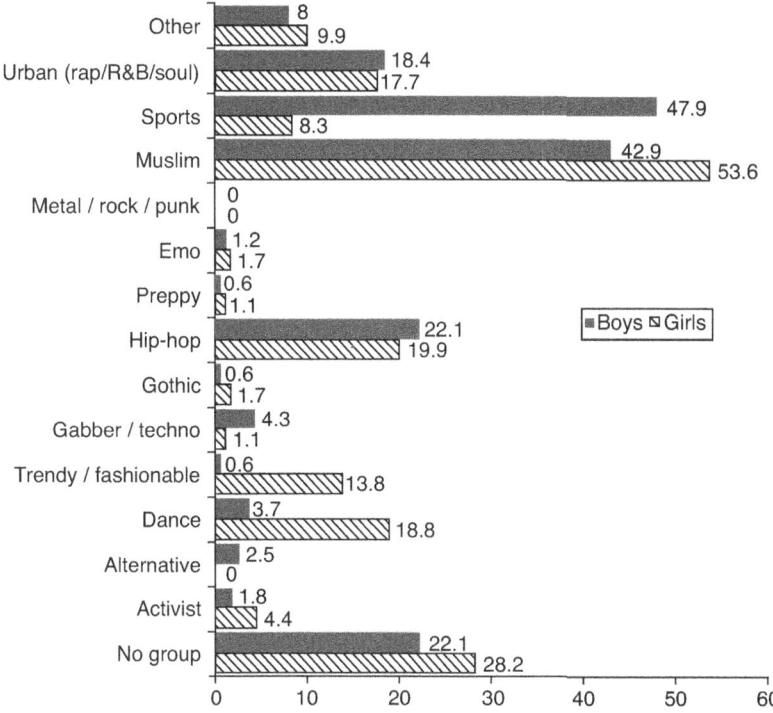

Figure 8.1 Subcultural youth group self-identifications among Moroccan-Dutch youths (percentages, multiple answers possible, n = 344)

'*Inshallah*' (God willing) in their nicknames or by showing they are a member of groups pertaining to Islam on their online profile page.

However, Safae (18 years old) reported that signalling Muslim affinities sometimes backfires: 'I have a girlfriend, and she wears a headscarf. On Hyves she got a message from someone stating "we live in 2010, a headscarf is outdated, it's something of the past". That was bad, you can't say that. I feel that is discrimination'. Such discriminatory practices were also, for instance, apparent in computer game culture. A fan of the game *Counter-Strike*, 15-year-old Oussema shared that he had bad experiences after he disclosed his ethnic and religious background to white Dutch players he encountered while playing the game: 'When saying I am Moroccan, I am a Muslim, I get called a terrorist'. Similarly, discussing YouTube videos pertaining to the country of Morocco, 16-year-old Naoul said: 'When you watch a video on YouTube, they shout "c**t-Moroccans" and this and that about Moroccans'. However, beyond such polarizing remarks that seek to categorize and essentialize Moroccan-Dutch youth identities, the following section demonstrates informants employ various tactics to express multiple belongingness. Signalling the cultural politics of global-local flows of people, technologies, and feelings, the affective encounter of bodies with media objects such as hyperlinks shifts attention from processes of meaning making towards apprehending them as experiences that matter (Karatzogianni and Kuntsman, 2012). Digital practices on their own do not determine feelings, but the affective relationship between groups of individuals with particular signs – such as a cool Islam – can make them matter as they 'weave' the virtual and the real (Gajjala, Yartey, and Birzescu, 2013: 50). The notion of the everyday as affective gets invoked, as religion is not something exceptional and visible only in the public sphere (where it gets attacked) but is also intimate, private, personal, and subject to multiple interpretations. How the online world captures this dynamic is of particular relevance for the younger generations located at the crossroads between traditional ideas of religious behaviour and more fluid, negotiable, transnationalized ideas of being a good Muslim/Muslima. Online, various sources can be found on how to do things properly, how to wear a *chador*, to pray, to read the Koran, and so forth. However the new spaces created online for religious subculture also hint at the tensions between expectations and choices, respect and self-determination, radicalized practices and fluid negotiations. The ambivalence and liboratory character of personal affective renderings of religion online can be traced by following hypertextual links. These are as Odin writes (cited in Landow, 2006) the ideal format to contest linear and authoritative narratives, applying through material practices the principle of postcolonialism and postsecularism.

Hypertextual selves

At the beginning of our interviews, informants were invited to reflect on their personal positioning. Thirteen-year-old Ilham for example described herself stating 'I am Moroccan, Berber and Muslim, but as you can see I hold the Dutch nationality'. Sixteen-year-old Amir states, 'I have my own personal style, and I don't belong to one group in particular, it is just multiculti, I feel'. In a similar vein, Oussema asserts: 'My religion is Islam, but it does not play a big role in my life. However, the projected image that [arises] when saying I have Islamic roots, does play a role. I like to surprise people by behaving in a way that does not [fit] with how they project my people'. We want to zoom in on hyperlinking practices to show how Moroccan-Dutch youth digitally destabilize narrow interpretations of Moroccan-Dutchness and Islam.

Social networking sites allow users to add hyperlinks to their personal profile pages, publish preferences, and participate in and affiliate with interest-based communities. Through the publishing of hyperlinks, informants render visible their distributed personal affective belongings. Jaishree Odin argued hyperlinking practices shape an aesthetic that can accommodate the multiplicity of postcolonial subjectivity: '[t]he perpetual negotiation of difference that the border subject engages in creates a new space that demands its own aesthetic'. Hypertext aesthetic, she proposes 'represents the need to switch from the linear, univocal, closed, authoritative aesthetic involving passive encounters characterizing the performance of the same to that of non-linear, multivocal, open, non-hierarchical aesthetic involving active encounters that are marked by repetition of the same with and in difference' (cited in Landow, 2006: 356–357). We would like to emphasize that hypertextual selves not only demonstrates a postcolonial aesthetic but also documents the workings of postsecular digital practices.

Upon joining a Hyves group, a small icon appears on a personal profile page. On her Hyves personal profile page, 13-year-old Midia hyperlinks to a variety of groups ranging from feminist interests ('Women in Charge') and Dutch nationalism ('I love Holland') to food cultures relating to both migration backgrounds ('Choumicha, the Moroccan and Turkish kitchen', 'Moroccan tea junky') as well as global junk food ('McDonald's'). She expresses belonging to religious interests ('Hijaab Style', 'Islam = Peace'), different clothing styles, from headscarves ('Respect is what I ask for the headscarf that I'm wearing') to Moroccan dresses ('Moroccan dresses 2009') and global fashion trends ('Skinny Jeans love' and the brand 'H&M'). Additionally, she joined the groups 'Moroccan Male Hotties' and 'Show you chose for Freedom – sign up for the Freedom-Hyves'. These different visual statements cover a wide spectrum of interests, belongings, and affiliations signalling distributed recognitions of 'sameness' (Karlsson, 2007). Taken together on a profile page, these different hyperlinks constitute an affective discursive space of intercultural encounter. In expressing a variety of affective belongings that Midia displays actively, she revalues her ethnic, religious, and gendered embeddings. This example shows the unexpected postsecular coalitions Moroccan-Dutch young people signal online rather than a straightforward continuation of migrant and religious cultures. They actively transform them in the context of the dominant youth cultures in which they grow up.

Conclusions

In this chapter, by addressing the articulation of religion through the use of digital media among urban, Muslim, Moroccan-Dutch, young people, links between postsecular debates, postcolonialism, and digital culture were established. Internet applications are one of the social stages where ethnic and religious minority youth struggle to stake out their individual identities by narrating themselves in various ways. Our analysis hopefully contributes to countering the implicit resurgent conservative reaction in the contemporary European and Dutch debates on the revival of religion, which tend to isolate Muslims as the locus of the return of religion as a challenge to democracy, secularism, and progress.

Contesting the association of religion with backwardness, or straight 'foreignness', Moroccan-Dutch youth appropriate Islam, through their digital practices, as a cool affective marker, not an essentialized category, removed from other markers of identity and belonging. Allowing like-minded youth to connect and inserting in the public sphere alternative configurations of believing, forum discussions are recognized in case study one for circulating self-presentations among like-minded peers. These under-the-radar processes are recognized to foster agency through democratization of belief systems and religious authority and resisting hegemonic renderings of Moroccan-Dutchness and Islam. Though religion figures as one of the dominant markers of identity formation it has become an affective everyday practice that is deeply embedded in digital affordances and networks. Case study two demonstrated religiosity is never articulated in isolation from other affective hyperlinked ties such as that of nationality, ethnicity, education, age, generation, class, and gender. The focus on affectivity is also useful to counteract prior utopian disembodied understandings of signification through digital practices.

Through the exploration of these connections it emerges that digital networks constitute a safe arena to unravel and display one's multiple networks of affective belongings. It constitutes also a safe space to practice piety and alternative forms of religious agency, not necessarily in conflict with the dictums of the host society which label religion, and Islam in particular, as blocking youth from integration and girls, in particular, from their path to emancipation. Countering these stereotypes and public pressures, forum discussions and hypertextual aesthetic indicate we should go beyond assessing the risk of isolation and radicalization of religious groups. It should not be forgotten, nonetheless, that the online world is not a separate sphere from the offline world, and that it often reproduces in more stark ways, and even reinforces, the dichotomy played out in society at large. However, as we have tried to show, youth migrant cultures in the Netherlands manage to create digital practices that both revive and revisit the notion of religion in everyday life, in playful and, at times, ironic ways. Hybridization, countering, carnivalesque, humour, parody, hyperlinking, and posting are some of the postcolonial and postsecular subversive strategies used that give an Islamic touch to everyday culture without resorting to violence or public defiance. At the same time, Islam or religion is re-appropriated and revisited from new perspectives. This makes the so-called revival of religion part of a cool endeavour that connect a more cosmopolitan public sphere with the everyday needs of a growing multicultural youth generation. This creates new forms of transnational ties and global branding along with new forms of religious affectivity and piety.

Notes

1. Postcolonialism has always been considered an offspring of postmodernism, though various critiques have focused on how the 'post' in postmodernism is not the same as in 'post' colonialism. In his famous essay 'Is the "Post" in "Postcolonial" the "Post" in "Postmodern"?' Appiah suggested, for example, that both 'posts' signal a spacing gesture through which the prefix remains inextricably connected to the root word ('modernism', 'colonialism') (Appiah, 1997: 428–429). Therefore, postcolonialism is bound to the legacy of colonialism it critiques and postmodernism to the modernism it continues. Obviously these relations are neither chronological nor teleological but are characterized by fracture and tense asymmetries. It is a 'post' that challenges master narratives and universalizing discourses, that aims at opening up the space for silenced histories and marginalized groups. Nonetheless, while the 'post' in postmodern emphasizes pluralism and multiplicities, the 'post' in postcolonialism wants to retain a certain humanism, or anticolonial humanism that can account for the suffering of colonial subjects while rejecting the master narratives of modernism (Appiah, 1997: 438).
2. This is in line with Huggan's argument in his 'Is the "post" in "Postsecular" the "post" in "Postcolonial",' who, paraphrasing Appiah on the relation of the 'posts' in postmodernism and postcolonialism, explains that postsecularism should be understood as a shift in the secularization paradigm which particularly applies to Western liberal democracies that 'are not postsecular at all but are rather caught in a continuing process of secularization, one symptom of which is the efflorescence of alternative spiritualities, and another the fundamentalist recoil against spiritual pluralism in the context of a consumer orientate late capitalist world' (Huggan, 2010: 753).

3. In the Netherlands, the term 'allochtoon' is widely used to refer to immigrants and their descendants. Officially the term 'allochtoon' is much more specific and refers to anyone who had at least one parent born outside the Netherlands. A further distinction is made between 'Western' and 'non-Western' 'allochtoon' people. The term is, however, often considered to refer to Moroccan, Surinamese, and Turkish immigrants to label specific immigrants groups. Therefore considered as stigmatizing, the city council of Amsterdam decided to stop using the term in 2013 because of its divisive effect.

References

Ahmed, S. (2004). *The Cultural Politics of Emotion*. London and New York: Routledge.
Appadurai, A. (1996). *Modernity at Large*. Minneapolis, MN: University of Minnesota Press.
Appiah, K.A. (1997). 'Is the "Post-" in "Postcolonial" the "Post-" in "Postmodern"?' In A. McClintock, A. Mufti, and E. Shohat (eds) *Dangerous Liaisons: Gender, Nation, and Postcolonial Perspectives*, 420–444. Minneapolis, MN: University of Minnesota Press.
Baban, F. and Keyman, F. (2008). 'Turkey and Postnational Europe: Challenges for the Cosmopolitan Political Community.' *European Journal of Social Theory* 11(1), 107–124.
Bakhtin, M.M. (1965). Trans. by H. Iswolsky, *Rabelais and His World* (1984). Bloomington, IN: Indiana University Press.
Balibar, E. and Wallerstein, I. (1991). *Race, Nation, Class: Ambiguous Identities*. London: Verso.
Beaumont, J. and Baker, C. (eds) (2011). *Postsecular Cities: Space, Theory and Practice*. London: Continuum.
Boubekeur, A. (2005). 'Cool and Competitive. Muslim Cultures in the West.' *ISIM Review* 16, 12–13.
Brouwer, L. (2006). 'Giving Voice to Dutch Moroccan Girls on the Internet.' *Global Media Journal* 5(9), Online source, available atlass.purduecal.edu/cca/gmj/fa06/gmj_fa06_brouwer.htm [last accessed 23 September 2014]
Buitelaar, M. (2008). 'De Islamisering van Identiteit onder Jongeren van Marokkaanse Afkomst [The Islamization of Identity among Youth of Moroccan Descent].' In M. ter Borg (ed.) *Handboek Religie in Nederland: Perspectief, Overzicht, Debat* [*Handbook Religion in the Netherlands: Perspective, Overview, Debate*], 239–252. Zoetermeer, Belgium: Meinema.
Byrne, D.N. (2008). 'The Future of (the) "Race": Identity, Discourse, and the Rise of Computer-mediated Public Spheres.' In A. Everett (ed.) *Learning Race and Ethnicity: Youth and Digital Media*, 15–38. Cambridge, MA: MIT Press.
Campbell, H. (2012). *Digital Religion: Understanding Religious Practice in New Media Worlds*. New York: Routledge.
CBS. (2011). 'Population: Sex, Age, Origin and Generation.' *Statistics Netherlands Statline*. Online source, available at http://statline.cbs.nl/ [last accessed 16 December 2011].
Couldry, N. (2003). *Media Rituals: A Critical Approach*. London: Routledge.

Crul, M. and Heering, L. (eds) (2008). *The Position of the Turkish and Moroccan Second Generation in Amsterdam and Rotterdam*. Amsterdam: Amsterdam University Press.
D'Haenens, L., Summeren, C. van, Saeys, F., and Koeman, J. (2004). *Integratie of Identiteit? Mediamenu's van Turkse en Marokkaanse Jongeren [Integration or Identity? Mediamenus of Turkish And Moroccan Youths]*. Amsterdam: Boom.
Farris, S.R. and Jong, S. de (2013). 'Discontinuous Intersections: Second-Generation Immigrant Girls in Transition from School to Work.' *Ethnic and Racial Studies*. iFirst. Online source, available at http://www.tandfonline.com/doi/pdf/10.1080/01419870.2013.774033 [last accessed 10 April 2013].
Fraser, N. (1990). 'Rethinking the Public Sphere: A Contribution to the Critique of Actually Existing Democracy.' *Social Text* 25/26, 56–80.
Gajjala, R., Yartey, F.N., and Birzescu, A. (2013). 'Producing the Global'. In R. Gajjala (ed.) *Cyberculture and the Subaltern: Weavings of the Virtual and Real*, 35–70. Plymouth: Lexington.
Gazzah, M. (2009). 'European Muslim Youth: Towards a Cool Islam?' In J.S. Nielsen (ed.) *Yearbook of Muslims in Europe*, 403–425. Leiden, Netherlands: Brill.
Højsgaard, M.T. and Warburg, M. (eds) (2005). *Religion and Cyberspace*. London: Routledge.
Hoover, S.M. (1988). *Mass Media Religion: The Social Sources of the Electronic Church*. London: Sage.
Hoover, S.M. (2006). *Religion in the Media Age*. New York: Routledge.
Huggan, G. (2010). 'Is the "Post-" in "Postsecular" the "Post-" in "Postcolonial"?' *Modern Fiction Studies* 56(4), 751–768.
Jong, J. de (2007). *Kapot Moeilijk. Een Etnografisch Onderzoek naar Opvallend Delinquent Groepsgedrag van 'Marokkaanse' Jongens*. [An Ethnographic Exploration of Delinquent Group behavior of `Moroccan' Boys]. Amsterdam: Aksant.
Karatzogianni, A. and Kuntsman, A. (eds) (2012). *Digital Cultures and the Politics of Emotion: Feelings, Affect and Technological Change*. New York, NY: Palgrave Macmillan.
Karlsson, L. (2007). 'Desperately Seeking Sameness. The Processes and Pleasures of Identification in Women's Diary Blog Reading.' *Feminist Media Studies* 7(2), 137–153.
Koning, M. de. (2005). 'Dit Is Geen Poep Wat Ik Praat. De Hirsi Ali Diss Nader Belicht [This Is No Bullshit. Assessing the Hirsi Ali Diss]'. *ZemZem* 1(1), 36–41.
Landow, G.P. (2006). *Hypertext 3.0. Critical Theory and New Media in an Era of Globalization*. Baltimore, MD: The Johns Hopkins University Press.
Leurs, K. (2012). *Digital Passages. Moroccan-Dutch Youths Performing Diaspora, Gender and Youth Cultural Identities across Digital Space*. PhD, Utrecht University. Available at http://igitur-archive.library.uu.nl/ [last accessed 9 April 2013].
Leurs, K., Midden, M., and Ponzanesi, S. (2012). 'Digital Multiculturalism in the Netherlands. Religious, Ethnic and Gender Positioning by Moroccan-Dutch Youth.' *Religion and Gender* 2(1), 150–174.
Lynch, G. (2010). 'Religion, Media and Cultures of Everyday Life.' In J.R. Hinnells (ed.) *The Routledge Companion to the Study of Religion*, 2nd ed., 543. Oxon: Routledge.
Mamadouh, V. (2001). 'Constructing a Dutch Moroccan Identity through the World Wide Web.' *Arab World Geographer* 4(4), 258–274.

Meyer, B. (ed.) (2011). *Aesthetic Formations: Media, Religion, and the Senses*. New York, NY: Palgrave Macmillan.
Mitchell, J. and Marriage, S. (eds) (2003). *Mediating Religion: Conversations in Media, Religion and Culture*. London: T&T Clark.
Morgan, D. (ed.) (2008). *Keywords in Media, Religion, and Culture*. London: Routledge.
Mufti, A. (1998). 'Auerbach In Istanbul: Edward Said, Secular Criticism, and the Question of Minority Culture.' *Critical Enquiry* 25, 95–125.
Nakamura, L. and Chow-White, P. (eds) (2012). *Race after the Internet*. Minneapolis, MN: University of Minnesota Press.
Nayar, P. (ed.) (2010). *The New Media and Cybercultures Anthology*. Oxford: Wiley-Blackwell.
Newman, N. (2009). 'That's All Concept; It's Nothing Real.' In S. Alim, A. Ibrahim and A. Pennycook (eds) *Global Linguistic Flows. Hip Hop Cultures, Youth Identities, and the Politics of Language*, 195–212. London: Routledge.
Nunley, V. (2004). 'From the Harbor to Da Academic Hood: Hush Harbors and an African American Rhetorical Tradition.' In E. Richardson and R. Jackson (eds) *African American Rhetoric(s): Interdisciplinary Perspectives*, 221–241. Carbondale, IL: Southern Illinois University Press.
Nynäs, P., Lassander, M. and Utriainen, T. (eds) (2012). *Postsecular Society*. New Brunswick, NJ: Transaction Publishers.
Pels, T. and Haan, M.J. de (2003). *Continuity and Change in Moroccan Socialization*. Utrecht: Verwey-Jonker Instituut/Utrecht University.
Piela, A. (2012). *Muslim Women Online*. London: Routledge.
Robbins, B. (2012). *Perpetual War. Cosmopolitanism from the Viewpoint of Violence*. Durham, NC: Duke University Press.
Said, E. (1983). *The World, the Text and the Critic*. Cambridge, MA: Harvard University Press.
Salvatore, A. (2004). 'Making Public Space: Opportunities and Limits of Collective Action among Muslims in Europe.' *Journal of Ethnic and Migration Studies* 30(5), 1013–1031.
Stekelenburg, J., Oegema, D., and Klandermans, B. (2011). 'No Radicalization without Identification: How Ethnic Dutch and Dutch Muslim Web Forums Radicalize over Time.' In A.E. Azzi, X. Chryssochoou, B. Klandermans, and B. Simon (eds) *Identity and Participation in Culturally Diverse Societies*, 256–274. Oxford: Blackwell.
Stolow, J. (2010). 'Religion, Media, and Globalization.' In B.S. Turner (ed.) *The New Blackwell Companion to the Sociology of Religion*, 544–562. Chichester: Blackwell.
Vis, F., Zoonen, L. van, and Mihelj, S. (2011). 'Women Responding to the Anti-Islam film *Fitna*: Voices and Acts of Citizenship on YouTube.' *Feminist Review* 97, 110–129.

9
Mentality, Fundamentality, and the Colonial Secular; or How Real Is Real Estate?

Pamela Klassen

What is a mentality, and when does it become a fundamentality? Technically speaking, these two words may not be etymologically linked, but their overlap is instructive for those pondering the meanings and effects of the 'secular'. A language of mentalities and imaginaries infuses writing about both fundamentalism and the secular. While scholars have often characterized a fundamentalist 'mindset' as one lacking in self-reflexivity or openness to democratic deliberation, so, too, have they turned to a language of mentality and related concepts – sensibilities, imaginaries, world views – as the dominant frame for explaining what the secular is, and how its power works (Marty, 1994; Derrida and Habermas, 2004; Taylor, 2007). Susan Harding, writing specifically of mid-twentieth-century US 'secularity' in its relation to 'fundamentalism', described the 'modern secular imaginary' as a 'hegemonic social mentality, a sensibility and code of etiquette' (Harding, 2009: 1283). Sociologist Jose Casanova offers a more precise definition, distinguishing the *secular* as a 'modern, epistemic category' from *secularization* as a social and historical process that worked to define and set apart 'religion' within civic and political institutions. *Secularism*, in turn, he described as a world view or ideology that can be both a principle of statecraft and a broader, taken-for-granted, modern *doxa* (Casanova, 2009).

This recent analysis of the secular has insisted that scholars ask hard questions about their own norms – their own 'social imaginaries', 'mentalities', and 'sensibilities'– including those that designate fundamentalism as rigidly dogmatic while celebrating secularism as a commitment to open critique (Derrida and Habermas, 2004; Asad, 2009). These debates about the secular, or what some now call the postsecular, are thus posing the question of when a mentality becomes a fundamentality, or when a group's implicitly shared way of thinking becomes articulated as an exclusive way of thinking to which others must accede, often with both their minds and their bodies (Scott, 2007).

By considering a different layer of etymology resident within the English-language concepts of fundamental and secular, we can set another illuminating frame onto the question, one that brings into relief not only mentalities and imaginaries but also matter and property. Fundamental, the *Oxford English Dictionary* (OED) attests, can be defined as the 'foundation' of a building or the 'base on which something is built' (OED, 1989b). Fundament, in turn, has a historical and geophysical definition of 'any landscape before colonization by man in general or by any particular group of men' (OED, 1989a). The gendered language may be accidental on the part of the OED, and the reference to colonization may not be meant to evoke the politics of imperialism; nevertheless, this definition marks the fundament as a land *not yet* spoken for by men who claim it and build upon it. In other words, the fundament is a 'wilderness' about to be 'civilized'. The word secular also has OED definitions that mark off matter in place and time. In its medieval meanings, the secular referred to what was worldly, neither 'spiritual' nor of the 'Church'. In later meanings, secular also denoted a long-term geophysical process 'having a period of enormous length; continuing through long ages' (OED, 1989c). Historically speaking, then, secular may refer to places not claimed by the Christian Church as well as to material processes that proceed according to the clock of science, not scripture.

In the twentieth century, fundamentalism and the secular took on new meanings as mutually constituting terms orbiting around the third concept of religion, a term not exactly denoting Christianity but largely dominated by it (Wenger, 2009; Asad, 1993). At least at a popular level, the secular largely came to be defined as that which is not based in religious authority, with fundamentalism as its most extreme, and religiously undergirded, opposite (Jakobsen and Pellegrini, 2008: 2). As feminist and other scholars have demonstrated, however, the fundamental and the secular, though both with Christian etymologies, do not have solely Christian genealogies and embodiments (Jakobsen and Pellegrini, 2008: 13). In this essay, I attend to one particular context in which the secular encompassed not only norms of democratic governance and legal recourse, but also the concepts of real estate or property as they emerged within a contested process of Christianization and colonialism. I show how Christianity has been one implicit and explicit foundation for not only secular mentalities, but also for their material habitations and legal effects. Put another way, fundamentalities and secularities draw not only from the mind but are also made out of matter (cf. Hirschkind, 2011).

In 'colonial secular' northwestern British Columbia, the focus of my current research, real estate became, quite literally, contested ground not only among First Nations, settlers, and colonial officials, but also among and between missionaries as representatives of the Church and as 'private' capitalist subjects. Texts and rituals coded as 'religious' – sermons, baptisms, school texts, bible translations, catechisms – were the most obvious of missionaries' tools for transforming both mentalities and materialities of Aboriginal peoples (Stevens, 2004). Missionaries, however, also used deeds of land, new zoning laws, and other legal documents of mapping to give them ownership of land that was newly subject to the juridico-political 'mentality' of real estate (DeRogatis, 2003; Neylan, 2002). In British Columbia, some missionaries literally represented both the 'law' and 'God' in their work – that is, they were both local magistrates and ministers of the gospel. In other cases, missionaries strongly resisted what they saw as unjust seizures of Indian land by both settlers and government (Patterson, 1967; Christophers, 1998; Foster, 2007b; Foster and Berger, 2008).[1] Missionaries' celestial visions paired with their earthly maps made them powerful yet unpredictable nodes in the creation of Canada, a nation that has never entirely extricated its secular, democratic authority from its underpinnings in a Christian mode of transcendence, by which the law could understand itself, at root, to be 'never wrong' (Berger, 2010: 117).

From the beginnings of 'British Columbia', ongoing struggles over the 'Indian Land Question' threw into high relief how the seemingly secular mentality of real estate was actually a fundamentality: an exclusive way of thinking enforced through a 'regime of private property' (Harris, 1997: 136). Real estate, also know as 'real property', is founded on the idea that an individual can gain 'title' to a section of land, its buildings, and its resources by exchanging money for the right; real property is an idea particular to certain legal cultures (Hann, 2007; Bell and Napoleon, 2009). 'Alienating' land through real estate is a practice that, with enough digging, is shown to be founded on claims of transcendence. In the Canadian case, the Crown claimed the title to the land both through negotiating treaties with First Nations and through a baldly imperialistic assertion of its own power. In the case of the vast territory of Rupert's Land, the Crown came to own most of northwestern Canada by purchasing it from the Hudson's Bay Company, a company which it had earlier chartered (Dickason, 1992). The Canadian state then slowly parcelled out much of this land to homesteaders, who were by law, men, and by preference, British (Carter, 2009; Harris, 1997).

This purchase was less than convincing to First Nations. As the 1913 'Statement of the Nishga Nation' exemplifies, First Nations throughout the northwest repeatedly petitioned the Canadian state (and sometimes the British Monarch) to acknowledge that they had never ceded 'title' to their land in any treaty:

> We lay claim to the rights of men. We claim to be aboriginal inhabitants of this country, and to have rights as such. We claim that our aboriginal rights have been guaranteed by Proclamation of King George Third and recognized by Acts of the Parliament of Great Britain. We claim that holding under the words of that Proclamation a tribal ownership of the territory, we should be dealt with in accordance with its provision, and that no part of our lands should be taken from us or in any way disposed of until the same has been purchased by the Crown. (Anon, 1915)

Though the Nisga'a were willing to play by some of the rules of the 'rights of men', such as adopting the language of title, they also contended that their own laws and their collective and ancestral presence on the land from 'time immemorial' were legitimate grounds for them to assert their claims (Harris, 2002; Foster, Raven, and Webber, 2007; Foster and Berger, 2008). Nisga'a writers were also astute observers of how the state used Christianity to undergird its territorial authority. They often turned to the state's recourse to Christian transcendence as an argument in support of their own challenges to white settlement, as Nisga'a chief (and Anglican Church member) Andrew Mercer argued in a 1911 letter to the editor of the Prince Rupert *Evening Empire*:

> If the surveyor and those that have staked pieces of land up in the Naas valley wish to come again, let them go to Ottawa first and make the government settle our land. And if our land is settle, then let the surveyor and those that have their stake come again, for we do not want to stop them. But we want a full settlement. Also we want to right of what is lawful. Same thing as you want to do right, as you all perceive it from the Holy Bible. Whenever the J.P. or a judge were in court they used Bible for to do right. We also see and read in it, in the Holy Bible, that 'Cursed is he that removeth his neighbor's land mark,' and that you break one of the Ten Commandments, 'Thou

shall not covet,' for you have knock us down and take our possession. (Mercer, 1911)

Andrew Mercer caught the state in the act of what Talal Asad has called 'transcendent mediation', by which the state proclaims its own authority to be rooted in the demos and yet also stakes itself on divine authority (Asad, 2003: 5). With a language of rights and commandments, Nisga'a drew on both secular and biblical norms, while also maintaining their own 'social imaginaries' that rooted authority in communal houses and ancestral clans (Taylor, 2004).

If to be postsecular is to be thinking and acting with a critical awareness of the powers of the secular, First Nations were postsecular long before the term was even coined. Their shrewd assessment of the state's appeal to Christian authority in claiming the land suggests they may also have been post-fundamental, or anti-fundamental, in two senses – they rejected the colonial designation of their land as a supposedly wild and unsettled 'fundament' waiting for settlers, while also naming the partiality and extremism of the state's claim to their land under the sovereignty of the 'Crown'.

To better understand the importance of these land disputes for the formation of the colonial secular, I first offer a reading of several key texts in the recent theorizing of the secular and its others – whether fundamentalism or the postsecular. I argue that the secular is partly created through the mutually constitutive relations of colonial modes of governance and Christian imaginations of moral order (Lutz, 2007: 31). In concert with this colonial Christian logic, the secular becomes a temporal category that both proclaims its own inevitability and asserts its ability to continue indefinitely through the ages. At a time when some accounts of the secular and postsecular seem to be drawing overly sharp divisions between Christianity and the secular, or even urging a 'reChristianization' of scholarship and/or the state, highlighting the ways that Christianity and the colonial state worked to create the secular seems particularly urgent (Smith, 2012; Sommerville, 2002).

Fundamentalism, the secular, and Christianization

Applying the label of fundamentalist is one of the most damning of insults from a 'secular' perspective – or, more particularly, from a perspective that understands 'religion' to be a voluntary affiliation that (ideally) carries no inherent legitimizing authority in the realm of the state. Understood in this sense, the secular is a space of public discourse and practice in which religious reasons are not admissible, or at least not very convincing, as arguments for laws, public policies, or communal norms. To be fundamentalist, in this reading, is to be outside the terms of secular agreement about the virtues and necessities of peaceful democratic debate: it is to be unyielding in one's views, to root one's 'world view' in a transcendent, divine authority, and to have a readiness for turning even to violence in support of one's convictions (Derrida and Habermas, 2004).

With the rise of 'fundamentalism' in many parts of the world, scholars from a range of disciplines turned sustained attention to the ways that fundamentalism, both as an ascribed and a native category, was more than just a stubborn, aggressive mentality – it was a set of practices and discourses with attendant contradictions, surprising alignments, and networks of power (Marty, 1994; Harding, 2001). Many scholars have shown how fundamentalism, while a 'native' term especially among some Christians, is also a pejorative term that, with its connotations of a threateningly violent transcendence, helps to constitute the 'secular' as a sphere of rational, peaceful debate (Jakobsen and Pellegrini, 2008). In turn, the secular has also become the focus of critique, and related concepts such as secularization and the postsecular have all been advanced as terms with more or less utility, and with more or less direct connection to Christianity. Where historian David Hollinger suggests that secularization in the United States would be better described as a process of 'deChristianization', sociologist James Beckford argues that in the context of Great Britain, Christianity continues to shape notions of both the secular and the postsecular (Hollinger, 2001; Beckford, 2012). Enumerating many meanings attributed to the postsecular, Beckford concludes that many scholars who employ the term in Euro-American settings are missing a critical historical awareness of the 'pragmatic settlement' between the state and religions, especially Christianity: '[state] policies, mechanisms, and practices have long been at work in Britain to recognize and summon religious identities' (Beckford, 2012: 13, 16). This summoning, I would add, calls forth very particular kinds of religion, namely ones that are willing to pragmatically settle, to accept the sovereignty of the state, and even to help to produce it.

Whether embodied in the 'state' or the 'public sphere', secularity's supposed freedom from religious obligations or compulsions is certainly not borne out in many of the European and North American nation-states that invoke the secular as an orientation. Self-professed secular states have long privileged certain religions – especially Christianity – in particular spheres such as education, health care, and charitable status, and many continue to collect taxes on behalf of 'established' churches (Casanova, 2009: 1061). Theorizing the secular or the postsecular, then, must involve asking the question of how key secular concepts require a settlement with state sovereignty, and how this settlement differentially recognizes the authority and 'sensibility' of particular religions. Perhaps 'religious reasons' undergird or support even such a 'secular' mode of authority as the right to buy and own land as property. As several political theorists have shown, prominent early modern theorists of property rights, such as John Locke, not only developed their theories in relation to Protestant theologies, but also engaged in political work entwined with Christian missionary colonialism directed at Aboriginal peoples (Waldron, 2002; Tully, 1993). Property rights and real estate are themselves acts of imagination surveyed and gridded onto the fundament; they are mentalities that in the course of colonialism became fundamentalities, rooted in the transcendence and violence of the state, sworn to with the authority of the Holy Bible at hand.

The complex relationships among fundamentalism, the secular, and the violence of the state were fruitfully explored in paired conversations with the philosophers Jürgen Habermas and Jacques Derrida in the wake of the 2001 Al Qaeda attack on the World Trade Center. In these parallel interviews, both Derrida and Habermas considered 'religion' and the 'secular' to be notably marked by their connection to fundamentalism or fanaticism, and both spoke with an awareness of themselves as 'Europeans' who sought to simultaneously defend and critique the viability of a rational, secular, violence-free public sphere. Wary of its 'pejorative ring', Derrida and Habermas nevertheless defined the concept of 'fundamentalist' as primarily a matter of mentality backed up by force: 'We use this predicate to characterize a peculiar mindset, a stubborn attitude that insists on the political imposition of its own convictions and reasons, even when they are far from being rationally acceptable. This holds especially for religious beliefs' (Derrida and Habermas, 2004: 31). Comparing contemporary Islam to Christianity, he suggested that the universalist, religious (i.e., mostly Christian) beliefs of early modern Europeans had become relativized both by confessionalization and by secularization. This relativizing also bred a self-reflexive 'cognitive thrust' that prompted religious 'believers' to realize that they could not successfully use violence to forward their own religious causes. Positing frozen fundamentalist mentalities vs. secularized cognitive thrusts, Derrida and Habermas's ideal mentalities had to keep moving, supple and adaptive, at the same time that he recognized that even to

182 Pamela Klassen

'deconstruct' the self-reflexivity of modernity was to participate in its mentality of critique (Derrida and Habermas, 2004: 32, 42).

By contrast, Derrida's recourse to the word 'fundamentalist' also turned to Islam as its object, but paralleled 'fundamentalist Islam' with 'the United States's fundamentally Christian professions of faith', pointing out the partiality of both (Derrida and Habermas, 2004: 117). Arguing that the 'secretly theological-political' sovereignty of the 'secular' state must be continually deconstructed, Derrida suggested that an understanding of today's 'fundamentalism' requires a deeper comprehension of 'our philosophical heritage', and an awareness of how and when justification is in play (Derrida and Habermas, 2004: 131). But this kind of awareness or comprehension did not come easily, in his view: '...the event is first of all *that which* I do not first of all comprehend. Better, the event is first of all *that* I do not comprehend' (Derrida and Habermas, 2004: 90). To be ever aware of the limits of one's comprehension, in Derrida's view, was not to 'relativize' into absurdity but to understand critique as an ongoing process better oriented by the risks of 'hospitality' than the grudging accommodation of 'toleration' (Derrida and Habermas, 2004: 128). Defining the job of the philosopher in a time of terror, Derrida said:

> A 'philosopher'...would be someone who analyzes and then draws the practical and effective consequences of the relationship between our philosophical heritage and the structure of the still dominant juridico-political system that is so clearly undergoing mutation. A 'philosopher' would be one who seeks a new criteriology to distinguish between 'comprehending' and 'justifying'. (Derrida and Habermas, 2004: 106)

Moving from a European context into a North American one, where the sovereignty of the state continues to be challenged by First Nations who make recourse to a different 'philosophical heritage' in which both land and religion are differently configured, Derrida's task of finding new criteria for comprehension and judgement requires rethinking the fundamentals that shape both mind and matter, laws and land. From a First Nations perspective, it is no secret that the sovereignty of the state and its claim on the fundament is, in part, justified through recourse to the theological-political.

Colonial secular spirits

Hovering between considering the secular as a matter of mind and as a matter of manners, scholars have recognized that their own thinking about the 'secular' is made that much more difficult by their own implication in both its ideologies and its habits (Scott, 2007; Asad, 2003; Modern, 2011). Charles Taylor, in one of the most influential of recent accounts of the secular, has provided perhaps the most widely adopted mentalist metaphor for thinking about the secular: the 'immanent frame'. For Taylor, the immanent frame is part of a 'modern social imaginary', which constructs the world as wholly natural and immanent – not supernatural and transcendent. The modern social imaginary of the secular reimagines political power, social organization, and human nature in such a way that an earlier respect for 'supernatural' spirits, transcendent forces, and social hierarchy has been displaced by a focus on the natural goodness of ordinary life and immanence, in a world of distinct individuals. While some scholars have argued that Taylor's immanent frame is not a mentalist, cognitive metaphor, nevertheless Taylor himself regularly placed the mind and what it believes at the centre of the frame (Warner, VanAntwerpen, and Calhoun, 2010). Inhabitants of the immanent frame are secular, modern 'buffered selves', people for whom 'it comes to seem axiomatic that all thought, feeling and purpose, all the features we normally can ascribe to agents, must be in minds, which are distinct from the "outer" world' (Taylor, 2007: 539). The buffered self is central to Taylor's argument – the secular age is rooted in a frame of mind, a world view, a mentality that is held by largely atomistic individuals in a world bereft of spirits.

Many scholars have demonstrated recently that the secular – at least in North America – has had plenty of room for a diversity of spirits (Bender, 2010; Klassen, 2011). Taylor's narrative of an immanent spiritless age, however, remains widely influential. Arguing that Western thinkers have largely framed the secular by a 'subtraction story' that proceeds via narratives that claim to 'strip away' religious illusions to get at the true, empirically derived nature of human desire and existence, Taylor insisted instead that secularity must also be understood as a *creative* process, by which freedom, power, mutual benefit, and rational debate are formed as modern virtues (Taylor, 2007: 579).[2] Understanding the secular as a creative process – that is, a process that made things happen – however, requires bringing back its spirits and spiritual moorings, especially as they were at play in the colonization of North America.

As several scholars have noted, Taylor's account of the secular pays little attention to the history of colonialism within the Christianity of the 'North Atlantic', thus severing the secular from the profound ways that it was structured by and created within colonial encounters. Saba Mahmood, for example, forcefully argues that attention to missionary expansion is crucial to any understanding of the secular, at the same time that she urges a genealogy of the secular that goes beyond its Christian formations: 'The modern nation-state, for example, with its juridical executive, and administrative functions, enfolds a variety of conceptions of the self, agency, privacy, publicity, religion, and ethics that have become globalized. The history of this transformation belongs less to the Christianization of non-Western societies and more to their secularization under modern rule' (Mahmood, 2010: 295). I agree with Mahmood, that attending only to Christianity will not tell a full story of the secular nation-state, but suggest that the place to draw the distinction between Christianization and secularization is not along the lines of law and governance.

To think the secular through mentalities or imaginaries that are rooted in individuals, or that separate state administration from Christianity too strictly, is to miss the social and political processes through which colonialism was effected. These social processes included law and governance enacted in what anthropologist Ronald Niezen has called a process of 'spiritual domination', in which Christian convictions about the necessity of converting Aboriginal people intertwined with a capitalist imagination of the landscape as ripe for 'resource extraction' (Niezen and Burgess, 2000).

In a different register, Courtney Bender has argued that colonialism and settlement have been crucial to 'emergent visions of sociality' in an America both secular and enchanted. Contending particularly with Charles Taylor's account of eighteenth- and nineteenth-century Romantic notions of the uninhabited and 'sublime wilderness', Bender argues that the idea of 'the wilderness continues to manifest not sublimity but the work of a transcendent order in which America's expansion is justified and sanctified' (Bender, 2008). The justification of settler expansion in North America – the production of the rural and the urban – was achieved partly by comprehending the land and the people as unsettled and 'wild' and partly by government efforts to actively deem First Nations land 'unproductive' when in Aboriginal hands (Klinger, 1995; Carter, 1993; Waisberg and Holzkamm, 1993).

The language of wilderness, civilization, and the 'unimproved' fundament prior to colonization were often invoked to justify the colonial secular against the threat of the Indian Land Question. As an unattributed article in the Prince Rupert *Evening Empire* put it in 1914, at a particularly active point in the Nisga'a land claims movement, 'The view has been expressed that, in appraising the Indian title, if admitted by the privy council, the government should go back to the time when the lands were a wilderness, when a wild people were found upon an unimproved state; that the Indian title cannot improve with civilized development – and that it were vain for the Indians to expect to be compensated to the extent of basing the intrinsic value of the land upon the activities of a white population; and that, therefore, there can be no claim for deferred benefit from the crown' (n.a., 1914). Or in other words, the author considered it to be an impossible task to calculate the value of the land now that the white people had transformed it from wilderness to civilization.[3] Turning the 'fundament' into urban centres, farmland, and mines required acts of sociality, violence, and governance undergirded by stories and laws that drew from both secular and spiritual authority (Lessard, Johnson, and Webber, 2011).

Missionary real estate

To demonstrate the varieties of spiritual authority drawn upon by the colonial secular state to claim land, I turn now to brief examples from the Northwest Coast region of Canada, where Anglican missionaries first ventured in the nineteenth century as one wing of the British colonization of a diversity of First Nations. Though many missionaries held very stubborn attitudes as to the rightness of their cause, they did not necessarily use explicit violence to effect their ends. The transcendence underlying their fundamentalisms was filtered through recourse to divine and state authority. Missionaries' main tools to 'convert' the Nisga'a and Tsimshian were forms of mediated communication: the biblical tracts, school books, and liturgical texts that had long shaped Christian subjects in domestic and foreign missions (Meyer, 1999; Keane, 2007). But they also used the texts of geographical surveys, 'real estate' deeds, and other documents to claim what they took to be the fundament – the wilderness – in both state-sanctioned and 'mythologically' grounded ways. To adapt Benjamin Berger's argument about how Canadian law has both transcendent authority and a will to convert at its core, missionaries were very aware of how the Bible and the law were powerful and complementary tools for their own task of conversion (Berger, 2010).

Anglican missionary James Benjamin McCullagh (1854–1921) well understood that competing mentalities and practices of claiming land were at the heart of conflicts between Nisga'a and colonial secular Christianity. McCullagh was a missionary based in Aiyansh, a small Christian settlement on the Nass River, within what the Anglican Church called the Diocese of Caledonia. In an address entitled 'The

Indian Potlatch' that he gave to the Church Missionary Society at the Anglican mission village of Metlakatla in 1899, McCullagh provided a detailed ethnographic account of the Nisga'a feasting system, worthy of any anthropologist of his day. Clarifying that 'potlatch' was a term invented by the 'white man' that conflated a variety of different feast systems, McCullagh argued that the potlatch was not primarily a religious event but a political act: 'the systematized form of tribal government based upon the united suffrages of the clans' (McCullagh, 1899: 2). The potlatch, McCullagh claimed, was the Nisga'a form of an election.

Though Nisga'a leaders contemporary to McCullagh used a similar kind of argument to argue for their land claims, McCullagh used his insights about the potlatch to argue for its eradication as a public form of governance that was at once 'socialistic' and selfish (McCullagh, 1899: 5). He also listed other 'negative' effects that anti-potlatch critics usually named, such as the potlatch being a waste of economically productive time and an opportunity for social and sexual licence (Cole and Chaikin, 1990; Bracken, 1997). But the government's 1885 ban of the potlatch was an ineffective legal approach, argued McCullagh. Instead, he pleaded for a law that would protect the 'Christian Indians' who had tried to step out of the potlatch system of social and economic debts. It was the potlatch system, McCullagh argued, that kept drawing his Christian converts back to traditional Nisga'a practices. The government should draw up a new law, he advised, ensuring that 'a chief wishing to become Christian and civilized should have his rights assured to him by law – the Potlatch should not be allowed to deprive him of his rights' (McCullagh, 1899: 19). McCullagh was referring here to rights of territory and inheritance, and he understood a conversion to Christianity to entail that a Nisga'a Christian would give up feasting as an inappropriately ritualized way to claim or redistribute land.

Ritual and territory, in fact, were profoundly linked in both Nisga'a and Christian social imaginaries. To participate in a Nisga'a feast was to acknowledge the host's legitimate right to territory and authority as the leader of a clan or house; to become a Christian was to renounce that authority and to claim territory under the laws of the state as an individual. To adapt Charles Taylor's terms, to become a Christian was to become a buffered self enclosed in the love of Jesus Christ, who would ideally be able to own real estate in his (and rarely her) own name.

Reconceptualizing land as real estate was central to missionary labours throughout the Northwest Coast. Under law, Indians could not pre-empt land or vote – two defining features of secular citizenship (Harris, 2002: 89). They could only own land collectively, in the form of 'reserves', and even that ownership could be threatened if the population of the reserve dwindled (Sterritt, 1998). With different emphases, both the Nisga'a and the missionaries contested this law, arguing that the right to own land would allow Indians to become full-fledged citizens. The Nisga'a, along with some missionaries, insisted that their collective land claims must first be settled before they would seek to own real estate as individuals (cf. McNally, 2010). First Nations were therefore stuck between two mentalities of real estate: to own land individually would weaken their collective land claims and the larger challenge to Canadian sovereignty that these claims embodied, while working within the reserve system forced them to conceive of and inhabit their land under this same Canadian sovereignty. Real estate had, in this case, very real effects.

At the same time that missionaries argued for individual landholding for Indians, they recognized the importance of collective landholding when it came to the Church. In an illuminating exchange of letters with a law firm in the provincial capital of Victoria, the Bishop of the Diocese of Caledonia, Frederick Du Vernet (1860–1924), argued repeatedly for the special privilege of the Church to own land as a 'corporate' or collective body, and even, in some cases, to do so on Indian reserves. In one dispute over land in the small river settlement of Port Simpson, Du Vernet challenged the claim of the previous Bishop of Caledonia, William Ridley, that he owned a small parcel of land privately, instead of as the representative of the Church. In Du Vernet's eyes, Ridley was confusing his roles as a church official and a private citizen (Du Vernet, 1909).

When Ridley tried to sell some of this land, Du Vernet argued that Bishop Ridley did not understand that he only 'owned' Church land as a common resource vested in him as long as he held the 'name' of bishop: 'It seems to me so highly improbable that Bishop Ridley in the days of his full mental vigor should have allowed his private property to be registered in the name of "The Lord Bishop of Caledonia" knowing as he did that such was a "corporation sole" that in the interests of the Church I must ask for further proof before I hand over Church property' (Du Vernet, 1909). The corporation sole had long been 'a curious freak of English law', as a concept that would help with maintaining the continuity of church property by designating an ecclesiastically sanctioned individual as holding the 'fee simple' or title to a piece of church land not as a 'person' but as legal entity (Maitland, 1901: 131; Maitland, 1900; O'Hara, 1988). Most commonly, for example, a bishop would own church property as cleric, who was a man but was also the 'secular, legal embodiment of the church' (Maitland, 1900, 1901; O'Hara, 1988). As

Perry Dane has argued, the corporation sole was an individual who was a collective representation, poised at the juncture of secular and church power as an 'extraordinary, irregular, custom-tailored effort at translating religious principles into secular terms' (Dane, 1998: 58).

In a manner ironically parallel to the way that Nisga'a territorial claims were ascribed to a ritually sanctioned individual holding the authority of a name through the potlatch or feasting system, the Canadian state recognized that an Anglican Bishop owned collective land as an individual sanctioned by appropriate ritual justification. The state could find a custom-tailored solution for Christian communal landholding via a name rooted in divine transcendence, but it could not accommodate comparable Nisga'a modes (McNeil, 2007: 141). This is an illuminating example of the fundamental Christianity of what legal scholar Marianna Valverde has called the 'epistemology of sovereignty' (Valverde, 2011). With the transcendent authority and honour of the 'Crown' in play, the Canadian juridico-political system grounds itself in 'the doctrine that the Crown is always already honourable, with this honour then seeping into the crown's 'mystical body' – the Canadian state, in this instance – just as Christ's virtues are deemed to seep into the mystical corporation that is the Christian church' (Valverde, 2011: 957).[4] Or as Andrew Mercer put it in 1911, judges and justices of the peace 'used [the] Bible for to do right' (Mercer, 1911).

Anglican missionaries should not be seen only as pious land grabbers. Some among them mounted some of the most dogged and innovative legal campaigns for Indian land claims in the early twentieth century (Foster, 2007). At the same time, they worked with a mentality of real estate that understood individual landholding to be both a civic and a spiritual virtue. They reiterated this virtue through testimonies, rituals, and deeds of title; they remade the fundament through both story and law, with both secular and spiritual reasons.

Conclusion

The nation-state (and the public sphere) within which First Nations, missionaries, and government officials were operating at the beginning of the twentieth century was already postsecular, if by that we mean a context in which communities with diverse mentalities, myths, and practices are (unequally) compelled to communicate and contend within the secular norms of liberal democratic polities. The European and Canadian settlers who followed the railroads, timber, and mines to northwestern British Columbia in the early twentieth century were relatively comfortable with securing their territory with cash and deeds of title. For the Nisga'a and the Tsimshian who greeted Christian (and 'unchurched') visitors to their Pacific Northwest homelands with a mixture of hospitality and hostility, the secular norms of communication – whether Christian testimony, newspapers, deeds of land, or school curricula – were literally written both in a foreign language and in a foreign mentality. Not always working in harmony with colonial officials, Christian missionaries in the new nation of Canada tried to abolish certain religious mentalities and practices among First Nations while instantiating others, as they sought to create secular, Christian citizens who could own land, build schools and churches, learn to read, and 'lay claim to the rights of men'.

Working with mentality of real estate, missionaries, settlers, and colonial officials did not comprehend their property regime as a fundamentality. Derrida's reflection on hospitality in a 'time of terror' prompted him to question the 'philosophical heritage' and criteria that enable comprehension and justification; reflecting on more mundane 'events' in the more distant past can have similar effects. Communication and comprehension are themselves so deeply cultural that, in the end, we likely all have something of the unexamined fundamentalist in our demeanors and our expectations. As a concept to think with, I would hope that the 'postsecular' could help to imagine and reimagine the clash and mixture of mentalities and practices – new and old – that give shape to the present. In the process, it is important to be mindful of one's own fundamentalities – those mentalities with rigid borders that may often be more like invisible fences than brick walls – and think carefully and honestly about what to retain and what to deconstruct.

In that spirit, Charles Taylor's magisterial account of the 'secular age' may have given short shrift to the place of colonialism in the creation of the secular. In other work on the 'politics of recognition', however, he has directly confronted issues of First Nations political authority. Commenting on the Nisga'a treaty in 1998, Taylor eloquently defended a vision of Canadian jurisprudence that would work to negotiate 'Aboriginal self-rule' with explicit acknowledgement of Canada's responsibility for the long and destructive history of colonialism (Taylor, 1998). His later reflections on the secular, however, did not bring these insights to bear on the ways that state sovereignty, working in concert with Christian authority, was a 'creative' process of destruction. To me, this suggests that any analysis of the secular that cuts too sharp a distinction between immanence and transcendence, or the earthly and the ethereal, misses the ways that secular authority – even in the form of real estate – depends on the infusion of matter and spirit.

The sovereignty of the Canadian state is not going away any time soon, but the assumptions that undergird it have been subject to some remarkably 'deconstructive' thinking of late. Canadian Supreme Court justices and legal theorists have come very close to acknowledging how the mentality of real estate and property operates as a fundamentality, underwritten by the coercive authority of the state, due in large part to First Nations' land claims including the cases that led to the Nisga'a of the Nass River becoming the Nisga'a Nation in 2000. Qualifying the state's sovereignty as *de facto* and acknowledging the sovereignty of First Nations, some Canadian legal thinkers (including some justices) are also acknowledging that the fundamentals of Canadian sovereignty are not necessarily rooted in time immemorial but are subject to 'secular' change, however slow and painful (Slattery, 2005). This change is unpredictable; within the last few years, real estate has made its way to the Nisga'a Nation. In a controversial decision, Nisga'a are now able to hold some fee simple land as individuals, and to sell their land to the highest bidder, whether those bidders are Nisga'a or not (Gutnick, 2012). Andrew Mercer and J.B. McCullagh both argued for this 'right', but at this moment, it is hard to say if the real estate signs that now dot the Nass Valley are markers of postsecular emancipation, colonial secular victory, or something else altogether.

Notes

For their comments on this paper, I thank the editors, Benjamin Berger, and the participants in Postsecular Publics, a collaborative workshop organized by the Jackman Humanities Institute at the University of Toronto and the Centre for Humanities at Utrecht University.

1. For the most part, I use the term 'First Nations' to denote Aboriginal peoples in the land settled as Canada but also use the term 'Indian' when it would have been the term used in early twentieth-century missionary and legal contexts.
2. Taylor, however, is no champion of the 'immanent frame' of the secular, and what he considers to be its corresponding humanist, therapeutic 'mentality' wreaking dangerous effects on human dignity and flourishing (Taylor, 2007).
3. This quotation is attributed to Deputy Superintendent of Indian Affairs Duncan Campbell Scott in Harris (2002).
4. Valverde is drawing both from John Borrows's discussion of the 'alchemy of sovereignty' and from Kantorowicz's discussion of medieval Christian 'political theology' (Borrows, 1999; Kantorowicz, 1997).

References

Anon. (1915). *The Nishga Petition to His Majesty's Privy Council: A Record of Interviews with the Government of Canada, Together with Related Documents* [S.l.]: Conference of Friends of the Indians of British Columbia.
Asad, T. (1993). *Genealogies of Religion: Discipline and Reasons of Power in Christianity and Islam.* Baltimore, MD: Johns Hopkins University Press.
Asad, T. (2003). *Formations of the Secular: Christianity, Islam, Modernity.* Baltimore, MD: Stanford University Press.
Asad, T. (2009). *Is Critique Secular?: Blasphemy, Injury, and Free Speech.* Townsend Center for the Humanities, University of California.
Beckford, J.A. (2012). 'SSSR Presidential Address Public Religions and the Postsecular: Critical Reflections.' *Journal for the Scientific Study of Religion* 51(1), 1–19.
Bell, C. and Napoleon, V. (eds) (2009). 'The Constitutional Role of Tangible and Intangible Property in Gitanyow.' In *First Nations Cultural Heritage and Law: Case Studies, Voices, and Perspectives*, 92–113. Vancouver, BC: University of British Columbia Press.
Bender, C. (2008). 'Every Meaning Shall Have its Homecoming Festival.' Lecture at the Varieties of Secularism in a Secular Age, Yale University, 5 April.
Bender, C. (2010). *The New Metaphysicals: Spirituality and the American Religious Imagination.* Chicago, IL: University of Chicago Press.
Berger, B.L. (2010). 'The Cultural Limits of Legal Tolerance.' In C. Bender and P.E. Klassen (eds) *After Pluralism: Reimagining Religious Engagement*, 98–123. New York: Columbia University Press.
Borrows, J. (1999). 'Sovereignty's Alchemy: An Analysis of Delgamuukw v. British Columbia.' *Osgoode Hall Law Journal* 37, 537–596.
Bracken, C. (1997). *The Potlatch Papers: A Colonial Case History.* Chicago, IL: University of Chicago Press.
Carter, S. (1993). *Lost Harvests: Prairie Indian Reserve Farmers and Government Policy.* Montreal and Kingston: McGill-Queen's University Press.
Carter, S. (2009). '"Daughters of British Blood" or "Hordes of Men of Alien Race" The Homesteads-For-Women Campaign in Western Canada.' *Great Plains Quarterly* 29(3), 267–286.
Casanova, J. (2009). 'The Secular and Secularisms.' *Social Research* 7(4), 1049–1066.
Christophers, B. (1998). *Positioning the Missionary: John Booth Good and the Confluence of Cultures in Nineteenth-Century British Columbia.* Vancouver, BC: UBC Press.
Cole, D. and Chaikin, I. (1990). *An Iron Hand upon the People: The Law Against the Potlatch on the Northwest Coast.* Vancouver, BC: Douglas & McIntyre.
Dane, P. (1998). 'The Corporation Sole and the Encounter of Law and Church.' In N.J. Demerath (ed.) *Sacred Companies: Organizational Aspects of Religion and Religious Aspects of Organizations.* Oxford and New York: Oxford University Press.
DeRogatis, A. (2003). *Moral Geography: Maps, Missionaries, and the American Frontier.* New York: Columbia University Press.
Derrida, J. and Habermas, J. (2004). *Philosophy in a Time of Terror: Dialogues with Jürgen Habermas and Jacques Derrida*, edited by G. Borradori. Chicago, IL: University of Chicago Press.

Dickason, O.P. (1992). *Canada's First Nations: A History of Founding Peoples from Earliest Times*. Norman, OK: University of Oklahoma Press.
Du Vernet, F. (1909). 'Letter to Crease & Crease, Barristers.' Victoria, BC, Archives of the Diocese of Caledonia, Box 77, No. 366.
Foster, H. (2007). 'We Are Not O'Meara's Children: Law, Lawyers, and the First Campaign for Aboriginal Title in British Columbia, 1908–28.' In H. Foster, H. Raven, and J. Webber (eds) *Let Right Be Done: Aboriginal Title, the Calder Case, and the Future of Indigenous Rights*, 61–84. Vancouver, BC: UBC Press.
Foster, H. and Berger, B.L. (2008). 'From Humble Prayers to Legal Demands: The Cowichan Petition of 1909 and the British Columbia Indian Land Question.' In A.R. Buck, B.L. Berger, and H. Foster (eds) *The Grand Experiment: Law and Legal Culture in British Settler Societies*. Vancouver, BC: UBC Press.
Foster, H., Raven, H., and Webber, J. (eds) (2007). *Let Right Be Done: Aboriginal Title, the Calder Case, and the Future of Indigenous Rights*. Vancouver, BC: UBC Press.
Gutnick, D. (2012). 'Nisga'a Real Estate 24 July.' *In the Field with David Gutnick*, CBC Radio. Online Source, available at http://www.cbc.ca/inthefield/2012/07/24/nisgaa-real-estate-july-24/ [last accessed 6 December 2012].
Hann, C. (2007). 'A New Double Movement? Anthropological Perspectives on Property in the Age of Neoliberalism.' *Socio-Economic Review* 5(2), 287–318.
Harding, S.F. (2001). *The Book of Jerry Falwell: Fundamentalist Language and Politics*. Princeton, NJ: Princeton University Press.
Harding, S.F. (2009). 'American Protestant Moralism and the Secular Imagination: From Temperance to the Moral Majority.' *Social Research* 76(4), 1277–1306.
Harris, C. (1997). *The Resettlement of British Columbia: Essays on Colonialism & Geographical Change*. Vancouver, BC: UBC Press.
Harris, C. (2002). *Making Native Space: Colonialism, Resistance, and Reserves in British Columbia*. Vancouver, BC: UBC Press.
Hirschkind, C. (2011). 'Is There a Secular Body?' *Cultural Anthropology* 26(4), 633–647.
Hollinger, D.A. (2001). 'The "Secularization" Question and the United States in the Twentieth Century.' *Church History* 70(1), 132–143.
Jakobsen, J.R. and Pellegrini, A. (2008). *Secularisms*. Durham, NC: Duke University Press.
Kantorowicz, E.H. (1997). *The King's Two Bodies: A Study in Mediaeval Political Theology*. Princeton, NJ: Princeton University Press.
Keane, W. (2007). *Christian Moderns: Freedom and Fetish in the Mission Encounter*. Berkeley, CA: University of California Press.
Klassen, P.E. (2011). *Spirits of Protestantism: Medicine, Healing, and Liberal Christianity*. Berkeley, CA: University of California Press.
Klinger, C. (1995). 'The Concepts of the Sublime and the Beautiful In Kant and Lyotard.' *Constellations* 2(2), 207–223.
Lessard, H., Johnson, R., and Webber, J. (eds) (2011). *Storied Communities: Narratives of Contact and Arrival in Constituting Political Community*. Vancouver, BC: UBC Press.
Lutz, J.S. (2007). *Myth and Memory: Stories of Indigenous-European Contact*. Vancouver, BC: UBC Press.
Mahmood, S. (2010). 'Can Secularism be Other-wise?' In M. Warner, J. VanAntwerpen, and C.J. Calhoun (eds) *Varieties of Secularism in a Secular Age*, 282–299. Cambridge, MA: Harvard University Press.

Maitland, F. (1900). 'The Corporation Sole.' *Law Quarterly Review* 16, 335–354.
Maitland, F. (1901). 'The Crown as Corporation.' *Law Quarterly Review* 17, 131–146.
Marty, M.E. (1994). *Fundamentalisms Observed*. Chicago, IL: University of Chicago Press.
McCullagh, J.B. (1899). 'The Indian Potlatch.' Substance of a paper read before CMS annual conference at Metlakatla, BC, 1899. Toronto, ON: Women's Missionary Society of the Methodist Church.
McNally, M.D. (2010). 'Native American Religious Freedom Beyond the First Amendment.' In C. Bender and P.E. Klassen (eds) *After Pluralism: Reimagining Religious Engagement*, 226–251. New York: Columbia University Press.
McNeil, K. (2007). Judicial Approaches to Self-Government since Calder: Searching for Doctrinal Coherence. In H. Foster, H. Raven, and J. Webber (eds) *Let Right Be Done: Aboriginal Title, the Calder Case, and the Future of Indigenous Rights*, 129–154. Vancouver, BC: UBC Press.
Mercer, A. (1911). 'Indians' View of Land Question.' *The Evening Empire*.
Meyer, B. (1999). *Translating the Devil: Religion and Modernity Among the Ewe in Ghana*. Edinburgh: Edinburgh University Press.
Modern, J.L. (2011). *Secularism in Antebellum America*. Chicago, IL: University of Chicago Press.
n.a. (1914). 'Indian Legal Status in Regards to Land.' *The Evening Empire*, 1–2.
Neylan, S. (2002). *The Heavens Are Changing: Nineteenth-Century Protestant Missions and Tsimshian Christianity*. Montreal: McGill-Queen's University Press.
Niezen, R. and Burgess, K. (2000). *Spirit Wars: Native North American Religions in the Age of Nation Building*. Berkeley, CA: University of California Press.
OED. (1989a). Fundament. *Oxford English Dictionary*. Available at http://www.oed.com.myaccess.library.utoronto.ca/view/Entry/75496?redirectedFrom fundament#eid [last accessed 28 June 2012].
OED. (1989b). Fundamental. *Oxford English Dictionary*. Available at http://www.oed.com.myaccess.library.utoronto.ca/view/Entry/75497 [last accessed 28 June 2012].
OED. (1989c). Secular. *Oxford English Dictionary*. Available at http://www.oed.com.myaccess.library.utoronto.ca/view/Entry/174620 [last accessed 28 June 2012].
O'Hara, J.B. (1988). 'The Modern Corporation Sole.' *Dickason Law Review* 93, 23–39.
Patterson, E.P. (1967). 'Arthur E. O'Meara, Friend of the Indians.' *The Pacific Northwest Quarterly* 58(2), 90–99.
Scott, J.W. (2007). *The Politics of the Veil*. Prineton, NJ: Princeton University Press.
Slattery, B. (2005). 'Aboriginal Rights and the Honour of the Crown.' *Supreme Court Law Review* 29, 433–445.
Smith, J.K.A. (2012). 'Secular Liturgies and the Prospects for a "Postsecular" Sociology of Religion.' In P.S. Gorski (ed.) *The Postsecular in Question: Religion in Contemporary Society*, 159–184. New York: NYU Press.
Sommerville, C.J. (2002). 'Postsecularism Marginalizes the University: A Rejoinder to Hollinger.' *Church History* 71(4), 848–857.
Sterritt, N. (1998). *Tribal Boundaries in the Nass Watershed*. Vancouver, BC: UBC Press.
Stevens, L.M. (2004). *The Poor Indians: British Missionaries, Native Americans, and Colonial Sensibility*. Philadelphia, PA: University of Pennsylvania Press.

Taylor, C. (1998). 'On the Nisga'a Treaty.' *BC Studies: The British Columbian Quarterly* 120, 37–40.
Taylor, C. (2004). *Modern Social Imaginaries*. Durham, NC: Duke University Press.
Taylor, C. (2007). *A Secular Age*. Cambridge, MA: Harvard University Press.
Tully, J. (1993). *An Approach to Political Philosophy: Locke in Contexts*. Cambridge: Cambridge University Press.
Valverde, M. (2011). '"The Honour of the Crown Is at Stake": Aboriginal Land Claims Litigation and the Epistemology of Sovereignty.' *UC Irvine Law Review* 1(3), 957–974.
Waisberg, L.G. and Holzkamm, T.E. (1993). '"A Tendency to Discourage Them from Cultivating": Ojibwa Agriculture and Indian Affairs Administration in Northwestern Ontario.' *Ethnohistory* 40(2), 175–211.
Waldron, J. (2002). *God, Locke, and Equality: Christian Foundations of John Locke's Political Thought*. Cambridge: Cambridge University Press.
Warner, M., VanAntwerpen, J., and Calhoun, C.J. (eds) (2010). *Varieties of Secularism in a Secular Age*. Cambridge, MA: Harvard University Press.
Wenger, T.J. (2009). *We Have a Religion: The 1920s Pueblo Indian Dance Controversy and American Religious Freedom*. Chapel Hill, NC: University of North Carolina Press.

10
Religious Aspirations, Public Religion, and the Secularity of Pluralism

Patrick Eisenlohr

The salience of religious activism and mobilizations throughout the contemporary world is perhaps the main reason for the popularity of the notion of the postsecular. The latter is inspired by hopes for greater inclusiveness towards religious groups and their aspirations, realizing that they are not necessarily incompatible with emancipatory political agendas, as well as the insight that religion remains a key component of social and political life that no amount of modernizing 'progress' and expansion of scientific knowledge can make disappear. At the same time, the term also owes much of its currency to the assumption that religion had actually been pushed back by modernization processes but has now 'returned.' However, an array of scholarship has demonstrated that religion actually never went away but was powerfully transformed by European imperial expansion and the rise of the nation state (Asad, 2003; Masuzawa, 2005; van der Veer, 2001). To make matters more complex, it is now increasingly clear that the modern comparative category of 'religion' that provides the basis for any discussion of secularization is actually the product of the same modernization processes that until relatively recently were widely believed to be responsible for an assumed decline of religion. Modern practices of governmentality delineated religion as a sphere of life separate from politics, law, economy, science, and society, and, as such, the universal category of religion is co-constituted through what is frequently regarded as its binary opposite, the secular. The concept of the postsecular, thus, evokes a rather contradictory scenario. On one hand, it is indebted to the classical secularization thesis according to which privatization of religion, the separation of religion from other aspects of social and political life, and the decline of the social significance of religion necessarily go hand in hand (see Casanova, 1994). Since, from a global perspective, no decline of the social significance of religion or increased privatization of religion appears to have taken place – indeed many argue the opposite – this invites the assumption that our contemporary world has somehow moved beyond the secular in a comprehensive sense. On the other hand, our comparative concept of religion which seems so fundamental to the current discussion about a religious 'revival' and a decline of the secular is actually unthinkable without the conceptual and governmental operations separating the religious from the nonreligious that constitute such a key part of the secularization thesis. One also has to add that European imperial expansion as a further key dimension of modernity and the resulting colonial encounter with religious others also helped bring about the universal and comparative category of religion that is often taken for granted in discussions about the putative retreat of the secular (van der Veer, 2001).

Perhaps the two most prominent theorists of the secular, Charles Taylor and Talal Asad, have both argued in different ways that certain aspects of the secular remain fundamental to our social and cultural life and are fully compatible with the instances of heightened religious activism and the visibility of religious practices and identifications so widely observed today. Locating the origin of the secular in the dynamics of Christian thought and politics, Taylor argues that people in Western societies and also large numbers elsewhere now live in an irretrievably 'secular age'. This is because, for them, even though not having declined in significance, religion has become an option only, requiring justification (Taylor, 2007: 3). Taylor argues that from such a perspective an immanent world has become the 'natural' baseline of our existence, which does not necessarily deny the existence of the transcendent or preclude engagement with it, but constitutes such a self-sufficient 'immanent frame' that it does not require the transcendent any more to appear as self-evident and real (Taylor, 2007: 549, 2010: 306–307). Taylor, thus, maintains that secularization in a very specific sense has become irreversible for a large and growing part of humanity. At the same time, the contemporary world is subject to dramatically visible 'religious mobilizations' (Taylor, 2006), which rely on the same modern techniques of moving and mobilizing people that are also used in nation-building, as well as on the same media-based interventions in the public sphere that democratic politics, advertising, and entertainment also make use of. According to Taylor, people need to be mobilized precisely because religion is not taken for granted any more and because they live in a world that from a phenomenological point of view does not require religion to be experienced as real and meaningful. Therefore, this 'disenchanted' condition and highly salient religious activism as well as a growing social significance of religion in much of the world seem perfectly compatible.

Taking a very different perspective on the genealogy of the secular, Talal Asad nevertheless reaches similar conclusions about the co-presence of the deeply secular and highly salient religious activism and mobilization today. As with Taylor, Asad suggests that our contemporary world is profoundly secular in a very specific way. Instead of emphasizing the role of a cosmological 'disenchantment' of the world that makes the transcendent an option only, for Asad the role of the modern nation-state is crucial in the secularization of certain aspects of our lives. Not only does the nation-state stand for the doctrine of popular sovereignty and is thus in contrast to the divinely legitimized rule of dynastic states firmly rooted in the history of humans – for 'the men and women of each national society make and *own* their history' (Asad, 1999: 186) – but it also seeks to regulate and remake individual life in the fulfilment of its own practical goals of governance and not those related to any sort of divine or transcendent agency. The modern nation-state, thus, aims to shape all social identities and spheres of action. 'It is not only that the state intervenes directly in the social body for purposes of reform; it is that all social activity requires the consent of the law, and therefore of the nation-state' (Asad, 1999: 191). This fundamental condition of modernity can certainly coexist with what Taylor has called 'religious mobilizations', in which the social significance and visibility of religion increases and religious activists forcefully participate in public spheres. It is only that religious activists such as Islamists have to contend with the regulatory powers of the modern nation-state that constitutes the secular ground for the management of the social: 'No movement that aspires to more than mere belief or inconsequential talk in public can remain indifferent to state power in a secular world' (Asad, 1999: 191).

However, what does such 'not remaining indifferent' to state power entail for religious activists and movements? How do the regulatory powers of the modern state grounded in a secular vision of social life intersect with what Taylor has called 'religious mobilizations'? In this chapter, I address these questions in order to contribute to a better understanding of how dimensions of 'deep secularity' that have become a taken-for-granted baseline for the political regulation of social and cultural life throughout the world relate to what is widely understood to be a greater visibility and importance of religion in the world today.

I examine two cases of religious mobilization among Muslims in contemporary Mauritius and in the global megacity Mumbai. Certainly, my examples could be added to many others confirming the salience of religious identifications and practices in the contemporary world. But my point is not to reiterate that such examples demonstrate the failure of the secularization thesis. Rather, I want to draw attention to the complex interplay between such religious mobilizations and the secular dimensions of modern nation-states.

Religion and globalization

One explanation for the greater salience of religious mobilizations in the contemporary world that is increasingly being put forward is the link between processes of globalization and religion. There is, for example, an established point of view that interprets religious activism, such as the growth of so-called fundamentalism, as a stress symptom among people suffering from the disruptions and insecurities brought about by globalization. Unable to make sense of the new complexities and dislocations that globalization brings along, they resort to purified and maximized forms of religion in a reactive way (Roy, 2004). Also, the workings of global markets often appear opaque to people in their local contexts and therefore, one argument goes, their effects are interpreted through a religious lens, resulting in 'occult economies' involving, for example, the agency of witches and sorcerers (Comaroff and Comaroff, 1999). More recent work in anthropology, however, has sought to avoid analysing the links between religion and globalization by reducing religion to the manifestation of something else (see Rudnyckyj, 2009). On the contrary, returning to a more Weberian approach to religion and political economy, scholars are now investigating the role religious cosmologies play in shaping the global political economy and examine the religious undertones in discourses about globalization.

For example, Joel Robbins (2009) and Thomas Csordas (2009) have recently argued that there are deep resonances between the centre-periphery structures of the globalized world and the cosmologies of major religious traditions such as Christianity and Islam that rest on a sharp distinction between this world and a realm of the transcendent. Many, perhaps most, people in the contemporary world view themselves as inhabiting peripheries of the globalized world, wanting to reach the desired centres. Religious cosmologies that reject this world in favour of travelling to a realm of a radically different and superior sphere of the transcendent structurally echo this contrast between real places that are lacking and the desired centres of the global political economy. Religious traditions built on such a contrast, such as Evangelical Christianity and reformist forms of Islam, provide people on the peripheries with workable plans to reach a desired realm so different from their present circumstances, and this is also the reason why they thrive and spread in the contemporary world. Among Sunni Barelvi Muslims in Mauritius and Twelver Shiite Muslims in Mumbai, where I have conducted ethnographic field research since 1996 and 2005, respectively, I have found evidence for such a link between religious activism and the dynamics of globalization. It is tempting to apply such an analysis to these two places, as Mumbai is one of the world's global megacities, and Mauritius an Indian Ocean island without a precolonial population that was settled in the course of European imperial expansion and has never known anything but globalization. Many Shiite Muslims in Mumbai as well as Sunni Barelvi Muslims in Mauritius consider involvement in religious activism and orthodoxy as a hallmark of a modern, cosmopolitan lifestyle, connecting them not only to the transcendent but also to centres of global importance in this world. In Mauritius, Muslims constitute 17 per cent of the population of approximately 1.2 million, the percentage of Hindus is now 52 per cent, while people of Indian origin taken as a whole constitute almost 70 per cent of the population. Among Mauritian Muslims, I have documented a steady trend towards standardized orthodoxy in the course of the last 100 years mainly driven by transnational Gujarati trader communities (Eisenlohr, 2012). This trend has greatly increased following the heightened integration of Mauritius into neoliberal processes of globalization since the 1980s having brought about what many consider an 'economic miracle'. Muslims constitute roughly 20 per cent of Mumbai's population, while Twelver Shiite Muslims comprise by far the largest number among the Shiite minority within the Muslim population.[1] Ithna Ashari Khojas, a Gujarati trader community, and the 'Mughals', a business community of Iranian origin, dominate the elites among Twelver Shiites and also most religious organizations. However, the great majority of Twelver Shiites in Mumbai is of North Indian migrant origin, and poverty among them is very widespread. In Mumbai, the growth of religious activism among Shiite Muslims has gone hand in hand with large flows of migration from the rural and small-town peripheries of Northern India to the global megacity. Here, migration that has been directly motivated by the role of Mumbai as a global centre has also led to increased engagement with the transnational networks of Twelver Shiite orthodoxy, especially the networks of widely respected senior scholars known as *marja-e taqlid* (sources of emulation) such as Ayatollah Sistani in Najaf. At the same time, such growth of religious orthodoxy also increasingly shapes the relationships Shiite Muslims entertain to their places of origin or ancestry in Northern India. Monetary remittances do of course play a key role in this relationship, as family members and other extended kin often depend on such remittances from migrants in the megacity. However, some of these resources are now also spent on religious activities and the building and support of Shiite institutions and places of religious remembrance such as miniature replicas of the tombs of Hussain and other members of the *ahl al-bayt* (the family of the Prophet) who lost their lives in the battle of Karbala in 680 AD. Moreover, migrants and their Mumbai-born descendants frequently time their periodic return visits from the city to coincide with religiously significant events in the ritual calendar, such as the months of Muharram and Ramadan. Also, religious mobilization among Muslims in both Mauritius and Mumbai to a considerable extent unfolds through the media technological and transport infrastructures of globalization. In both places, religious traditions are now firmly integrated with contemporary media practices. Sermons and devotional poetry recitals circulate transnationally and provide more opportunities for honing one's piety also outside the established ritual and performative contexts associated with these religious genres. Moreover, media strategies adopted from modern marketing and advertising now feature prominently in promoting particular traditions of Islam, such as the South Asian Sunni Barelvi tradition in Mauritius or Twelver Shiism in Mumbai.

State regulation of religious diversity

All these developments illustrate the broad links between processes of globalization and religious activism in the contemporary world. But it is also important to realize that such activism has to reckon with the regulatory powers of the modern nation-state. Such engagement with state power remains also central to other kinds of social activism. However, the boundary between religious and nonreligious movements of protest and affirmation is especially fleeting today, as the example of contemporary feminism attests (Braidotti, 2008). Both in Mauritius and India, the managing of religious diversity is subject to state controls and visions of pluralism, and religious mobilizations are also, in part, a response to such national regimes of diversity. One important dimension of the secularity of these modern nation-states is that their institutions regard certain relationships between religious institutions and traditions and the state as desirable, because they consider these relationships as essential for the maintenance of public order and the formation of loyal and productive citizens. Among both Barelvi Muslims in Mauritius and Twelver Shiite Muslims in Mumbai there is a pronounced tendency to combine religious activism with pledges to good citizenship and, above all, to stress the role Islamic piety can play in promoting peaceful coexistence among citizens. There is a great concern to display the conformity of religious mobilization with the ideal arrangements of religious pluralism promulgated by the respective nation-states. In Mauritius, where there was no precolonial population, the postcolonial state has embarked on a policy to promote so-called 'ancestral cultures' of the various 'communities' of Indian and Chinese origin, that in turn largely consist of religious traditions. The dominant ideology of Mauritian pluralism suggests that full citizenship involves the cultivation of such 'ancestral cultures' with religious biases and turns Mauritians into morally grounded and productive citizens capable to peacefully coexist with others. For Mauritian Muslims, Islamic traditions represent their 'ancestral culture' which the state supports by subsidizing religious bodies and institutions and by teaching so-called 'ancestral languages' such as Urdu and Arabic in state schools – languages that Muslims almost exclusively use in religious contexts and settings. By cultivating Islam as their 'ancestral culture', Mauritian Muslims not only reinforce transnational links and solidarities and establish connections to centres of religious authority located elsewhere but also demonstrate their adherence to the Mauritian state vision of governing the marked diversity of the Mauritian population. Ministers and other senior state representatives attend major events in the Islamic ritual calendar such as *yaum-un nabi* (the birthday of the Prophet), where Muslims combine public displays of piety with a claim to be model citizens whose grounding in a major, recognized, religious tradition enables them to peacefully and respectfully coexist with non-Muslim citizens as a matter of ethical conduct.

This is also the case in Mumbai, where public expressions of Islamic practice and belonging are constrained by the status of Muslims as a beleaguered minority in India that is constantly asked to prove their good citizenship and routinely suspected of involvement in subversive activities such as terrorism and collaboration with archenemy Pakistan. At the same time, postcolonial India has followed politics of pluralism and secularism that recognize the great importance of religion in the lives of Indian citizens, including its collective dimensions. Discourses that connect moral values grounded in religious tradition, good citizenship, and peaceful coexistence are very widespread in India. Responding to this special and problematic position within the regime of religious pluralism promoted by the Indian state, a Shiite Muslim media centre in Mumbai affiliated with Ayatollah Sistani in Najaf, annually launches a 'Muharram Awareness Campaign' in the Islamic month of Muharram. This month is a time of ritual mourning for Shiite Muslims who commemorate the death of the Prophet Muhammad's grandson Hussain and other members of the family of the Prophet in the Battle of Karbala. Through its website, as well as advertising banners on buses and trains and in other public places, the 'World Islamic Network' headquartered in the centrally located Mumbai Muslim neighbourhood of Dongri, seeks to connect Islamic piety with the claim that Muslims are exemplary Indian citizens. For example, many Shiite Muslims consider Gandhi's anti-colonial struggle as being inspired by Hussain's struggle against tyranny at Karbala. The billboards set up by the network feature reported sayings by Gandhi according to which, 'If India ever desires to become a great nation it should follow the example of Imam Hussain.' Also, the Muharram 2010/2011 campaign made reference to the 26 November 2008 terrorist attacks in Mumbai by portraying Shiite Muslims as model citizens who, through the tragedy of Karbala, represent the world's original victims of terrorism. For example, on World Islamic Network advertising banner images of the iconic Taj Mahal hotel, as it burned during the attacks, were juxtaposed with images of the golden minarets of the splendid tomb of Imam Hussain at Karbala, together with the statement: 'The Grandson of the Prophet Muhammad (s.a.w.s.) Imam Hussain (a.s.) sacrificed his life to unite all who oppose terrorism and injustice.' Such a combination of promoting Muslim piety during the month of Ramadan with raising awareness of Indian Muslims' good citizenship and moral grounding among non-Muslims was not only evident from the placement of the billboards and digital banners outside Muslim enclaves but also through the choice of English and Hindi – the latter especially indicates the addressing of a national but clearly non-Muslim public.

Both examples demonstrate that modern religious mobilizations are intensely driven by the forces of globalization while making ample use of its media infrastructures. In this, they not only respond to but are also crucially shaped by the regulations and ideologies of governing religion in the respective nation-states. Both Muslims in Mauritius and in Mumbai cannot ignore state visions of religious diversity and the relationships between state institutions and religious groups they stipulate. Indeed, especially in the media-driven parts of religious mobilization, both Barelvi Muslims in Mauritius and Twelver Shiite Muslims in Mumbai seek to align themselves with such official ideals of diversity.

In different ways, they combine calls for Islamic piety and orthopraxy with claims to be good citizens that contribute to national cohesion and are engaged in tolerant and fruitful coexistence with citizens of other religious affiliation. This in turn indicates that the religious activism, among Barelvi Muslims in Mauritius and Shiite Muslims in Mumbai I have described, intersects in complex ways with techniques of modern governance that constitute a key dimension of secularity in the contemporary world.

Standardized religion

Religious mobilizations among Muslims in Mauritius and Mumbai clearly respond to state regimes of regulating religious diversity among its citizens. But this is not the only way in which highly visible piety and religious activism interacts with what authors such as Talal Asad have described as the core secular dimensions of our contemporary world. Let us return to the issue of the modern, universal concept of religion that is the combined result of modern practices of governance separating a sphere of the religious from other fields of social and political life and the intensified encounter with religious others in the course of European imperial expansion. Perhaps no other issue illustrates the deep entanglement of religious mobilization and dimensions of the secular as forcefully than the important role that standardized, universal notions of religion play in what appears to some as a contemporary 'return of religion.' In my Mauritian example, the centrality of standardized religion is already obvious in the official policy of promoting 'ancestral cultures' largely based on officially recognized religious traditions. Mauritians are thus expected not to adhere to popular religious traditions and heterodoxy but to officially recognize 'world religions', and this adherence, in turn, reinforces their membership in the nation. For Mauritian Muslims, major Islamic traditions represent their 'ancestral culture', and the South Asian Barelvi school is currently still the most significant of these transnational, standardized forms of religion. The Mauritian policy of privileging 'ancestral cultures' based on such religious orthodoxies is the endpoint of a long history of religious debate and purification among Mauritians. For Muslims, who – like Mauritian Muslims in their great majority – came to Mauritius as indentured labourers, this has resulted in the decline of forms of popular and 'hybrid' religiosity that were characteristic of Hindus and Muslims of rural nineteenth-century North India, and especially the shared world of the sugar plantations and emerging Indo-Mauritian villages in the countryside. There, forms of neighbourly solidarity between indentured immigrants of Hindu and Muslim background were the norm, and the shared memory of migration and its circumstances was long kept alive through forms of ritual kinship across religious lines among those of whose ancestors had arrived on the same ship (*jahaji bhai*). Such shared Indo-Mauritian life-worlds, under indenture and in its immediate aftermath, also included forms of reciprocal participation in religious practices. It was common for Hindus to participate in the 'Ghoon' or 'Tazzia', processions in memory of the martyrdom of Hussain, the grandson of the Prophet Muhammad at the Battle of Karbala (Edun, 1984). My older informants in Mauritius remembered that Muslims, in turn, joined in the chanting of the popular version of the Ramayana epos on ritual occasions and also left offerings such as flowers and candles at village trees for local guardian deities. Muslim and Hindu wedding rituals were more influenced by the shared rural background of indentured labourers in Uttar Pradesh (UP) and Bihar than by separate religious orthodoxies. In the course of the twentieth century, and greatly accelerating in the decades before independence in 1968, this shared world of popular and alternative religiosity came gradually to an end and was increasingly replaced by religious purification and the accentuation of boundaries with religious others. Among Mauritian Muslims, Gujarati merchant elites, who had settled in Mauritius as free immigrants with their own capital and dense networks of business, kinship, and religion with India and other locations in the Indian Ocean world, played a key role in spreading more standardized and orthodox forms of Islam among Mauritian Muslims. The Kutchi Memons, for a long time the wealthiest and most influential among these merchant elites, introduced the Barelvi tradition to Mauritius, to which they cultivate a longstanding relationship. The Memons' chief competitors, the Sunni Surtees, also engaged in mosque building and invited missionaries of the rival Deobandi tradition to Mauritius. Barelvis, for a long time the large majority, probably still constitute little more than half among the Mauritian Muslims. Their influence is steadily pushed back by the Deobandis, above all the transnational missionary movement Tablighi Jamaat, while there is also a growing number of Salafis. The competition between rival Islamic traditions in Mauritius introduced through the cosmopolitan networks of Gujarati merchant communities led to a growing trend towards standardized, orthodox versions of Islam which were in turn recognized as Mauritian Muslims' 'ancestral culture' after independence in 1968 (Eisenlohr, 2006a).

The deployment of standardized religious orthodoxies in seeking to achieve peaceful coexistence among citizens is another salient example of how highly visible religious mobilization and secular forms of governance intermingle. Both in Mauritius and in India there are strong traditions assigning religious orthodoxies key roles in the formation of peaceful, tolerant, and productive citizens. According to these visions, citizens are in need of moral grounding to be able to acquire these qualities, and the moral values citizens should adhere to are, in turn, inseparable from religious traditions. Even though religious values and practices play key roles in this vision of productive and tolerant citizenship, they are also part of a secular regime of modern governance. This is because the state promotes such religiously undergirded notions of citizenship not in the name of a realm of the divine. The state does so in order to create more compliant and productive citizens who will, in turn, support and strengthen its own power. Crucially, both in Mauritius and India the modern nation-state legitimizes its role in claiming to be the concrete realization of the right of self-determination of the nation, which in turn does not belong to the world of the divine.

In Mauritius, the state draws on a discourse of the possible destabilization of social bonds brought about by economic development in the context of globalization. Mobilizing a familiar narrative of globalization as potentially disruptive and destabilizing on the local level, the state legitimizes its broad support for 'ancestral cultures' based on religious traditions in terms of the latter's presumed integrative effects. Here, Mauritian state representatives partake in a particular Gandhian tradition of regulating religious diversity in India according to which religious commitments are essential building blocks for shaping disciplined and peaceful citizens (Parsuraman, 1988; see also Eisenlohr, 2006b: 398–399). Far from banishing religion to a sphere of the private, the task of the state is actually to encourage and mobilize benign religious values across the boundaries of religious traditions to make successful nation building possible (compare Nandy, 1990; Madan, 1998). This take on Indian secularism, so eagerly adopted by the Mauritian government, contrasts with the vision of India's first Prime Minister Jawaharlal Nehru, who was convinced of the necessity for the state to control dangerous religious passions. However, Nehru's understanding of secularism, certainly the most influential among the range of Indian secularisms since independence, did not insist on a strict separation of state from religious institutions. Recognizing religious rights also in their collective dimension, Nehru allowed for the state to intervene in the affairs of religious communities to reform or ban 'backward' practices, amounting to an arrangement of the relations between the state and religious communities described as 'principled distance' (Bhargava, 2007). Both dominant strains of Indian secularism, Nehruvian and Gandhian, are projects to regulate religious diversity through the state. This is also the case in the Gandhian vision. Even though the latter contains romantic appeals to presumably unsullied and benign popular religiosity rooted in an old Indian tradition of religious conviviality and tolerance, the mobilization of religion for the making of good citizens ultimately turns out to be also a modern technique of governance, a point especially salient in the Mauritian policy of regulating diversity through the promotion of 'ancestral cultures'. But also in Mumbai, Shiite Muslims' portrayal of themselves as the world's original victims of injustice and terrorism, supporting their public claims to be good and peaceful Indian citizens, is taking place against the background of increasing standardization of religion. Since the late 1970s, for Shiite Muslims in Mumbai this has, above all, been evident in the much greater importance of practices and doctrines that are explicitly authorized by leading religious scholars in the world of Twelver Shiism that are recognized as *marja-e taqlid*. For Mumbai, this has meant a greater influence of Ayatollah Sistanti in Najaf, Iraq, who is also the most influential *marja* in India as a whole. The spread of contemporary religious media, such as formerly cassettes and now audio and DVDs – as well as cable TV networks that circulate various kinds of religious performances, such as speeches and sermons of leading clerics, poetry recitals, and recordings of Shiite mourning practices for the victims of Karbala – has played a key role in this process of increasing orthodoxization. Here, the connection between state regimes of governing religious diversity and the spread of standardized transnational religious orthodoxies is less explicit than in the Mauritian policy of 'ancestral cultures'. Unlike in Mauritius, state institutions do not directly encourage the increasing standardization of Islamic practice. Nevertheless, representatives of transnational religious orthodoxy are also at the forefront in positioning Shiite Muslims as good citizens, as in the 'Muharram Awareness Campaign'. One important reason for this is the change from quietist stances connected to religious practices to more activist engagement in Shiite religious mobilization, a development that many of my informants attributed to the impact of the Iranian revolution. While the concept of *vilayat-e faqih* (rule of the jurisprudent), institutionalized by Ayatollah Khomeini as the foundational principle of the Islamic Republic of Iran, was never popular in India and was also never approved by Ayatollah Sistani, the idea that remembrance of the injustice of Karbala should not be confined to elaborate rituals of mourning but should also propel practical public engagement against suffering and oppression has gained greater ground since the Iranian Revolution throughout the transnational Shiite world. Among Shiite Muslims in Mumbai this has, above all, resulted in increased charity work and support of education among Shiite Muslims, as well as public efforts in claiming good citizenship and loyalty to the Indian nation on the basis of Islamic values. The foundations and activists tied to transnational networks of *marjaiyya* have, in turn, dominated all these forms of activism, at the same time greatly increasing their influence among Shiite Muslims in Mumbai.

Conclusion

In this chapter, I have engaged with the contradictions that underlie the notion of the postsecular. I have suggested that those who consider highly visible religious activism as evidence for a movement beyond a secular world tend to ignore the crucial role that modern techniques of governance play in the making of religion and religious mobilization in the world today. My examples of religious vitality among Muslims in Mumbai and Mauritius show that processes of globalization are important driving forces for religious mobilization. They, however, intersect with varying state regimes of regulating religion and religious plurality, to which religious mobilizations respond. This dynamic results in greater public visibility of religion and, at the same time, also gives secular forms of modern governance ample opportunities to shape religious mobilization. One of the original ironies of the notion of the postsecular is that modern, standardized notions of religion that underlie discussions of a possible transition to a postsecular world are themselves the product of specific processes of secularization. My examples show that notions of standardized 'world religions' have become increasingly important for religious activism and state attempts to regulate religion. The spread of such understandings of religion as major, transnational and standardized orthodoxies can be understood as one of the dimensions of cultural globalization. It is also the point where processes of globalization and state regimes of regulating religion converge, both favouring major, standardized forms of religion. The multilayered relationships between processes of globalization, state regimes of regulating religion, and religious mobilization in the world today suggest a complex intermingling of the religious and the secular that affords no easy answers about processes of secularization and puts in doubt expectations of an unambiguously postsecular future.

Note

1. Ismaili Bohras and Ismaili Agha Khani Khojas are other, smaller Shiite communities in the city of Mumbai.

References

Asad, T. (1999). 'Religion, Nation-State, Secularism.' In P. van der Veer and H. Lehmann (eds) *Nation and Religion: Perspectives on Europe and Asia*, 178–196. Princeton: Princeton University Press.
—— (2003). *Formations of the Secular: Christianity, Islam, Modernity*. Stanford, CA: Stanford University Press.
Bhargava, R. (2007). 'The Distinctiveness of Indian Secularism.' In T.N. Srinivasan (ed.) *The Future of Secularism*, 20–53. Delhi: Oxford University Press.
Braidotti, R. (2008). 'In Spite of the Times: The Postsecular Turn in Feminism.' *Theory, Culture & Society* 25(1), 1–24.
Casanova, J. (1994). *Public Religions in the Modern World*. Chicago: University of Chicago Press.
Comaroff, J. and Comaroff, J. (1999). 'Occult Economies and the Violence of Abstraction: Notes from the South African Postcolony.' *American Ethnologist* 12(2), 291–343.
Csordas, T. (2009). 'Introduction: Modalities of Transnational Transcendence.' In T. Csordas (ed.) *Transnational Transcendence: Essays on Religion and Globalization*, 1–30. Berkeley, CA: University of California Press.
Edun, E.H. (1984). 'Tajjia (Tazzia).' In Uttam Bissoondoyal (ed.) *Indians Overseas: The Mauritia Experience*, 28–34. Moka, Mauritius: Mahatma Gandhi Institute.
Eisenlohr, P. (2006a). 'The Politics of Diaspora and the Morality of Secularism: Muslim Identities and Islamic Authority in Mauritius.' *Journal of the Royal Anthropological Institute* (N.S.) 12(2), 395–412.
—— (2006b). *Little India: Diaspora, Time and Ethnolinguistic Belonging in Hindu Mauritius*. Berkeley, CA: University of California Press.
—— (2012). 'Cosmopolitanism, Globalization, and Islamic Piety Movements in Mauritius.' *City & Society* 24(1), 7–28.
Madan, T.N. (1998). 'Secularism in Its Place.' In R. Bhargava (ed.) *Secularism and Its Critics*, 297–320. New Delhi: Oxford University Press.
Masuzawa, T. (2005). *The Invention of World Religions, or How European Universalism Was Preserved in the Language of Pluralism*. Chicago: University of Chicago Press.
Nandy, A. (1990). 'The Politics of Secularism and the Recovery of Religious Tolerance.' In V. Das (ed.) *Mirrors of Violence*, 69–93. Delhi: Oxford University Press.
Parsuraman, A. (1988). *From Ancestral Cultures to National Culture: Mauritius*. Moka, Mauritius: Mahatma Gandhi Institute Press.
Robbins, J. (2009). 'Is the *Trans-* in *Transnational* the *Trans-* in *Transcendent*? On Alterity and the Sacred in the Age of Globalization.' In T. Csordas (ed.) *Transnational Transcendence: Essays on Religion and Globalization*, 55–72. Berkeley, CA: University of California Press.

Roy, O. (2004). *Globalized Islam: The Search for a New Ummah*. New York: Columbia University Press.
Rudnyckyj, D. (2009). 'Spiritual Economies: Islam and Neoliberalism in Contemporary Indonesia.' *Cultural Anthropology* 24(1), 104–141.
Taylor, C. (2006). 'Religious Mobilizations.' *Public Culture* 18(2), 281–300.
—— (2007). *A Secular Age*. Cambridge, MA: Harvard University Press.
—— (2010). 'Afterword: Apologia pro Libro suo.' In M. Warner, J. Vanantwerpen, and C. Calhoun (eds) *Varieties of Secularism in a Secular Age*, 300–321. Cambridge, MA: Harvard University Press.
van der Veer, P. (2001). *Imperial Encounters: Religion and Modernity in India and Britain*. Princeton, NJ: Princeton University Press.

11
Towards a More Inclusive Feminism: Defining Feminism through Faith
Eva Midden

Introduction

In 1991, the conservative liberal politician Frits Bolkestein published the article *'Integratie van minderheden moet met lef worden aangepakt'* ('Integretation of minorities should be handled with guts'), which is generally considered to be the start of a long range of debates about minorities in the Netherlands. Even though many already believed that more attention should be given to the integration of migrants, the words of Bolkestein shocked the country (Prins, 2002). His main thesis is that multiculturalism should be limited; Western principles like freedom and equality are to be protected by all means (Bolkestein, 1991). Furthermore, he argues that more attention should be paid to the integration of minorities: because it is such a difficult problem, we have to deal with it with courage and creativity. There is no room for taboos or taking the easy way out (Bolkestein, 1991: 188).

Despite the long history of immigration, which was closely linked to colonization, most accounts of Dutch migration history start with the arrival of the so-called 'guest workers' in the 1950s (Ghorashi, 2003). They, mostly from Turkey and Morocco, were seen as temporary migrants who came to the Netherlands to work for a few years. When the government realized that these people would not go back to their country of birth, integration policies became an issue. However, this was not until the 1980s, when many migrants had already lived in the country for several decades. In these years, policy was mostly based on the idea that migrants should integrate into Dutch society, while maintaining their own identities: *'integratie met behoud van eigen identiteit'* (Ghorashi, 2003).

The beginning of the migration critical discourse can be connected to the first statements against this approach towards migrants and other cultures, such as the one by Bolkestein (Prins, 2002). In *Voorbij de Onschuld* (*Beyond Innocence*), Baukje Prins argues that the harsh discussions about multiculturalism and Islam in the Netherlands show that since the 1990s a new public discourse has arisen (Prins, 2004). An essential element of this 'neorealist' discourse is emancipation. Even though none of the neorealists seem to have shown any interest in women's rights before, they now use gender relations to define their own identity as opposite to the 'Other'. For most of the neorealist opinion leaders gender is an important example to explain what is wrong with multiculturalism/Islam/minority cultures, but none of them saw emancipation really as the main issue. In 2001, however, one of the well-known feminists of the Netherlands spoke out. In an interview with a national newspaper on International Women's Day, Ciska Dresselhuys (at that time chief editor of the popular feminist magazine *Opzij*) says that women who wear headscarves cannot work for her: 'In a coffee shop I don't endure sexism; circumcision is a taboo for me and editors with a headscarf can't work for *Opzij*' (Dresselhuys, 2001).

The feminist believes that the headscarf is a sign of women's oppression; any woman wearing one, therefore, cannot be a feminist and thus cannot work for a feminist magazine. Dresselhuys's words led to a hot discussion in the Netherlands, first of all because it was probably illegal for her, as an employer, to judge possible employees on their appearance. But besides this legal problem, the claims of Dresselhuys pointed out that the so-called problems with migration and multiculturalism were not only a problem of right-wing politicians but also an essential issue within feminism.

Mainstream Western feminism is generally known as secular. Women in this movement have fought religious dogmas and paternalistic gender patterns in religious texts and traditions. However, for many women all over the world religion is also an important part of their lives. Some of them try to combine their religious beliefs and feminist ideals. For a long time, their discussions remained in the margins, but in the last few years, 'mainstream' feminists are forced to rethink their standpoint about religion. Many of them remain critical about the relationship between religion and feminism, but others emphasize the importance of recognizing differences between women and reinvestigating the relationship between religion, secularism, and feminism. In her article on the feminist postsecular turn, Rosi Braidotti, for example, states, 'feminists cannot be simply secular, or be secular in a simple or self-evident sense. More complexity is needed' (Braidotti, 2008: 4).

In this chapter, I will discuss the results of the nine focus groups that I held with women from various women's organizations in the Netherlands. The interviews were semi-structured and covered the main aspects of the discussions about culture, religion, and feminism. The aim is to combine the arguments of women who are actively involved in organizations with critical theory on the postsecular turn. The final goal is to redefine the relationship between religion, secularism, and feminism in a more affirmative and inclusive manner.

The research project is set in the Netherlands for two reasons. First, the debate in the Netherlands has been rather heated and at the top of the political agenda; think, for example, of the violent occurrences in the past (the murder of film director Theo van Gogh and the constant threats to kill politicians like Ayaan Hirsi Ali), but also of the recent dismissal of Tariq Ramadan, both as advisory of the city of Rotterdam and as professor at the University of Rotterdam.[1] Secondly, due to my background and location, the Netherlands is the most logical starting point for my research. I am familiar with the political, social, and historical context and can therefore explore parameters in the debate that only someone who has lived in this location can. But even though this research is first of all based on a particular location, it is not solely a particular case. The debates about multiculturalism, integration, and Islam are not only important in the Netherlands but in many other (European) countries as well. And even though some of the historical, political, and social contexts differ in these countries, other aspects of the debate are similar. The recurrent debates about headscarves and *burqas* in, for example, Britain, France, Germany, and Belgium show that ideas about womanhood, gender equality, agency, cultural difference, and religious practices play an important role in public discourses all over Europe (and probably beyond).

Thinking feminism through the postsecular

This chapter has been much inspired by the so-called postsecular turn and more affirmative perspectives on the relationship between religion and feminism. I would like to make it explicit that even though I write this as a non-religious or secular feminist, I believe that feminism can no longer afford a strict secular approach. First of all, this would exclude a large group of women for whom religion/culture are very important. And secondly, it seems impossible to disconnect this approach from

Islamophobist politics. As we could see in the introduction of this chapter, in many public debates, gender equality functions as one of the arguments against multiculturalism in general, or Islam specifically. Sometimes this means that feminism is (mis)used for racist purposes. I do not mean to argue that this kind of misuse of feminist theories should automatically mean that feminists have to change their ideas, but I do think that we might need to reconsider our strategies. In my view, postsecular theory can be an important step in that direction and help to rethink the relationship between religion and feminism.

Bracke and Schmitt argue that despite the 'historic reluctance of traditional left wing and feminist movements, we can already recognize a greater interest in religious issues and identities within these groups' (Bracke and Schmitt, 2006: 11). This is connected to the above-mentioned conservative claim on secularism and the consequential link to racism and Islamophobia. Another important reason to commit to religious or postsecular dialogues could be the creation of a pluralist alternative to the current polarization. I argue that feminism cannot be strictly secular anymore and that the postsecular turn needs to be taken into account in the discussions about religion and feminism. In other words, a critical perspective on secularism and its relation to religion is a necessary aspect of a productive and inclusive (re)definition of feminism. Among other things, this includes critical analyses of what secularism is and does in our society.

Secularism builds on a certain concept of the world and the problems in that world (Asad, 2003: 191–192). This means that it has different meanings depending on time and location. Thus, above all, secularism is not the logical and reasonable 'successor' of faith. Bolette Blaagaard refers to this simplistic dichotomous use of secularism and religion as 'secular illiteracy' (Blaagaard, 2007). She argues that both secularism and the Enlightenment have strong ties to Christianity and that only forgetfulness makes the strict opposition between a religious 'them' and a secular 'us' possible. Furthermore, the ignorance of the secular legacy is closely connected to whiteness, or the invisibility of the white norm. Therefore, we need more knowledge and understanding of the relationship between Christianity, secularism, and so-called enlightened Western societies (Blaagaard, 2007: 13). I absolutely agree on this and would like to argue that an inclusive feminism should invest more in critically evaluating feminism's (assumed) relation to secularism. This would remove the 'Other' from the centre of attention and create space for a feminist analysis on a broader basis, without stigmatizing certain groups of women.

This chapter is also inspired by the recent debates on agency and subjectivity, which I would also connect to the postsecular turn. The women in the focus groups mentioned that they want to become emancipated in a non-self-centred way and take into account the wishes and needs of their families and friends. This connects to the work of Saba Mahmood, who, among other things, reconceptualizes the traditional conception of agency by detaching it from the simply dichotomous relation of subversion and subordination and leaving open the possibility of learning from others (Mahmood, 2005). However, despite the fact that it is important to note that there is agency beyond oppositional consciousness, the comments of the women in the focus groups on religion and knowledge also show that we need alternative analyses of what oppositional consciousness is. I would like to refer here to Rosi Braidotti's conceptualization of political subjectivity that starts from 'multiple micro-political practices of daily activism or interventions' (Braidotti, 2008: 16). This interpretation of subjectivity is a crucial instrument in many debates about religion and feminism because it helps us to conceptualize a feminism that can fight certain harmful traditions or customs without condemning religions or cultures in a general and stigmatizing way.

The final aspect that I would like to mention at this point in regard to rethinking religion and feminism through critical and postsecular theory is the concept of 'affirmative ethics'. One of the consequences of this approach is that we have to acknowledge the fact that we cannot change the world in a second; change takes time. Or as one of the women said: we have to see this as a process and not try to pin everything down beforehand. I would argue that we could theorize these remarks further through Braidotti's ideas on 'affirmative ethics'. This interpretation of ethics is not 'tied to the present by negation' but is instead 'affirmative and geared to creating possible futures' (Braidotti, 2008: 11). Thus, instead of trying to deconstruct or criticize certain identities or subjectivities, we should affirm them and think about the possibilities they create and the alternatives they can offer to current views on these issues. This means that difference is regarded as positive (instead of negative) and can form the basis of transformation or 'creative becoming' (Braidotti, 2008: 11).

Approach and sample

In the previous sections, I have shown that the public discourse in the Netherlands has for a long time not only focused on migration

Towards a More Inclusive Feminism 215

and integration issues but also often connected minority cultures, and especially Islam, to gender- and emancipation-related issues. The main purpose is to broaden the perspectives on the relationship between religion, secularism, and feminism by referring to the arguments and experiences of women who are active in grass-roots women's organizations (see Harding, 2004 for an elaborate analysis of the value of women's experiences in knowledge production). A total of nine focus groups were held in order to discuss topics of religion and emancipation.[2]

In order to get an adequate range of answers to these questions, it was necessary to obtain a broad sample that would be representative of the diversity in women's organizations in the Netherlands. Nine different organizations were chosen to cover the major groups that have a say in the debate.[3] The organizations differed in terms of main target group (country of origin, religious affiliation, civil status), action process (discussion, self-help, or information centres), and focus of intervention (emancipation, empowerment, or experience sharing). The aim was to bring together as many different organizations as possible, in order to produce as many different arguments as possible. The organizations in the sample were selected because they were interested in feminism or emancipation-related issues and in cultural and religious issues (or diversity).[4]

The main approach for this paper is based on critical discourse analysis (CDA), following especially the work of Norman Fairclough (Fairclough, 2001). The reason for this is that power and power relations are central in his work. Fairclough has a background in linguistics but developed an approach to discourse, which is also useful for social scientists and philosophers. Social relations, he argues, are for a large part determined by linguistics, and language is not just a tool we use to express social processes but part of these processes themselves.

Thinking about inclusive feminisms

Religion and culture: knowledge is power

Muslim women have developed various strategies when it comes to thinking about and working with their religion and emancipation, such as emphasizing the multiple discourses connected to religious traditions and reinterpreting and re-translating holy texts (Cooke, 2002). They criticize individuals and institutions that limit and oppress them (both within and outside Islam) and argue that we need to invest in alternative explanations of the Qur'an, which start from the main messages of the Qur'an, and also contextualize the texts (Barlas, 2005).

The women in the focus groups also referred to these kinds of strategies in order to navigate between religious traditions and obligations and emancipation. The differences between religion and culture are also part of this. One woman from Al Nisa, for example, argued:

> We cannot just blame culture; religion also plays a part in it, and therefore it is so important that women have proper knowledge on, for example, the Hadith. If a man for instance uses a Hadith ... which is very negative about women. ... As a woman you should have knowledge of the Hadith so that you can say, ok, you have one, I can show you ten that say the opposite. (Al Nisa, 43 min.)

Another woman adds to this that we have to acknowledge the relation between culture and religion:

> The traditional interpretations of the Qur'an and the Hadith are cultural and date from the seventh-century Arabic peninsula, which was a patriarchal society. So it is not just culture. We have to be aware how culture has influenced religion and the interpretation of religion, and how it has become oppressive to women in certain ways. (Al Nisa, 43 min.)

The interesting aspect of this woman's argument is that she, on the one hand, tells us to recognize how culture and religion are interwoven in the interpretation of religion as we now know it (see above), but that, at the same time, we have to be aware of the distinction between religion and culture and recognize that Islam often leaves more space to women than culture does (Al Nisa, 44 min.). This way, she can both criticize certain practices within her religion and resist those same practices by referring to holy texts. The key here is to recognize both the power relations involved and the possible differences within religious traditions and, finally, to give more attention to the distinction between certain practices (or in this case, religious traditions) and theory (or the holy texts). This approach opens a road to resistance from within, which is necessary, the women from Al Nisa add, because just recognizing the differences between culture and religion and text and interpretation does not change anything about the interpretations that are still dominant (Al Nisa, 44 min.). An interesting example of this kind of resistance from within is the remark of one woman, who recalls the moment when a woman on the street addressed her about her blouse:

supposedly my blouse was to tight on the back, because she saw a man looking at me. The only thing I told her was: then, why did you not approach that man then? (Al Nisa, 53 min.)

Of course this is just an innocent incident, but it does show how one can make others conscious of the fact that being modest is not just expected from women but also from men and, hence, that it is a mistake to only hold women responsible for this. I would argue that this also relates to Rosi Braidotti's interpretation of subjectivity. This woman's remarks are closely connected to the 'multiple micro-political practices of daily activism or interventions in and around the world we inhabit' (Braidotti, 2008: 16) of which political subjectivity consists in Braidotti's words.

Would you call yourself a feminist?

When the word 'feminism' was brought up in the focus groups, often the atmosphere changed almost immediately. Laughter and yelling were, in many cases, an important part of the response. Some women instantly confirmed they were feminists, others opposed to using the term. In the focus group with Al Nisa, for example, there was a discussion about calling yourself a feminist or not. All the women in the group were interested in Islam and emancipation (those were also the central themes of their organization), but the term feminism led to a rather heated debate. 'What is a feminist?' was their main question. The first woman, who tried to answer the question, argued that if there were any term she would like to use to describe herself it would be 'Muslim woman'[5] (Al Nisa, 30 min.). In her view, this word automatically entails all the other things that are important in life. This connects to remarks made by the women in Daral Arquam as well. The argument is that as a Muslim you are already committing to constant learning and developing the self and hence to emancipation. This means that she does not just argue that emancipation and Islam are compatible or that Islam inspires her in her struggle for emancipation, but that Islam *is* emancipation.

The differences and similarities between feminism and emancipation were mentioned in almost all the focus groups. In most groups, women could not agree on what feminism was or is, but very often it was associated with a struggle for and by *women* (for example, Al Nisa, FNV, Daral Arquam), contrary to emancipation, which was considered to apply to *everybody*. Some women did not want to call themselves feminists because they associated it with 'hating men' or 'being against men' (for instance, in Yasmin group). Besides the above-mentioned and rather stereotypical argument, the most mentioned reason was a general feeling of alienation with Western mainstream feminism, or 'Cisca Dresselhuys feminism',[6] as the women from Al Nisa called it (Al Nisa, 37 min.). It appeared that many women associated feminism with the standpoints of the Dutch feminist magazine, *Opzij*, and for that reason do not call themselves feminists (Al Nisa, 37 min.). Feminism, in this view, is too much based on the male norm:

> They [feminists who write for *Opzij*, EM] want women to become 'less female'[7] and that goes against my views on the relationship between men and women. And also within Islam you can't work on feminism and emancipation this way. ... You should actually stay close to the people that are close to you. Within Islam there is more than enough space to emancipate and become feminist. So I would suggest making a clear distinction between *Opzij* feminism ... and Islam feminism. All women in this group would support the latter. (Al Nisa, 37 min.)

As becomes clear from this quote, it is almost impossible to discuss the relationship between feminism and emancipation without addressing the negative associations many Muslim women have with (mainstream, secular) feminism. These women are interested in a feminist struggle, but not as it is interpreted by certain Western feminists at this moment. Or, as one of the women in the focus groups argued:

> All kinds of ideals related to women's appearance are not criticized – nudity, having to look young, and all the photoshopping – and the women who want something else, than what men want, are not accepted. (Al Nisa, 37 min.)

This is an often-heard comparison or complaint: women with a headscarf are criticized for being anti-feminist and women in mini-skirts are considered to be feminists. These different views on feminism can be related to religion but also seem to refer to a different interpretation of sexual difference. Or, to put it in other words, religion might not have so much influence on these women's views on emancipation but more on their perspective on sexual difference.

This is confirmed by the work of historian Joan Scott on the politics of the veil in France. She argues that French Republicanism deals with sexual difference by denying it; Muslim communities, on the other hand, acknowledge that sexual difference can cause problems in society and therefore aim to manage them. Hence, the discussions about the headscarf might not be about equality between men and women but about making Muslim women equal to French women (Scott, 2005). Apparently, French women could only be 'equal' by openly displaying their sexuality and sexual desire. The real problem of the headscarf, from this perspective, is thus that by 'covering women's sexuality', the Western secular view of sexual difference is countered. Of course, the French debates on headscarves are particularly located in the French context and cannot too easily be compared to discussions in other European countries, but we can use the argument proposed above. For example, if we apply the ideas about the importance of sexual difference to the remarks made by the women of Al Nisa, we see that these women not only have different ideas about the relationship between religion and feminism but, from there, also make a different feminist analyses about sexual difference. This perspective makes it possible to move the focus of the debate from religion and could open up new possibilities for dialogue.

'Jumping generations'[8]

When the women of SCALA discussed the problematic associations with the word feminism and asked themselves whether 'feminists' should for that reason come up with a new term, it was argued that this would be disrespectful to the generations before us who had achieved so much already in respect to women's rights (SCALA, 50 min.). Quickly after agreeing on having respect for previous generations, however, also the tensions between these different generations turned up. Especially with the women from SCALA and ZAMI, the discussions on this subject showed very explicitly how we have to find a middle ground between respecting the achievements of previous generations and, at the same time, accept the fact that different circumstances can lead to new feminist analyses. The women of SCALA experienced the differences between generations in their own group. A 'younger' woman made the following argument:

> Second wave feminists made it possible for us to make our own choices but are now also preventing us from making choices that they don't like. (SCALA, 55 min.)

Besides the issue of making your own choices, also other points of criticism on 'Second Wave' feminism were mentioned in the focus groups. In the ZAMI group, for example, it was argued that they focus too much on gender alone in their analyses and neglect to pay attention to other axes of difference, such as ethnicity or religion (ZAMI, 17 min.). This causes them to investigate only certain issues and to make limited analysis of problems and solutions. Another point, which is related to this, is that most 'second-wave feminists' are too much focused on the issue of work: 'the only thing women still have to achieve is to work more and to get to higher positions' (Al Nisa, 38 min.). Even though more and more research is published on the relationship between different generations of feminists, in general, or third-wave feminism, specifically (e.g., Henry, 2004; Tuin, 2009; Redfern and Aune, 2010), the particular relationship between feminist generations and religion is still underresearched. As becomes clear in the previous statements, many women in my interviews have certain complaints about 'second-wave feminism' and they connect it to the issue of religion and difference. To put it bluntly: second-wave feminism is associated with a limited interpretation of feminism, that focuses on sexual difference and socio-economic issues, such as work, and does not leave much space for other interpretations. Even though this might be an unfair accusation, the remark does bring many questions to mind about the relationship and conceptualization of various feminist generations.

In her work on epistemology of different generations of feminism, Iris van der Tuin investigates how we can capture generational change (Tuin, 2009). She proposes a methodology of 'jumping generations', in order to use and implement parts of 'second-wave' feminism, where it is useful for current generations, without falling into the trap of linear thinking. We should neither idealize previous feminist generations nor reject them completely. This is exactly how I read the remarks of one of the women in SCALA: they do not want to let go of the word feminism, but would like to start from the struggles that previous generations have fought and think how we can conceptualize feminism from there, taking into account changes in our societies. One of these changes, I would argue, is that religion has become such an important issue that secular feminists have to take it into account in their analyses as well. The women in ZAMI, who also described how problematic it is to ignore religion as an important factor in feminist analyses, confirm this:

> For these older white women religion apparently is not an issue, but for black/migrant and refugee women it is. But also politically it is an important issue, aren't these women looking at our society? It is on the political agenda. These were all second-wave feminists, and they are completely outside of reality. (ZAMI, 16 min.)

This woman's remarks are rather generalizing second-wave feminists and seem to ignore the importance of, for example, black feminists during the second wave of feminism, but I would agree with this statement on one point: as a secular/atheist feminist, you couldn't ignore the political developments in the world. As religion is such an important issue in local, national, and international politics nowadays, feminists cannot simply ignore it in their analyses. The concept of 'jumping generations' would be a good starting point for this. One of the women from SCALA connects to this with her remarks on the third wave: 'if you want to make the new wave a vibrant one, you have to create a situation where women can be themselves, where women ... can choose to do what they want at this moment' (ZAMI, 57 min.). Or, as she put it earlier in the interview, the third wave should be a 'warm wave' (ZAMI, 36 min.). In this context she proposes to think through connections instead of all working in our own niches.

Back to basics?

One of the things that came back in many of the interviews was the question: how do we frame the subjects that we are fighting for? One can, for instance, focus on something like circumcision, but another possibility would be to concentrate on broader issues that can connect more people; violence against women, for example. This vision seems to correspond to the remarks described above where a woman proposes to think through connections instead of 'working on our own little corners'. Also in the E-Quality focus group, the women aim to work through such a model. The starting point for E-Quality is the concept of 'equal opportunities'. This makes it possible to produce a more nuanced analysis of the problems and solutions at hand. It also helps them to go beyond the dichotomous relation of the supposedly oppressed Muslim women and the emancipated 'autochtonous' women:

> Autochtonous women can learn from, for example, Surinamese women, because they dealt with work issues and participation in a different way. Allochtonous women are not in all cases in a disadvantaged position. There are areas in which black/migrant and refugee women are ahead, we can learn from that and there are areas where it is the other way around, or where men are in a worse position, that also needs attention. In that context all inequality is problematic. (E-Quality, 27min.)

Even though this approach holds on to a form of linear thinking, the advantages of defining feminist struggle on such a broader basis is that it will probably appeal to more women, but also that there is less chance of denigrating women from certain cultures/religions. The women emphasize the importance of not focusing on specific issues connected to specific groups but to building alliances and joined struggles between women. One of the ways to achieve this is to work on broader themes that prevent women to be divided into oppressed and emancipated but make space for more dynamic cooperation. Furthermore, more attention should be given to the different interpretations of emancipation. For most of the women in the focus groups this term is, first of all, about making your own choices. For example, not all women want to emancipate through work or having a career. A woman in Daral Arquam explained very clearly that, in her opinion, emancipation should not be confused with self-centredness:

> Emancipation is about making your own choices, but everybody makes those choices within a certain framework. For me this means that I am emancipated because I, most of the time, choose to do what I want, but I also take into account the needs and wishes of my husband and children. (Daral Arquam, 17 min.)

If we bring these remarks about emancipation together with the above, we can conclude that the women in the focus groups are constantly emphasizing the importance of broadening and contextualizing the debates and struggles for emancipation: work with broader themes to enhance solidarity, work with broader definitions to include more women's perspectives, and adjust your analysis to current and local situations.

Approaching feminism and diversity

In many of the interviews, the women in the group put forward that if we want a more inclusive feminism, we need to contextualize and be open to alternative interpretations of feminism. Furthermore, we have to be conscious of the fact that everybody brings his/her background into the feminist struggle and that these backgrounds are constructed through many different axes of meaning (gender, ethnicity, race, sexuality, ability, etc.). Feminist standpoints cannot be formed (automatically) through one's gender alone. This connects to the remarks of the women in the ZAMI group; feminism in their view is always about diversity (ZAMI, 34 min.). In that context one woman in this group also introduces the (as she calls it) 'and/and strategy'[9]:

Towards a More Inclusive Feminism 223

We should let go of the either/or strategy of referring to people as either woman, or black. You are a black woman, a mother maybe. That perspective gives you the total image. (ZAMI, 37 min.)

When I asked the women in the group whether they are sometimes confronted with issues that make it difficult to think through the 'and/and strategy', they indeed mentioned some cases in which it is difficult to see whether something needs to be respected as a different interpretation of emancipation or considered as a harmful tradition. But according to another woman in the group, it is important to realize that:

> The and/and strategy does not mean that you cannot be critical or search for dialogue. Being critical and the search for dialogue also help with consciousness raising. (ZAMI, 43 min.)

This important remark can be helpful when one combines it with the contextualizing strategy, but it also shows a certain tension within these women's thinking on feminism. On the one hand, they want feminism to be inclusive and respectful towards diversity; on the other hand, they want to raise consciousness among women. One woman in the ZAMI group emphasizes the importance of getting to know each other's standpoints and working together, despite certain differences:

> Try to find reciprocity and create something new that way, use your creativity. This way you do not hold on to your own thing, but by working together you create something new ... a new society, that starts from working together. (ZAMI, 45 min.)

So, the starting point for the women in this group is respect for difference, being open to other women's standpoints, experiences, and strategies, and to create a dialogue and maybe cooperation from that. As I mentioned before, this does not necessarily mean that you agree on everything; rather, it means you begin with an open mind. If you really believe something needs to be changed or that women should become more conscious on certain issues, you can always try to convince them, but only in an open dialogue. The women in this group were also still in favour of consciousness raising and developing laws that help women to get a better position in society. Or, as one woman put it: 'you have to work on different levels, you have to fix things in more areas than one' (ZAMI, 52 min.). In some cases these different levels will work simultaneously; in other cases, there might be tensions that need to be discussed in their own context: 'we shouldn't try to pin everything down beforehand' (ZAMI, 58 min.). In my view, these remarks, especially in regard to dialogue, respect for difference, and openness, very much connect to the arguments of Rosi Braidotti about 'affirmative ethics', specifically, and the postsecular turn, in general. This interpretation of ethics is not 'tied to the present by negation' but is instead 'affirmative and geared to creating possible futures' (Braidotti, 2008: 11). Thus, instead of trying to deconstruct or criticize certain identities or subjectivities, we should affirm them and think about the possibilities they create and the alternatives they can offer to current views on these issues. This means that difference is regarded as positive (instead of negative) and can form the basis of transformation or 'creative becoming' (Braidotti, 2008: 11). Central to Braidotti's approach is that we affirm otherness and hence do not focus on sameness. According to Braidotti, we can do this by changing our view on pain and suffering. Instead of dealing with pain by denying it, or trying to go against it, we should find ways to work through the pain (Braidotti, 2008: 16). This confirms the argument of the women in the focus groups that we should approach the relationship between multiculturalism and feminism as a process, rather than trying to achieve instant change. Furthermore, it connects to the idea that it is more productive to develop alternative interpretations of certain traditions and practices, rather than dismissing them altogether.

Concluding remarks: towards a more inclusive feminism

In this article I have described and analysed the results of the nine focus groups I held with women from various women's organizations in the Netherlands. The main aim of these group interviews was to produce alternative and situated knowledges about the relationship between culture, religion, and feminism.

Many women in the interviews emphasized how important it is to know more about their religion and the holy texts and to develop a better understanding of the relationship between religion and culture. This way, women can criticize certain religious traditions by referring to holy texts. The key here is to recognize the power relations involved, acknowledge the possible differences within religious traditions, and create distinctions between certain practices (or in this case, religious traditions) and theory (or the holy texts).

Feminism was a rather contested term among the participants of the focus groups; something they associated with anti-religious statements, limited interpretations of emancipation, and the exclusion of men. Some mentioned that particularly 'second-wave' feminists are ignoring religion and culture in their feminist analyses. In several groups, the women theorized what a third wave should look like; warm and inclusive was the general outcome of these discussions. Other conclusions that came out of the interviews were related to the issues at stake for feminism and the approaches to take towards them. Several women warned against fighting for 'your own little corners' and instead proposed to frame problems in a larger context in order to make it possible for women to connect on these issues. Finally, they argued for a contextualized and intersectional approach towards feminism.

Interpretations of feminism and emancipation varied greatly between the different women in the focus groups. Some women instantly defined themselves as feminists, while others were opposed to using the term. In the case of the latter, many preferred to think of themselves as 'emancipated'. These women are interested in a struggle for equality but not as it is interpreted by certain Western feminists at present. Some women, therefore, argue that we have to struggle for different interpretations of feminism; others prefer to use the more neutral term emancipation. For most of the women in the focus groups, emancipation was about making your own choices and not just about having a career. Furthermore, the women made the important point that emancipation is about making choices within a certain framework, such as the needs and wishes of your friends and family. In that sense, they explicitly criticized individualistic interpretations of emancipation that ignore these ties.

Another point that is important in this context is the interpretation of subjectivity. Alternative views on this key concept can help feminists to open up alternative ways of structuring one's life and achieving change. This approach would also make it possible to start a dialogue amongst women about feminism, without asking minority women to give up their beliefs or cultural background. A radical dismissal of these beliefs and traditions on the basis of certain dominant views would completely erase these women's struggles and power to achieve change. Furthermore, it prevents feminists from actually discussing the issues at stake, rather than constantly emphasizing certain principles.

In short, the results of the focus groups show that a more inclusive feminism can be applied in practice by working with overlapping themes in order to enhance solidarity, developing alternative definitions of emancipation to include more women's perspectives, and adjusting analyses to current and local contexts and power relations.

Notes

1. See, for instance, http://www.nrc.nl/international/article2332245.ece/Rotterdam_fires_Tariq_Ramadan_over_Iranian_TV_show.
2. The interaction and multi-vocal narratives that occur in focus groups make them a highly suitable method for accessing certain marginalized or 'subjugated' voices (Leavy, 2007). First of all, focus groups are generally considered to create the most equal relationship possible between researcher and interviewees (Wilkinson, 2004). Contrary to a one-to-one interview, in a focus group the researcher is outnumbered by the interviewees. This can make it easier for them to take control of the conversation and shift the balance of power. The effect is strengthened by the fact that focus groups are often only partly structured by the researcher. In other words, there are plenty of possibilities for the interviewees to influence the development of the discussion and to steer it in a different direction from the one the researcher might have planned.
3. BIZ, ZAMI, FNV Vrouwenbond, Daral Arquam, Yasmin, Al Nisa, E-Quality, SCALA, and Interreligieuze Dialoog.
4. All focus groups were held in the period between April and June 2008. The amount of women for one interview ranged from 4 to 20. I always started the conversation by introducing myself, in order to be accountable for my own position and background. The interviews were semi-structured, which means that I prepared certain questions on important themes, such as culture, religion, emancipation, empowerment, participation, and current political issues, while also allowing for free association on the relationship between multiculturalism and feminism. Considering the main aim of these interviews (exploring different ways of thinking about multiculturalism and feminism), it was important to discuss certain themes, but also to leave enough space for the interviewees to put forward other issues.
5. She used the Dutch term 'Moslima'.
6. See also the introduction of this paper: Cisca Dresselhuys was, for a long time, the chief editor of a feminist magazine in the Netherlands. She is very much known for her critical view on religion.
7. She said, 'Ze doen aan ontvrouwelijking'.
8. See Tuin (2009), 'Jumping Generations'.
9. She used the word 'en/en strategie'.

References

Ali, A.H. (2004a). 'De Maagdenkooi.' In *De Maagdenkooi*, 7–25. Amsterdam: Augustus.
Ali, A.H. (2004b). 'Hoezo, Uiting Van Trots?' In *De Maagdenkooi*, 36–39. Amsterdam: Augustus.
Asad, T. (2003). *Formations of the Secular. Christianity, Islam, Modernity*. Stanford, CA: Stanford University Press.
Barlas (2005). 'Globalizing Equality: Muslim Women, Theology, and Feminisms'. In F. Nouraie-Simone (ed.) *On Shifting Ground: Muslim Women in the Global Era*. New York: Feminist Press.
Blaagaard, B. (2007). 'Gender or Discrimination: Rethinking the Cartoon Controversy.' *Historica* 2(30), 15–19.

Bolkestein, F. (1991). 'De integratie van minderheden moet met lef worden aangepakt.' *Volkskrant*. 12 September. Reprinted in F. Bolkestein (1992) 'Integratie van minderheden.' *Woorden hebben hun betekenis*, 181–188 Amsterdam: Prometheus.

Bracke, S. (2008). 'Conjugating the Modern/Religious, Conceptualizing Female Religious Agency: Contours of a "Postsecular" Conjuncture.' *Theory, Culture, & Society* 25(6), 51–67.

Bracke, S. and Schmitt, M. (2006). 'The Postsecular and the Battle over Transcendence.' Paper presented at 'Restating Religion: A Conference Reconsidering the Rules', Columbia University, 23–24 March 2006.

Braidotti, R. (2008). 'In Spite of the Times: The Postsecular Turn in Feminism.' *Theory, Culture, & Society* 25(6), 1–24.

Buruma, I. (2006). *Murder in Amsterdam: The Death of Theo van Gogh and the Limits of Tolerance*. New York: Penguin Press.

Cooke, M. (2002). 'Multiple Critique: Islamic Feminist Rhetorical Strategies'. In L.E. Donaldson and K. Pui-lan (eds) *Postcolonialism, Feminism and Religious Discourse*. London/New York: Routledge, 142–161.

Dresselhuys, C. (2001) Cited in X. van Gelder Miriam Schöttelndreier 'Het feminisme bloeit waanzinnig, in Overijssel.' *De Volkskrant*. 8 March.

Fairclough, N. (2001). *Language and Power*. London: Longman.

Ghorashi, H. (2003). 'Ayaan Hirsi Ali: Daring or Dogmatic? Debates on Multiculturalism and Emancipation in the Netherlands.' *Focaal: European Journal of Anthropology* 42, 163–173.

Harding, S. (2004). 'Rethinking Standpoint Epistomology: What is 'Strong Objectivity'?' In S. Harding (ed.) *The Feminist Standpoint Theory Reader. Intellectual and Political Controversies*, 127–141. London/New York: Routledge.

Henry, A. (2004). *Not My Mother's Sister: Generational Conflict and Third-Wave Feminism*. Bloomington, IN: Indiana University Press.

Leavy, P.L. (2007). 'The Practice of Feminist Oral History and Focus Groups Interviews.' In S. Nagy Hesse-Biber, and P. Leavy (eds) *Feminist Research Practice: A Primer*, 149–187. London: Sage.

Mahmood, S. (2005). *Politics of Piety. The Islamic Revival and the Feminist Subject*. Princeton, NJ and Oxford: Princeton University Press.

Okin, Moller S. (1999a). *Is Multiculturalism Bad for Women?* Edited by J. Cohen, M. Howard, and M.C. Nussbaum. Princeton, NJ: Princeton University Press.

Prins, B. (2002). 'Het lef om taboes te doorbreken. Nieuw realisme in het Nederlandse discours over multiculturalisme.' *Migrantenstudies* 18(4), 241–254.

Prins, B. (2004). *Voorbij de Onschuld. Het debat over integratie in Nederland*. Amsterdam: Van Gennip.

Redfern, C. and Aune, K. (2010). *Reclaiming the F Word: The New Feminist Movement*. New York: Zed Books.

Scott, J.W. (2005). 'Symptomatic Politics: The Banning of Islamic Head Scarves in French Public Schools.' *French, Politics, Culture & Society*, 23(3), 106–127.

Tuin, I. van der. (2009). 'Jumping Generations: On Second- and Third-Wave Feminist Epistemology.' *Australian Feminist Studies* 24(59), 17–31.

Wilkinson, S. (2004). 'Focus Groups: A Feminist Method.' In S. Nagy Hesse-Biber and M. Yaiser (eds) *Feminist Perspectives on Social Research*, 271–296. Oxford: Oxford University Press.

12
Blasphemous Feminist Art: Incarnate Politics of Identity in Postsecular Perspective

Anne-Marie Korte

Introduction: 'blasphemous' feminist art

Among the increasing number of publicly exhibited works of art that have become accused of blasphemy or sacrilege in the context of cultural identity politics in Western societies, religiously connoted feminist art works and performances seem to stand out and to fulfil a particularly provocative role. The concerned works of art have remarkable common traits in their disputed imagery. They connect almost palpable and often naked human bodies to iconic sacred scenes of Western Christian culture and art, such as the suffering Jesus Christ on the cross, the Last Supper, the Virgin Mary with the child Jesus, or the Pietà (Mater Dolorosa). Well known examples are works such as *Ecce Homo* by Elisabeth Ohlson (Sweden), *I.N.R.I.* by Serge Bramly and Bettina Rheims (France), *Yo Mama's Last Supper* by Renée Cox (USA), *Our Lady* by Alma López (USA), *The Blood Ties* by Katarzyna Kozyra (Poland), and *Passion* by Dorota Nieznalska (Poland). More recently, also songs and acts consisting of social, political, and religious critique, performed 'provocatively' by pop and punk artists such as Madonna, Lady Gaga, and the Russian formation Pussy Riot, have become publicly contested for comparable reasons. All these works of visual or performative art have been accused – more or less formally – of blasphemy or sacrilege, which contributed to both their notoriety and their controversiality by causing huge media attention. Not only conservative religious interest groups and religious leaders and representatives have targeted these art works and performances, but also secular politicians and civil authorities have declared them offensive, and both parties have tried

Blasphemous Feminist Art 229

or even succeeded to stop, prohibit, or ban their public exhibition or performance.[1]

The works of art and performances involved are created by predominantly female artists, performers, and activists who explicate their aim to contribute to the emancipation of women and ethnic or sexual minorities. They explain that, for this end, they address and in some aspects re-enact or rework the faith traditions they have been raised in. (In all these cases this pertains to particular forms of Christianity, as will be discussed later.) In their work, they consciously bring together emancipatory issues and core religious imagery of their own upbringings. They focus in particular on the presentation and staging of human bodies (including their own) in their most sensitive aspects (i.e., as naked, delicate, sensuous, vulnerable, wounded, tortured). According to them, this is the material or medium by which they envision both their most hurtful and their most hopeful and joyous experiences, while at the same time this offers them ammunition for political, cultural, and religious criticism. They often use the controversy that their work evokes as an enlarged public podium to state their political and artistic views (cf. Heartney, 2003, 2004, 2007; Korte, 2009b; Papenburg and Zarzycka, 2013).

In this contribution, I aim to clarify why at present precisely these 'religiously embodied' feminist works of art so easily fall prone to controversy, public upheaval, and legal pursuit, in particular to accusations of blasphemy and sacrilege. The case of Madonna's crucifixion scene in her *Confessions on a Dance Floor* show (2006) will be my core example, and the disciplinary fields that inform my analysis are religious studies, theology, and gender studies. I will argue that the controversy that these feminist works of art and performances evoke is related to the identity politics of ethnic and sexual minorities, and of religious communities, interest groups, and lobbyists, involved in a fight over shifting positions of privilege and marginalization in modern neoliberal societies. The deliberate and ostentatious interplay of gendered corporeality and (homo)sexuality with religious themes forms the symbolic arena of this fight. The clashes that these works of art engender are positioned on the fault line of religion and secularity, and their controversiality is deeply embedded in the ideological debates over this demarcation.

It is my contention that the many instances of alleged blasphemous imagery featuring gendered corporeality and non-heteronormative sexuality that make up the so-called culture wars of the past two decades are related to a particular social and cultural shift in modern and predominantly secularizing societies regarding the public meaning of both religion and sexuality. This shift concerns the position and public perception of both religion and sexuality as identity markers in their mutual interrelatedness. At stake is an oscillating relationship of religion and sexuality as modern individual and collective markers of identity. Significant for this instability is the emergence of a dichotomous public discourse in which a secular position is equated with acceptance of sexualities in the plural and a religious position with rejection thereof. The cultural shift this implies could be seen as a reshuffling of prominence, power, and visibility in relation to the former established social and personal meaning of both religion and sexuality (Jakobsen and Pellegrini, 2004; Jordan, 2011). Until late into the twentieth century in Western countries, religious identity counted as a primary marker of one's social position, while sexual preference and behaviour were privatized to the degree of invisibility. Most recently, the affirmation of sexuality in the plural, in all its (public) manifestations, for many has come to count as a core value of modern Western life, while religious identity has become far more privatized, or is supposed to be so (Dudink, 2011; El-Tayeb, 2012; Puar, 2007, 2011; Kuntsman, 2009). The many current cultural conflicts gravitating around religion, gender roles, and sexual diversity thus are not only indicators of changing views of sexuality and its role in the formation of individual and collective identity, but also of the fundamentally changing role of religion in modern society (Van den Berg et al., 2014). This is why I think that an attentive investigation of these interrelated changes, both in a postsecular perspective and *in a gender critical perspective*, should be at the forefront of the analysis of contemporary accusations of 'blasphemous' works of art. Before starting to discuss my casus I will first elaborate these perspectives of analysis.

Blasphemous art in postsecular and gender-critical perspective

On 23–26 October 2012, the World Conference on Artistic Freedom of Expression took place in Oslo, Norway, under the heading of 'All that is banned is desired'. It included a brief appearance of a member of the besieged Pussy Riot punk formation. A central cause of concern was expressed that censorship by religious organizations and the phenomenon of religiously argued bans on artistic freedom of expression are on the rise, against the expectations of 'many in the West' (Denselow, 2012:15). However, since the fatwa against Salman Rushdie in 1989, Western attention has actually centred predominantly on censorship and attacks originating from militant fundamentalist Islam. This tendency of interest also became visible at the Oslo conference. The fact that there is also an increase of Christian groups and institutions in the USA and Europe that raise objections to or try to ban works of art is less publicly discussed. But actually already in 1987, the exhibition of Andres Serrano's controversial photograph *Piss Christ*, winner of the Southeastern Center for Contemporary Art's Awards in the Visual Arts competition and partly sponsored by the National Endowment for the Arts, opened a national and recurrent debate in the USA, fuelled by Christian organizations, on the conditions and restrictions for the creation and exposition of art funded by public means. The subsequent exhibition of Serrano's *Piss Christ* in museums in Australia, Great Britain, and France raised similar debates and confrontations on a local and national level, including physical attacks on the exposed photograph at the National Gallery of Art of Victoria in 1997 (cf. Verrips, 2008). When, in September 2012, *Piss Christ* was on display at the Edward Tyler Nahem gallery in New York, at the Andres Serrano overview *Body and Spirit*, religious groups and politicians called for President Obama to denounce this work of art, comparing it to the anti-Islamic film *Innocence of Muslims* (2012), which had been condemned by the White House earlier that month.

In these and similar instances a resurging and pugnacious discourse on blasphemy and sacrilege can be found in which both religious and non-religious parties have a particular stake. At first sight, the manifestation and spread of this discourse during the past two decades seems to belie the fact that in the course of the twentieth century the legal prohibition of blasphemy and sacrilege in most European countries (as well as in the USA, Canada, and Australia) has gradually been waived, diluted, or become obsolete. This paradoxical state of affairs has given rise to discussion, initiated by philosophers, historians, theologians, and scholars of religion, on the reappearance and meaning of (accusations of) blasphemy and sacrilege in contemporary public debate.[2] Cultural historian David Nash, specialized in the European history of blasphemy, argues that blasphemy's history unsettles both the historiography of Christian religion and the twentieth-century secularization theory engrafted in this history. Blasphemy's present manifestations in Europe disturb the idea of a progressive rationalization and privatization of religion. 'Blasphemy's illumination of conflict models and incidents showed that belief was capable of ebbing and flowing and appearing at pressure points in the interaction of individuals and societies' (Nash, 2008: 16). I subscribe the general observation that the increased recourse to (the discourse of) blasphemy and sacrilege to oppose or ban culture critical statements and performances reflects power struggles and cultural identity politics – also addressed as 'culture wars' – in postsecular, neoliberal, and multi-religious societies. However, I do not consider the accusations of blasphemy and sacrilege only to be rearguard actions, relics of old times, or simply mistakes of categories. Following scholar of religion Brent Plate, author of the fascinating book *Blasphemy: Art That Offends*, I want to emphasize the (co)incidental and composed character of blasphemy accusations in their relation to political and religious power struggles. The discourse of blasphemy emerges *between* the production and reception of artworks or performances, and needs to be studied by 'taking into account the proleptic and analeptic dimension of blasphemous events' (Plate, forthcoming). As a scholar of religion, Plate defines blasphemy as fundamentally consisting of acts of transgression, 'crossing the lines between the sacred and the profane in seemingly improper ways' (Plate, 2006: 43). He proceeds that although there are no specific formal qualities that blasphemous images and acts share, sexuality, nudity, and bodily fluids seem to register in a great many of them. According to Plate, they collectively point towards modern society's dis-ease with the human body itself, 'that most intimate and yet most foreign of entities' (Plate, 2006: 47). Concurring with Mary Douglas's symbolic anthropological interpretation in *Purity and Danger*, Plate observes that 'impure mixings' with these ingredients abound in contemporary contentious imagery.

But these observations, although highly relevant to understand the staging and impact of current public discourse on blasphemous art, do not yet touch upon the pressing question of why gendered corporeality and non-heteronormative sexuality are the very target of accusations of blasphemy and sacrilege in so many contemporary cases. They do not clarify why precisely the interplay of iconic religious imagery with female corporeality and (homo)sexuality is perceived as endangering the distinction between the sacred and the profane. As theologian Sarah Maitland has shown, pointing to the famous accusations against Jesus, Paul, Dante, Galileo, and Darwin, blasphemy and sacrilege in consecutive periods of Western cultural history have often been located in areas other than those of gendered corporeality and sexuality, as the fights over the operation of salvation, the shape of the cosmos, and the definition of the civic state that have been at stake in these accusations indicate (Maitland, 1997). Contentious imagery has its own history and genealogy, which means that the question of the prominence of instances of 'blasphemous' imagery featuring gendered corporeality and sexual diversity in the culture wars of the past two decades should be addressed in its particular details, imagery, and resonance. Over and against art critics and other scholars, who claim that allusions to gendered corporeality and (homo)sexuality will per definition work provocatively in the context of iconic religious imagery because of the strong and potentially conflicting affective registers that are involved (cf. Freedberg, 1989; Verrips, 2008), I esteem more fruitful an approach that explores these contested works of art in relation to historical processes of shifting gender positions and changing stances towards sexual diversity in Western modernity. For instance, as theologian Margaret Miles has shown, in the Renaissance period when the first collective shift of women from the private to the public sphere took place in Europe, female nakedness and sexuality became the focus of a newly explicit public and controversial figuration in the arts (Miles, 1989). Feminist historians and art critics have suggested that nineteenth and twentieth century's movements of women's emancipation, and the strong political and cultural opposition that these movements have met, created a similar impulse to explore gendered corporeality and sexuality in artistic imagination and cultural expressions.

Also, the modern transformations of religion with regard to the distinction between the public and the private sphere should be incorporated in this analysis. In her seminal lecture 'Sexularism', Joan Scott points to the nineteenth century's increasing sexualization of women – the reduction of women to body and sexuality – as inherent part of the upcoming modern ideal of secularity in which the political and the religious, and the public and the private, became opposed along patterns of strengthened gender dichotomy, conceived as a natural distinction rooted in physical bodies. According to Scott, it has to be acknowledged that the 'domestication' of women, or their increasing assignment to the private sphere, as well as the simultaneous 'feminization of religion' took place in the context of the fast expansion of the modern Western political and cultural ideal of secularity. 'The public-private demarcation so crucial to the secular/religious divide rests on a vision of sexual difference that legitimizes the political and social inequality of women and men' (Scott, 2009: 4). In modernity's secular ambitions, in its struggle with the hegemony of religious institutions and world views for liberal ends, 'feminized' religion, women's religiosity, and female sexuality have become intertwined in their position as 'the other' of secular reason and modern citizenship, when in the processes of secularization in the West women became more and more exclusively associated with both religion and the private sphere. As Scott argues:

> The assignment of women and religion to the private sphere was not – in the first articulations of the secular ideal – about the regulation by religion of female sexuality. Rather feminine religiosity was seen as a force that threatened to disrupt or undermine the rational pursuits that constitute politics; like feminine sexuality it was excessive, transgressive and dangerous. (Scott, 2009: 4)

The above developed, analytical perspectives help to clarify why contemporary works of art and performances that openly combine 'feminized' religion, women's religiosity, and female sexuality while intending to make critical feminist statements – works such as the ones I introduced at the opening of this contribution – are potentially transgressive in multifaceted ways and run the risk of being accused of offence, insult, and defamation, not only by conservative religious groups and leaders but also by secular politicians and civil authorities. I will now turn to a more detailed analysis of Madonna's crucifixion act to further elaborate my position.

Madonna's controversial crucifixion scene[3]

In her 2006 *Confessions* tour, America's greatest female pop star ever, Madonna, managed to upset many people around the world by staging a crucifixion scene. Although Madonna had toyed with Christian symbols such as crosses and crucifixes already frequently in her oeuvre, here she launched a new incorporation of this symbol by staging herself as the one who is crucified. Suspended on a huge shining silver disco cross and wearing a crown of thorns, Madonna sung one of her famous songs, 'Live to Tell', supported by an organ-laden, 'churchly' sounding orchestration. Pictures of African AIDS orphans and texts from the New Testament were projected on a big screen behind her. At the end she stepped down from the cross, put down her crown and kneeled on stage in a gesture of praying, while texts like: 'For I was hungry and you gave me food' (Matt. 25:35–36) and 'Whatever you did for one of these least ones, you did for me' (Matt. 25:40) shone in large letters above Madonna's head.

In most countries where Madonna performed during her *Confessions* tour the crucifixion scene was heavily criticized. It was disqualified as outrageous and blasphemous, in particular by Christian groups and organizations, who often sought to prohibit the show. Catholic Church leaders confronted with Madonna performing her show in Rome declared her crucifixion act to be disrespectful, provocative, and a publicity stunt in bad taste: 'Being raised on a cross with a crown of thorns like a modern Christ is absurd. Doing it in the cradle of Christianity comes close to blasphemy'.[4] Female Lutheran Bishop of Hannover Margot Kässmann, the first woman ever to hold this position in Germany, commented that 'to put oneself in the place of Jesus is an extraordinary form of overestimation of one's self'.[5]

In response to these accusations of hubris and of insulting God as well as Christian believers by identifying herself with Jesus on the cross, Madonna remarkably *affirmed* that she wanted to imitate Jesus by staging this act. Taking up one's cross and pleading to pay attention to Africa's AIDS orphans is, so she claimed, fully in the spirit of Jesus's teachings. 'I believe in my heart that if Jesus were alive today he would be doing the same thing,' she stated (2006). The fact that, in the wake of her *Confessions* tour, Madonna adopted an AIDS orphan from Malawi – who later turned out to be not a full orphan – also contributed to the controversial and paradoxical aspects of her performance. For Madonna's act could be seen as a glamorous rendition of the leading role of the crucified Christ from the script of the gospels, passion plays, and folk devotion, but also as a quite personal appropriation – almost even an incarnation – of the suffering Christ. Her act could be seen as a cheap moralistic call to 'do like Jesus', but also as an engaged popularization of contemporary theological readings of the crucifixion, followed by a highly visible exemplary act of charity. It could be perceived as a sincere attempt to revitalize the Christian symbol of crucifixion but also as a shameless exploitation of this symbol by making a spectacle of it. And, of course, it could be considered as sheer provocation, for it is obvious that religion plays a major role in Madonna's teasings and provocations. To quote French literary critic Georges-Claude Guilbert, who wrote a book on Madonna as 'Postmodern Myth':

> Madonna, star, queen and divinity, but also sometimes scapegoat, is a privileged source of scandal and mythology. ... Goddess and priestess of her own cult, she (continuously) upsets the adepts of the more traditional cults: Christians, Muslims and Jews. (Guilbert, 2002: 160)

Although I agree that Madonna constantly and deliberately shocks and provokes to attract attention, I do not want to reduce her ingeniously designed shows and compositions to this label. Nor do I consider her repertoire of religious themes a sheer manipulative toolbox. Provocation I esteem part of her profession as an artist and performer. I am not interested in these provocations as such, but in the themes, forms, and media Madonna actually uses to provoke and in the comments and reactions they evoke.[6] To address Madonna's crucifixion performance in its controversiality, I esteem an important element of a postsecular analysis. To approach this act from this perspective does not take away its fundamental ambiguity nor its controversiality, but it opens a perspective of analysis that acknowledges this ambiguity and controversiality, and reflects on this complexity without repeating and reinstalling the modern opposition of secularism versus religion and the ways this opposition is interwoven with secular feminist as well as contemporary theological claims (cf. Asad, 2003; Taylor, 2007; Braidotti, 2008; Habermas, 2008; Casanova, 2009a; Göle, 2010). This reading, in particular, aims to explain how critical appropriations of core religious images and practices partake in emancipatory identity politics in postsecular conditions.

Female crucifixion as iconoclash

The actual transgression that determines the controversiality of religiously embodied feminist works of art such as Madonna's crucifixion scene can be located on various levels of tension, depending on whom or what is held most sacred and what is seen as most threatening to violate this. From an intra-religious perspective, this transgression consists of violating the interdiction of representation of the divine and of trespassing against God as giver of this rule. Andreas Häger, a scholar of religion who has studied the use of the image of the Christian cross in Madonna's earlier oeuvre, argues that judging this use to be blasphemous does not depend on whether the cross is understood as a religious symbol or not. According to Häger (1997), the judgement of blasphemy is founded upon the idea that the (religious) symbol of crucifixion is confined and closed in its actual form, content, and meaning (because of its transcendent or God-given nature). The offence of blasphemy here involved concerns the violation of established, authorized, and familiar representation of the crucified Christ.

On a more general level of mythic conception and cultic practice, the disputed status of these works of art is related to the problematic role and meaning of gendered corporeality in the religious imagination of the great monotheistic religions (Judaism, Christianity, and Islam). As Christian feminist theology argues, where in these religions God is seen as transcendent, sovereign, male, and not bound to material existence, women are conceived to be totally 'other' than this God (cf. Ruether, 1983; Christ, 1987; Plaskow, 1991; Adler, 1999; Althaus-Reid, 2006). So to connect female corporeality to the established symbols of divine reality, in particular to the figure of Jesus as God incarnate, easily generates the judgement of blasphemy or sacrilege. From this perspective, not individual acts of hubris or mockery but more general perceptions and demarcations of what counts as sacred determine the perceived offensiveness.

Thirdly, these accusations of blasphemy and sacrilege can be considered as core disputes about religious identity and meaning in multicultural and multi-religious societies, as clashes between various understandings and imaginations of what is found to be sacred. Cultural philosopher Bruno Latour has coined the term 'iconoclash' to address these situations, using a neologism that combines the aspects of clash and iconoclasm. Iconoclash names an object, image, or situation that embodies or creates an unsettled – and unsettling – clash between different scientific, religious, and artistic world views. Characteristic of these iconoclashes is that they create ambiguity and hesitation of interpretation, because they counter images with images and combine aspects of image breaking with those of image making (Latour, 2002). This concept of iconoclash acknowledges the multi-directional transgressions taking place in contemporary accusations of blasphemy and sacrilege, and it considers them as manifestations and collisions of different but not necessarily opposing or exclusive world views.

Against this background, Madonna's crucifixion act becomes a very interesting case to reflect on: what exactly effects transgression(s) here? What is so problematic in Madonna's staging of herself in the role of the crucified Christ? By which aspects of her act does a symbol that counts as sacred become ridiculed, affected, or obscured? Is this the central presence of female corporeality, or the high-handed personal identification with Jesus? Or is it the fact that the person who identifies with Jesus is *Madonna*, the pop star and extremely successful businesswoman whom we, willingly or unwillingly, associate with the provocative, sensualized, and eroticized exhibition of her own body? In order to answer these questions in terms of the specificity of Madonna's performance, I first discuss two other examples of disputed female crucifixion in their own distinct contexts.

Female crucifixion in medieval devotional practices

As I have argued elsewhere in more detail, the visualization or staging of female crucifixion has not per definition been judged blasphemous in Christian cultural history.[7] On the contrary, the exposition of female crucifixion has been incorporated into devotional practices over a long period of time. The commemoration of crucified female saints and martyrs, such as Blandina, Julia, or Eulalia, has been cultic practice since early Christianity. However, indicative of the social and religious tensions that female crucifixion harbours, there has been a continuous reservation to portray these female saints as actually hanging on the cross; the cross is mostly shown only as one of their attributes.[8] A remarkable exception to this iconographic tradition is the popular devotion concerning a female crucified saint, depicted as such, that existed all over in Europe from the fourteenth to the sixteenth century (cf. Friesen, 2001, 2007; Nightlinger, 1993; Schweizer-Vüllers, 1997; Zänker, 1998). A long-standing explanation of the existence of these extraordinary visualizations speaks of a misunderstanding: the crucified saint portrayed could not have been a woman, because it was Jesus, depicted in the majestic style of Eastern Christianity. This tradition perceived Jesus on the cross in the role of the divinely ordained High Priest, fully and richly dressed. From the twelfth century onwards this image of the royally dressed, crucified Christ was venerated in Western Christianity, alongside the upcoming Gothic depiction of the almost naked suffering Christ (Belting, 1981). The adoration of the so-called 'robed Christ' existed, in particular, in connection to the famous sculpture of the *Volto Santo* (Holy Face) or *Sante Croce* (Holy Cross) in the Cathedral of Lucca in Tuscany, which became a famous place of pilgrimage (Lazzarini, 1982). According to the misunderstanding thesis, the many copies of this image that were created and spread over the centuries were not interpreted any longer as signifying Jesus with his symbols of sacred kingship and royal priesthood. The particular details of this image, such as the precious robe, the ornaments, the crown, and the shoes contributed to the growing idea that the statue was, in fact, that of a woman rather than of Jesus (Schnürer and Ritz, 1934).

But more interesting than this misunderstanding thesis is the question: why and how did the practice of veneration of a crucified female saint become so important and accepted that even an established and popular image of the crucified Christ could be taken to be representative of her? This interpretive shift took place in the bedding of the cultural and religious transition towards a lower Christology and a more personal devotion to Jesus and the saints in the late Middle Ages, following the radical religious reform movements of the mendicant orders in the thirteenth century. In this context, the triumphal nature of the earlier crucifixes, which had reflected the conviction that the crucifixion necessarily implied Jesus's resurrection, increasingly gave way to a more pessimistic vision of human nature and existence, and this changed the religious interpretation of suffering and death considerably. Jesus became preferably depicted as suffering, bleeding, and dying on the cross, which rendered him more human and more connected to ordinary human existence. As church historian Caroline Walker Bynum has shown, this implied that in the late Middle Ages women could identify themselves more directly with the suffering Christ, and, vice versa, that Jesus could be perceived as being more close to women, in particular in his human aspects of suffering, bleeding, and dying to further new, eternal life (cf. Friesen, 2001; Gibson, 1992; Beckwith, 1993; Newman, 1995).

The fact that the visual presence of female crucifixion was widely accepted in late medieval Europe – until it was swept away in the broad iconoclastic gesture of the Reformation – probably was related to the profound gender ambiguity and the gender bending that characterized its depictions. They point to the redemptive significance of female crucifixion and the gender inclusiveness of divine incarnation in Jesus – not overtly or provocatively but in a rather subtle and ambiguous way. The agony and cruel death of the female saint are implied but not overtly shown, which offers an affective and imaginative space to call up the suffering of the saint, of Jesus, as well as that of the believers. And the richly dressed and adorned crucified body refers simultaneously to femaleness and to maleness, to the suffering Christ as well as to the risen Christ. This gendered ambiguity apparently did not diminish, but rather emphasized and reinforced the sacred dimensions of the crucified Christ.

Female crucifixion as twentieth-century feminist iconoclasm

The last quarter of the twentieth century has seen the rise of so-called *Christa* sculptures and paintings, made in the context of women's political, cultural, and religious emancipation in Western countries. These works, created individually by female artists, each aim to present the crucified Christ in a female form. Famous examples are the bronze sculpture *Christa* by the American Edwina Sandys (1974),[9] the bronze sculpture *Crucified Woman* by the Canadian Almuth Lutkenhaus-Lackey (1976),[10] and the three-dimensional panel *Bosnian Christa* by the British Margaret Argyle (1993).[11] These sculptures were not made as, or intended to be, religious works of art in the sense of objects of devotion or meditation, nor were they meant to be installed or handled in religious settings. They reflect, according to their makers, a creative reworking of the central sacred symbol of Christianity, the crucifixion of Jesus.

One of these artists, Margaret Argyle, has stated that she sees this female Christ as a symbol that addresses the situation of Bosnian women during the ethnical cleansings and civil war in former Yugoslavia in the early 1990s of the twentieth century: 'A Christa which would speak about the obscenity of rape clearly and graphically.'[12] The suffering woman on the cross Argyle created re-awakened for her the symbolic meaning of the cross of Jesus and of the faith in God, who is in the world and is present wherever a human being suffers. Her panel refers to the specific suffering of women during the conflicts and slaughters in former Yugoslavia, while at the same time it suggests the idea of the Christian cross guarding the vulva and prohibiting the violation of women's bodies.

These *Christas* all gave rise to similar reactions of indignation, illustrated here by considering the vicissitudes of Sandys's *Christa* in more detail (for detailed information on this case, cf. Clague, 2005b). This sculpture, created in 1974 by an artist known for her monumental works, is rather small and reserved. It shows a slender female nude with arms outstretched in cruciform and with a crown of thorns on her bent head. It was the first of the works of art mentioned here that was publicly exposed. But it only became perceived and disputed as controversial when it was exhibited, ten years after its creation, in a Christian ecclesiastical and liturgical setting. In 1984, it was placed near the main altar in the Episcopal Cathedral of St. John the Divine in New York City during Holy Week. The display of the sculpture in this context evoked very emotional stances pro and contra, expressed by church leaders and publicists on both sides of the debate. The opponents declared that the sculpture, by showing a naked suffering woman on the cross, was 'symbolically reprehensible' and 'theologically and historically indefensible' (Briggs, 1984), while the defending party argued that the sculpture revealed in a confronting way the inclusiveness and depth of the theological meaning of God's incarnation in Jesus (Farrell, 1985).[13] After 11 days, the sculpture had to be removed from the Cathedral due to ongoing protests. When six months later the sculpture was displayed at the Memorial Chapel of Stanford University in California, the same mixed reactions occurred.

In the reactions to the public exposition of these *Christas*, two aspects are remarkable. Firstly, these three works of art only became contested when they were put in ecclesiastical and liturgical settings, as has happened several times with all these works of art. They were not disputed while displayed in other public spaces like museums or galleries. Only in these religious settings, when the *Christas* entered the sacred space of collective Christian remembrance and imagination, they became forms of iconoclash. Secondly, in this context, these contested works of art proved to be capable of bringing about theological debate on the meaning of one of the central tenets of Christian faith: God becoming human and fully participating in humanity's existence and suffering. For by suggesting similarity and comparability between the suffering of women and the crucifixion of Jesus, the *Christas* more or less deliberately put a gender-critical strain on the familiar meanings of this symbol. This strain can be interpreted as a threat of erasure and destruction, but also as an invitation to reconsider and re-appropriate the meaning of this central symbol of Christianity.[14]

I would suggest that one of the reasons why these works of art did not only bring about shock and aversion but also generated incentives to theological debate and reflection lies in the particular gender aspects of these visualizations of female crucifixion. The *Christa*s clearly show the naked body of a woman, but in all cases this body is very restrained and tenuously stylized in the characteristic pose of a crucifixion. The difference between these thin female bodies and that of the commonly depicted naked suffering Christ on the cross is minimal. Pictured this way, the crucified female body has a great figural likeness to the suffering body of Jesus, and in this fusion of images the naked crucified bodies of women seem to transcend their primarily sexual connotation. The sacred, solemn, and non-sexual associations summoned by the suffering body of Jesus can counter or absorb the ambivalent reactions that are commonly evoked by the exposure of the naked bodies of women. Here the maleness of the traditional crucifixion symbol is contested by an act of feminist iconoclasm that does not replace the male figure with the female figure but blurs the established distinction between them. This specific constellation of images has supported the acceptance of these *Christas* and generated the rise of the *Christa* as a theme in works of art all over the world during the past two decades.

Madonna's crucifixion act reconsidered

Madonna's 2006 crucifixion scene was staged as part of a show, in the form of a play, and as an artistic expression. What needs to be evaluated is the way she staged and enacted the theme of female crucifixion and the effects that her artistic choices produced. One possible proceeding of such an evaluation I have developed in the foregoing parts of this contribution. That is why now, to conclude, I will look at the gender strategy of Madonna's crucifixion scene and its effects compared with those found in the two other contested cases of female crucifixion that I have discussed above. At first sight, looking at Madonna's crucifixion scene as actually performed on stage, we can notice a striking resemblance to the staging of gendered corporeality in the medieval devotional practices regarding female crucifixion. Madonna, surprisingly, has left out all her usual provocations while taking on the role of the crucified Christ: she does not take off her clothes in this scene, and she is not provocatively dressed either. Rather, she shows herself on the cross in a very modest, androgynous style, fully dressed with a blouse, trousers and boots. The modesty and serenity Madonna displays resemble the gender ambiguity and the gender bending of the medieval devotional paintings of Saint Uncumber. Madonna, embodying the crucified Christ discretely within an energetic show composed of passionate confessions of herself and her dancers, comes closest to 'the spiritual transmutation of the life of the body' that Luce Irigaray ascribes to Jesus as 'human totem': 'a bridge between totemic cultures and patriarchal cultures, the cultures of life and the cultures of the mind, confused by the patriarchy with the Word' (Irigaray and Burke, 2007: 362).

But looking at Madonna's crucifixion scene while taking into account Madonna's openly stated intentions of this act, it seems that the staging of her act resembles more strongly the restrained feminist criticism of the makers of the *Christas*. Like them, Madonna strives for a critical appropriation of the symbol of crucifixion as a protest against injustice, violence, and suffering, in particular the suffering caused by AIDS that often is not noticed or tends to be forgotten. Like the *Christa* artists, Madonna fuses the symbol of the suffering Christ with the figure of a not-too-corporal woman to put a gender-critical strain on the familiar meanings of this symbol. And like these artists, Madonna has restaged the crucifixion scene with references to contemporary situations of suffering and injustice. In Madonna's crucifixion act, abandoned mourning women – Jesus's mother and his female friends – are *not* below and behind the cross, as in classical Christian iconography, but instead the faces of abandoned mournful children, who are orphans and victims of AIDS, fill in these spaces.

It is possible, considering Madonna's staging of the crucifixion scene and in view of her intentions, to interpret this performance theologically as a contemporary, gender-inclusive representation of Jesus's suffering. In doing so, we may value this act as an affirmation of the agenda of feminist and liberation theology, as has been suggested by some theologians (Häger, 1997; Thienen, 2007). However, although the *Christas* indeed evoked a theological impetus like that, it is doubtful if Madonna's act could ever bring about a similar effect. In the case of Madonna, provocation dominates the scene: Madonna's objective clearly is to advance the iconoclash itself, not to contribute to its effacement.

But leaving aside Madonna's more or less outspoken intentions, I maintain that the form and style of her act *qua* gender strategy enhances the controversiality of female crucifixion. For, finally, I think that Madonna's staging of the crucifixion scene resembles most the works of the female artists and performers who explicitly pose *themselves* as Jesus or Mary in their works of art: Renée Cox, Alma López, and Katarzyna Kozyra, whose works gave rise to huge controversies and insurmountable conflicts. The *presentia realis*, the real, ineluctable presence of women of flesh and blood in these works of art, intensifies the iconoclash between sacred symbol and female corporeality and sexuality.[15]

Probably here the most challenging tension of Madonna's crucifixion act can be identified, which also clarifies why this act has come to play a crucial role in contemporary identity political clashes. On the one hand, Madonna's performance is highly susceptible to accusations of hubris and blasphemy, neither because of the presence of female corporeality *per se*, nor because of the fact that a female crucifixion as such is staged, but because Madonna poses as a recognizable individual and a woman of stature and fame who intentionally stands for and in the place of Jesus. On the other hand, Madonna's act is also in an unexpected way intriguing because of her personal, 'lived', and confessed identification with the crucified, suffering Christ. An uncanny admixture of secular and religious values is demonstrated here. By putting on a fragile and broken body, Madonna seems to have acknowledged that the visceral and vulnerable body is both a potent signifier of lived experience and a medium of formal and aesthetic inquiry – which brings her on speaking terms with old traditions of 'spiritual exercise' in Christian devotional practices and imagination. More generally spoken, her act attests to the fact that in postsecular conditions the individual body's role as a challenge to constricting social codes has increased, while the gendered and sexuate body simultaneously has become profiled as the principal arena for the politics of identity, as well as a facilitator and marker of belonging.

Notes

1. For comprehensive and critical overviews of contemporary art accused of blasphemy see Brent Plate (2006); Coleman, and White (2006); Coleman and Fernandes Dias (2008); Verrips (2008); Heartney (2011).

2. For discussions of blasphemy and sacrilege in their contemporary forms see also Lawton (1993); Levy (1993); Fisher and Ramsay (2000); Nash (2007);Wils (2007); Coleman (2011).
3. To analyse Madonna's crucifixion scene I have followed the threefold approach of cultural phenomena in the context of theological evaluation as proposed by Lynch (2005): an author-focused approach (researching the scene in relation to Madonna's life, oeuvre, and published intentions), an object-focused approach (research into the visual and symbolic specificity of this scene), and a reception-orientated approach (investigation of the reactions and comments the scene has evoked). See also Korte (2009, 2010, 2011).
4. Media reactions to Madonna's performance as described and commented on in this paragraph have been gathered from national and international newspapers and the Internet from the period of June to December 2006.
5. See note above.
6. For critical analyses of Madonna's life and works see a.o. Schwichtenberg (1993); Grigat (1995); Dresen (1998); Fouz-Hernández and Jarman-Ivens (2004).
7. See note 5.
8. See for instance the portrayal of Margaret of Antioch (died AD 305) (Lanzi and Lanzi, 2004: 92).
9. Edwina Sandys, *Christa*, bronze sculpture (54" x 40" x 8"), 1974.
10. Almuth Lutkenhaus-Lackey, *Crucified Woman*, bronze sculpture (8 feet tall), 1976.
11. Margaret Argyle, *Bosnian Christa*, mixed textile panel (48" x 29"), 1993.
12. Clague (1995) 'Interview with Margaret Argyle', *Feminist Theology* 10(1), 58.
13. See also 'Reflections on the Christa' (1985) *Journal of Women and Religion*, Special Issue, 4(2).
14. For more in-depth feminist-theological discussion of these works of art, see also Clague (2005); Strahm Bernet (1991); Meyer (1997); Raab (1997).
15. For extended discussions of these works of art in this context see my earlier publications in note 5.

References

Adler, R. (1999). *Engendering Judaism: An Inclusive Theology and Ethics*. Boston, MA: Beacon Press.
Althaus-Reid, M. (2006). *Liberation Theology and Sexuality*. Aldershot, UK: Ashgate.
Asad, T. (2003). *Formations of the Secular: Christianity, Islam, Modernity*. Stanford, CA: Stanford University Press.
Beckwith, S. (1993). *Christ's Body: Identity, Culture, and Society in Late Medieval Writings*. London: Routledge.
Belting, H. (1981). *Das Bild und sein Publikum im Mittelalter: Form und Funktion früher Bildtafeln der Passion*. Berlin: Mann.
Berg, M. van den, Bos, D.J., Derks, M., Ganzevoort, R.R., Jovanovic, M., Korte, A.-M., and Sremac, S. (2014). 'Religion, Homosexuality, and Contested Social Orders in the Netherlands, the Western Balkans, and Sweden.' In G. Ganiel, H.Winkel, and C. Monnot (eds) *Religion in Times of Crisis*. Leiden: Brill, 116–134.

Bracke, S. (2008). 'Conjugating the Modern/Religious, Conceptualizing Female Religious Agency: Contours of a 'Post-Secular' Conjunction.' *Theory, Culture & Society* 25(6), 51–67.
Braidotti, R. (2008). 'In Spite of the Times: the Postsecular Turn in Feminism.' *Theory Culture & Society* 25(6), 1–24.
Brent Plate, S. (Forthcoming). 'Eventual Blasphemies: Setting the Offensive Work of Art in Time.' In Michiel Leezenberg, Anne-Marie Korte and Martin van Bruinessen (eds) *Gestures: Religion Qua Performance*. New York: Fordham. University Press, forthcoming.
Briggs, K.A. (1984). 'Cathedral Removing Statue of Crucified Woman.' *New York Times* 28 April.
Butler, J., Habermas, J., Taylor, C., and West, C. (2011). *The Power of Religion in the Public Sphere*, edited by E. Mendieta and J. VanAntwerpen. New York: Columbia University Press.
Casanova, J. (2009a). *Religion, Politics and Gender Equality: Public Religions Revisited*. United Nations Research Institute for Social Development (UNRISD).
Casanova, J. (2009b). 'Nativism and the Politics of Gender in Catholicism and Islam'. In H. Herzog and A. Braude (eds) *Gendering Religion and Politics: Untangling Modernities*, 21–50. New York: Palgrave Macmillan
Christ, C.P. (1987). *Laughter of Aphrodite: Reflections on a Journey to the Goddess*. San Francisco, CA: Harper & Row.
Clague, J. (1995). 'Interview with Margaret Argyle.' *Feminist Theology* 10(1), 58.
Clague, J. (2005a). 'The Christa: Symbolizing My Humanity and My Pain.' *Feminist Theology* 14(1), 83–108.
Clague, J. (2005b). 'Divine Transgressions: The Female Christ-Form in Art.' *Critical Quarterly* 47(3), 47–63.
Coleman, E.B. (2011). 'The Offenses of Blasphemy: Messages in and through Art.' *Journal of Value Inquiry* 45, 67–84.
Coleman, E.B. and Fernandes Dias, M.S. (eds) (2008). *Negotiating the Sacred II: Blasphemy and Sacrilege in the Arts*. Canberra: ANU Press.
Coleman, E.B. and White, K. (eds) (2006). *Negotiating the Sacred: Blasphemy and Sacrilege in a Multicultural Society*. Canberra: ANU Press.
Denselow, R. (2012). *All That Is Banned Is Desired*. Report of the World Conference on Artistic Freedom of Expression, Oslo, 25–26 October 2012. Copenhagen: Freemuse.
Dresen, G. (1998). *Is dit mijn lichaam? Visioenen van het Volmaakte Lichaam in Katholieke Moraal en Mystiek*. Nijmegen: Valkhof.
Dudink, S. (2011). 'Homosexuality, Race, and the Rhetoric of Nationalism'. *History of the Present* 1(2), 259–264.
El-Tayeb, F. (2012). '"Gays Who Cannot Properly Be Gay": Queer Muslims in the Neoliberal European City.' *European Journal of Women's Studies* 19(1), 79–95.
Farrell, M.J. (1985). 'Christa: Woman Climbs on the Cross to Challenge Christianity's Male Dominance.' *National Catholic Reporter*, 5 April 1985, 11–12.
Fisher, A. and Ramsay, H. (2000). 'Of Art and Blasphemy.' *Ethical Theory and Moral Practice* 3(2), 137–167.
Fouz-Hernández, S. and Jarman-Ivens, F. (eds) (2004). *Madonna's Drowned Worlds: New Approaches to Her Cultural Transformations, 1983–2003*. Aldershot, UK: Ashgate.

Freedberg, D. (1989) *The Power of Images: Studies in the History and Theory of Response*. Chicago and London: Chicago University Press.
Friesen, I.E. (2001). *The Female Crucifix: Images of St. Wilgefortis since the Middle Ages*. Waterloo, ON: Wilfrid Laurier University Press.
Friesen, I.E. (2007). 'Virgo Fortis: Images of the Crucified Virgin Saint in Medieval Art.' In B. MacLachlan and J. Fletcher (eds) *Virginity Revisited: Configurations of the Unpossessed Body*, 116–127. Toronto, ON: University of Toronto Press.
Ganzevoort, R., Van der Laan, M., and Olsman, E. (2011). 'Growing up Gay and Religious: Conflict, Dialogue, and Religious Identity Strategies.' *Mental Health, Religion, and Culture* 14(3), 209–222.
Gibson, J. (1992). 'Could Christ have been Born A Woman? A Medieval Debate.' *Journal of Feminist Studies in Religion* 8(1), 65–82.
Göle, N. (2010). 'The Civilizational, Spacial, and Sexual Powers of the Secular.' In M. Warner, J. VanAntwerpen, and C. Calhoun (eds) *Varieties of Secularism in a Secular Age*, 243–264. Cambridge, MA: Harvard University Press.
Grigat, N. (1995). *Madonnabilder: Dekonstruktive Ästhetik in den Videobildern Madonnas*. Frankfurt am Main: P. Lang.
Guilbert, G.C. (2002). *Madonna as Postmodern Myth: How One Star's Self-Construction Rewrites Sex, Gender, Hollywood, and the American Dream*. Jefferson, NC: McFarland & Co.
Habermas, J. (2008). 'Notes on Post-Secular Society,' *New Perspectives Quarterly* 25(4), 17–29.
Häger, A. (1997). 'The Interpretation of Religious Symbols in Popular Music.' *Temenos* 33: 57–61.
Heartney, E. (2003). 'Thinking through the Body: Women Artists and the Catholic Imagination.' *Hypatia* 18(4), 3–22.
Heartney, E. (2004). *Postmodern Heretics: The Catholic Imagination in Contemporary Art*. New York: Midmarch Arts Press.
Heartney, E. (2007). 'Kiki Smith: A View from the Inside Out.' In E. Heartney, H. Posner, N. Princenthal, and S. Scott (eds) *After the Revolution: Women Who Transformed Contemporary Art*, 189–207. Munich: Prestel.
Heartney, E. (2011). 'The Global Culture War.' *Art in America* (October) 119–123.
Irigaray, L. and Burke, K.I. (2007). 'Beyond Totem and Idol, the Sexuate Other.' *Continental Philosophical Review* 40: 353–364.
Jakobsen, J. and Pellegrini, A. (2004). *Love the Sin: Sexual Regulation and the Limits of Religious Tolerance*. Boston, MA: Beacon Press.
Jordan, M. (2011). 'The Return of Religion during the Reign of Sexuality.' In L. Martin Alcoff and J. Caputo (eds) *Feminism, Sexuality, and the Return of Religion*. Bloomington, IN: Indiana University Press.
Korte, A.-M. (2009a). 'Madonna's Kruisigingscène: Blasfemie of Theologische Uitdaging?' *Tijdschrift voor Theologie* 49: 125–140.
Korte, A.-M. (2009b). 'Madonna's Crucifixion and the Female Body in Feminist Theology.' In R. Buikema and I. van der Tuin (eds) *Doing Gender in Media, Art and Culture*, 117–133. New York: Routledge.
Korte, A.-M. (2010). 'Dying to Tell: Madonna's Kruisigingscène als Icoon van Heiligheid en Zonde.' In D. Polleyfelt (ed.) *Wil Er Iemand Mijn Messias Zijn?* 29–57. Leuven, Belgium: Acco.
Korte, A.-M. (2011). 'Madonna's Kruisiging: Van Theatraal Passiespel tot Publiek Steekspel.' *Religie & Samenleving* 6(1), 81–101.

Kuntsman, A. (2009). *Figurations of Violence and Belonging: Queerness, Migranthood and Nationalism in Cyberspace and Beyond.* Oxford: Peter Lang.
Lanzi, F. and Lanzi, G. (2004). *Saints and Their Symbols: Recognizing Saints in Art and in Popular Images.* Collegeville, MN: Liturgical Press.
Latour, B. (2002). 'What is Iconoclash? Or is there a World Beyond the Image Wars?' In B. Latour and P. Weibel (eds) *Iconoclash: Beyond the Image Wars in Science, Religion, and Art.* Karlsruhe: Zentrum für Kunst und Medientechnologie.
Lazzarini, P. (1982). *Il Volto Santo Di Lucca, 782–1982.* Lucca: Fazzi.
Levy, L. (1993). *Blasphemy: Verbal Offense Against the Sacred, from Moses to Salman Rushdie.* New York: Knopf.
Lynch, G. (2005). *Understanding Theology and Popular Culture.* Malden, MA: Blackwell.
Maitland, S. (1997). 'Blasphemy and Creativity.' In D. Cohn-Sherbok (ed.) *The Salman Rushdie Controversy in Interreligious Perspective,* 115–130. Queenston, ON: The Edwin Mellen Press.
Meyer, J.M. (1997). 'Profane and Sacred: Religious Imagery and Prophetic Expression in Postmodern Art.' *Journal of the American Academy of Religion* LXV(1), 19.
Miles, M. (1989). *Carnal Knowing: Female Nakedness and Religious Meaning in the Christian West.* Boston, MA: Beacon Press.
Nash, D. (2007). 'Analyzing the History of Religious Crime: Models of "Passive" and "Active" Blasphemy since the Medieval Period.' *Journal of Social History* 41(1), 5–29.
Nash, D. (2008). 'Blasphemy and Sacrilege: A Challenge to Secularization and Theories of the Modern?' In E.B. Coleman and M.S. Fernandes Dias (eds) *Negotiating the Sacred II: Blasphemy and Sacrilege in the Arts,* 11–22. Canberra: ANU Press.
Newman, B. (1995). *From Virile Woman to womanChrist: Studies in Medieval Religion and Literature.* Philadelphia: University of Pennsylvania Press.
Nightlinger, E. (1993). 'The Female *Imitatio Christi* and Medieval Popular Religion: The Case of St.Wilgefortis.' In B. Wheeler (ed.) *Feminea Medievalia: Representations of the Feminine in the Middle Ages,* 291–328. Dallas, TX: Academia Press.
Papenburg, B. and Zarzycka, M. (eds) (2013). *Carnal Aesthetics: Transgressive Imagery and Feminist Politics.* London/New York: I.B. Tauris.
Plaskow, J. (1991). *Standing Again at Sinai: Judaism from a Feminist Perspective.* San Francisco, CA: HarperSanFrancisco.
Plate, S.B. (2006). *Blasphemy: Art That Offends.* London: Black Dog.
Puar, J. (2007). *Terrorist Assemblages: Homonationalism in Queer Times.* Durham, NC: Duke University Press.
Puar, J. (2011). Citation and Censorship: The Politics of Talking about the Sexual Politics of Israel. *Feminist Legal Studies* 19(2), 133–142.
Raab, K.A. (1997). 'Christology Crossing Boundaries: The Threat of Imaging Christ as Other than a White Male.' *Pastoral Psychology* 45(5), 389–400.
Ruether, R.R. (1983). *Sexism and God-Talk: Toward a Feminist Theology.* Boston, MA: Beacon Press.
Samson, J., Jansen, W.H.M., and Notermans, C.D. (2011). '"The Gender Agenda": New Strategies in Catholic Fundamentalist Framing of Non-Heterosexuality in Europe.' *Journal of Religion in Europe* 4(2), 273–299.

Schnürer, G. and Ritz, J.M. (1934). *Sankt Kümmernis und Volto Santo: Studien und Bilder* Düsseldorf: L. Schwann.
Schweizer-Vüllers, R. (1997). *Die Heilige am Kreuz: Studien zum Weiblichen Gottesbild im späten Mittelalter und in der Barockzeit*. Bern: P. Lang.
Schwichtenberg, C. (1993). *The Madonna Connection: Representational Politics, Subcultural Identities, and Cultural Theory*. Boulder, CO: Westview Press.
Scott, J.W. (2009). Sexularism. Ursula Hirschman Annual Lecture on Gender and Europe. Florence, Italy, 23 April 2009. RSCAS Distinguished Lecture 2009/01.
Strahm Bernet, S. (1991). 'Jesa Christa.' In D. Strahm and R. Strobel (eds) *Vom Verlangen nach Heilwerden: Christologie in Feministisch-theologischer Sicht*, 172–181. Fribourg, Switzerland: Exodus.
Stychin, C. (2009). 'Faith in the Future: Sexuality, Religion and the Public Sphere.' *Oxford Journal of Legal Studies* 29(4), 729–755.
Taylor, C. (2007). *A Secular Age*. Cambridge, MA: Harvard University Press.
Thienen, J. van. (2007). 'Madonna's Kruis: De Vrouwelijke Verbeelding van Christus.' *Lover* 34(1), 8–10.
Verrips, J. (2008). 'Offending Art and the Sense of Touch.' *Material Religion* 4(2), 204–225.
Wils, J.P. (2007). *Gotteslästerung*. Frankfurt am Main: Verlag der Weltreligionen.
Zänker, J. (1998). *Crucifixae: Frauen am Kreuz*. Berlin: Gebr. Mann.

13
Conclusion: The Residual Spirituality in Critical Theory: A Case for Affirmative Postsecular Politics

Rosi Braidotti

Introduction

The highly politicized context in which issues linked to religion in the public sphere are being discussed, in Europe and elsewhere in the world today, raises a number of questions that go beyond the study of religion itself. Throughout this volume, the issue of the postsecular has been addressed as one of the defining features of the material and discursive conditions that structure our social context. The starting assumption for this volume was the determination to disrupt the dominant equation between Christianity and secularism, so as to open up new spaces for critical theory. Stathis Gourgouris put it admirably: 'the ultimate point is not merely to disrupt the antinomic complicity between the religious and the secular, but to take away from the religious the agency of determining what is secular' (Gourgouris, 2013: 62).

While the general focus of this volume is on this particular challenge, the contributors have been encouraged to roam freely and address this issue from a range of transdisciplinary fields and methods. In this process, they have constructed several relevant and multifaceted intersections of the postsecular condition.

The nodal points of the book are: firstly, the manipulative framing of debates on secularism by conservative and populist political forces in the European Union today, in terms of the cultural and philosophical legacy of Christianity and the Western project of modernity (Hemel; Sørensen; Lentin and Titley); secondly, the repercussions of these political and social movements for the terminology and the agenda of contemporary philosophical debates (Lambert; Baumgartner; Egginton; Braidotti); and thirdly, the implications of this politically loaded context for the status of women and LGBT people (Midden; Korte) and for contemporary neo- and postcolonial geopolitical relations, including their socio-economic and technological aspects (Eisenlohr; Klassen; Leurs and Ponzanesi). These are not merely single and isolated thematic cross references; they compose a multi-dimensional web of dynamically linked social and discursive effects. The volume does not aim to provide even a synoptic view, let alone a synthesis, of these complex phenomena. What we have attempted instead is a cartographic account of their multiple and subtle resonances and of their mutual reinforcement through the reiteration of common themes, tropes, and concerns. The shared belief in the materiality of a complex historical event we call 'the postsecular predicament' therefore does not detract from, but rather constitutes, the core of this volume's theoretical complexity. As the essays gathered here clearly demonstrate, whatever the postsecular predicament may or may not be – and the positions on this question differ considerably – it nonetheless touches some raw nerves in the theory and practice of critical thought. The volume focuses on the strength and relevance of the postsecular moment and its impact upon ethical and political citizenship in the twenty-first century. The authors propose a range of critical responses and political reactions to the web of complex social relations that constitute 'the postsecular predicament' and thus contribute to a more sharply defined and socially responsible agenda on this issue. In this volume, the political critique of a Eurocentric and Western supremacist ideology of coercive secularism – as intrinsically linked to religion by negation – works in tandem with a rigorous scientific investigation of the renewed vitality of the theme of religion in the public sphere. In this intense collective endeavour, critique and creativity reinforce and co-define each other.

Given that the volume deals so extensively with the complex and multi-layered phenomenon that is the postsecular predicament, far from attempting to resolve or dissolve this complexity, I think the next step needs to take the argument further by connecting it to the issue of post-secular subjectivity. The key question I want to discuss consequently is: how does the project of critical theory and the ethical drive that sustains it relate to the postsecular predicament? What kind of subject need one be, in order to actively desire to undertake the demands and expectations of critical theory in a postsecular context? I do not mean to refer back to moral intentionality or rational choice, but rather to explore and deploy the question affectively and ethically in terms of process-oriented nomadic subjectivity.

My starting assumption is twofold: firstly, there is a strong sense of socio-political urgency about the postsecular predicament. Secondly, this complex phenomenon constitutes the backdrop against which I want to defend an affirmative politics, resting on a vital materialist vision of subjectivity. It is precisely because they touch such raw nerves in people's sense of identity and identification that critical theories of the subject are so important in a postsecular age. Contemporary subjects have to confront the complex challenges of living in a fast-changing, globally interlinked, technologically mediated world. We need to let go of the familiar while resisting the pull of fear, anxiety, and nostalgia that come with departing from set habits and known mental landscapes. We need to learn to think differently about what kind of subjects we are in the process of becoming.

In this postface, I will take the unusual step of developing a personal position on the issue of the residual spirituality of critical theory through the analysis of postsecular subjectivity. I want to argue for a vision of consciousness that links thinking to affectivity, critique to affirmation instead of negativity, and that does not hesitate to show traces of residual – albeit it non-theistic – spirituality. The conceptual punch of something we may call the postsecular turn consists in the notion that agency, or political subjectivity, is not mutually exclusive with spiritual values and that civic engagement as well as militant activism may involve significant amounts of spirituality. For as long as I believe in civic values such as justice, freedom, equality, and democratic criticism, I can be said to be a believer, albeit of the non-theistic kind. This provocative statement has an important corollary – namely that political agency need not be critical in the negative sense of oppositional and it need not rely on a dialectical scheme of production of counter-subjectivities. This leads me to put the case for affirmative politics and to suggest that subjectivity is a monistic-process ontology of embodied and embedded – and hence situated – practices, through autopoiesis or self-styling. This view of the subject involves complex and continuous negotiations with others – human and non-human – and it therefore entails multiple forms of ethical accountability. We are confronted with a double challenge: firstly, we need to disengage subjectivity both from oppositional consciousness and from critique defined as negativity. Secondly, subjectivity needs to be linked to affects, to the imagination and transformative becoming, in ways that are perfectly compatible with postsecular spirituality.

Why can this argument be taken as provocative? Because a sort of secularist consensus has forged the practice of critical theory, installing a number of criteria and rules of intellectual behaviour that in due course have become set habits and canonical procedures. They rest on the antinomy reason-emotions, that is to say thinking-believing, which translates into other binary subsets: rational arguments versus acts of faith; public activity versus private beliefs; socio-political citizenship versus spiritual rituals; material versus spiritual; and, by extension, critical theory versus irrational factors such as spirituality (Asad et al., 2009).

The feminist movement was historically the first to seriously challenge the public-private distinction by proclaiming that the personal is the political. Feminists have also shown both the power structures that frame the separation of the public from the private and the many discrepancies and contradictions that characterize it. Feminism has a long and rich genealogy in terms of pleading for creative alternatives. From the very early days, Joan Kelly (1979) typified feminist theory as a double-edged vision, with a strong critical function and an equally strong creative function. Faith in the creative powers of the imagination is an integral part of feminists' appraisal of embodiment and the bodily roots of subjectivity.

The question of the public-private distinction raises also the issue of citizenship and of the role of women in the social contract (Pateman, 1988); it lies at the core of what Joan Scott has aptly labelled: 'sex-ularism' (Scott, 2007). The latter refers to the co-option of feminist and emancipatory politics into the neo-nationalist discourse of contemporary populist movements which claim exclusive rights to the legacy of Enlightenment secularism. In this respect, feminist theory and politics today cannot avoid a head-on collision with the very secularism that has historically been its point of reference (Braidotti, 2008). Mindful of this critical legacy, I want to argue that the postsecular predicament invites and somehow demands a reappraisal of the role of affective and even spiritual values at the core of the analytical tasks of critical theory. Let me develop this argument.

Vital materialism, affect, ontology

The residual spirituality at work in critical theory is best expressed in contemporary vital materialist thought (Braidotti, 2006, 2013) and in the 'affective turn' (Clough, 2008). They foreground the political impact of processes of becoming, defined as materially grounded transformative acts that reflect both the ontological relationality of the human subject and the social complexity of our network societies (Braidotti, 2011b). The return to vitalism, redefined through machinic autopoieses

(Guattari, 1995), supplements the bio-political analysis of the age of intelligent machines (De Landa, 2002) and enables more accurate accounts of contemporary power in terms of vital politics. This switch to vitalism is itself a symptom of the postsecular turn in political theory. Whereas classical vitalism is a flawed holistic notion, which became historically linked to the organicist philosophies of European fascism, contemporary vitalism is a philosophy of relations, flows, and assemblages. It moves beyond the fixity, the Eurocentric racism, and the sacralization of Life of nineteenth-century vitalism.[1] Vital materialism presupposes and builds upon the philosophical monism that is central to a relational and non-unitary vision of subjectivity (Ansell Pearson, 1999; Grosz, 2004; Protevi, 2009; Patton, 2000; Braidotti, 2011a).

The core notion in both vital materialism and the affective turn is the autonomy of affect itself (Massumi, 2002). Psychoanalytic theory introduced this insight last century through the notion of desire and the primacy of unconscious processes. Lacan developed this into a fullfledged theory of the subject as built by Lack and Law. The psychoanalytic vision stresses that the subject is split, or 'di-vidual', and what divides it – but also constitutes it – is the linguistic signifier. Language as the mediator between self and the natural and social environment functions like a third party that separates the human subjects from the conditions that engendered them in the first place, namely the 'other'. In a patriarchal system, this 'other' is embodied and embedded institutionally in the maternal body. The task of splitting the native mother-child dyad is fulfilled by the Father. Therefore, the phallic Law-of-the-Father is not only the abstract master code of language, but also the key symbolic political rule in our social system, according to the isomorphism between the psychic and the social realms, which is central to psychoanalytic theory. The linguistic branch of poststructuralism sees language as the phallogocentric system (Derrida, 1978) and as the trace of an 'other' within (Kristeva, 1991), while its feminist critics see it as the master code of phallic patriarchal power (Irigaray, 1985; Cixous, 1976).

The political economy of domination and exclusion, which is institutionalized in language as a socio-symbolic system adds an extra dimension to the psychoanalytic vision of the 'di-vidual' subject. If language is both an ontological precondition and an ethical interpellation, then we are faced here with a seeming contradictory statement: that language, as an ontological *a priori*, is external to the self, but it is also a constant presence at the heart of the self, thereby inscribing the relation to others as the defining feature of our common humanity. In the linguistic turn tradition, this is taken as a productive double bind: language has no object other than itself, but in so far as it is always tied to others, it is already quite a crowd. The writers – philosophers, critics, and poets – have the obligation to deploy the analytical premises of language itself and to labour to share them with the readers. As Maurice Blanchot (2000) argued, dealing with language, in theoretical or poetical writing, entails the visualization of ethical relationality. In other words, the use of language in writing critical theory is a secular activity imbued with spirituality in so far as it both evokes and approximates the presence of the other.

These insights need to be read within the firmly secular structure of psychoanalytic thought. Psychoanalysis is a non-theological account of desire, passion, and affect, based on the Law of the Father and on the constitutive role of Lack. In this respect, Lacan differs from Freud who, as a champion of atheism and anti-clericalism, provided one of the most scathing analyses of the psychic function of religion in *The Future of an Illusion* (1927). The psychoanalytic approach consists in emphasizing the pathological aspects of the religious attitude, which is delusional at heart. Significantly, Freud includes a blind faith in the powers of scientific reason among these pathological formations and warns the scientific community against it. Diehard champions of atheism, like Dawkins (2006), would do well to heed this warning.

Linguistically based psychoanalysis recognizes the importance of affect but codes it negatively and defines the task of thinking as to both the yearning for and the mourning of the death of the Father as sociosymbolic carrier of Lack and Law. Psychoanalysis acknowledges both the constitutive and the unfulfillable character of the ethical demand made by the other which is inscribed as the heart of the split subject. The Law – both psychic and social – as well as psychoanalytic ethics consist in accepting this presence, while honouring the subject's unconscious desire. Ultimately, the psychoanalytic affect consists in enacting the destitution of the unitary subject and the end of the totality of truth and meaning, while acknowledging the enduring power of our individual and collective yearning for the very totality we lost.

The non-theistic spirituality of psychoanalytic theory is developed in interesting directions by Simon Critchley (1999, 2012, 2013) who combines it with the philosophical work of Levinas (1969) and Derrida (2002). Building on their insights, Critchley argues that the subject is constitutionally split by the ethical demand by the other, which it can never fully meet. This 'demand' is an ethical interpellation that exceeds the subject's ability to fulfil it and yet constructs the subject around this impossibility. Critchley consequently stresses the importance of subject formation through negativity, not affinity or wonder. He believes in the relational nature of the subject but defines it in terms of the structural and constitutive function of the relationship to otherness. By extension he takes a stand against the ontology of vital politics, to which he opposes a pragmatic relationship to the real, messy world that calls both for oppositional politics and for the healing power of love.

There are significant differences between contemporary manifestations of affective relational ethics that continue to rely on social constructivist methods and monistic vitalism. Whereas a social constructivist approach within the linguistic turn tradition responds to this analysis oppositionally – in the case of Critchley, by returning to Gramsci (2012); in the case of Butler (2004), by appealing to Levinasian-inspired ethics; in the case of Derrida (1978), by advocating the open-ended and relational structure of language itself – vital materialism takes a different route. The nomadic subject is not linguistically ordained and therefore not subjected to the normative rules of Law and Lack. It rather expresses the vital, generative force of desire as the ontological drive by intelligent matter to express itself in as manifold a manner as it can sustain at any given point in space and time. Vital materialism is a practice of negotiations with the negative and of affirmation, not of negativity, and this fatal attraction for the positive constitutes not only its core ethical value but also its political ontology.

Under the impact of Spinozist monism, a different emphasis has been placed on the affective elements of human subjectivity under advanced capitalism and on the process of political subject formation. Rejecting the Lacanian conceptual structure and terminology, vital materialist thinkers stress the generative importance of affects and connect them to a positive view of desire as plenitude, not as Lack (Braidotti, 2006). The unconscious affects and drives, instead of being played back upon a sort of negative filter linked to the 'black box' of desire as Lack with its corollary of negative passions like envy, resentment, and perennial frustration, are approached affirmatively. Affects are the autonomous visceral elements of our allegedly rational and discursive belief system (Connolly, 1999). What they express is the profoundly relational nature of human subjectivity and its constitutive drive for the freedom of expression of its powers (*potentia*).

Vital materialism expresses the postsecular predicament in that it stresses a spiritual sense of intimacy with the world and a sense of entanglement in a web of ever-shifting relations and perpetual becoming. Bataille's agnostic spirituality is of great inspiration for nomadic thought in that it leads to a non-theistic form of naturalism that rejects all transcendental mystifications (Bataille, 1988). Mary Bryden calls it: 'a dynamism of the void' (Bryden, 2001: 5), which generates alternative visions of how matter and mind interact. Intimacy with the world speaks of our ability to recollect it and reconnect to it and hence of our capacity to find our 'homes' within it, in the pursuit of nomadic sustainable relations (Braidotti, 2006). Relational nomadic subjects engage in transversal connections – Haraway speaks of 'becoming-with' (Haraway, 2007) – multiple human and non-human others. Such webs of connections and negotiations define belonging not as attachment to static identity lines but as dynamic transversal moves across ecosophically interconnected categories. Relationality consists of a deep sense of negotiations with multiple ecologies – social, environmental, and psychic (Guattari, 1995) – that constitute us. A sense of familiarity with the world flows from the simple fact that we are the products of such ecological interconnections and notably of the nature-culture continuum (Haraway, 1997) that marks our era.

Theoretically and politically, vital materialism stands against the emphasis on political theology that, adapted from Carl Schmitt (1996), shaped the thinking of Leo Strauss and the American neo-cons through the Bush Jr years (Norton, 2004). The difference between the two approaches is that political theology in its classical enunciation as well as in the contemporary reinterpretation by Agamben (1998) reduces modern political theories to the secularized version of theological concepts. This fundamentally authoritarian reduction overemphasizes the ruthlessly dichotomous ('friend or enemy') and polarizing nature ('you are with us or against us') of the political relation. By stressing the antagonistic dimension as the defining core of politics (Mouffe, 2005), this theory ends up endorsing negativity and the necessity of violence. It also expresses an indictment of Western modernity and the democratic process as being structurally flawed.

Materialist vital ethics, on the other hand, while being resolutely atheistic, is ontologically pacifist. Deleuze's notion of the univocity of being and the immanence of matter is a vitalist anti-theology. Starting from the recognition of our intimacy with the world, it defends this claim on conceptual grounds by reference to a non-unitary subject immersed in the intelligent and self-organizing structure of life itself. It, therefore, infuses affect and endurance at the heart of its definition of materialism and of matter itself as a nature-culture continuum. The proposed methodology is not social constructivism, but rather neo-Spinozist expressionism (Braidotti, 2013). That is to say that events, phenomena, and subject formations are approached as actualizations of differential modes of becoming within a monistic universe. The univocity of being means that we have to deal with one matter, which is intelligent, embedded, embodied, and affective. It requires a subtler analysis of differential variations in the process of subjectivation in order to account for the actualization of transversal subject formations, also known as 'assemblages' (Deleuze and Guattari, 1987).

The Deleuzian position shares the same commitment to overturning the dialectical model of intersubjectivity as the linguistic tradition of semiotic, psychoanalysis, and deconstruction but takes a different road. It assumes the de-familiarization or relative de-territorialization of established values and habits of thought as a starting point to explore and experiment with alternative forms of subjectivity. This qualitative shift engages our collective imaginings (Lloyd and Gatens, 1999) and desire (Braidotti, 2011b) – in response to world-historical structural transformations. The nomadic subject is a materially embodied and historically embedded 'di-vidual' in that it is a bound instantiation of a common and ever-shifting matter. Each singular self is an actualized and temporarily bound expression of the ongoing process of becoming. Matter is intelligent and self-organizing; specific forms of individuation are carved out of this vital material, according to the monistic vision of matter. In the specific case of the human organism, it implies the embrainment of the body as well as the embodiment of the mind (Marks, 1998). It is a materialist non-theistic vital philosophy.

Spinoza is not the only philosopher Deleuze and Guattari enlist to the task of defining vital materialism. Nietzsche, Bergson, and Leibnitz also play a role as well as writers like Artaud, Melville, Kafka, Woolf, and Beckett. They are approached as spiritual thinkers of matter in that they combine a shared awareness of the death of God with renewed trust in 'the rebirth of immanence' (Ansell Pearson, 2001: 141). This entails a spiritual affirmation of joy, or life, as creation.

The renewed emphasis on immanence and on monism or the univocity of being is an affirmative response to Nietzsche's proclamation of the death of God. In a move that Dan Smith (2001) assesses as the most anti-Heideggerian moment in Deleuze's thought, vital materialist philosophy rejects the onto-theological paradigm (which, on the other hand, continues to haunt Derrida). Linking this move to the critique of the Lacanian notion of the Law as Lack, Deleuze and Guattari (1997) announce and explore the implications of the end of the judgement of God, the demise of the despotic power of the signifier, and the Oedipalized terror it exercises. They replace it with the joyful assertion of disobedience, anti-Oedipal disloyalty to the master, and lines of flight toward becoming-nomadic.

We have here two radically different postsecular scenarios and two opposite views as to what constitutes the spiritual roots of this predicament and their political relevance. They differ considerably: I see the ethical vision of Otherness proposed by Levinas and Derrida as melancholy, fatalistic, and passive. Critchley's celebration of the aporetic as the political moment is, in my eyes, unethical, disguising its profound pessimism behind a thin veneer of tragic affectivity. Nomadic theory prefers to produce energizing affects and to look instead for the ways in which otherness prompts, mobilizes, and allows for flows of affirmation of values and forces which are not yet sustained by the current conditions. Critchley's position is moreover uncritically anthropocentric and closes off all relations to the non-human environment. Nomadic ethics, on the other hand, includes *zoe*-centred relations to external and non-human forces: cells (Franklin, 2007), viruses and bacteria (Parisi, 2004), and the planet as a whole (Haraway, 2007). All differences notwithstanding, however, we do also have a consensus about the relevance of a non-theistic spiritual dimension in critical theory and on its ethical and affective implications.

Another significant point of contrast between the two traditions of thought concerns the crucial importance of the imaginary (that is to say, of narrative and representations of social and cultural constructions), especially the emotional and visual impact of totemic and iconic figures as fundamental structures of psychic order and social cohesion. This emphasis on the imaginary rests conceptually on the isomorphism between psychic and social structures, which in Lacanian psychoanalysis, as I argued before, are equally subjected to the rule of the Master signifier and of desire as Lack.

Psychoanalysis offers important insights into the crucial role played by the social imaginary and its unconscious interpellations. It does so, however, within a social constructivist approach that privileges the structural importance of the social and psychic codes that implement the phallic Law. Thus, imaginary representations fulfil both a psychic and a social function, fuelling the powers of identification with dominant icons. If in the past these icons were religious in origin and function, today they are dominated by popular culture images and by political figures, ranging from the ubiquitous face of Che Guevara or the young Angela Davis, to the images of Nelson Mandela and other secular saints like Princess Diana. These iconic representations fulfil a totemic function in the sacrificial sense of the term: 'they suffered so that we may be better off'. The irrational and even 'mystical' elements of mass popular culture have been commented upon – mostly negatively – by critical theorists as diverse as Adorno and Horkheimer, and Deleuze and Guattari. Contemporary digital techno-culture has intensified this trend, encouraging viral links between visual culture, the faces of global icons, and a postsecular social imaginary that fetishizes them into the 'sacred monsters' of global consumption. An opportunistic and profit-driven pseudo-spirituality is therefore integrated into the cultural logic of advanced capitalism. It is marketed by visually driven popular culture, which both sacralizes and cannibalizes a fast turnover of icons.

Deleuze goes further than psychoanalysis and offers a different theory of the social imaginary, arguing productively against the primacy of linguistic process of signification. The imaginary is not the emanation of a symbolic system that allegedly structures both our psychic and our social existence, but rather the material implementation of social relations of power. Accordingly, Levinas's emphasis on transcendence and on the face as the ethical boundary of the other (Levinas, 1999) is explicitly critiqued by Deleuze and Guattari. The face is for nomadic thought a decoding and over-coding machine fully inscribed in the market economy and in despotic power relations. Faces produce representational codes and practices – a surplus value function which Deleuze analyses in terms of the immanence of power and the notion of 'faciality'[2] (Deleuze and Guattari, 1987). This function is made manifest in the market economy through the process of hyper-individualistic branding of the faces of celebrities and the overwhelming role they play in the construction of the collective cultural imaginary. The theoretical advantage of this approach is the ability to account for the fluid and contradictory workings of power in advanced capitalism by grounding them in immanent relations and hence resisting them by the same means.

Affirmative politics

I have argued so far that the residual spirituality of psychoanalytic theory consists in highlighting the affective dimension of subject formation in three interrelated ways. Firstly, through the sober and non-theistic acknowledgement of the importance and the autonomy of affects and desire. Secondly, by stressing the constitutive role played by the ethical demand of the other in constructing subjectivity. Thirdly, by exploring the role of the imaginary as visual recognition of the (face of the) other and the social significance of iconic images. On all three counts the affective turn introduced by psychoanalysis is a major element in the postsecular predicament and it paves the way for the further developments proposed by vital materialism.

The major point of difference between this tradition and Deleuze is paradigmatic and it corresponds to the switch from Hegel to Spinoza I mentioned at the beginning. Psychoanalysis incorporates and perpetuates a negative Hegelian vision of desire as Lack and a dialectical understanding of the self-other opposition in the constitution of the subject. Whatever spiritual dimension may be at work in psychoanalysis, it bears a privileged bond to negativity. Spinoza-based vital materialism on the other hand takes a firm stand against this tradition of thought and proposes an alternative based on Spinozist monism and the idea of desire as plenitude and the expression of freedom. The postsecular spiritual dimension here entails the notions of the monistic univocity of being, or radical immanence, positivity, and the productivity of desire. Affirmative politics challenges the traditional equation between political subjectivity and critical oppositional consciousness and the reduction of both to negativity. What this means is that the political cannot be assumed to equate the rational, or the public sphere, and that the spiritual is not the same as the irrational, or the private sphere. We need more dynamic and porous demarcation lines between these domains; I will start by discussing political subjectivity.

Deleuze and Guattari diversify political subjectivity along multiple axes, each of which spells a different location in space and time. Standard oppositional politics is advocated, in a post-Foucauldian mode, as a necessary form of resistance to the social manifestations of injustices, violence, and oppression. This kind of political intervention – also labelled as 'la politique', or politics as usual – is postulated on the temporal axis of *Chronos*, linear institutional time. This political stance acknowledges human vulnerability, on the one hand, and despotic power relations, on the other.

The political – or 'le politique' – on the other hand, is postulated on the axis of *Aion* – the non-institutionalized time of becoming and of affirmative critical practice. It is minoritarian and it aims at the counter-actualization of alternative states of affairs in relation to the present. Based on the principle that we do not know what a body can do, the becoming-political ultimately aims at transformations in the very structures of subjectivity. It is about engendering and sustaining processes of 'becoming-minoritarian'. This specific sensibility combines a strong historical memory with consciousness and the desire for resistance. It rejects the sanctimonious, dogmatic tone of dominant ideologies, left or right of the political spectrum, in favour of a production of affirmative acts of transformation. The creative aspects of this practice combine with a profound form of asceticism; that is to say, with an ethics of non-profit to build upon micro-political instances of activism, avoiding overarching generalizations or new master discourses (Lyotard, 1984). This humble yet experimental approach to changing our collective modes of relation to the environment, social and other, our cultural norms and values, our social imaginary, our bodies, ourselves, is the most pragmatic manifestation of the politics of radical immanence.

This distinction between politics and the political is relevant to discussions of the postsecular predicament. In the work of Michel Foucault, it is postulated along the double axis of power as restrictive or coercive (*potestas*) and as empowering and productive (*potentia*). The former focuses on the management of civil society and its institutions, the latter on the transformative experimentation with new arts of existence and ethical relations. Politics is made of progressive emancipatory measures predicated on chronological continuity, whereas the political is the radical self-styling that requires the circular time of critical praxis. Critical theory consists in connecting thinking not so much to '*la politique*' (organized or majoritarian politics) as to '*le* politique' (the political movement in its diffuse, nomadic, and rhizomic forms of becoming). Thinking is about the creation of new concepts as navigational tools or 'conceptual personae' that can assist us in negotiating temporary analytical frames to capture complexity in its manifold manifestations.

The political is the shared acknowledgement of ethical relationality and it is postulated upon Spinozist monism (Macherey, 2011) and the rejection of the legacy of Hegelian-Marxist dialectics of consciousness and otherness. This school of critical theory banks on negativity and in a perverse way even requires it, because it builds on the assumption that the critical position consists in analysing negative social and discursive condition in order to better overthrow them. In other words it is the same conditions that construct the negative moment – for instance, the experience of oppression, marginality, injury, or trauma – and also the possibility of overturning them. The same analytic premises provide both the damages and the possibility of positive resistance, counteraction, or transcendence (Foucault, 1977a; Brown, 2006). What triggers and, at the same time, is engendered by this process of both analysis and resistance is called 'oppositional consciousness'. In other words, the negative experience can be turned into the matter that critical theory engages with and thus into the productive source of counter-truths and values, which aim at overthrowing not only the real-life negative instances but also their representations.

This process has become canonized as the equation of critical political subjectivity with negativity, oppositional, or, in Hegel's terms from

Phenomenology of Spirit, the 'unhappy' consciousness (Hegel, 1977: §230). As an alternative, I want to suggest a non-Hegelian, monistic, and vital-materialist analysis that foregrounds the relational, negotiation-bound, and affirmative elements of this process. My point is that the political – as *'le* politique' – is defined by a relational, affirmative ethics that aims to cultivate and produce the condition of its own expression: it is a praxis based on a positive definition of the subject and process-driven, relational 'di-vidual'. This assumes that a subject's ethical core is clearly not his/her moral intentionality, as much as the effects of power (as repressive – *potestas* – and positive – *potentia*) his/her actions are likely to have upon the world. It is a process of engendering empowering modes of becoming (Deleuze, 1990; Braidotti, 2006).

Here is the punchline of contemporary vital-materialist politics: given that the ethical good is equated with radical relationality aiming at affirmative empowerment, the ethical ideal is to increase one's ability to enter into modes of relation with multiple others. Oppositional consciousness is replaced by affirmative praxis; political subjectivity is a process or assemblage that actualizes this ethical propensity. The view of subjectivity I have been arguing for does not condition the emergence of the subject on negation but on creative affirmation; not on loss but on vital generative forces. The propensity for affirmation is a key feature of neo-Spinozist nomadic subjects and it explicitly acknowledges its residual spiritual connotations. Affirmation is the key ethical value for the postsecular turn in critical theory, which imagines a subject whose existence, ethics, and politics are not indexed on negativity but on production of affirmative affects.

The rejection of the dialectical scheme implies also a shift of temporal gears. It means that the conditions for political and ethical agency are not dependent on the current state of the terrain: they are not oppositional and thus not tied to the present by negation. Instead, they are projected across time as affirmative praxis, geared to creating empowering relations aimed at possible futures. Ethical relations create possible worlds by mobilizing resources that have been left untapped in the present, including our desires and imagination. They are the driving forces that concretize in actual, material relations and can, thus, constitute a network, web, or rhizome of interconnection with others.

Such a vision, moreover, does not restrict the ethical instance within the limits of human otherness, but also opens it up to interrelations with non-human, post-human, and inhuman forces. The eco-philosophical dimension is essential to the postsecular turn in that it values one's reliance on the multiple ecologies that sustain us in a nature-culture continuum (Haraway, 1997; Guattari, 1995, 2000) and within which subjects must cultivate affirmative ethical relations. Critical theory is rather about strategies of actualization of affirmation as an ethical practice that consists of multiple micro-political practices of daily activism or interventions in and on the world we inhabit for ourselves and for future generations.

The essence of my argument is that there is no logical necessity to link political subjectivity to oppositional consciousness and reduce critique to negativity. Critical theory can be just as critical and more persuasively theoretical if it embraces philosophical monism and vital politics and disengages the process of consciousness-raising from the logic of negativity, connecting it instead to creative affirmation. The corollary of this shift is twofold: firstly, it proves that political subjectivity or agency need not be aimed solely at the production of radical counter-subjectivities. It is not a social constructivist oppositional strategy that aims at storming the Bastille of capitalism, or undoing the winter palace of phallogocentrism. It rather involves discontinuous and heterogeneous negotiations with dominant norms and technologies of the self. Secondly, it argues that political subjectivity rests on a postsecular ethics of otherness that values reciprocity as mutual specification or creation. It does not pursue the recognition of sameness, but rather the quest for creative alternatives and sustainable futures.

This position is postsecular in the sense that it actively works towards the creation of affirmative alternatives by working through the negative instances, including their representations. This shift is central to the postsecular turn in critical theory, which imagines a subject whose existence, ethics, and politics are not indexed on negativity and hence on the horizon of alterity and melancholia. This subject is looking for the ways in which otherness prompts, mobilizes, and allows for the affirmation of what is *not yet* contained in the present conditions, namely sustainable futures.

Postsecular spirituality

The emphasis on affirmation, desire as plenitude, and consequently the creation of possible futures is one of the key aspects of the residual spirituality in critical theory. For instance, the system of feminist civic values rests on a social notion of faith in progress as the hope for the construction of alternative social horizons, new norms, and values. Faith in progress itself is a vote of confidence in the future. Ultimately, it is a belief in the perfectibility of Wo/Man, albeit it in a much grounded, accountable mode that privileges partial perspectives (Haraway, 1988). It is a postsecular position, in that it is an immanent, not transcendental theory, which posits generous bonds of cosmopolitanism, solidarity, and community across locations and generations. It expresses sizable doses of residual spirituality in its yearning for social justice and sustainability.

At some level, postsecular spirituality has all the appearance of a logical paradox, which conceals deeper levels of complexity. We are confronting today a postsecular realization that all beliefs – their different propositional contents notwithstanding – are acts of faith. The operational concept is faith itself; that is to say, the belief in a social narrative, in its imaginary hold, and its normative implications. All belief systems contain a hard core of narrative normativity and of spiritual hope. Nietzsche put it with customary wit: if you believe in grammar, you believe in God[3] (Kauffman, 1982).

To which I am tempted to reply that God is dead, Marx is dead, and I am not feeling too well myself,[4] so the very scaffolding of contemporary belief systems is rather shaky. Postsecular subjects today are at best believers without belief systems. This is not a crisis, however, but the opening of multiple possibilities. The vital-materialist vision of the subject speaks to and of a post-Nietzschean world without monotheistic faith. A world without Lack and Law, free from the role of judgement defined as the expression of the negative and despotic face of power (*potestas*). It is the universe of Kafka and Beckett, re-read with Deleuze: a world that has exhausted all faith in traditional values and eschatological vision of the future, to seek for transformative energy in the immanence of a continuous present. This world has worked through the powers of icons and magical thinking, it has sobered up after the transcendentalist delirium, and has landed here and now in the humble reality of just a life, just a continuous present that never forgets the future.

Ontological monism and Spinozist ethics are often criticized as aristocratic, detached from the contingencies of real life and potentially authoritarian in political terms (Hallward, 2006). I, as most Deleuzians, on the other hand, praise the ontological pacifism and non-violence of vital materialism. The awareness of ontological relationality is neither elitist, nor naïve. It does not exclude the awareness of negative relations and destructive affects. Elsewhere I have outlined the frame of a nomadic vital ethics that consists in the praxis of actively constructing conditions and relations conducive to affirmation (Braidotti, 2006). The ethical good is a praxis, not a given. It is the collective pursuit of social relations aiming at constructing affirmative values and practices.

The argument for postsecular spirituality draws strength from the politics of global consumption of Life itself today and redesigns the relation to otherness within its opportunistic political economy. We need to attend to the forces of life and matter that are traversed by and not exhausted by 'politics as usual'. This implies giving centre stage to the vital materialism of *zoe* as multiple relations or flows of interaction, production or generative power of the inhuman. This has two major implications. The first one is ethical: we need to rethink responsibility in terms of eco-philosophical principles. A diffuse sort of ontological gratitude is needed in the post-human era, towards the multitude of non-human agents that is supporting us through the present anthropological mutation. Bio-centred egalitarianism aims instead at dispersing and transcending anthropocentrism by dissolving it into a network of bio-agencies and eco-sophical relations. This is not techno-paganism but radical immanence in its ethical version, its most concrete form: it points to the becoming-imperceptible of the former anthropocentric subject. I will return to this issue.

The second implication is political: we need to organize communities that reflect and enhance this vision of the subject. This is a community that acknowledges difference as the principle of non-Oneness as its founding myth of origin – anti-Oedipal, post-humanist, vitalist, non-unitary, and yet accountable. Not bound together by the guilt of shared violence, or irreparable loss, or unpayable ontological debts – but rather by the compassionate acknowledgement of our common need to negotiate thresholds on sustainability with and alongside the relentless and monstrous energy of a 'Life' that does not respond to our names. A political economy of non-compensation needs to be installed – that is to say, a fundamental principle of non-profit. This rejects the liberal vision of the subject, which inscribes the political economy of capitalism at the heart of subjectivity in terms of losses, perpetual debt, savings, recognition, and production. Moreover, it moves further than the histrionic post-psychoanalytic quip about the trappings of the surplus value of *jouissance* (Žižek, 2013). Acknowledging instead the importance of proximity and relation, it turns the margins of unspeakable-ness, the traumatized nature of our being-in-the-world and our shared fragility into the praxis of co-construction of affirmative social practices. It is an affirmative approach to the tragedy of 'existence in a worldly universe that lacks all guarantees' (Gourgouris, 2013: 23). It is a form of *amor fati*, a way of living up to the intensities of life, so as to be worthy of all that happens to us – to live out our shared capacity to affect and to be affected.

Postsecular spirituality is the unspectacular, humble acknowledgement of ontological relationality, which assumes the monistic ontology and the nature-culture continuum. It consequently involves eco-sophical interrelations of the non-theistic but vital kind with both human and non-human others. Postsecular spirituality, redefined as a topology of affects and affirmative ethics, is one of the attributes of nomadic subjectivity and it designs an ethics of affirmation and an eco-philosophy of relations. The process of unfolding affects is central to the composition of radically immanent bodies and thus it can be seen as the actualization of enfleshed materialism within a monistic ontology. The selection of the forces of becoming is regulated by an ethics of joy and affirmation, which functions through the transformation of negative into positive passions. These are essentially a matter of affinity: being able to enter a relation with another entity whose elements appeal to one produces a joyful encounter. They express one's empowerment as *potentia* and increase the subject's capacity to enter into further relations, grow, and expand. This expansion is time-bound: the nomadic subject by expressing and increasing its positive passions empowers itself to last, to endure, to continue through, and in time defined as *Aion*, not as *Chronos*. This is the politics of becoming: a collective assemblage of forces that coalesce around commonly shared elements, webs of sustainable interconnections that empower us to grow and to endure.

Ways of dying

Spiritual practices are embodied and embedded, active and affective. They do not take place in a fight from the flesh but through it. I want to take this a step further and argue that nomadic subjectivity as radical immanence implies a practice of postsecular spirituality which also redesigns the idea and the experience of death (Braidotti, 2006). Whereas psychoanalysis indexes the unconscious libidinal processes in the all-powerful death drive, whose entropic force is central to human desire (Laplanche, 1976), nomadic materialism offers a vital vision of death.

Conceptually, death has to do with the ultimate phase of the process of becoming, according to Deleuze and Guattari, namely becoming-imperceptible, in keeping with the deep materialism of my Spinozist roots. What we humans truly desire as humans is to disappear, to step on the side of life and let it flow by, without actually stopping it. What we really aspire to is to self-style our own death (Phillips, 1999). Our fundamental drive (*conatus*) is to express the potency of life (*potentia*), by joining forces with other flows of becoming. The great animal-machine, the 'chaosmosis' (Guattari, 1995) of the universe is the horizon of becoming that marks the resilience of life as *bios/zoe* and its generative power also through what we usually call death.

Death is our becoming-imperceptible. That is the point of fusion between the self and his/her habitat, the cosmos as a whole. It marks the point of evanescence of the self and its replacement by a living nexus of multiple interconnections that empower not the self, but the collective; not identity, but affirmative subjectivity; not consciousness, but affirmative interconnections. The distinction Deleuze draws from Spinoza and Blanchot – the distinction between personal and impersonal death – is relevant here (Deleuze, 1983, 1990, 1995). Personal death of the self as social identity is the suppression of the individualized ego. Impersonal death, on the other hand, is beyond the ego: a death that marks the extreme threshold of my powers to become.

Impersonal death is the incorporeal or intensive event that opens up a proliferation of generative options of a qualitative different kind. The becoming-corpse of the body is another phase in the impersonal Life of the species. What matters is the ethical or intensive Life, which is ascetically lived as virtual suicide in the pursuit of the destitution of the unitary self. Ultimately, all one has left is what one is propelled by, namely affects, relations, and becoming. One is constructed in these transitions and through these encounters. Impersonal death is the ultimate destitution of selfhood into embodied and embedded relations, that is to say, into radical immanence.

As I argued elsewhere (Braidotti, 2006), death is the inhuman conceptual excess: the unrepresentable, the unthinkable, and the unproductive black hole that we all fear. Yet, death is also a creative synthesis of flows, energies, and perpetual becoming. Because humans are mortal, death, or the transience of life, is written at our core: it is the event that structures our time-lines and frames our time-zones, not as a limit but as a porous threshold. In so far as it is ever-present in our psychic and somatic landscapes, as the event that has always already happened (Blanchot, 2000), death as a constitutive event is behind us, it has already taken place as a virtual potential that constructs our inscription into Time, which is the other matter Life is made of. The temporality of death is time itself, by which I mean the totality of time.

The full blast of the awareness of the transitory nature of all that lives is the defining moment in our existence. It structures our becoming-subjects, our capacity and powers of relation, and the process of acquiring ethical awareness. Being mortal, we all are 'have beens': the spectacle of our death is written obliquely into the script of our temporality, not as a barrier but as a condition of possibility. This death that pertains to a past that is forever present is not individual but impersonal; it is the precondition of our existence, of the future.

This proximity to death is a close and intimate friendship that calls for endurance, in the double sense of temporal duration or continuity and spatial suffering or sustainability. As an individual occurrence, it will come in the form of the physical extinction of the body; but as impersonal event, in the sense of the awareness of finitude, of the interrupted flow of my being there, death has already taken place. We are all synchronized with death – death is the same thing as the time of our living, in so far as we all live on borrowed time. Making friends with the impersonal necessity of death is an ethical way of installing oneself in life as a transient, slightly wounded visitor. We build our house on the crack, so to speak. We live to recover from the shocking awareness that this game is over even before it started. The proximity to death suspends life, not into transcendence, but rather into the radical immanence of 'just a life' (Deleuze, 1995), here and now, for as long as we can and as much as we can take. It is indeed the case that the Life in me will go, but it is *zoe*, not the rational conscious, sovereign individual, without a 'self' that could even claim to supervise, let alone control the process. Life does go on, as *zoe* always does; so much so that the injunction is not the classical 'give me life (*bios*) *or* give me death', but rather 'give me life (*zoe*) *and hence* give me death'.

This does not mean, however, that Life unfolds on the horizon of death. This classical notion is central to the metaphysics of finitude that, especially in the Heideggerian tradition, sacralizes death as the defining feature of human consciousness (Agamben, 1998). I want to stress instead the productive differential nature of *zoe*, which means the productive aspect of the life-death continuum. It does not deny the reality of loss, but rather to re-work it so as to assert the vital powers of healing and compassion. This is the core of post-human affirmative ethics in a contemporary Spinozist mode (Braidotti, 2011b). Nomadic processes of becoming-imperceptible lean towards a spirituality, which is the opposite of mysticism in the sentimental mode dear to Christianity, and definitely not a stepping stone to the final redemption. It is not a morality of fringe benefits, but rather an ethics of non-profit that points beyond metaphysical life insurance politics. It enjoys gratuitous acts of kindness in the mode of a becoming-world of the subject.

'Becoming-imperceptible' is a way of configuring the transmutation of values which propels us out of the black hole of critical negativity into the paradoxically generative void of positivity, or full affirmation. It is a seduction into life that breaks with the spectral economy of the eternal return of the Same, and involves friendship with impersonal death. At that point of becoming-imperceptible, all a subject can do is mark his/her assent to the loss of identity (defined as a by-product of *potestas*) and respectfully merge with the process of *potentia* itself, and hence with one's environment. It is the absolute form of de-territorialization and its horizon is beyond the immediacy of life.

Conclusion: of possible futures

The core of postsecular spirituality is programmatic and forward-looking. This volume has been conceived very much in this spirit and as an affirmative contribution to this ongoing social and symbolic project. The authors gathered here agree that we need new cosmologies and world views that are appropriate to our own high level of complexity and the technological development and to the ferocious and insidious sets of structural injustices and violent modes of dispossession that mark the global economy. We need original cultural, spiritual, ethical creativity, be it myths, narratives, or representations that are adequate to this new civilization we inhabit (Haraway, 1997).

This project requires more visionary power or prophetic energy, qualities which are neither especially in fashion in critical theory academic circles, nor highly valued in these times of commercial globalization. This combination of sensitivity to representational issues and awareness of the materialist workings of power is the force of critical intellectuals (West, 1994). More conceptual creativity and theoretical courage are needed in order to confront the challenges of the global era. Creativity is unimaginable without some visionary or spiritual fuel.

Prophetic or visionary minds are thinkers of the future. The future as an active object of desire propels us forth and we can draw from it the strength and motivation to be active in the here and now of the present. The present is always the future present: it will have made a positive difference in the world. Only the yearning for sustainable futures can construct a liveable present. The anticipation of endurance, of making it to a possible 'tomorrow', transposes energies from the future back into the present. This is a non-entropic model of energy flow and hence of transferral of desire as creative becoming. This is not a leap of faith, but an active transposition, a transformation at the in-depth level, a praxis that enacts a change of critical culture, also at the ethical level. As Deleuze put it: we need both a future and a people.

A prophetic or visionary dimension is necessary for critical theory to secure the one element that advanced capitalism is systematically depriving us of, namely, sustainable transformations. The propositional core of the postsecular predicament takes a stand against the cynicism of neo-Marxists and the nostalgia of neo-Hegelians, with their perpetual infatuation with violence, antagonism, and confrontation, against the sterility of the vision of critique as the work of negativity. The residual spirituality of critical theory resides in acknowledging that we need to actually dare take the risk of affirmative politics and the collective construction of social horizons of hope. A qualitative and creative leap induced by a prophetic, visionary dimension is a way to repair and compensate for that which we are running out of: time.

Notes

With thanks to Tobjn de Graauw and Ernst van den Hemel for their constructive comments.

1. In this respect, I concur with Foucault's claim that Deleuze and Guattari's project of *Capitalism and Schizophrenia* is an introduction to anti-fascism and to non-fascist ethics (Foucault, 1977b).
2. Faciality is the function of re-territorialization of the subject. It consists in branding the self as the private property of the capitalist individual, so as to make it recognizable, consumable, and profitable.
3. Ernst van den Hemel pointed out to me the exact quote: 'I am afraid we are not rid of God because we still have faith in grammar' (Kaufmann, 1982: 483). Deleuze cites it in *The Logic of Sense* (1990: 281): 'Nietzsche's predictions about the link between God and grammar has been realized.'
4. This is the text of a graffiti I read on the walls of Paris in the 1980s.

References

Agamben, G. (1998). *Homo Sacer: Sovereign Power and Bare Life*. Standford, CA: Stanford University Press.
Ansell Pearson, K. (1999). *Germinal Life. The Difference and Repetition of Deleuze*. London and New York: Routledge.
Ansell Pearson, K. (2001). 'Pure Reserve: Deleuze, Philosophy and Immanence.' In M. Bryden (ed.) *Deleuze and Religion*. New York and London: Routledge.
Asad, T., Brown, W., Butler, J. and Mahmood, S. (2009). *Is Critique Secular? Blasphemy, Injury and Free Speech*. Berkeley: UC Press.
Bataille, G. (1988). *The Accursed Share*. New York: Zone Books.
Blanchot, M. (2000). *The Instant of My Death*. Stanford, CA: Stanford University Press.
Braidotti, R. (2006). *Transpositions. On Nomadic Ethics*. Cambridge: Polity Press
Braidotti, R. (2008). 'In Spite of the Times: The Postsecular Turn in Feminism.' *Theory, Culture & Society* 25(6), 1–24.
Braidotti, R. (2011a). *Nomadic Subjects: Embodiment and Sexual Difference in Contemporary Feminist Theory*, 2nd edition. New York: Columbia University Press.

Braidotti, R. (2011b). *Nomadic Theory: The Portable Rosi Braidotti*. New York: Columbia University Press.
Braidotti, R. (2013). *The Posthuman*. Cambridge: Polity Press.
Brown, W. (2006). *Regulating Aversion. Tolerance in the Age of Identity and Empire*. Princeton, NJ: Princeton University Press.
Bryden, M. (ed.) (2001). *Deleuze and Religion*. New York and London: Routledge.
Butler, J. (2004). *Precarious Life*. London: Verso.
Cixous, H. (1976). 'The Laugh of the Medusa.' *Signs* 1(4), 875–893.
Clough, P. (2008). 'The Affective Turn: Political Economy, Biomedia and Bodies.' *Theory, Culture & Society* 25(1), 1–22.
Connolly, W. (1999). *Why Am I Not a Secularist?* Minneapolis, MN: University of Minnesota Press.
Critchley, S. (1999). *Ethics, Politics, Subjectivity*. London: Verso Books.
Critchley, S. (2012). *The Faith of the Faithless: Experiments in Political Theology*. London: Verso.
Critchley, S. (2013). *Infinitely Demanding. Ethics of Commitment, Politics of Resistance*. London: Verso.
Dawkins, R. (2006). *The God Delusion*. London: Black Swan.
De Landa, M. (2002). *Intensive Science & Virtual Philosophy*. London: Continuum.
Deleuze, G. (1983). *Nietzsche and Philosophy*. New York: Columbia University Press.
Deleuze, G. (1990). *Expressionism in Philosophy: Spinoza*. New York: Zone Books.
Deleuze, G. (1995). 'L'immanence: une vie….' *Philosophie* 47: 3–7.
Deleuze, G. and Guattari, F. (1987). *A Thousand Plateaus: Capitalism and Schizophrenia*. Minneapolis, MN: University of Minnesota Press.
Deleuze, G. and Guattari, F. (1997). *Essays Clinical and Critical*. Minneapolis, MN: University of Minnesota Press.
Derrida, J. (1978). *Writing and Difference*. Chicago, IL: Chicago University Press.
Derrida, J. (2002). *Acts of Religion*. London and New York: Routledge.
Foucault, M. (1977a). *Discipline and Punish*. New York: Pantheon Books.
Foucault, M. (1977b). 'Preface.' In G. Deleuze and F. Guattari (eds) *Anti-Oedipus*, xi–xiv. New York: The Viking Press.
Franklin, S. (2007). *Dolly Mixtures*. Durham, NC: Duke University Press.
Freud, S. (1927). *The Future of an Illusion*. Standard Edition, vol. 21. London: Hogarth Press.
Gatens, M. and Lloyd, G. (1999). *Collective Imaginings. Spinoza, Past and Present*. London and New York: Routledge.
Gourgouris, S. (2013). *Lessons in Secular Criticism*. New York: Fordham University Press.
Grosz, E. (2004). *The Nick of Time. Politics, Evolution and the Untimely*. Durham: Duke University Press.
Guattari, F. (1995). *Chaosmosis: An Ethico-Aesthetic Paradigm*. Sydney: Power.
Guattari, F. (2000). *The Three Ecologies*. London: Athlone.
Hallward, P. (2006). *Out of this World: Deleuze and the Philosophy of Creation*. London: Verso.
Haraway, D. (1988). 'Situated Knowledges: The Science Question in Feminism as a Site of Discourse on the Privilege of Partial Perspective.' *Feminist Studies* 14(3), 575–599.

Haraway, D. (1997). *Modest Witness@ Second Millennium. Female Man Meets Oncomouse*. London and New York: Routledge.
Haraway, D. (2007). *When Species Meet*. Minneapolis, MN: University of Minnesota Press.
Hegel, G.W.F. (1977). *Phenomenology of Spirit*. Oxford: Carlendon Press.
Irigaray, L. (1985). *Speculum of the Other Woman*, Trans. by Gillian Gill. Ithaca, NY: Cornell University Press.
Kaufmann, W. (ed.) (1982). *The Portable Nietzche*. London: Penguin Books.
Kelly, J. (1979). 'The Double-edged Vision of Feminist Theory.' *Feminist Studies* 5(1), 216–227.
Kristeva, J. (1991). *Strangers to Ourselves*. New York: Colombia University Press.
Laplanche, J. (1976). *Life and Death in Psychoanalysis*. Baltimore, MD and London: John Hopkins University Press.
Levinas, E. (1969). *Totality and Infinity: An Essay on Exteriority*. Pittsburgh, PA: Duquesne University Press.
Levinas, E. (1999). *Alterity and Transcendence*. New York: Columbia University Press.
Lyotard, J.F. (1984). *The Postmodern Condition*. Manchester: Manchester University Press.
Macherey, P. (2011). *Hegel or Spinoza?* Minneapolis, MN: University of Minnesota Press.
Marks, John (1998). *Gilles Deleuze. Vitalism and Multiplicity*. London: Pluto Press.
Massumi, B. (2002). *Parables for the Virtual. Movement, Affect, Sensation*. Durham, NC: Duke University Press.
Mouffe, C. (2005). *On the Political*. New York: Routledge.
Norton, A. (2004). *Leo Strauss and the Politics of American Empire*. New Haven, CT: Yale University Press.
Parisi, L. (2004). *Abstract Sex. Philosophy, Biotechnology, and the Mutation of Desire*. London: Continuum Press.
Pateman, C. (1988). *The Sexual Contract*. Cambridge: Polity Press.
Patton, P. (2000). *Deleuze and the Political*. London and New York: Routledge.
Phillips, A. (1999). *Darwin's Worms*. London: Faber & Faber.
Protevi, J. (2009). *Political Affect*. Minneapolis, MN: University of Minnesota Press.
Schmitt, C. (1996). *The Concept of the Political*. Chicago, IL: Chicago University Press.
Scott, J.W. (2007). *The Politics of the Veil*. Princeton: Princeton University Press.
Smith, D. (2001). 'The Doctrine of Univocity: Deleuze's Ontology of Immanence.' In M. Bryden (ed.) *Deleuze and Religion*. New York and London: Routledge.
West, C. (1994). *Prophetic Thought in Postmodern Times*. Monroe, ME: Common Courage Press.
Žižek, S.J. (2013). *Enjoy Your Symptom!: Jacques Lacan in Hollywood and Out*. New York: Routledge.

Index

Abdul-Ahad, Ghaith, 133
accomodationist approach, 25
advanced capitalism, 3
affect, 152–71, 252–9
affective belongings, 155–6, 165–9
affirmative ethics, 214, 262
affirmative politics, 251, 259–63
Afghan women, 7
Agamben, G., 115, 256
agency, 4, 5, 214
Ahmed, Sarah, 165–6
Ali, Hirsi, 7, 8, 27, 38–9, 86–7, 164–5, 212
allegory, 119–20
anti-Muslim sentiment, 8–9, 11, 27–9, 135, 137, 142–3, 164–5, 213
anti-racism, 136–9, 141
anti-Semitism, 59, 60, 71
Appadurai,, 153–4
Appiah, K. A., 171n1
Aquinas, Thomas, 106–7
Arab Spring, 133
Arendt, Hannah, 111
Argyle, Margaret, 239–40
art, blasphemous, 228–44
Asad, Talal, 2, 40–5, 70, 179, 196, 197
asceticism, 260–1
assemblages, 257
assimilationism, 85, 89–90
atheism, 6, 98, 144, 147
Australia, 136, 138
autonomy, 2, 5, 253

Back, Les, 142
backlash politics, 136–7
backwardness, 10, 136
Badiou, Alain, 10, 115, 117–25, 128–30
Bakhtin, Mikhail, 164
Bataille, G., 255–6
Battle of Karbala, 200, 202, 204, 206–7
Baumgartner, Christoph, 10, 77–94
Baur, Ferdinand Christian, 59

Beauvoir, Simone de, 6
Beckford, James, 72n6, 180
Bender, Courtney, 184
Benedict XVI, Pope, 26
Benhabib, Seyla, 3
Berger, Benhamin, 185
Berger, Peter, 30n3
Berg-Sørensen, Anders, 9, 35–50
Bhargava, Rajeev, 15, 30n2
biotechnology, 3
Blaagaard, Bolette, 213
Blair, Cherie, 7
Blair, Tony, 22
Blanchot, Maurice, 254
blasphemous feminist art, 10, 228–44
Board, Gerard, 134
Boe, Carolina, 86
Bolkestein, Frits, 54–5, 63, 210, 211
Bouteldja, Houria, 148, 149
Bracke, S., 213
Braidotti, Rosi, 12, 71–2, 135, 211–12, 214, 249–70
Breivik, Anders, 8
Brink, B. van den, 82
British Columbia, 177–90
Brouwe, Lenie, 162–3
Brown, Wendy, 70
Bruckner, Pascal, 38, 39
Bryden, Mary, 256
Buruma, Ian, 38–9
Bush, George W., 7
Butler, Judith, 70, 255
Bynum, Caroline Walker, 239
Byrne, Dara, 155, 159–60

Caldwell, Christopher, 139–40
Campbell, Heidi, 154
Canada, 136, 138, 177–90
capitalism, 3, 6, 7, 10, 60, 98
carnivalesque, 164–5, 171
Casanova, Jose, 175, 181
Catholic Church, 26, 84, 177, 187–8, 235

273

censorship, 133, 230–1
Christa sculptures/paintings, 239–43
Christian-Democratic parties, 58, 62
Christian identity, 25–6
Christianity, 1–3, 43, 54, 70, 176
   colonialism and, 177–9, 183–90
   crucifixion and, 234–43
   early, 59
   in Europe, 15–16, 25–6, 154
   Evangelical, 199
   Orthodox, 6
   Saint Paul and, 115–31
   secularism and, 176–7, 179–82, 213, 249
Christian theology, 106–7
Christian values, 25–7
Church of England, 20, 23, 25
citizenship, 64
   democratic, 80–1, 83
   ethics of, 77–94
   religious, 15, 79–81, 91–2
   secular, 79–81, 89, 91–3, 186–7
civilizations
   clash of, 3, 7–8, 49, 60–1, 64–5, 86
   colonialism and, 184
class struggles, 129
Cliteur, Paul, 63
Cold War, 6, 60
colonialism, 4, 17, 71, 148, 176–90, 196
communism, 6, 60, 110–12, 117
Confessions on a Dance Floor show, 229, 234–43
Connolly, William, 2
conservative nationalism, 53–74
conservativism, 64–8, 71
'cool Islam', 156, 168
Copé, Jean-François, 141
counter-discourses, 155
counter-publics, 155, 159–65
counter-subjectivity, 5
crisis, 115
Critchley, Simon, 254–5, 258
critical secularism, 46–9
critical theory, 3, 12, 115–16, 249–70
critique, 115
crucifixion, 234–54
Csordas, Thomas, 198
cultural identity, 62
cultural racism, 28

culture
   digital, 154–72
   global, 153–4
   popular, 258–9
   race and, 139–40
   religion and, 215–17
   youth, 156, 164, 169, 170–1

Dawkins, Richard, 98
death, 266–9
Deleuze, Gilles, 100–1, 257, 259, 260, 262, 265–7
deliberative democracy, 78–9, 81–3
democracy, 1, 2, 9, 11, 14, 37, 39, 43, 44, 48, 49, 60, 78–9, 81–3, 86, 87, 92, 110–12
democratic citizenship, 80–1, 83
de Mul, Jos, 69
Denmark, 25, 27, 40
   Muhammad cartoon controversy, 10, 35, 78, 81–93, 134–5, 145–6, 154–5
Derrida, Jacques, 181, 182, 189, 253–5, 258
desecularization, 15, 18, 30, 97
DHC, 164–5
difference, 124
digital culture, 154–72
digital spaces, 152–72
digital postsecularism, 153–6
Dillon, Michele, 80
disorientalism, 147
diversity, 16–17, 144, 200–3, 206, 222–4
domination, 253–4
Douglas, Mary, 232
Dresselhuys, Ciska, 211
Dutch society
   conservative nationalism in, 53–74
   values of, 53–4
Du Vernet, Frederick, 187
Duyvendak, Jan Willem, 64

Eastern Europe, 154
Eastern European churches, 6
egalitarian universalism, 56
Egginton, William, 10, 97–113
Ego, 123–5, 127
Egypt, 43, 133
Eisenhower, Dwight D., 60

Eisenlohr, Patrick, 11, 195–208
elites, 98–100, 110
emancipation, 2–5, 7, 20, 71–2, 163, 170, 190, 211, 215–18, 222–5, 229, 233, 239
emancipatory politics, 3, 4, 7
empathy, 103–5
empirical subjectivity, 100–1
"end of history," 60–1
English Defence League (EDL), 141
Enlightenment, 2, 3, 9, 35–6, 37, 100, 115, 213, 252
 critique of religion, 37–9, 46–9
 ideals, 47
 radical, 37–9
equality, 2, 39, 40, 60
ethics, 100, 214, 255, 258, 260–3
ethics of citizenship, 77–94
ethnic identity, 17
ethnicity, 10
ethnic minorities, 21–2, 136–7, 210
ethnocentrism, 3–4, 7
Eurocentrism, 2, 253
Europe
 see also Western Europe
 Christianity in, 15–16, 25–6, 154
 Islamophobia in, 137
 Muslims in, 154–5
 postsecularism crisis in, 14–31
 public discourse in, 35–50
Europeanism, 28–9
European Parliament, 5
European Union (EU), 61
Evangelicals, 60, 199
exceptionalim, 122
exclusion, 253–4
extremism, 28, 35, 143, 157, 164

fable, 119–20, 122–3, 130n2
Facebook, 152
faciality, 259
faith, 1, 72, 106–7, 115, 116, 130n1
false consciousness, 129
Farage, Nigel, 72n1
Fekete, Liz, 142
female bodies, 232–3
female crucifixion, 234–43
feminism, 5, 7, 8, 11, 57, 64, 72, 210–26, 252
 blasphemous feminist art, 228–44

diversity and, 222–4
 inclusive, 215–21, 224–5
 postsecular and, 212–14
 religion and, 213–17
 second-wave, 219–21
financial crises, 5, 7
First Nations people, 177–9, 184–90
Fitna, 35, 154
Forman-Barzilai, Fonna, 112n1
Fortyun, Pim, 27, 62–3
Foucault, Michel, 42, 117, 261
France, 16, 17
 headscarf case in, 22–4, 40–5
 Islamophobia in, 28
 secularism in, 20–1, 40–5
Francis, Pope, 3
Fraser, Nancy, 155, 159
freedom, 10, 98
free speech, 35–6, 39, 57, 81, 83–4, 133–5, 142, 145, 146
Freud, Sigmund, 254
Fukuyama, F., 3, 60
fundamentalism, 36, 98, 109, 111, 175–82, 189, 196, 230

Garcia, Cindy Lee, 145
Garton, Timothy, 38
gay rights, 57, 64, 71, 148–9
Gellner, E., 2
gender, 157, 166, 218–19, 232–3
 equality, 29, 142, 221–2
 Muslims and, 26–7, 145
 relations, 5, 11–12
 violence, 5
generations, 21, 156, 160, 161, 166, 168, 170, 171
Germany, 25
global culture, 153–4
global economy, 3
global financial crisis, 5
globalization, 3, 4, 6, 198–200, 202, 207
God, 106, 109, 112, 257, 264
Goldberg, D. T., 139, 142
governmentality, 42, 117, 195
Gramsci, A., 255
Grotenhuis, M. te, 58
Guattari, F., 253, 257, 259, 260, 266
guest workers, 210
Guilbert, Georges-Claude, 235
Gunnell, John G., 66–7

Habermas, Jürgen, 1–3, 9, 15, 45, 46, 55–6, 77–94, 97, 155, 181–2
Häger, Andreas, 236
Hall, Stuart, 139
Haraway, D., 256
Harris, Sam, 98
headscarves, 22–4, 40–5, 211, 212, 218–19
Hedehaard, Lars, 145
Hegel, G.W.F., 59, 260, 261–2
Heidegger, M., 116, 126, 128
hermeneutic theology, 110–12
Hervik, Peter, 86, 145
Hesse, Barnor, 136, 137, 138, 140
'Hirsi Ali Diss', 164–5
Hitchens, Christopher, 98
Hobbes, Thomas, 100
Hollinger, David, 180
homo-nationalism, 8, 64
homophobia, 5, 148–9
homosexuality, 29, 64, 148–9, 232–3
hospitality, 189
Hudson' Bay Company, 177–8
Huggan, G., 171n2
humanism, 2, 153
human rights, 39
Hume, David, 100–3
Huntington, Samuel P., 8, 60–1, 64–5, 86
Husserl, E., 115
Huxley, A., 137, 138
hyperlinks, 169
hypertextual selves, 168–9, 170–1
Hyves, 152, 169

Ibrajim, Yasmin, 147
iconclash, 236–7
iconclasm, feminist, 239–41
identity, 17, 19, 67–8
  cultural, 62
  formation, 8
  national, 64, 68, 71, 72
  politics, 123, 125–6, 143–4, 228–44
  religious, 17, 25, 53, 54, 64, 165–9, 230
  secular, 57
  shifting, 116–17
  Universalist, 117–18
imaginaries, 175, 184, 258–9

immanent frame, 183
immigrants, 16–17, 136
immigration/immigrants, 27, 54, 153–4, 210–11, 214–15
imperialism, 195
India, 200–2, 204–7
Indian Land Question, 177–8, 184–5, 186–7
individualism, 2, 5, 7
Innocence of Muslims, 35, 132–5, 145, 155, 231
Institute of Public Policy Research (IPPR), 20–1
integration, 54, 146, 212
Internet discussion forums, 159–65
intersubjectivity, 127–8, 129, 257
intertexuality, 147
intolerance, 61, 146
Islam, 2, 5, 81, 181, 212, 213
  see also Muslims
  affective belongingness and, 165–9
  anti-Muslim sentiment and, 8–9, 11
  'cool Islam', 156, 168
  democracy and, 86, 87, 92
  exclusion of, from public sphere, 57
  fundamentalist, 182, 230
  gender and, 157
  reformist, 199
  reimagining of, 147
  as threat, 54
Islamification, 142
Islamophobia, 27–9, 137, 142–3, 213
Israel, Jonathan, 37–9

Jakobsen, Janet, 97
Jewish theology, 105–6
John-Paul II, Pope, 6, 26
Judaism, 60, 70
Judeo-Christian roots, 53–74
Judeo-Christian values, 9, 62–3, 71
Juste, Carsten, 85
justice, 101–2

Kant, Immanuel, 107–8, 109, 112
Karlsson, Lena, 166
Kelly, Joan, 252
Kennedy, James, 71
Kinneging, Andreas, 67
Klassen, Pamela, 11, 175–90

Klausen, Jytte, 86
knowledge, 106–7
Korte, Anne-Marie, 11, 228–44
Kundnani, Arun, 141
Kuyper, Abraham, 57
Kymlicka, Will, 19

labour markets, 17
Lacan, Jacques, 253, 254
Lambert, Gregg, 10, 115–31
language, 253–4, 255
  of God, 108
  philosophy of, 94n3
  religious, 79, 81, 89, 94n3
Latour, Bruno, 237
law, rule of, 2, 39, 80
laws, against religious discrimination, 22–3
Leibniz, Gottfried, 108–9
Lentin, Alana, 10–11, 132–49
lesbian, gay, bisexual, and transgender (LGBT) people, 3, 4, 250
Leurs, Koen, 10, 11, 152–72
Levinas, Emmanuelle, 10, 121, 123–30, 254, 258, 259
liberal democracy, 110–12
liberalism, 25–8, 55, 57, 60, 63–4, 90–1, 98, 99–105, 143–4
liberal-secularism, 10
liberty, 39, 40
life, sanctity of, 3
Lilla, Mark, 97–8, 99–100, 105, 107–8, 109
linguistic turn, 253–4, 257
Locke, John, 100, 181
Lutheran Church, 20
Lutkenhaus-Lackey, Almuth, 239

MacKinnon, Rebecca, 133
Madonna, 11, 229, 234–43
Mahmood, Saba, 10, 70–2, 89–90, 183–4
Maimonides, 105–6
Maitland, Sarah, 232
Mamadough, Virginie, 159
March, Andrew F., 90–1
Mark, Karl, 6
Martin, Marie, 112n2
Marx, Karl, 110, 119, 261

Marxism, 6, 117, 129
materialism, 12, 252–9
Mauritius, 198–206
McCullagh, James Benjamin, 185–6, 190
media, 83
  coverage of Muhammad cartoon controversy in, 87–8
  religion and, 154
  role of, 10
Meeks, Wayne A., 119, 121
Memoms, 204
mentality, 175–7, 184, 189
Mepschens, Paul, 64
Mercer, Andrew, 178–9, 190
Merkel, Angela, 138
message boards, 159–65
Midden, Eva, 11, 210–26
migrant youth, religion in online practices of, 152–72
migration theory, 153–4, 210–11
Miles, Margaret, 233
minarets ban, 28, 146
minorities, 15, 21–2, 136–7, 210
missionaries, 177, 181, 183–8
Mitropolous, Angela, 143
modernity, 1–4, 9, 14, 107, 152, 181–2, 195–7, 249
Modood, Tariq, 9, 14–31
monism, 253, 255, 257, 260, 263, 264
morality, 3, 59, 62, 79, 100–5
moral panic, 3
Moroccan-Dutch, 155–72
Mufti, Aamir, 153
Muhammad cartoons, 10, 35, 78, 81–93, 134–5, 145–6, 154–5
multiculturalism, 5, 9–11, 16–19, 29, 31n13, 54, 55, 61, 123, 125–6, 136, 138–41, 143, 144, 149, 210–13
Mumbai, 198–203, 206–7
muscular liberalism, 25–7
Muslim Council of Britain (MCB), 22–3
Muslim issue, 10–11, 135, 147, 149
Muslims
  see also Islam
  anti-Muslim sentiment, 8–9, 11, 27–9, 135, 137, 142–3, 164–5, 213
  assertiveness by, 21–5

278 Index

Muslims – *continued*
 in Europe, 154–5
 female dress, 17, 22–4, 26–7, 211, 212, 218–19
 gender issues and, 26–7, 157, 166, 218–19
 Moroccan-Danish youth, online practices of, 155–72
 Muhammad cartoons and, 83–93
 religious mobilization among, 198–208
 solidarity with, 84–5, 88–9
 stereotypes of, 157, 163–5, 170
 in Western Europe, 16–19, 21–30
 women, 17, 23–4, 26–7, 29, 215–19

Nakoula, Nakoula Basseley, 132, 133, 154
Nash, David, 231
national identity, 64, 68, 71, 72
nationalism, 6, 26, 28–9, 136, 153
 conservative, 53–74
 homo-nationalism, 8, 64
nation-state, 43, 184, 188, 195, 197
natural law, 3
Nazism, 87, 122, 128, 137
neoconservative politics, 5, 10, 53–74, 256
neo-imperialism, 4
neoliberalism, 6–7, 10
neo-materialism, 12
neorealism, 211
neo-secularism, 16
Netherlands, 20, 21, 27, 154, 212
 immigration to, 210–11, 214–15
 Judeo-Christian roots in, 53–74
 minorities in, 210
 Moroccan-Danish youth in, 155–72
 multiculturalism in, 54, 55
 politics in, 57–8
 progressive critics in, 68–70
 public discourse in, 214–15
new atheism, 144
New Labour, 22
New Right, 58
Nietzsche, Friedrich, 59, 257, 264
Niezen, Ronald, 184
9/11, 61
Nisga'a Nation, 177–90

noble lies, 65–6, 67
nomadic theory, 258
Nordic Bishops' Conference, 84
norms, 19, 82
Nunley, Vorris, 160
Nussbaum, Martha, 3

Obama, Barack, 136, 138
Odin, Jaishree, 169
online communication, 8, 153–6
ontology, 123, 125–7, 128, 252–9
oppositional consciousness, 261
Orthodox religion, 6
"Other," 125–6, 127, 128, 213, 253, 261

Pakistan, 201
Parekh, Bhikhu, 19
particularism, 125, 127
Party for Freedom, 35
Paul, *see* Saint Paul
Pellegrini, Ann, 97
performative construction, 10
Peters, Bernhard, 82
Peters, John Durham, 134–5
phenomenology, 117
Philips, Anne, 143
philosophy, 59, 116, 182
piety, 5, 170, 171, 200–3
pillarization, 20, 21, 57
Piss Christ, 231
Pitcher, Ben, 139
Plate, Brent, 232
Plato, 66
pluralism, 200–3
Poland, 6
political agency, 5
political debates, 81–93
political economy, 98, 253–4
political institutions, 40, 48
political secularism, 14–31, 40
political subjectivity, 5
political theology, 41–6, 98, 100, 112, 256
politics
 affirmative, 251, 259–63
 backlash, 136–7
 democratic, 78
 emancipatory, 3, 4, 7

politics – *continued*
  identity, 123, 125–6, 143–4, 228–44
  neoconservative, 5, 10, 53–74
  religion and, 41–2, 44–9, 55, 70–2
  theology and, 105–9
  unframed, 105–9
Ponzanesi, Sandra, 10, 11, 152–72
popular culture, 258–9
postcolonial contexts, 11, 152–3
postcolonialism, 154, 155, 171n1
postmodernism, 171n1
post-racial, 135–6, 137–41
postracialism, 144
postsecularism, 1–5, 9–12, 53, 55–6, 171n2, 175–6, 195–6, 250
  Christianity and, 180
  crisis of, 14–31
  critical theory and, 249–70
  critics of, 69–70
  defined, 56
  digital, 153–6
  feminism and, 212–14
  historical background, 6–9
  postcolonialism and, 152–3, 155
  spirituality and, 263–9
postsecular societies, 3, 9, 15, 46
  ethics of citizenship in, 77–94
power, 37, 39, 46, 48, 261
Prins, Baukje, 211
profit motive, 7
progress, 1, 2, 7, 11
progressives, 68–72
property rights, 181
  see also real estate
Protestantism, 55, 181
protests, against Muhammad cartoons, 84–8
psychoanalysis, 117, 253–5, 258–60
public culture, 82–3, 93
public discourse, 35–50, 87, 91, 93, 179–80, 211, 214–15
public sphere, 56, 155
  political, 79
  religion in, 5–6, 36, 57
Pussy Riot, 230

Al Qaeda, 181
Qur'an, 39, 64, 215

race, 10, 136, 137, 139–40, 149, 152, 154, 155
racism, 4, 8, 11, 28, 135, 137–43, 149, 157, 253
radical Enlightenment, 37–9
Ramadan, Tariq, 212
rationality, 2
Ratzinger, Cardinal, 2, 3
Reagan, Ronald, 60
real estate, 176–90
reason, 1–2, 6, 116–17
relationality, 256
religion, 15, 176, 195
  see also Christianity; Islam
  activism, 195, 197, 200–1
  backwardness and, 1, 10
  blasphemous feminist art and, 228–44
  critique of Enlightenment, 37–9
  culturalization of, 72
  culture and, 215–17
  Enlightenment critique, 46–9
  feminism and, 213–17
  fundamentalism, 7–8
  globalization and, 198–200, 202, 207
  liberalism and, 99–105
  marginalization of, 15
  media and, 154
  mobilization of, 196–208
  in online practices, 152–72
  Orthodox, 6
  politics and, 41–2, 44–9, 55, 70–2
  postsecularism and, 195–6
  privatization of, 196
  Protestant notion of, 89, 90
  public, 15, 20–1, 29
  in public sphere, 5–6, 36, 57
  race and, 136, 137, 152, 154, 155
  regulation of, 36–7, 44, 200–3
  sexuality and, 229–30
  standardized, 203–7
  violence and, 83
religious beliefs, 97, 98, 108–9, 112
religious citizens, 15, 79–81, 91–2
religious communities, 80, 91
religious discrimination, laws against, 22–3
religious identity, 17, 25, 53, 54, 64, 165–9, 230

religious language, 79, 81, 89, 94n3
religious minorities, 15, 136–7, 210
religious pluralism, 11
reverse racism, 136, 141
Ridley, William, 187
Rieman, Rob, 68
"right to offend," 133–5
right-wing parties, 28, 35, 65, 143, 157
riots, Paris, 17
Robbins, Bruce, 153
Robbins, Joel, 198
Roman Empire, 120, 130
Rose, Flemming, 86
Rose, Nicholas, 3, 81
Rouhs, Manfred, 134
Rousseau, Jean Jacques, 107–8
Roy, O., 15
Rupert's Land, 177–8
Rushdie, Salman, 22–3, 230

Sadek, Morris, 133
Said, Edward, 153
Saint Paul, 115–31
Sandys, Edwina, 239, 240
Sarkozy, Nicolas, 24, 72n4
The Satanic Verses (Rushdie), 22–34
Scherer, M., 15
Schmitt, Carl, 41–2, 43, 44, 45, 213, 256
science, 2, 3, 79, 117
scientific knowledge, 107
Scott, Joan, 71–2, 233, 234, 252
secular citizens, 15, 79–81, 89, 91–3, 186–7
secularism, 1–4, 40, 175–6
  alternative, 47
  anti-Muslim sentiment and, 8–9
  Christianity and, 1–3, 176–7, 179–82, 213, 249
  colonialism and, 179–90
  concept of, 49, 50n1
  critical, 46–9
  critics of, 39–45, 55
  discourses, 40
  doctrine of, 36–7
  feminism and, 210–26
  fixed notions of, 142–7
  forms of, 4
  France, 20–1, 40–5
  ideology of, 5
  Indian, 205–6
  liberal-secularism, 10
  moderate, 20–1
  modernity and, 9
  political, 14–31, 40
  self-critical, 48
  varieties of, 44
secularization, 50n1, 54–5, 97, 135, 175, 181, 195–7, 207, 233–4
secularization myth, 1, 9, 97–9, 153
secular values, 61
self-censorship, 83
self-critical secularism, 48
self-determination, 39
sensibilities, 175
separation of church and state, 2, 57, 80
Serrano, Andres, 231
sexual freedom, 5, 142
sexuality, 149, 219, 229–30, 233–4
sexual orientation, 27, 29, 64, 148–9, 232–3
sex-ularism, 252
Sloterdijk, P., 3
Smith, Adam, 103–4
Smith, Dan, 257
Smith, Rogers M., 46–7
social imaginaries, 175–6, 258–9
social movements, 3
social networking sites, 152, 169
social progress, 2
social relations, 126, 129
sovereignty, 41–4, 62, 98, 181, 182, 190, 197
Spaemann, Robert, 72n3
Sparrow, Jeffrey, 144, 147
Spinoza, Baruch, 38, 257, 260, 264
spiritual domination, 184
spirituality, 16, 152, 251, 255–6, 263–9
Spruyt, Bart Jan, 64, 67–8
state churches, 181
stereotypes, 157, 163–5, 170
Stevens, Christopher, 133
Stop the Islamization of Europe (SIOE), 137
Strauss, Leo, 65–7, 256
structuralism, 117
subaltern counterpublics, 155

Index 281

subculture, 166
subjectivity, 5, 88–90, 100–1, 115,
    214, 225, 252, 255, 257, 261–3
Submission, 35, 154
Switzerland, 28, 146

Taguieff, Pierre-André, 138
Tax, Meredith, 133, 144
Taylor, Charles, 2, 19, 98, 135, 183,
    184, 189–90, 190n2, 196–7
Tebble, Adam, 143
technology, 3, 6, 8, 153–6
terrorism, 6, 28, 61, 142, 201
theology, 59, 98, 100, 105–9, 126
    democracy and, 110–12
    hermeneutic, 110–12
    philosophy and, 116
    political, 41–6, 98, 100, 112, 256
Titley, Gavan, 10–11, 132–49
tolerance/toleration, 25, 39, 54, 64,
    68–9, 107, 144, 206
totalitarianism, 36, 142
tradition, 64–8
transcendence, eradication of, 97–113
Tuin, Iris van der, 220

underdevelopment, 7
United Kingdom, 20–1, 31n6
    Islamophobia in, 28
    Rushdie affair in, 22–3
United States, 16, 60, 65–6, 118, 120,
    138
universalism, 3, 19, 56, 119, 121–2,
    125–6, 129–30
univocity, 256–7, 260
utility, 102–3

Valenta, Markha, 71
values, 82
    Christian, 26–7
    Dutch, 53–4
    Judeo-Christian, 62–3, 68–9, 71
    liberal, 57
    Muslim, 26–7
    progressive, 71–2
    secular, 61
    Western, 6, 210
Valverde, Marianna, 188, 190n4
van den Hemel, Ernst, 9–10, 53–74

van der Veer, Peter, 71
van Gogh, Theo, 35, 154, 212
Vattimo, Gianni, 110, 111–12
violence, 81, 83
vital materialism, 252–9
Voltaire, 58–9

Wade, Peter, 137
war on terror, 6, 8, 61, 135
Western Europe
    see also Europe
    Islamophobia in, 27–9
    Judeo-Christian roots in, 53–74
    multiculturalism in, 18–19, 29
    Muslims in, 16–19, 21–30
    postsecularism crisis in, 14–31
    secularism in, 20–1
Western values, 6, 210
whiteness, 213
white supremacy, 7
Wilders, Geert, 8, 10, 27, 35, 61–2, 64,
    70, 71, 73n7, 142, 146, 154–5,
    157, 163–4
women, 3, 7, 250
    Afghan, 7
    bodies of, 7, 232–3
    emancipation of, 4, 5, 71–2, 163,
        170, 211, 215–18, 222–6, 229,
        233, 239
    feminism and, 210–26
    headscarves worn by, 23–4, 211,
        212, 218–19
    Muslim, 17, 23–4, 26–7, 29, 215–19
    self-determination, 8
World Conference on Artistic Freedom
    of Expression, 230–1
World Islamic Network, 202
world views, 175

xenophobia, 8, 135

Yilmaz, Ferruh, 146, 149
Young, Iris, 19
youth culture, 156, 164, 169, 170–1
YouTube, 35, 132, 133, 158, 167

Zabala, Santiago, 110, 111–12
Žižek, S. J., 116, 265
Zuckerman, Ethan, 133

The manufacturer's authorised representative in the EU is Springer Nature Customer Service Centre GmbH, Europaplatz 3, 69115 Heidelberg, Germany. If you have any concerns regarding our products, please contact ProductSafety@springernature.com

Printed and bound by CPI Group (UK) Ltd, Croydon, CR0 4YY
23/03/2026
02076734-0011